AUGUSTINE AND POLITICS

AUGUSTINE IN CONVERSATION: TRADITION AND INNOVATION

Series Editors: John Doody and Kim Paffenroth

This series produces edited volumes that explore Augustine's relationship to a particular discipline or field of study. This "relationship" is considered in several different ways: some contributors consider Augustine's practice of the particular discipline in question; some consider his subsequent influence on the field of study; and others consider how Augustine himself has become an object of study by their discipline. Such variety adds breadth and new perspectives— *innovation*—to our ongoing conversation with Augustine on topics of lasting import to him and us, while using Augustine as our conversation partner lends focus and a common thread—*tradition*—to our disparate fields and interests.

TITLES IN SERIES
Augustine and Politics
Edited by John Doody, Kevin L. Hughes, and Kim Paffenroth

Augustine and Literature
Edited by Robert P. Kennedy, Kim Paffenroth, and John Doody

AUGUSTINE AND POLITICS

Edited by John Doody,
Kevin L. Hughes, and
Kim Paffenroth

LEXINGTON BOOKS
Lanham • Boulder • New York • Toronto • Oxford

LEXINGTON BOOKS

Published in the United States of America
by Lexington Books
An imprint of The Rowman & Littlefield Publishing Group, Inc.
4501 Forbes Boulevard, Suite 200, Lanham, Maryland 20706

PO Box 317
Oxford
OX2 9RU, UK

British Library Cataloguing in Publication Information Available

Library of Congress Cataloging-in-Publication Data

Augustine and politics / edited by John Doody, Kevin L. Hughes, and Kim Paffenroth.
    p. cm.
  Includes bibliographical references and index.
  ISBN 0-7391-0556-6 (cloth : alk. paper) — ISBN 0-7391-1009-8 (pbk. : alk. paper)
  1. Augustine, Saint, Bishop of Hippo—Political and social views. 2. Political science—
History—To 1500. I. Doody, John, 1943– II. Hughes, Kevin L. III. Paffenroth, Kim, 1966–
JC121.A8A94 2005
320'.092—dc22   2004023921

Printed in the United States of America

∞™ The paper used in this publication meets the minimum requirements of American
National Standard for Information Sciences—Permanence of Paper for Printed Library
Materials, ANSI/NISO Z39.48-1992.

Dedicated to the memory of
Fr. John Rotelle, O.S.A.

Contents

Dedicatory Preface

ON SEPTEMBER 1, 2002, THE WORLD of Augustinian scholarship lost an able and indefatigable collaborator with the death of Father John E. Rotelle, O.S.A. Fr. Rotelle had both deep love for and extensive knowledge of St. Augustine and the Augustinian tradition and dedicated his considerable talents to the editorial and publishing task of making that tradition known. His lasting contribution to the English-speaking world in this regard is the now-underway multivolume series, *The Works of Saint Augustine: A Translation for the 21st Century*, published by New City Press of Hyde Park, New York. The emergence of the first volume in the series in 1990 was followed by twenty-six further volumes to date, and when the project is completed all the writings of Augustine of Hippo will be available in English for the very first time. Fr. Rotelle brought to this task many years of experience and acknowledged significant mentors in his life who prepared and equipped him for these tasks. He noted in particular the influence of Fr. Agostino Trapè, O.S.A., the renowned Italian Augustinolgist, who instilled in him both the necessary knowledge and enthusiasm to pursue the task of publishing the works of Augustine. After the Second Vatican Council, Fr. Rotelle served for a number of years on ICEL, the International Committee on English in the Liturgy, involved in the translation and publication of liturgical texts. It was this experience that gave him first-hand knowledge of the demands that would be involved in bringing to the English-speaking world the writings of Augustine. Beyond this project, his work as director of the Augustinian Press (Villanova, Pennsylvania) brought to the public a variety of other texts and studies associated with the Augustinian tradition. His presence will be deeply missed and it is to him that we dedicate this volume.

—Thomas F. Martin, O.S.A.

Introduction

John Doody, Kevin L. Hughes, and Kim Paffenroth

O UR TOPIC FOR THIS VOLUME is as timely as that of our earlier volume on *Augustine and Liberal Education* (Ashgate Publishing, 2000). The study of Augustine's political teachings has suffered from a history of misreadings, both ancient and modern. It is only in recent years that the traditional lines of "Augustinian pessimism" have been opened to question. Scholars have begun to explore the broader lines of Augustine's political thought in his letters and sermons, and thus have been able to place the "classic text," the *City of God*, in its proper context. The contributions in this volume take stock of these recent developments and revisit old assumptions about the significance of Augustine of Hippo for political thought. They do so from many different perspectives, examining the anthropological and theological underpinnings of Augustine's thought, his critique of politics, his development of his own political thought, and some of the later manifestations or uses of his thought in the Middle Ages, Renaissance, and today. This new vision is at once more bracing, more hopeful, and more diverse than earlier readings could have allowed.

Phillip Cary begins our study by looking at Augustine's social ontology—how he thinks humans exist in relation to one another and in relation to their group. This is the most fundamental question to start with, for it forces us to look closely at how Augustine defines a society, its essence and its goals. Cary takes us carefully through an examination of interpersonal relations in Augustine's works, concluding that we are better off without the Augustinian nostalgia for inward unity, together with its ideal of seeing into each other's thoughts. Instead, our social theory really needs more respect for externals (words and bodies) than one finds in the Augustinian tradition, which admits that these externals are there, but always longs to see beyond and beneath them.

In his chapter, Robert Kennedy argues that Augustine's thoughts on truthfulness and the role of language in forming communities show how Augustine can affirm the value of secular institutions, even for Christian morality, while refusing to admit that there can be salvation outside a community that lives by grace. Although he denies any salvific value to anything that does not share in Christ's grace, his nuanced view of the relationship between truthfulness as personal integrity and the worship of the true God that completes it and makes it beatifying explains why the tension in his attitude toward secular societies is necessary.

The next chapter examines another bond within society, the deep and vital bond of friendship that Augustine experienced and described so vividly. Paffenroth shows how the Platonist, Ciceronian, and Christian elements give Augustine's idea of friendship its personal, social, and theological dimensions, thereby perfecting in these different spheres of life the people and communities who experience such friendship.

In his chapter, David C. Schindler argues that Augustine is not, as some claim, the first to articulate the modern notion of freedom (namely, as the power to choose), but in fact offers a profound alternative: freedom as the fruit of beauty, and as original participation in goodness. After showing that the view of freedom as mere choice entails nihilism, the chapter explains how Augustine's notion of consent allows him to avoid falling into the trap of determinism, while at the same time to avoid making the will something "arbitrary."

Under the heading of Augustine's "political activity" or "activism," Robert Dodaro illustrates some of Augustine's aims and strategies in engaging the political process of his day in favor of individuals and classes of persons who required legal assistance in their dealings with public officials. By drawing on a number of cases from the bishop's letters to imperial and local officials, Dodaro is able to show something of the nexus between Augustine's political thought and action. The author also draws upon various canons from African episcopal councils in which Augustine participated that demonstrate a high level of coordinated, pastoral activity among his colleagues in favor of changes in imperial legislation that would benefit the poorer classes of society.

Michael Hanby next considers Augustine's critique of Roman civil religion and the function of "just wars" within it, exposing a demonic sacrificial order incompatible with the sacrifice of Christ. He goes on to show how the church might appropriate this critique to confront contemporary imperial power and state violence.

In his chapter, Kevin Hughes explores Augustine's political vision on a smaller, practical scale. Augustine sees the household as a crucial sphere of political life, one essential to the cultivation of habits of humility and charity. His household politics offered his late antique Christian audience strategies to resist Rome's imperial "colonization of the imagination," and, Hughes suggests, it may offer surprising possibilities to households and families in an age of consumerism.

Thomas F. Martin, O.S.A., next shows how Augustine's monastic initiatives in Hippo Regius offer a concrete example of an organized, social community (the monastery), buttressed by his ample theoretical explanation. The fact that he chose to do so "in the city" rather than "in the wilderness" gave his monasticism a deliberate public face. Martin argues that this is not without political implication, offering an alternative model of the *vita socialis* to his Roman African world.

Thomas W. Smith guides us through the *City of God*, demonstrating how Augustine's treatment of politics there must be considered in light of his overarching pedagogy, which is aimed at transforming his audience's loves. A person whose life has been reoriented by love of God and neighbor uses political action as a vehicle for self-giving. Augustine thinks this reorientation, characteristic of the City of God, is the basis for a just, peaceful political life in this world.

Contemporary political theory presents the meaning of the destiny of human beings in political terms. Augustine, by contrast, presents the meaning of politics in terms of the twin destinies of human beings. Todd Breyfogle's chapter sketches the various and contradictory contemporary appropriations of Augustine's political thought and draws attention to some fundamental ambiguities in Augustine's own thought. Breyfogle argues that we misunderstand Augustine's political theory in large measure because we struggle to force Augustine's thought into the vocabulary and conceptual framework of modern liberalism, rather than listening to Augustine speak to us in and on his own terms. Breyfogle identifies three central Augustinian terms—society (societas), friendship (amicitia), and truth (veritas)—as indicative of ways in which Augustine helps us to rethink the fundamental framework of contemporary politics. While the chapter is ultimately suggestive rather than conclusive, it helps capture the non-institutional spirit of Augustine's rich reflections on politics in ways that illuminate the structure of Augustine's (and our own) political theory.

In his chapter, Louis Hamilton connects Donatism to the eleventh-century reforms of the Roman Church. His contribution to the debate is twofold. First, that Peter Damian's *Book of Gommorah* actually sets out the very Donatist argument that he would later try to counter. His was an argument against the purity of the sacraments performed by sinning clerics expressed in sexual terms, specifically an anxiety over clerical celibacy and homosexuality. Second, that anxiety about the purity of the sacraments was deeply rooted enough for the reformers to adopt an essentially Donatist position regarding the (re)dedication of altars and churches.

Eugene McCarraher contends that although modernity is thought to be marked by a "secular" or "disenchanted" world-view, an Augustinian reading of political and economic culture suggests a very different account. Seen through an Augustinian lens, modern political culture becomes a form of false worship (or fetishism) in which redemptive power is ascribed to the nation-state. Similarly, modern economic culture becomes a fetishism in which salvation depends on the commodity form. Both fetishes comprise the perverse enchantments of the modern earthly city, whose true redemption lies, as Augustine contended, in the political economy of the heavenly city—that is, in the ecclesial and sacramental practices of the Church.

Finally, Paul Wright argues that the political eschatology of Machiavelli's most provocative texts is at heart a volatile mixture of his peculiar classicism and Augustine's ambivalent relationship to the earthly city he would transcend. Their overlapping anthropologies are reflected in Augustine's struggle to sustain a critique of Rome with language borrowed from it, and Machiavelli's failure to develop a misanthropy free of theological dimensions. Ultimately, Augustinian typology fuels the civil religion of Machiavelli, which in the *Discourse on Remodeling Florence* takes on its most ambitious, perilous, and strangely pragmatic form.

These contributions together provide us not with a view of Augustine's politics, but, as the title of the series implies, a conversation with Augustine about politics. It has been our pleasure as editors to learn from our colleagues' work, though we remind readers that the views of individual chapters are not necessarily shared by us or the other contributors. Both the pleasure and learning are now increased by sharing these ideas with other partners in this vital and ongoing conversation.

Part I

HUMAN NATURE AND VIRTUE IN RELATION TO POLITICS

1

United Inwardly by Love: Augustine's Social Ontology

Phillip Cary

To UNDERSTAND AUGUSTINE'S political theory it helps to understand his ontology, his theory of being. Augustine is a Platonist, and his Christian Platonist ontology makes a sharp distinction between three levels of being: God, soul, and bodies.[1] The levels are ordered hierarchically: God is ontologically higher and better than the soul, which is ontologically higher and better than bodies. Augustine's ontology thus includes a sharper distinction between soul and body (treating them as two different kinds of being), as well as a higher valuation of the soul than most of us are comfortable with today. As a result there is much to make us uncomfortable in Augustine's political theory, which, like his theology, assumes an ontology most of us don't really like. But to begin with, let us set aside discomfort and try to understand. There is much to discover about Augustine's ontology that is exciting and beautiful, and even those of us who are not Platonists may find ourselves falling under the spell of its beauty. Once we have felt this attraction, we are in a better position both to learn from Augustine and to be responsible critics. We will also understand better some elements of Augustine's political theory that have long troubled his readers, such as his apparent "pessimism" (as it has been called) about political life, as well as other elements that are so troubling they are hardly ever mentioned, such as his observation that the ultimate difference between the city of God and the earthly city, is that the one is predestined to salvation and the other to damnation.[2]

Love Unites

What *is* a society, really? What makes a community of human beings a different kind of group than a pile of stones? This is the fundamental question of
social ontology: the question about what it is for a society, a community, or a
people to have being. It is a question that preoccupies Augustine in the *City of
God*, as he comes back over the course of many books of that work (which
means in effect over the course of many years of his life) to Cicero's definition
of a community or people (*populus*) as "a group brought together by agreement in law and common interest."[3] He had in fact already been preoccupied
by this question for over a decade before beginning the *City of God*. He saw
the nature of social unity as an underlying issue in the disagreement between
Donatists and Catholics about who was the true Church, the community of
God's people in Christ. In both the Donatist controversy and the *City of God*,
Augustine's fundamental point about social ontology is that love makes one
community out of many souls. That is why he corrects Cicero by putting love
rather than law at the center of his definition of a people. For societies can be
lawless, existing without justice,[4] but they cannot have existence at all without
love. So Augustine proposes a new definition: a community or people is "a
group of many rational beings that is brought together by shared agreement
in the things it loves."[5] The ontological concept underlying this definition is
that unless a group of persons agrees in loving the same things (whether this
love be good or evil), it has no more unity than a mere collection of bodies in
one place, like a pile of stones.

The question about the being of society is an example of a kind of ontological problem familiar in the tradition of Platonist philosophy: a one-many
problem. How is it that many horses make up one species of animal? How is
it that many bricks make one house? How is it that many thoughts belong together in one mind? And how is it that many rational beings are one society?
Each kind of being has the kind of unity appropriate to it. The unity of a hap-
hazard pile of stones is different from the unity of a house constructed by the
skill of a builder, which is different again from the unity of a system of ideas
known by one mind, which is different finally from the unity of souls in one
society. And make no mistake about it: for Augustine the question of social
ontology comes down to a question about the unity of souls, not bodies. It is
by our souls that we are rational beings, as Augustine's definition requires. So
a social unity is not like a pile of stones or even like a house (whose unity is
imposed on it from without, by the agency of its builder), but is rather an inward unity of love, which is possible only for souls.

What joins human beings together is something distinctive to souls, not
bodies, as Augustine makes clear at the beginning of his most important anti-

Donatist treatise, which concerns the relation of baptism to the unity of the church. He explains how the Donatist schismatics are separated from the unity of the Catholic church:

> In the views they share with us they are with us, but in their dissent from us they withdraw from us. This kind of approach or departure should not be measured by bodily rather than spiritual movement. For as bodies are joined by continuity of place, so agreement of wills is a kind of contact of souls. (*On Baptism against the Donatists* 1.1.2)

Souls come together by means of a power they have but bodies don't—the will, which is the power of the soul by which we love. So agreement in willing the same things joins souls together by virtue of their shared love, and disagreement separates them into divided communities. Disagreement in will is also the root of dissension in mind. For it turns out that in Latin, dissent of mind implies disagreement in will, as speakers of Latin state their opinions by indicating what they intend or mean, using the verb *volo*, "I will." (For example, where we would say, "Plato thinks the philosopher is a lover of God," Augustine literally says that Plato "wills the philosopher to be a lover of God."[6]) So Augustine can use the language of will to indicate differences of opinion as well as conflicting desires. By the same token, for Augustine agreement of wills makes for a unity of thought as well as unity in love—precisely the unity appropriate to rational beings.

This is not a kind of unity bodies can have. Augustine relates it to a kind of motion souls can have but not bodies. Readers of the *Confessions* will be familiar with how love moves us, not simply by stirring up our emotions, but by attracting us to what we love. Love is like weight, which in ancient physics was more like what we now call specific gravity. Each kind of thing has its own specific weight, which may move it up or down. As the weight of a stone pulls it downward to its natural place of rest on the earth, the weight of fire draws it upward toward the celestial fire of the stars, which is where it belongs. That is the explanation given in ancient physics for why flames never move downward and stones don't rise to heaven when you throw them upward. Augustine turns this into a metaphor for the movement of the soul. A soul's earthly loves attract it to earthly things while charity, the love of God, is like fire ascending to heaven. In that sense, says Augustine, "My love is my weight: wherever I am carried, it carries me."[7]

This is not a movement in space. Here lies a crucial point of Augustine's ontology, to which we will frequently return. Only bodies literally move from place to place.[8] The soul's journey to God, as Augustine learned from Plotinus, is not a journey for the feet but for the will.[9] Charity (i.e., the state of the will which loves God above all things) is the motive force that brings us home to our place of eternal rest with God, for love is a desire for union with what is loved, as Augustine says: "What is all love? Does it not will to be one with what it loves?"[10] By the same token, when we find what we love we embrace it and keep it near. So the lover not only moves toward what he loves but "is glued to it by love" and "makes it part of his own soul" (*On Free Choice* 1.33). As Augustine explains, "such is the power of love, that what the mind has thought about for a long time with love, clinging to it by the glue of caring about it, it pulls in with itself."[11] Thus by love the soul both seeks unity and establishes it.[12] A drunkard's soul, for instance, seeks union with alcohol in the only way possible, by pouring it into his belly. A miser's soul seeks union with money in the only way possible, by acquisition and possession. A friend's soul seeks union with her friend, and it enjoys a unity that is possible only for souls, by which the two become one soul.[13] And charity seeks the ultimate union, which is possible only with God, by which we enjoy eternal life and happiness.

The great question of Augustine's politics is about the relation between the two latter kinds of unity, both of which are incorporeal. How is the union of one soul with another related to the union of the soul with God? Both are essential goals of the Christian life, as Jesus himself commanded that after loving God with our whole heart and mind and strength we must also love our neighbor as ourselves.[14] As Augustine's ethics revolves around these two kinds of love, so his politics revolves around the two kinds of unity they make possible. The city of God is the community of rational beings (humans and angels) brought together by love for God but also looking forward to eternal fellowship (*societate*) with one another.[15] What is unique about it is not that it is a community, but the particular kind of love that makes it a community. Augustine brings this out by comparing it to a group of people brought together by their shared love for a particular actor.[16] Their love draws them not only to the actor's performances, but also to each other's company. Moreover, they try to attract more people into the group, inducing them to join in the same love. Thus an enthusiastic fan club is a fine example of what Augustine means by a community. In the same way the city of God is a community, for "this fits what we do who are brought together by the love of God, to enjoy whom is to live in happiness" (*On Christian Doctrine* 1.30).

Thus a plurality of souls can be brought together (*sociatus*), not just by loving one another, but also by sharing a love for the same thing. This love changes who they are, for "what is loved necessarily affects the lover with itself" (*On Eighty-three Different Questions* 35.2). The soul takes on the character of what it loves, so "to see what a people is like, we should look at what they love" (*City of God* 19.24). The fan club imitates what they love in their favorite actor, while souls in the church become more and more like God—just, wise, and holy. Above all, the character of one's happiness too is dependent on the

character of what one loves. The drunkard's happiness is merely a bodily pleasure that quickly wears off,[17] the fan club's happiness is as false as the actor's
persona, and the happiness of the city of God is eternal life, because it loves
the one eternal God.[18]

Thus the happiness of all loves other than the church's is temporary, for
they lead in the end not to union but separation. The soul cannot love mortal
things without losing them sooner or later, which is why it is a deep unhappiness to "love one who will die as if he will not die"(*Conf.* 4.8.13). Because
friendship means a union of two souls, grief for a lost friend means a soul
ripped in two—as when Augustine's concubine was torn from him because
she stood in the way of a profitable marriage, and "my heart, where I was attached to her, was cut up and wounded, and it shed blood" (*Conf.* 6.15.25).
The good news is that things are different for souls united by love for God, as
Augustine sums it up in a principle that governs the whole narrative of the
Confessions: "Happy is he who loves You, and his friend in You, and his enemy
for Your sake. For he alone loses nothing dear to him, to whom all are dear in
Him who is never lost" (*Conf.* 4.9.14). There is no final separation of souls in
the church. Therefore if we would be happy we must love our friends in God,
because outside of God no soul keeps its beloved forever—all is ultimately
grief and eternal loss. That is the destiny to which the earthly city, with all its
multitude of competing and conflicting loves, is headed—an ultimate scatter-
ing, dissolution, and frustration.

Only the grace of God rescues some of the children of Adam from this reign
of death and makes a new community, built around the undeserved gift of a
love that never fails.[19] For according to Augustine's theology of grace, our love
for God is "poured into our hearts by the gift of the Holy Spirit."[20] Augustine's
argument with the Donatists centered on the outward sign marking the presence of this gift in the soul. His key point is that the means by which grace is
given are internal, not external. For it is possible to possess baptism as a valid
outward sign of unity, yet falsify it by inner dissent of will. It is like soldiers who
receive the official tattoo marking their membership in the army, but then
desert.[21] The tattoo remains valid and indelible, but the deserters' wills are in
conflict with what it signifies and thus render it false and ineffectual. They no
longer belong in heart to the army, even though they still have a bodily sign
that says they do. In the same way, Augustine argues, Donatist baptism is valid
but ineffectual. The Donatists are truly baptized, but they do not share the
inner love which binds the Catholic church in one and leads it to eternal happiness. Their souls dissent from the unity and peace of the Catholic church,
and "it is the peace of the Church that remits sins," which is the same as to say,
"unity remits" (*On Baptism against the Donatists* 3.23). So heretics and schismatics such as the Donatists possess the valid external sign of baptism, but not

the inner grace of forgiveness that it signifies, because "the love which 'covers a multitude of sins' is a gift proper to Catholic unity and peace" (*On Baptism against the Donatists* 3.21, quoting 1 Peter 4:8). Here we have the key elements of Augustine's social ontology in their original theological setting, years before he began writing *City of God.* His political theory grows out of this understanding of what it means for human beings to be social creatures, brought together with other souls by bonds of love and peace, where everything depends on precisely what it is they love.

Two Kinds of Tears

All loves outside the unity of the city of God lead to ultimate loss and irremediable grief. Of course Catholic Christians also grieve from time to time in this mortal life, but their loss cannot be lasting and they should take care not to grieve "like the others who have no hope."[22] This explains the puzzling episode in *Confessions* Book Nine when Augustine tries so hard to hold back his tears during his mother's funeral: he does not want to weep as if she had died unhappy or indeed had altogether died.[23] This episode offends most modern readers, who may be hazy about the nature of the afterlife, but are quite certain of the importance of expressing one's grief. An examination of the way this puzzling episode is rooted in Augustine's understanding of love and loss will lead us more deeply into his social ontology.

Augustine does not want to weep for his mother the same way he had wept earlier over the unnamed friend in *Confessions* Book Four, grieving like a man who feels his loss to be irrevocable, so that "only tears were sweet to me" (*Conf.* 4.4.9). At that time he had no real comfort, as he was ignorant of the true God and therefore had no ground of hope: it is as if everything was emptiness and absence. But now, Augustine the author explains to us, even that loss has turned out to be a comfort to him, for by death his friend "was snatched away from my insanity, to be kept safe with You for my consolation" (*Conf.* 4.4.8). Young Augustine's insanity was his devotion to the Manichaean heresy, into which he had led this friend and many others. He began to lose his friend— and gain him for eternity—on the day when, unconscious from a deadly fever, his friend was given a Catholic baptism. Augustine, the heretic, made fun of this ritual as soon as his friend woke up, but the response he got stunned him. His friend "shuddered at me as if I were his enemy" and told him to quit it "if I wanted to be his friend" (*Conf.* 4.4.8). And then shortly afterwards he died, put forever out of reach of the deadly heresy into which Augustine would have led him back. Imagine how differently Augustine the bishop would now feel if his friend had lived a year or two more, long enough to be lured back into heresy and then die in dissension from the Catholic church. In that case the soul of the man he loved would be permanently separated from the unity of the people of God, which means he would die eternally, suffering the penalty of unending punishment.[24] But instead, to Augustine's lasting comfort, his old friend now enjoys eternal life in God, just like his more recent friend Nebridius, of whose death Augustine speaks in tones of deep consolation, because he also died newly-baptized and now lives forever "in the bosom of Abraham" (*Conf.* 9.3.6). Both friends enjoy the eternal unity of the city of God to which Augustine himself now looks forward in confident hope.

So not all grief is alike. Monica herself, Augustine's devout Catholic mother, had to learn the difference between the two kinds of grieving. On the one hand, she wept because her son had fallen into heresy, the false faith that would eventually mean the death of his soul if he were not converted back to the Catholic church. To this weeping is addressed the prophetic assurance, "it cannot be that the son of these tears shall perish" (*Conf.* 3.12.21). These words are simply the most memorable instance of the principle we have already noticed, that "he alone loses nothing dear to him, to whom all are dear in Him who is never lost" (*Conf.* 4.9.14). As Augustine later explains, God could not have broken his mother's heart by rejecting "the tears with which she begged from you not gold or silver, nor any mutable and transient good, but the salvation of her son's soul" (*Conf.* 5.9.17). But He could refuse to answer her more earthly prayers. For she wept not only for her son's soul, but also for his body. Even a mother's love can be carnal. Like many mothers "but much more than most" (*Conf.* 5.8.15), she wanted to keep her child near her all the time. This was a kind of "smother love," as we might call it now, which had to be purged, punished, and overcome. So God takes her brilliant boy out of her sight in order to bring him eventually to conversion in Ambrose's Milan. It was a painful separation, for Augustine quite simply ditched his mother, telling her a lie to get away from her and sail off to Italy while she was left behind on the African shore, ignorant of his departure, still weeping and praying that God would not take him from her. Yet by taking away his body, God answered her prayers for his soul: "hearing the key point of her desire, You did not take care of what she was then asking for, in order to do in me what she was always asking for" (*Conf.* 5.8.15). Augustine will return to Africa a Catholic, but once again he will have to set sail without his mother, and this time the hard lesson will be for him to learn.

For by the time of her death, Monica has thoroughly learned her lesson, but Augustine has not. At least such is Augustine's portrait of her last days, spent in Italy where she has rejoined him and been the first to hear of his conversion. With her true prayers answered, she has nothing more to look forward to in this life and is more than willing to give up every earthly hope. In fact she begins to wonder "what I am still doing here and why I am here" (*Conf.* 9.10.26). Where she really is, it turns out, is the key question. It is the first question she asks after waking up from a faint which caused her to be "briefly withdrawn from present things" (*Conf.* 9.11.27). This carefully-phrased description could apply just as well to the conversation she has with Augustine a few days earlier at Ostia, when the two of them ascend together beyond the whole sensible world to touch, ever so briefly, the eternal Wisdom that feeds souls forever with the food of Truth in a region of unfailing plenty (*Conf.* 9.10.24–25). Is this not where they both hope to be in the long run? Monica is ready to leave here and go there, "her devout and pious soul released from the body" (*Conf.* 9.11.28) as Augustine puts it in describing her death. But first she has one last lesson for her children. As she lies on her deathbed, Augustine's brother reminds her of her old desire to die in her own country and be buried beside her husband, but she is long past that. "See how he talks!" (*Conf.* 9.11.27) she says to Augustine, and warns them both against caring more for her body than for her soul. She herself no longer cares where her corpse ends up, as she is convinced that "Nothing is far from God" (*Conf.* 9.11.28).

Yet at her funeral Augustine weeps as if she has gone away. He is disappointed with himself because he knows better. He misses her bodily presence and the habit of seeing her, but he knows he has not really lost her. Still, he cannot control his emotions and is "vehemently displeased that these human things, which had to happen in the due order and destiny of our condition, could have so much power over me" (*Conf.* 9.12.31). His are still the mixed tears that Monica once wept, caring not only for the soul (a care whose tears he always thoroughly approves), but for her body, as a son who misses seeing his mother—as if in burying her body he had lost *her*. He eventually allows himself to weep for her, but keeps telling himself he ought to know better.

No Separation in Space

Behind this remarkable episode of Augustine's reluctant tears is an ontological point. What Monica understands, and what bishop Augustine writing the *Confessions* has been trying to teach us, is that only bodies have the kind of being that is defined by locality and confined to one place, so only bodies can be distant from each other in space. God is present everywhere and undivided, so no spatial distance can separate anything from him ("Nothing is far from God"). Such presence is impossible to conceive unless one notices that the soul too is a being not extended in space.[25] Though not immutable, the soul is like God in its nonspatial mode of being. It changes in time (for instance, from ignorant to wise, or from unhappy to happy), but it does not move around in space.[26]

Therefore, like God, it cannot be separated from anything in space (as if it needed to travel some number of miles to be reunited with it), but unlike God it can be separated by disordered will and misdirected attention.

Only sin separates us from God, as Augustine explains, quoting the prophet Isaiah.[27] This is a point of Platonist ontology expressed in biblical language. To put it in more philosophical language: "No one can lose Truth or Wisdom unwillingly. For no one can be separated from it in space. What is called separation from Truth or Wisdom is actually a perverse will, by which lower things are loved" (*On Free Choice* 2.37). Or, in Augustine's most brilliant combination of biblical and Platonist imagery, it is like when the Prodigal Son runs away from God his father and goes into a far country. No spatial distance separates the two, Augustine explains, using imagery from a favorite passage in Plotinus, for the Prodigal does not travel by feet or chariot or ship. Rather, "to be far from Your face is to be in lustful, which is to say darkened, affections" (*Conf.* 1.18.28). The soul's separation from God is not in space, but in its own proper dimension of will and love and vision, the inner space of the soul which is not literally a space ("an inner place, not a place," as Augustine puts it).[28] God is always within us, as He is present in all things He has made,[29] but we can be separated from God by turning outward, away from our inmost self. The soul is capable of turning its back on its own insides, looking away from the light within,[30] and seeking among external things the beauty that would make it happy. Thus our separation from God, our failure to love Him with our whole heart and soul and will, can be described in the stunning paradox: "You were within, and I was outside" (*Conf.* 10.27.38). But by the same token, a soul that loves God, once released from the cares of the body and the concerns of this visible world, can in no way be separated from Him—nor from any soul who shares in the same love. That is the ontological grounding of the principle, "He alone loses nothing dear to him, to whom all are dear in God." It is as if Augustine were telling himself at his mother's funeral, "I should know that by now!"

Mother and son get a taste of this true and lasting union when, in their vision at Ostia, they succeed for a moment in touching eternal Wisdom together. As throughout the *Confessions*, Wisdom here means Christ, the second person of the Trinity, who is the Wisdom of God.[31] However, this is not Christ in the flesh, for Augustine is very clear about excluding all bodily things from what they see. Their vision is not of things that could be seen with the eyes of the body (like Julian of Norwich having visions of Christ on the cross). Picturing bodily things only gets in the way of seeing what God is really like, as Augustine has already explained to us.[32] To see God we must turn to look at our own soul, whose nonspatial mode of being is the best clue to God's incorporeal presence, undivided and unextended yet

everywhere in the universe.[33] Thus for Augustine the love of God demands
an inward turn: "Who is this above the head of my soul? Through my soul
itself will I ascend to him" (*Conf.* 10.7.11).

What the vision at Ostia shows us is that this inner ascent need not be solitary. The inner space of the Augustinian soul is not solipsistic, inviolably separated from other souls by the kind of inner privacy imagined in modern philosophy. It is not like a dark room in which we view only our own private
ideas, as described by John Locke.[34] Augustine's inner self is a place to see Platonic ideas like Truth and Wisdom and the supreme Good, which are not private property but common to all souls.[35] We turn inward, look upward, and
all see one and the same Sun shining with divine light. The vision at Ostia in
Confessions Book Nine has the same structure as the visions Augustine describes earlier in the *Confessions* in connection with his reading of the books
of the Platonists.[36] These descriptions in turn are based on the ascent to the
vision of God he had worked out many years before in his treatise *On Free
Choice*. In all three settings the soul is the great clue to the incorporeal nature
of God.[37] The true seeker of God turns inward to examine the soul's powers,
ascending from sense perception to the intellectual power of the mind, and
then looks above the mind at the light by which it was made. What it sees then
is described in various terms, such as Wisdom and Truth, eternal Beauty and
supreme Good, but all are names for God.

Inner Unity

The treatment of inner ascent in *On Free Choice*, which is by far the longest of
the three, insists on the point that the ultimate object of inner vision is the
same for everyone. Once again, what we need to see is eternal Wisdom, the
second person of the Trinity, but not the incarnate Christ, for it is feminine
(like the Latin term *sapientia*), not masculine like the man Jesus. It is precisely
her presence within the soul rather than in the externality of flesh that makes
divine Wisdom equally accessible to all who love her, a good we can all share
without dividing it or cutting it up in pieces like a bodily thing:

> So we have what we can all enjoy equally and in common: there is no shortage
> or deficiency in her. All her lovers can have her without being jealous; she is com-
> mon to all and chaste for each. No one says to anyone else: "Get back so I can get
> to her" or "Hands off, so I can get a hug too." Everybody can cling to the same
> one and touch her.[38]

This is why Monica and Augustine could touch the same Wisdom together.
She belongs to everyone who longs for her, and she can feed them all with her

very self without being divided up into separate portions so that one person has less than another:

> None of her food is torn apart; there is nothing you drink from her that I can't drink. You don't change anything of hers from common to private property; what you get from her, remains whole for me. . . . . For nothing of her ever becomes property of any one person or persons, but the whole of her is common to all together. (*On Free Choice* 2.37)

The One imparts herself to the many without division or loss. Thus the inner vision of Wisdom can be shared not only by Augustine and Monica, but by the whole city of God together, without fear of shortage or deficiency. Each one of them can have it all. This is why the city of God is immune from the endemic warfare of the earthly city, whose members are united in a love of external goods for which they must compete.

Augustine's concept of the inner union of love thus affords him a powerful analysis of the roots of human division: in the earthly city, precisely the source of social unity is also the source of social conflict.[39] Whenever people agree in loving something other than God they are prone to fight over it, because there is never enough to go around and what there is must be divided before everyone can have a piece. Such is the ontological basis of war and peace. Those whose hearts are devoted to temporal goods do not know lasting peace, because they seek happiness in beings that cannot remain whole and uncorrupted; while those who love God with their whole hearts are made happy by a good they cannot fight over, because it belongs as an undivided whole to each one of them. The nonspatial being of the divine, indivisible and incorruptible, thus makes possible true unity and undisturbed love among souls, instead of the ever-imminent conflict and divisions of the earthly city.

By the same token, the indivisible unity of the inner Good means that the inner world of the soul is by nature a space shared in common, not a private world in which each soul is separated and alone. If this is hard to imagine, try using an image from Plotinus which influenced Augustine.[40] Picture the inner world as a huge sphere shining with divine light, at whose center is the supreme Good. Call this sphere "soul." On its surface are many faces looking outward. We could call these our individual souls, though Plotinus would call them rather divided souls. They are separated from each other, unaware of each others' interior, only insofar as their attention is riveted on the world outside, the external world of bodies. But if they turned "into the inside," as Plotinus puts it, they would see both the truth and their own inward unity. For in reality, Plotinus teaches, all souls are one.[41] The One they all love is at their common center, if they would only turn inward and see it. So in Plotinus, as in Augustine, the inward turn does not end in privacy and isolation, but in the common Good in which all souls are united.

But Plotinus stands in need of correction before Augustine can fully endorse his inward turn. For the Christian, God must be found not only within us but above us, as the Creator is ontologically superior to the soul he created. Thus Augustine's project of inward turn always includes a crucial second turning point, where the mind recognizes that God is not only within but above, so that to see him it must turn inward but also upward.[42] This extra step is what makes inward privacy conceivable for the first time in the history of Western thought. For once we assume the necessity of this twofold movement of the soul we can imagine taking the first step without the second, entering the inner space of the self, but not looking up to see the divine light. In that case we find ourselves in a world all our own, exploring images and memories that we do not have in common with others.[43] In fact, given the sinfulness of our loves, we usually inhabit not the shared inner space of those who embrace true Wisdom, but the external world of transitory beauties,[44] and what we find in ourselves is not God, but only our own ignorance and sin. Thus our disordered loves, separating us from God, separate us also from one another. Our inner selves are obscured and hidden from each other, not because they have to be, but because of our darkened affections. The private inner self is born in sin.[45]

This means that the purity of heart with which we finally see God will also give us a new clarity in seeing one another's souls. Picking up on a passage of Plotinus,[46] Augustine puts into circulation a notion that will become the basis for a deep form of nostalgia in the Western tradition: the desire to see what is in the minds of our friends. What can be seen in this mortal life is the mere bodily exterior; the inner content of our friend's soul is hidden from us so that we can only believe it, not see it for ourselves.[47] But the city of God looks forward to a deeper and more inward unity in which we will all see through mere exteriors to the depths of the inner self:

> For there will be but one city out of many minds that have one soul and one heart in God, and the perfection of our unity after this present pilgrimage will be that everyone's thoughts will not be hidden from one another nor in conflict among themselves on any point. (*On the Good of Marriage* 21)

In Augustine's version of heaven "our thoughts will be obvious to one another" (*City of God* 22.29), because God is "the light by which all those things which are now hidden in human hearts shall be made manifest" (Letter 92.2). This powerful fantasy informs Dante's *Paradiso*, where the souls of the blessed see each others' thoughts, and it has come to be taken as the standard for attempts to explain our knowledge of other persons, as if we *really* know one another only to the extent that our knowledge approaches this ideal.

It is nostalgia as well as fantasy, because the underlying notion is that the inability to see into each other's hearts is not natural, but a terrible loss, a punishment due to our primal Fall from transparency. For Augustine, the sin of Adam and Eve brought with it not only the death of our bodies, but the hiddenness of our souls:

> Abandoning the face of Truth, they craved the pleasure of lying, and God changed their bodies into this fleshly mortality, where lying hearts are hidden. For we should not believe that thoughts could be hidden in those heavenly bodies as they are in these bodies. Rather, I think that just as some of the movements of our souls appear in the face and especially in the eyes, so in the transparency and simplicity of heavenly bodies none of the movements of our souls will be hidden in any way. (*On Genesis against the Manichaeans* 2:32)

The corruption of human nature due to sin has given us bodies that are not only mortal but opaque, blocking the vision by which one soul sees another. As the blessedness of heaven undoes our mortality, therefore, so it will undo the opacity of our bodies and the hiddenness of our souls. In contrast to most modern social theories, where language is the fundamental glue of human society by which we escape inner privacy, Augustine sees all outward forms of signification as inadequate remedies for the loss of this true inward unity in which everyone's thoughts are directly visible to everyone else. "The reason all these words are uttered bodily is the abyss of this world and the blindness of the flesh, by which thoughts cannot be seen and there is need of rattling in the ears" (*Conf.* 13.23.34). It is as if language began at Babel, or the confusion of tongues at Babel took place right after the expulsion from Eden.[48] In the *City of God* language is seen to divide as much as unite us, as Augustine observes that a dog is better company for a man than a fellow human being who can't speak his language.[49] In the *Confessions*, the baby learning to express his inner thoughts in external words is entering "the stormy fellowship [*societate*] of human life" (*Conf.* 1.8.13), where he will be beaten for not learning the eloquence needed to manipulate others' minds.[50] Mere external words represent for Augustine not the glue of society, but the deceptive and domineering power of rhetoric.[51] We need words in our lives only because of the way our minds and bodies have been corrupted by sin.

Unnatural Politics

Augustine's social ontology thus assumes a primal unity of human souls prior to the Fall, which was lost in Adam but is being restored in Christ. In the beginning all souls were one in Adam, and indeed Augustine makes the absolutely

startling claim that, "we all were that one man."[52] Evidently we are to understand that all our souls began together as one, which is why the sin of the first
man is the original sin for which every human being is rightly held guilty. Augustine does not say exactly how this works, but it seems clear that something
like the Plotinian notion of the unity of all souls is at work here.[53] That unity
has been shattered by the Fall, which divides souls from one another in conflicting loves. But in the final happiness, that unity will be restored and renewed, as souls are brought together no longer in Adam, but in Christ. The
consequence of this for political theory is that the site of true human unity is
not the State, but the Church, which is the part of the heavenly city that is still
on its earthly pilgrimage. The earthly city, by contrast, consists of all those who
came from the original unity in Adam but will be excluded by damnation from
the final unity in Christ.[54]

    That is why the source of the difference between the two cities is divine pre-
destination, by which God chooses to give the saving grace of Christ to some
souls rather than others. Predestination is simply God's foreknowledge of how
he will give his gifts,[55] which means that "the only difference between predestination and grace is that predestination is the preparation of grace and grace
is the giving itself" (*On the Predestination of the Saints* 19). Predestination dif-
ferentiates the two cities because grace makes the ultimate difference between
the saved and the damned. "Who makes you different?" the apostle Paul asks,
and follows up with another rhetorical question: "What do you have that you
have not received?"[56] As Augustine reads these two questions, the answers are
clear: every good gift (including the grace to believe and love God and any
other goodness in our will that leads to salvation) is received from God, who
alone makes anyone different from the mass of damnation that all humanity
has become in Adam. For there is a terrible remnant of the original unity in
Adam, consisting of the guilty and corrupted human nature we all share because of our participation in original sin. Picking up on a metaphor from
Paul, Augustine compares the whole human race to a lump of clay, from some
of which a potter chooses to make vessels fit for honor, leaving the rest to become vessels fit for destruction.[57] In the same way all humanity is lumped together in common guilt because of original sin, but God by his grace chooses
to save some undeserving sinners, leaving the rest to earn their own damnation (since there are none who can save themselves). The earthly city is the
bearer of this residual unity of sin in Adam, the lump or mass of damnation.

    That is why the politics of the earthly city is not essential to human nature.
It is rooted not in the way God created human nature, but in the way Adam
corrupted it. So Augustine does not treat "politics," as we ordinarily conceive
it today, as a natural form of human life.[58] The life of the earthly city is a sinful dead end in the story of human social life. This does not mean human be-

ings are naturally asocial (as in the typical assumption of social contract sce-
narios in modern political theory, which posit a "state of nature" prior to society). Rather, it means that the true and natural human society is that of the
heavenly city. For the Good that fulfills our nature as rational beings is eternal
rather than temporal, which means our natural happiness consists in a heavenly rather than an earthly life. So it is the heavenly city rather than earthly
city that lives naturally, in the sense of seeking and enjoying those goods
which are most truly appropriate to human nature.

This point is easy to miss if one makes a habit of distinguishing between natural and supernatural happiness, as many readers of Augustine have done ever
since Thomas Aquinas. Augustine knows no such distinction.[59] For him eternal
life in God is our natural fulfillment, the only good that can make us truly
happy, which means it is the state in which human nature is whole, pure, uncorrupted by sin, and therefore most truly itself. So the earthly city is not related
to the life of the heavenly city as natural is to supernatural, but as a nature corrupted by sin and mortality is to a nature being restored by grace to purity and
immortality. Augustinian politics concern earthly peace, but earthly peace is
only a concern so long as we are mortal,[60] and we are not mortal by nature. Augustine underlines this using the language of natural law: "even the death of the
body was not inflicted on us under the law of nature, by which God made no
death for humanity, but under the desert of sin" (*City of God* 13.15). Hence it is
not the natural state of things when the heavenly city is on its earthly pilgrimage, sharing for a time the condition of mortality with the earthly city. Although
it makes use of the peace proper to the latter, obeys its laws and preserves harmony with it on things pertaining to earthly peace, this is only "until mortality
itself, which makes such peace necessary, passes away." (*City of God* 19.17). This
is not human nature, but a temporary state of affairs until the restoration of
human nature in Christ is made perfect in eternal happiness.

The Ontology of Peace

We can see why Augustine does not think of politics as belonging to human
nature if we watch the theme of peace as it unfolds in the nineteenth book of
the *City of God*, the *locus classicus* of Augustine's political theory. But to do so,
we must be careful not to replace Augustine's assumptions with Thomistic or
modern assumptions of our own. For instance, we must not neglect the fundamental context he establishes for his political theory at the beginning of
Book Nineteen—namely, the quest for our ultimate end, which is happiness.
As Augustine points out, this is the overarching quest of all ancient philosophy, for "there is no reason for human philosophizing but to be happy" (*City*

of God 19.1). For modern readers, this is an assumption that takes some getting used to. Augustine is operating in a context where he can take it for
granted (as we after Kant cannot) that the point of philosophy in general and
of ethics in particular is to find happiness. It helps to realize that the Latin
term for happiness (*beatitudo*) is the same word that we translate "blessedness" when we run across it in a medieval author. In the ancient philosophical tradition since Aristotle, happiness always means the ultimate end of
human life, the final fulfillment beyond which there is nothing more to seek.[61]
That is why Augustine speaks of happiness as a kind of rest: it is the goal in
which all our restless desires come to ultimate rest, seeking nothing further.[62]
This is closely related to Augustine's notion of peace, though it is not quite the
same thing. "Rest" means the ultimate fulfillment of desire; "peace" means the
ordered harmony of those who have found rest. So rest always brings peace,
and true peace is only possible when we have found eternal rest.

The great question of ancient philosophy is what the ultimate goal or final
end of humanity really consists in.[63] This is the same as asking: what is it that
makes us truly happy? There are a great many possible answers, which Augustine (using the schema of Varro's treatise *On Philosophy*) spells out for us.
What is most important for modern readers to be clear about in this welter of
possibilities is that Augustine never assumes happiness must be a feeling. That
would require that it be a form of pleasure (i.e., of good feeling) which is the
hedonist view (where "hedonism" does not mean living a wild life, but is a
technical term for the philosophical view that happiness is a form of pleasure,
hedone in Greek). Augustine operates within an anti-hedonist consensus
shared by Stoic, Platonist, and Aristotelian philosophers, who identify the
happy life with some combination of virtue and wisdom. Augustine's theological variation on this crucial pair of philosophical terms is the righteousness of faith and the vision of God, respectively.

The initial treatment of happiness leads to the point on which Christianity
differs from the philosophers: the question of whether we can be happy in this
life. The theme of peace emerges in the course of Augustine's answering this
question with a resounding no. Even those who are virtuous or righteous in
this life are not yet happy in reality, but only in hope, because as long as they
live in this mortal life they are not yet at peace. Even their virtues are really a
constant warfare against the vices that remain in their corrupted nature.[64] The
concept of peace becomes a theme at this point because that is how Augustine
has always explained the imperfection of human righteousness in the context
of Paul's doctrine of law and grace. In his exegesis of Paul, Augustine divides
our journey toward happiness into a sequence of four stages: before law, under
law, under grace, and *in peace*.[65] This sequence applies to individuals as well as
to the human race as a whole. Each stage is defined in terms of our warfare

against sin: before we know the law we do not struggle against it; when we are under the law we struggle and lose; when divine grace is given we struggle and win; and when we reach our ultimate goal we no longer struggle but live in perfect righteousness, happiness and peace.

So prior to the *City of God*, Augustine's use of the term "peace" centered on the happy life (i.e., after this mortal life) in which we are no longer even capable of sinning.[66] This happiness involves a special kind of peace between body and soul, in which the former readily obeys the latter instead of leading it into carnal desires. This peace in turn follows from a higher and more fundamental peace in which the soul obeys God. So the soul's disobedience to God in the sin of the first man meant the loss not only of peace with God, but also of peace with its own body, resulting in a warfare between the two parts of human nature. This is one of the fundamental punishments of sin: because the soul disobeyed God, the body disobeys the soul.[67] (The most wrenching form of this disobedience is death itself, as the first task the soul has in governing the body is to give it life.) Both forms of peace are ordered hierarchically: the soul, which exists at the middle level of Augustine's three-tiered hierarchy of being, lives in perfect peace when it obeys God, its ontological superior, and is obeyed by the body, its ontological inferior.

What makes the theme of peace in *City of God* Book Nineteen so complex is that this Pauline strand of Augustine's concept of peace is combined with another, which I will call the Cyprianic strand. Cyprian was the great African bishop and theologian of a previous century (d. 258) to whose writings both Donatists and Catholics appealed. He was a champion of the unity of the church,[68] as well as its peace.[69] So Augustine's polemics against the Donatists dwell on the unity and peace of the church, as we have already seen. What Augustine adds to Cyprian is an ontological understanding of the nature of unity and peace. Everything is what it is insofar as it is one, as Augustine explains in one of his earliest writings: "In order for a stone to be a stone, all its parts and its whole nature must be solidified in one. And how about a tree? Does a tree really exist if it is not one tree? . . . A people (*populus*) is one city, which is threatened by dissension—and what is dissenting but not consenting as one?"[70] In a slightly later treatise, he very briefly says something similar about how peace is necessary for being: "Even a bodily thing has a certain harmony of its parts, without which it could not exist. . . . A body has a kind of peace because of its form, without which it would not exist at all" (*On True Religion* 21). This ontology of unity and peace undergirds Augustine's contributions to the Catholic side of the controversy with the Donatists. The unity of the church that Cyprian championed and the peace of the church that he would not violate, are essential to the very being of the church as a community of souls brought together by love of one God.

Augustine develops the ontology of peace at some length in Book Nineteen of the *City of God*,[71] as he turns to a point on which Christianity agrees with the philosophical tradition: that the happy life for human beings is a social life. In the course of his argument that human beings cannot be happy in this mortal life, Augustine spends several chapters describing the unhappiness specifically of social life, concentrating especially on the miseries we suffer because other souls are unknown to us, their inner thoughts hidden from our mind's eye. That is why judges must torture innocent witnesses, for instance.[72] Even friendship, that sweetest of all human bonds, is not certain to be a lasting good, because we cannot be sure of our friend's heart or how it might change.[73] There is no lasting peace in this mortal life, yet there is a kind of peace which is necessary for the very being of mortal things (and here the Cyprianic strand is introduced), without which living bodies could only dissolve like corpses and social life would be impossible.[74] Even rebels and robbers must be at peace among themselves if they are to join in fighting or stealing. So Augustine's ontology of peace implies that there is always some sort of peace on earth that is worth preserving, though it is not the true and lasting peace for which the heavenly city hopes.

The ontological problem with the earthly peace is that it introduces hierarchy among ontological equals. Whereas the (Pauline) peace between soul and body and between soul and God is a peace of hierarchical obedience, the (Cyprianic) peace of a community of souls preserves the unity of those who all belong at the same ontological level. So when Augustine uses the language of natural law to explain that we are naturally social beings, he immediately proceeds to the implication that we are naturally equal as well. After noting that even nonsocial animals like tigers and eagles come together for sexual intercourse, reproduction, and raising of young, Augustine proceeds:

> How much more is a human being led by a law of his own nature to enter into society and obtain peace, as far as is in him, with all human beings! For even evil people fight for the peace of those who are their own—and want as much as possible to make everyone their own, so that everybody and everything serves one person. And how can this be unless they agree to his peace, whether from love or fear? Thus pride is the perverse imitation of God. For it hates equality with its fellows (*sociis*) under Him, but would impose upon its fellows its own domination in place of Him. For it hates the just peace of God and loves its own wicked peace. But what it cannot avoid doing is to love peace of some kind or other. For no vice is so contrary to nature that it destroys the very last vestige of nature. (*City of God* 19.12)

To seek peace is not a moral but an ontological law, a law of human nature. Even the wicked cannot but seek some kind of peace or other, but they seek the peace of conquest, lusting for domination over other souls with a pride that aims to replace God's rule with their own, thus replacing the natural equality of souls under God with slavery under themselves. So the ontology of peace allows for a certain sort of human fellowship or society (*societas*) which does not fit Augustine's definition of a community or people (*populus*), because it need not be based on shared love, but only on fear and domination. Yet even without love, peace can preserve a certain real though inadequate level of human unity. This kind of peace is a vicious injustice that corrupts human nature and society, but also preserves it in being, affording a certain stability to various unhappy forms of social life. Such is typically the peace of the earthly city.

Earthly Peace

The peace desired by the earthly city should therefore not be confused with the natural gift of peace that God gives to all mortal creatures. When Augustine lists ten kinds of peace ordained under the laws by which God makes peace among mortal things through "the tranquility of order," the peace of the earthly city is not on the list.[75] The members of the earthly city belong to the category of "the unhappy," who are in a state of perturbation rather than tranquility.[76] Yet they must have some sort of peace if they are to exist at all, just as evil things must have some sort of goodness in order to remain in being. Thus the ontology of peace works just like Augustine's ontology of good, which denies the possibility of pure evil. Even the devil must have something good in him, else he could not have being, since all being is created by a good God.[77] In the same way, the earthly city must have some kind of peace, else it could not be at all. Therefore the temporal peace by which God preserves the being of mortal men applies to the earthly city too.[78]

Yet "temporal peace" should not be confused with "earthly peace." The one is a temporal good given by God, the other is the result of the earthly city's sinful attempt to enjoy temporal goods. "Enjoyment" (*fructus*) is a technical term from Augustine's ethics, which is based on his distinction between using and enjoying (*uti* and *frui*). Temporal goods are not to be enjoyed for their own sake, but should be used in such a way that we may come to enjoyment of the eternal good.[79] So the difference between the earthly city and the heavenly city is that the one enjoys, the other only uses, the earthly peace: "In the earthly city every use of temporal things is related to enjoyment of earthly peace, while in the heavenly city it is related to the enjoyment of eternal peace" (*City of God* 19.14). This is the familiar theme in new dress: the earthly city is united by love of temporal goods, the heavenly city by love of the one eternal Good.

Augustine proceeds to relate this theme to his ontology of peace, discussing each of the ten kinds of peace in turn.[80] The crucial point in Augustine's political theory comes in the transition between the seventh and eighth kinds of peace: that is, from the peace of the household to the peace of the city (not to be confused with the peace of the *earthly* city, which is not among the ten on the list).[81] But to understand this transition the ethical context must be kept in mind (again, it is a matter of paying attention to Augustine's own assumptions), which means we must back up two steps and start with the fifth kind of peace, that between human beings and God. This consists in obedience to the two commands that "God the teacher teaches," that we love first God and then neighbor (*City of God* 19.14). Obedience to the second command is in turn the basis of peace between human beings (the sixth kind of peace). To love our neighbors as ourselves means counseling them to love God, so that they too might come to the same Good we desire for ourselves. The giving and receiving of this kind of counsel is the peace that is natural to human beings in the state of their mortality, when they have not yet reached eternal happiness. It begins with those neighbors who are nearest, "such as wife, children, domestic servants (*City of God* 19.14). Thus the peace of the household is a certain kind of counsel, which fits the definition of "an ordered harmony of commanding and obeying among those who live together," as Augustine proceeds to explain: "Commanding is done by those who give counsel, as man to wife, parents to children, and master to slave; whereas obeying is done by those who receive counsel: as woman to husband, children to parents, and slaves to master" (*City of God* 19.14). Here we come upon the central conundrum of Augustine's political theory, which is how the unnatural relationship of slavery finds its way into the peace of the household, and what that means for its relationship to the peace of the city.[82] Augustine evidently takes the subordination of women and children to be natural, due to their bodily inferiority,[83] but he devotes a whole chapter to showing that slavery is unnatural, a result of our sinful condition which can be just only in a context of just punishment.[84]

The problem is that "our just fathers" (Augustine is thinking especially of the Old Testament patriarchs) had slaves.[85] But slavery in a household ruled by a member of the city of God is different from what you might expect. Augustine admits that with regard to temporal goods, the patriarchs treated their slaves differently from their children (for of course slaves were not heirs). "But when it comes to worshiping God, in whom eternal goods are hoped for, they counseled all members of the household with equal love" (*City of God* 19.16). So at the most fundamental level, both ontologically and ethically, all souls are treated equally in the household that lives by faith. The true paterfamilias is the father who "counsels everyone in the family to worship and serve God as if they were his own children, desiring and preferring to come to that heavenly household where the duty of commanding mortals is no longer necessary, because there will be no more duty of giving counsel to those who are happy in that immortality" (*City of God* 19.16). Until that final happiness is reached, the good paterfamilias keeps order and peace in the household by punishment when necessary, but never out of a lust for domination. In such a house, "fathers must endure more in ruling [*dominantur*] than slaves in serving" (*City of God* 19.16).

So why would Christian households have slaves at all? This is precisely the point at which Augustine makes the transition from the peace of the household to the peace of the city. He accepts the commonplace of classical political theory that makes the household an integral part of the city, so that "it behooves the paterfamilias to take up from the laws of the city the precepts by which he rules his own house, so it may be adjusted to the peace of the city."[86] Slavery belongs in the Christian household, it seems, only because it is present in the city of which the household is part.

Which city is that, one might ask? Certainly not the city of God. When Augustine speaks of "the peace of the city" here, he refers to a definition modeled on that of the peace of the household: both are "an ordered harmony of commanding and obeying," the one "among those who live together" (*cohabitantium*), the other "among citizens" (*civium*). This definition has conceptually more in common with Cicero's definition of a community (brought together by agreement in law) than with Augustine's (brought together by loving the same things). It is in fact the closest Augustine comes to a notion of a political life that is natural to us. The city to which the household contributes might conceivably be some actual empirical city like Rome or Carthage, though Augustine does not say so. This kind of city would include members from both the heavenly and the earthly city, and would therefore be bound into one not by loving the same things, but by obeying the same laws, as Cicero's definition suggests.

But that is a road Augustine does not take. Instead he proceeds to distinguish between two sorts of household, those which live by faith (which would include the households of faithful Old Testament patriarchs like Abraham) and those which do not. The difference (we should not be surprised) is that the latter "pursues an earthly peace in things advantageous to this temporal life" while the former "looks for eternal things promised in the future" (*City of God* 19.17). Of course they both use the things that are necessary for this mortal life, but the end for which they use them is entirely different. In other words, the two kinds of household turn out to be exactly parallel to the two cities, which Augustine proceeds to discuss next. At this point we immediately lose sight of empirical cities like Rome and Carthage (if they were ever really in view) and come to the central theme of Augustine's political theory, the earthly peace that is shared by both cities. For the earthly city "does not live by faith but desires earthly peace," and thus takes "the ordered harmony of commanding and obeying among citizens," which defines the peace of the city, and fixes it on "a certain settlement [*compositio*] of human wills concerning the things that pertain to mortal life" (*City of God* 19.17). Earthly peace means we do not fight too much over the temporal goods that all mortals need. The heavenly city has use for such a peace while it is still on its pilgrimage on earth, but unlike the earthly city does not seek to enjoy it for its own sake, but longs rather for eternal peace.

What disappears from sight with this quick move to the two cities theme is the possibility of a Christian ruler analogous to the Christian paterfamilias. For while the households that Augustine describes as living by faith are empirical groups ruled by particular human fathers, the two cities are not empirical cities and have no merely human rulers. The heavenly city has God for its king, and the earthly city has no place for Christian kings in any of its parts, for its very being consists in the refusal to love and worship the one true God. Thus the key move of a patriarchal politics, which makes the king to be the father of his country and legitimates his power as an extension of parental power, is blocked from the outset.[87] With the possibility of a Christian political ruler goes the possibility of imagining a politics where all are treated equally, as in the Christian father's rule over his family. For equality in the Christian household depends on the ontology of the soul and its true happiness, which consists in enjoyment of eternal rather than temporal goods. Precisely for this reason Augustine does not expect to find the equality that is natural to all souls in the earthly city, the community whose being is wrapped around a damnable love for temporal goods.

This "pessimism" about politics, which has troubled so many scholars of Augustine, locates him in a unique place on the conceptual map of ancient political theory. On the one hand, he has absolutely none of the utopian tendency to imagine an earthly politics free of the lust for domination. On the other hand, he cannot be classed together with more realistic versions of ancient political theory. For instance, his views are almost exactly opposite to those of Aristotle, who affirms politics as a natural human activity together with the naturalness of slaves being part of the property of the household.[88] Augustine on the contrary recognizes the unnaturalness of slavery, but at the price of seeing all politics as unnatural, pervaded as it is with servitude and domination.

My conclusion is one that most Augustine scholars have been resisting for a long time: insofar as politics concerns the life of the earthly city, Augustine must regard it as an unnatural activity, allowing no room for a specifically

Christian politics. Augustine's schema of the two cities does not exclude Christians from making positive contributions to the earthly peace, but it leaves no place for the concept of a Christian ruler outside the household. I know this is rather astonishing to find in a treatise written by a citizen of an empire that had been ruled by Christians for over a century. But it is the inevitable consequence of the very being of the two cities, according to Augustine's social ontology. And in point of fact Augustine does not have anything to say to or about Christian rulers in the political theory developed in Book Nineteen of the *City of God*.[89]

Corrections

Western Christian political theory may begin with Augustine, but it does not end there. Medieval theologians come along and correct Augustine's deficiencies without quite realizing the changes they are making in his political theory. Above all, they supply the notion of a Christian ruler and of political life that can and should be ordered in a specifically Christian way. Thus Augustine's two cities is transformed into church and empire, both Christian: the Roman Catholic Church and the Holy Roman Empire. In much the same vein, Reformation theologians speak of two kingdoms, church and state, the latter to be ruled by Christians if possible. Both traditions differ from Augustine in offering a great deal of advice to political rulers concerning the Christian conduct of their office. These changes cohere with the deep Thomistic correction of Augustine's ontology, which makes this earthly life natural to human souls, elevating our heavenly beatitude to supernatural status. The Thomistic correction makes for better political theory than Augustine and perhaps for sounder Christian doctrine as well, but it also makes for inaccurate and anachronistic readings of Augustine.

This is not the only case in which I believe creative misreadings of Augustine have done us a fair amount of good. Strictly for purposes of Augustine scholarship, however, it is important to correct the corrections. In summary, here is how I propose to do that. We could define Augustinian politics as the promotion of the peace of the earthly city, and ask whether Augustine thinks this is a natural feature of human life. He clearly thinks it is a good thing, the proper responsibility of the state, to which the church also ought to contribute in its way. But that is not the same as to say it is natural. Surgery is a good thing if needed, but it is not a natural procedure. The standard correction of Augustine's political theory proposes that politics is not only good but natural, as if the earthly city's pursuit of earthly peace were a natural concern for lower goods, rather than what Augustine says it is: a sinful desire to enjoy temporal goods as if they were our ultimate happiness, rather than merely to use them for the ulterior purpose of arriving at eternal life. So the two cities are not related as natural to supernatural or as secular to sacred, but as damned to saved. The earthly peace is the social good which is possible even for the community of the wicked destined for damnation.

One could try to defend the standard correction using a different analogy, based on a distinction that is more clearly Augustinian than the natural/supernatural distinction. Suppose the earthly city were related to the heavenly city as body to soul, so that caring for earthly peace is like caring for our health, which Augustine identifies as one of the goods of temporal peace.[90] On that supposition one could suggest that just as the soul ought to give due care to bodily health (not of course loving the body more than God), so the church also ought to assist the state in caring for the natural, earthly peace of its citizens. Certainly nothing in the two cities schema requires Augustine to see anything wrong in the church providing such assistance from time to time.

But there is a disanalogy which wrecks this as an overall strategy for interpreting Augustine's two cities schema. As we have seen, Augustine believes it is not natural for the human body to die, but a punishment due to sin. When mortality comes to an end, the resurrected human body will live forever in heaven (a point of Christian doctrine which Augustine defends at great length elsewhere in the *City of God*),[91] while the earthly city and its peace based on domination and warfare will be no more. The human body, which truly belongs to human nature, will live forever together with the soul that rules it, but the earthly city passes away because its being is due not to nature, but to the corruption of human nature by sin and death. Unlike the earthly city, the path of the human body is not a dead end. Its health will be renewed, perfected, and established forever in the resurrection of the body. In the end, human life, even in the body, is by nature heavenly, not earthly.

So the peace of the earthly city should not be compared to health in the human body. Not the state, but the church, the body of Christ, is where the wound to human unity is being healed. Political peace, rather, is like a painful and inadequate remedy for the diseased condition of our flesh. It is not like good health, but like a wheelchair, an artificial thing for which we have every reason to be grateful, one we should use well and take good care of; but by the same token it is one we can look forward to leaving behind in the resurrection of the dead, when the true happiness of human nature arrives at last, in an eternal life that also means eternal health for the body.

In conclusion, I would propose a different correction, using Protestant and Eastern Orthodox resources, which unlike the Thomistic correction frankly acknowledges disagreement with Augustine. I would suggest that Augustine got it all backwards when he adopted the Platonist notion of intellectual vision, which implies that our eternal happiness consists in seeing God with the eye of our mind, enjoying him "not like a friend enjoying a friend but like the eye enjoying the light."[92] Rejecting this Christian Platonist notion of the vision of God means altering our notion of friendship as well. It means rejecting the fantasy of inward unity along with the desire to see into each other's hearts. It means being content with a knowledge of other persons that comes through external means and especially through listening and trusting what they have to say, on the model of the biblical notion of hearing God's word and believing it (the Protestant corrective).[93]

What then would eternal life look like? One biblical image is a marriage supper,[94] a gathering where diverse families are joined, bodies are fed, and people talk, sing, and dance. The vision of God then would mean something like seeing our host sitting at table with us, wiping all tears from our eyes and sharing with us his own body, as he is both God in the flesh and the first human being to be raised bodily from the dead. This is not the Platonist vision of a disembodied Idea of the Good beyond the whole sensible and temporal world,[95] but rather what the disciples saw on the Mount of Transfiguration (this is the Eastern Orthodox corrective)[96] when they beheld the glory of God in the face of Jesus Christ. A political theory that took this as the model of human community would, like Augustine, think of slavery and domination as unnatural, but would be able to give up the nostalgia for inner unity and replace it with an understanding of love that respects the external distance separating (but also joining, like a supper table) each one of us with the others whom we love. Respect for such external things as bodies and words is needed if we are really to know other persons, for in order to love others *as* other than ourselves, we must be happy to find them outside the space of our own self.

Notes

1. Letter 18.2. This and other texts in which Augustine spells out his three-tiered ontology are anthologized in Vernon Bourke, ed., *The Essential Augustine* (2nd ed; Indianapolis: Hackett, 1974) 43–66. For exposition, see Bourke's lecture, *Augustine's View of Reality* (Villanova, PA: Villanova University Press, 1964) 3–5.

2. *City of God* 15.1.

3. *City of God* 2.21 and 19.21: *coetum juris consensu et utilitatis communione sociatum.* All translations are mine.

4. Hence Cicero's definition fails because it leads to the preposterous conclusion that in a fallen world full of injustice there can be no such thing as human community: *City Of God* 19.21.

5. *City of God* 19.24: *coetus multitudinis rationalis, rerum quas diligit concordi communione sociatus.*

6. *City of God* 8.8: *Plato . . . vult esse philosophum amatorem Dei.*

7. *Conf.* 13.9.10. The same comparison appears also in *City of God* 11.28; and the physics of objects seeking their natural place of rest plays a role in the striking meditation on the unnaturalness of a human body hanging upside down in *City of God* 19.12.

8. In Letter 18.2, the being of God, soul, and bodies is distinguished according to their vulnerability to change. God is unchanging, bodies change in space and time, and the soul is changeable in time but not in space. To be utterly unchangeable is to be free from suffering, corruption, and death. To be unchangeable in space means, of course, that something does not move from place to place.

9. See *Conf.* 1.18.28 and 8.8.19, which echo Plotinus' imagery of feet, chariots, and ships in *Ennead* 1.6.8. This passage of Plotinus has an importance for Augustine that goes far beyond mere verbal echoes: see Robert J. O'Connell, *Soundings in St. Augustine's Imagination* (New York: Fordham University Press, 1994) 176–79.

10. *On Order* 2.48. See also *On the Trinity* 8.14: "What is love, then, but a kind of life that couples two things, the lover and the beloved, or desires to couple them?"

11. *On the Trinity* 10.7. Love as the soul's glue is a metaphor found also in *Conf.* 4.10.15. One of the things to which love can glue the soul is God: *On the Psalms* 62.17.

12. For a general discussion of love as a unitive force, see John Burnaby, *Amor Dei: A Study in the Religion of St. Augustine* (London: Hodder and Stoughton, 1938) 100–103.

13. *Conf.* 4.6.11.

14. For the centrality of this twofold command of love in Augustine's ethics, see *On Christian Doctrine* 1.20–29, whose import is briefly summarized in *City of God* 19.14 (a passage examined below). For an introduction to Augustine's ethics of love and its Platonist underpinnings, see Burnaby, *Amor Dei,* chapters 4–6.

15. *City of God* 14.28.

16. *On Christian Doctrine* 1.30.

17. See *Conf.* 6.6.9.

18. *City of God* 7 (preface). Note the conclusion of *City of God* 14.25: our life will not be happy until it is eternal. Thus the classical concept of happiness (*eudaimonia*) becomes in Augustine's medieval successors the theological concept of eternal blessedness (*beatitudo*). The key identification is between *beata vita* (Augustine's Ciceronian translation of *eudaimonia*) and the biblical phrase *aeterna vita* (eternal life). This identification is central to Augustine's synthesis of classical and biblical thought. For this identification, see in addition *On Eighty-three Different Questions* 35.2, Sermon 150.10, and *On the Trinity* 13.11 (which concludes, "there is no way life can be truly happy unless it is eternal").

19. *City of God* 14.1.

20. Romans 5:5, a central text in Augustine's doctrine of grace beginning with *Exposition of Some Propositions from Romans* 26 and 60, but most characteristically in *On the Spirit and the Letter* 5 and 42.

21. *On Baptism against the Donatists* 1.5.

22. 1 Thessalonians 4:13; see Augustine's Sermon 172 on this text, which takes a position on the value of grief consistent with both the moving defense of grief in *City of*

God 19.8 and his regrets about how he grieved over his mother in *Confessions* Book Nine, which we are about to examine. In this sermon he tells his congregation: "Pious hearts are permitted to be saddened by the death of their dear ones, with a sorrow that is curable, and they pour out for this mortal condition tears that can be consoled. These are soon restrained by the joy of faith, with which they believe that when believers die, they are gone from us a little while and pass on to better things."

23. *Conf.* 9.12.29.

24. When Augustine speaks of eternal death, he does not mean the extinction of the soul (for the soul is created immortal) but its eternal punishment and separation from God (see *City of God* 6.12). Eternal death is thus a specific kind of life after death: the kind that is opposite to "eternal life," a New Testament term which refers not to any old life after death, but specifically to the life of eternal happiness. So "eternal life" and "eternal death" are biblical terms for what are popularly called "heaven" and "hell."

25. *Conf.* 7.1.2.

26. Letter 18.2.

27. *Retractations* 1.5.2, quoting Isaiah 59:2, "Your sins make a separation between you and God."

28. *Conf.* 10.9.16—*interiore loco, non loco.*

29. *Conf.* 1.2.2.

30. *Conf.* 7.7.11.

31. 1 Corinthians 1:24, "Christ the Virtue of God and the Wisdom of God," is a keynote of Augustine's thinking throughout his early writings up to the *Confessions*: see P. Cary, *Augustine's Invention of the Inner Self* (Oxford: Oxford University Press 2000) 51–53.

32. *Conf.* 7.1.1.

33. *Conf.* 7.1.2.

34. Locke, *An Essay concerning Human Understanding*, 2.11.17; see discussion in Cary, *Augustine's Invention of the Inner Self*, 122–24.

35. See *On Free Choice* 2.27–29.

36. *Conf.* 7.10.16 and 7.11.23.

37. Readers of the *City of God* can find a brief exposition of the same notion in Augustine's explanation of the superiority of Platonist epistemology in *City of God* 8.5.

38. *On Free Choice* 2.37. I have translated using informal idiom here to bring out the erotic overtones that Augustine clearly has in mind, but it is worthwhile to note that the verbs for "get back" (*recedere*) and "get to" (*accedere*) are at the root of the words rendered "withdraw" and "approach" in the quotation from *On Baptism against the Donatists* 1.1.2, above. See the similarly erotic treatment of divine Wisdom in *Soliloquies* 1:22, which also emphasizes the point that she can be shared by all who love her without competition or diminution.

39. See *City of God* 15.4 (and contrast with the end of 15.3, which reflects the same view of shared goods of the soul that has just been examined).

40. Plotinus, *Ennead* 6.5.7. See Cary, *Augustine's Invention of the Inner Self*, 29, with discussion of the ontological background, 24–30. Robert O'Connell argues for the importance of this Plotinian image both in Augustine's early thinking, in *St. Augustine's Early Theory of Man* (Cambridge: Harvard University Press, 1968) 62–64, and in his

mature doctrine of original sin, in *The Origin of the Soul in St. Augustine's Later Works* (New York: Fordham University Press, 1987) 348.

41. *Ennead* 4.3.1–8. For the traces of this doctrine of the unity of all souls in Augustine's writings, see the work of Roland Teske, "The World-Soul and Time in St. Augustine," *Augustinian Studies* 14 (1983) 75–92, as well as his *Paradoxes of Time in Saint Augustine* (Milwaukee: Marquette University Press, 1996) esp. 46–55. In addition to citing texts where Augustine hints at the unity of all souls, Teske argues that Augustine's famous account of time as a distention or stretching out of the soul (in *Conf.* 11.14.17–31.41) is incoherent and hopelessly subjectivist unless something like the Plotinian doctrine of the unity of all souls underlies it.

42. For this correction of Plotinus by Augustine, see Cary, *Augustine's Invention of the Inner Self*, 38–40.

43. *Confessions* 10.8.12–15. See Cary, *Augustine's Invention of the Inner Self*, chapter 10 and Conclusion.

44. *Confessions* 10.27.39.

45. See Cary, *Augustine's Invention of the Inner Self*, chapter 9.

46. *Ennead* 4.3.18; see O'Connell, *St. Augustine's Early Theory of Man*, 163–65.

47. *On Faith in Things Unseen* 2.

48. See *On Christian Doctrine* 2.5.

49. *City of God* 19.7.

50. *Conf.* 1.9.14.

51. See *On Music* 6.41 and the comments of Ulrich Duchrow, "*Signum* und *superbia* beim jungen Augustin (386–390)," *Revue des Études Augustiniennes* 7/4 (1961) 369–72.

52. *City of God* 13.14. See the important discussion in O'Connell, *The Origin of the Soul in St. Augustine's Later Works*, 294–309, showing how Augustine uses this claim in his mature doctrine of original sin. O'Connell comments on a whole series of passages that make the same startling claim, that we all *were* Adam: *On the Psalms* 84.7, *On Marriage and Concupiscence* 2.15, *Against Julian (Incomplete Work)* 2.178 (this passage explicitly makes Eve part of that original unity in Adam) and *On the Merits and Remission of Sins* 3.14—a series to which I would add *On the Merits and Remission of Sins* 1.11 and Sermon 165.7.

53. See O'Connell, *The Origin of the Soul in St. Augustine's Later Works*, 337–50; also John Rist, *Augustine: Ancient Thought Baptized* (Cambridge: Cambridge University Press, 1994) 121–29.

54. *City of God* 15.1.

55. See the definition of predestination in *On the Gift of Perseverance* 35.

56. 1 Corinthians 4:7. See Augustine's use of this passage in *Against Two Letters of the Pelagians* 2.15, *On Rebuke and Grace* 12, and Letter 186.4 (the whole letter, which is an important document in the anti-Pelagian controversy, can be read as a comment on this verse of Paul).

57. For the metaphor of the mass of damnation, see in addition to the references in the previous note, *City of God* 15.1 and 15.21, *Enchiridion* 107, as well as the early texts *On Eighty-three Different Questions* 68.3 (the first time Augustine uses the Pauline passage for this purpose) and *To Simplicianus* 1.2.16–20 (the first time he works out the

consequences of the metaphor carefully, in what remains his most extensive treatment of the topic).

58. As Robert Markus points out, for Augustine the "archetypal society" is "not a *polis*," and the "Aristotelian theologians in the middle ages" were mistaken in "claiming the weight of Augustine's authority in support of their belief that the political order formed part of the natural order established by God in the universe"; see R. A. Markus, *Saeculum: History and Society in the Theology of St. Augustine* (Cambridge: Cambridge University Press, 1970) 103.

59. See P. Cary, "The Incomprehensibility of God and the Origin of the Thomistic Concept of the Supernatural," *Pro Ecclesia* 11:3 (Summer 2002) 340–55.

60. *City of God* 19.17.

61. See Aristotle, *Nichomachean Ethics* 1.7, an account that deeply influenced the whole subsequent tradition of ancient ethics, which was resolutely teleological, as Augustine's discussion of Varro in *City of God* 19.1 shows.

62. See for instance the opening and concluding chapters of *Confessions.*

63. *City of God* 19.1.

64. *City of God* 19.4.

65. *On Eighty-three Different Questions* 66 and *Exposition of Some Propositions from Romans* 13–18. For helpful commentary see William S. Babcock, "Augustine's Interpretation of Romans (A. D. 394–396)," *Augustinian Studies* 10 (1979) 55–74. This four-stage schema is implicit in much of Augustine's later polemics against the Pelagians, as is especially clear in Letter 145.

66. On being unable to sin (*non posse peccare*) which is a kind of heavenly freedom, see *On Rebuke and Grace* 33 and *Enchiridion* 105.

67. *City of God* 14.15.

68. See Cyprian, *On the Unity of the Church*, as well as his Letters 72 and 73 (I use the numbering in the *Ante-Nicene Fathers* edition; other editions number these as 73 and 74) and especially the famous saying in 72.21, "outside of the church, no salvation."

69. Cyprian, Letters 71.2 and 72.26 (keeping peace with his fellow bishops on a contentious issue). Augustine praises him because he "wanted to be in the unity of peace even with those who had a different view of the matter" (*On Baptism against the Donatists* 2.1.2, end).

70. *On Order* 2.48. The Latin for the last clause is untranslatable: *quid autem est dissentire, nisi non unum sentire?*

71. John Milbank has put articulating an ontology of peace on the agenda for theology today in his *Theology and Social Theory* (Oxford: Blackwell, 1990), where he contrasts Augustine's ontology of peace (pp. 389–392) with Nietzschean ontologies of violence (pp. 278–296).

72. *City of God* 19.6.

73. *City of God* 19.8.

74. *City of God* 19.12.

75. The list is in the beginning of *City of God* 19.13, but it should be seen in the context of the immediately preceding reference to laws "of the supreme Creator and Ordainer, by whom the peace of the universe is administered," laws which "are diffused

through the whole for the health of those mortal kinds [i.e., both humans and animals], making peace by fitting one thing with another."

76. The discussion of the *miseri* (often translated "those who are miserable" or "wretches," but strictly speaking the opposite of *beati*, "those who are happy") begins immediately after the list of ten kinds of peace natural to mortal life, and concerns precisely the issue of their ambiguous relation to this list. Like *miseri* and *beati, perturbatio* and *tranquillitas* are strict opposites, taken from Stoic ethics as represented by Cicero.

77. *City of God* 19.13.

78. The phrase "temporal peace" appears at the end of *City of God* 19.13, but is immediately replaced by the phrase "earthly peace" at the beginning of 19.14, quoted next.

79. *On Christian Doctrine* 1.3–5. For the meaning and development of these key terms in Augustine's ethics, see the fundamental study by Oliver O'Donovan, "Usus and fruitio in Augustine, De Doctrina Christiana I," *Journal of Theological Studies* (n.s.) 33/2 (October 1982) 361–97.

80. *City of God* 19.14–17.

81. Note: some editions of the Bettenson translation of *City of God* unaccountably leave "the peace of the city" off the list.

82. See Markus's similar reading of the text on this same point: *Saeculum*, Appendix B, 197–210.

83. That children are inferior to their parents in body but not in soul seems obvious; that women are inferior to men in body but not in their rational souls is an explicit teaching of Augustine in *On the Trinity* 12.12.

84. *City of God* 19.15.

85. *City of God* 19.16.

86. *City of God* 19.16. On the integral relation of household (*oikos*) to city (*polis*) see of course Aristotle, *Politics* 1.2–3.

87. Contrast the argument made by John Locke's opponent, Robert Filmer, in *Patriarcha: Or the Natural Power of Kings*, included in Locke, *Two Treatises of Government* (New York: MacMillan, 1974) 249–308.

88. Aristotle, *Politics* 1.4–6.

89. Augustine is capable of acknowledging that there have been good Christians in positions of political authority (most notably in *City of God* 5.24–26), but tends to think of anything specifically Christian in their duties as stemming from their membership in the church, not the state. See Markus, *Saeculum*, 148–149.

90. *City of God* 19.13.

91. *City of God* 13.16–18 and 22.25–28. Augustine realizes that the nature of human bodies makes them seem very out of place in heaven (22.11) and he is sensitive to criticism coming from the Platonist tradition with its hope for a disembodied afterlife. But in fact he is not willing to give up on the Platonist tradition so easily, and argues that if the best insights of differing Platonists were combined, the result would agree with the Christian view (22.27).

92. *City of God* 8.8. For the centrality of the Platonist concept of intellectual vision in Augustine's theology, see Cary, *Augustine's Invention of the Inner Self*, chapter 5.

93. For the thesis that knowing others requires us to believe their words, see Cary, "Believing the Word: A Proposal about Knowing Other Persons," *Faith and Philosophy* 13/1 (1996) 78–90, which includes an argument against the fantasy ideal of seeing into each other's minds, which I think is not only untrue but bad for us, because it fails to respect the otherness of other persons.

94. Revelation 19:7; see also 21:2–4 and Isaiah 25:6–8, bound together by the image of the host wiping all tears from the faces of his guests.

95. Plato, *Republic* 757b (the Allegory of the Cave). Cf. the conclusion of *City of God* 8.8: "Now this true and supreme Good is precisely what Plato calls God."

96. The light seen in the event of Jesus' Transfiguration (Matthew 17:2) is the key to beatitude according to the great Eastern Orthodox theologian Gregory Palamas, *The Triads* (Mahwah, NJ: Paulist Press, 1983) 71–92.

2

Truthfulness as the Bond of Society

Robert P. Kennedy

Truthfulness and Truth

IN HIS MOST MEMORABLE PHRASE, Augustine identifies a creative void at the core of human existence, "our restless heart" (*inquietum est cor nostrum*) that spurs us to search for peace.[1] Every person yearns to be filled with a completely sufficient goodness which will give order to the soul and bring rest to the frenetic search for genuine happiness.[2] In the *Confessions*, Augustine presents himself as seeking to fill himself with truth. Manicheism, Platonism, and Catholicism each offer him a dish that promises a sense of repletion, the food of truth that will nourish and sustain him.[3] When he does manage to experience a sense of peace, it takes the form of an insight into, or contact with, Truth. The narrative of Augustine's life culminates in a fleeting taste of truth:

> If the tumult of the flesh fell silent for someone,
> and silent too were the phantasms of earth, sea and air,
> silent the heavens,
> and the very soul silent to itself, that it might pass beyond itself by not thinking of its own being;
> if dreams and revelations were silent,
> if every tongue and every sign, and whatever is subject to transience
> were wholly stilled for him
> —for if anyone listens, all these things will tell him,
> "We did not make ourselves;
> he made us who abides for ever"—
> and having said this they held their peace

for they had pricked the listening ear to him who made them;
and then he alone were to speak,
not through things that are made, but of himself,
that we might hear his Word, not through fleshly tongue or angels' voice, nor
thundercloud,
nor any riddling parable,
hear him unmediated, whom we love in all these things,
hear him without them,
as now we stretch out and in a flash of thought
touch that eternal wisdom who abides above all things.[4]

The most basic meaning of truth is found in these fleeting moments when the mind reaches upward and attains a glimpse of reality from God's eternal perspective. This union of the mind with God bestows peace by conferring a sense of the unshakeable goodness of all creation. The confidence in reality that comes with the knowledge of God's eternal design supplies the foundation for all Augustine's discussions of truth. In the state of ecstasy, the transience of all created goods disappears and the mind enjoys them completely in God, and discovers the voice of God in them. Truth, here identical with God, is convertible with being and goodness. From this experience, a person is able to recognize all beings calling him to transcend their limited being and to perceive the common good of creation.

Augustine is certainly not alone in proclaiming that love for God enables human beings to see the world accurately. What is more distinctive to him is the insistence on the complete congruence between love of God and respect for truth. Any love that does not accord with truth is not love at all but rather a kind of abuse.[5] For Augustine, the question of love boils down to the one criterion of whether this love brings oneself and others closer to God. If it does, then it is God's love working in us to make all things flow together into Him.[6] If it does not, then it does not merit the name of love.

Love must be joined with truth in order to bring genuine fulfillment. Yet this is still not the whole story. Augustine had had fleeting contact with Truth as a Platonist, but this philosophical attainment did not serve to bring him a taste of lasting happiness.[7] It is only when he has become a Catholic and makes his ascent in the company of his mother, who represents the Catholic faith, that his vision can become a source of salvation for himself and others. Here we have a tension that runs through Augustine's thought on truth: Augustine's affirmation of all truth, wherever it might be found, along with his absolute denial of any salvific value to truth outside the context of grace. This paradox is basic to his ideas about virtue, truthfulness, and the nature of community. Since God is the source of all being and all truth, Augustine must be open to the presence of truth in sources outside the Christian community. But the uniqueness of Christ's role as the mediator of divine truth would seem to mandate a rejection of any claim to truth from non-Christian sources.

For Augustine, this paradoxical tension explains the necessary conflict Christians will experience as they engage with other communities while striving to remain faithful to their fundamental identity in Christ. Attempts to remove this tension, whether by sectarian withdrawal or by irenic compromise, will either deny God's creative goodness or undermine Christian identity and thereby amount to a denial of God's grace. To maintain both sides of this tension, Augustine holds that truthfulness in the fullest and most important sense is impossible without God's grace while also insisting that all human beings owe it to each other not to conceal their minds by lying. The injunction to shun all lying has special force among Christians, because they have a duty to make God's revelation apparent not only in what they believe and say, but in how they try to defend and propagate their faith. At the same time, lying tends to undercut the basis of any social life, even among bands of robbers or in demonic pacts. Positively, Augustine commends the integrity he finds in any community, and it is this integrity, which is an incomplete form of truthfulness, that can serve as an example to Christians. In the end, therefore, Augustine does find a constructive role for "secular" politics. Nevertheless, political pursuits can never in themselves constitute true virtue, which comes only when one's life is directed by grace.

Much of Augustine's thought on truthfulness emerges from his attempts to convince his fellow Christians that lying cannot be justified on any grounds, and so we will begin with his analysis of the vice of lying. The next section explicates the connection between truthfulness and community-building through an examination of the way in which language constitutes human societies. Augustine's emphasis on language as a moral practice that forms individuals and reinforces their commitment to a society's values deepens the problem of how he can reconcile his affirmation of non-Christian cultures with his denial of any salvific potential in them. In the third section, I will argue that in *The City of God* Augustine's discussions of truth and virtue, respectively, show that truthfulness can not finally be divorced from living the truth, and yet that a community that lives in God's grace should seek both to discover truths outside its own boundaries and to incorporate these truths into a fuller appreciation of the gift of God's Word.

The Vice of Lying

Augustine shows a strong repugnance toward lying throughout his writings. In this section we will examine why Augustine held that every lie is a sin. We will begin with his definition of lying, which is very narrow in its specification of what types of action count as lies. Although his rejection of lying might seem unduly to restrict options to ward off harm, his definition does allow latitude to maintain secrets and to mask one's intentions even if this tactic is deceptive. We will consider some illustrations of his thoughts on deception in order to see how he draws the line between deception and lying. Getting to the heart of the matter, we will next analyze why Augustine holds all lies to be wrong. He gives two main arguments for regarding every lie as a sin. The first is a philosophical argument that has taken many forms: lying is wrong because it frustrates the capacity for communication.[8] Augustine's use of this reason depends on his premise, inherited from Platonism, that truth and goodness are convertible with each other; ethically, this means that there cannot be goodness where there is a denial of truth. His second argument is theological and derives from the necessity of believing that the authors of Scripture never lie. As Christians are called to represent the teaching of Scripture, they have a primary obligation to be truthful. Finally, we will see how Augustine sets his position on lying within the wider context of the virtue of truthfulness.

In one of his early works, *The Teacher*, Augustine is discussing with his son Adeodatus how signs communicate knowledge from one mind to another. What they find is that words do not impart knowledge, but that we learn things by an illumination of their reality. Christ, the Word of God, is the only real teacher. In the course of showing this, Augustine raises a number of examples of ways in which words fail. One of these is when the speaker is lying:

> Hence words do not even have the function of indicating the mind of the speaker, if it is uncertain whether he knows what he is saying. There are liars too and deceivers, so that you can easily understand that words not only do not reveal the mind, but even serve to conceal it. I do not of course in any way doubt that the words of truthful people are endeavouring to reveal the mind of the speaker and make some claim to do so, and would do so, all would agree, if only liars were not allowed to speak.[9]

The note of exasperation in Augustine's wish that liars be silent resonates with his views on language generally. Augustine felt that the need to use signs was a punishment that came with the fall of Adam and Eve, an unfortunate necessity brought about by their being trapped for their disobedience in mortal bodies instead of the spiritual bodies God had bestowed on them in Paradise.[10] The focus is on the search for knowledge in a world that is filled with obstacles, such as misunderstandings and slips of the tongue. Lying is an especially pernicious example of the difficulties we face in trying to gain access to wisdom through signs.

Augustine will continue to relate the problem of lying with the problem of error, but the emphasis gradually changes as he sees language in a more positive light. This reevaluation of the status of language leads him to identify the vice of lying more precisely. In his treatise *On Lying*, he begins with the assertion that we must not rashly accuse someone of lying. To avoid false accusation, Augustine engages in a lengthy discussion of what lying is and is not. He concludes that lying refers to a willed discrepancy between one's thought and one's utterance:

> That person lies, therefore, who has one thing in mind and states something else either by words or by significations of any kind. This is why a liar is said to have a double heart, that is, a double thought: One thought is of that thing which he either thinks or knows to be true but does not produce; another is of that thing which he produces in place of that thought, either knowing or thinking it to be false.[11]

Almost thirty years later, Augustine reaffirms that to have one thought in one's mind and another on one's lips is "the very essence of lying."[12] Augustine points out that it is the relationship between what the speaker says and what he or she thinks that determines whether he or she is lying, not the truth or falsity of the speaker's belief or statement. If someone states a falsehood while believing that it is true, this is an error but not a lie. (Thus, George Costanza in an episode of the sitcom *Seinfeld* perversely but correctly advises Jerry that he can pass a lie-detector test if he can make himself believe his own lies.) Conversely, the fact that a person states a truth does not necessarily mean that she is not lying; if she believes that her true statement is false, then this is a lie. But the most remarkable feature of this definition is that it does not entail a desire to deceive. Aquinas will later include some types of jokes among lies (i.e., "jocular lies");[13] in this, he was following the logic of Augustine's definition, which does not require that one attempt to deceive by lying. Although Augustine normally treats lying as a means of deception, he himself asserted that joking lies, even those with no deceptive aim, are lies.[14]

Augustine recognizes that people usually tell lies in order to deceive others about what they know, yet he is careful to keep lying and deception distinct and separate issues. He is also well aware that this can be a very fine line. On the one hand, he cannot condone lying, while, on the other, he will not accept naivete as an excuse for causing unnecessary harm. Thus, commenting on Christ's injunction not to give what is holy to the dogs or cast one's pearls before swine, he warns against a false guilelessness:

> But because the word "guileless" can convey a false impression to some who are desirous to obey God's precepts, so that they think it wrong to conceal the truth on occasion just as it is wrong to say at times what is false; and because in this

way, by revealing things which they to whom they are revealed are not able to as-similate, they may do more harm than if they had completely and always con-cealed them, He very properly enjoins: *Give not that which is holy to dogs. Neither cast your pearls before swine, lest perhaps they trample them under their feet, and turning upon you, they tear you.*[15]

He goes on to clarify this statement by explicitly excluding lying:

> One, therefore, who desires to have a clean and guileless heart ought not to feel guilty if he conceals anything from him who cannot receive it. Nor must the im-pression be taken from this that lying is a licit thing; for it does not follow that in concealing the truth falsehood is uttered.[16]

A misguided zeal for truth can often do more harm than lying. Augustine was not insensitive to the fact that someone can be devastated if he is told that a person he admires has belittled his talents or accomplishments or that a loved one has betrayed him. He also forcefully defends the obligation to keep secrets; his treatise *Against Lying* is, in one sense, an argument for maintaining the es-sential difference between secrets and lies. He also knows that truth can be used maliciously as a weapon to inflict deliberate harm. A truthful person desires above all to encourage and inspire others to love truth. The gossip and the per-son who compulsively relates his thoughts, even when ill-informed, show a carelessness about truth that belies their claim to truthfulness. And, of course, the malicious bearer of truths intentionally subordinates truth to his own in-terests. At one point, Augustine contends that the fault of lying is the will to de-ceive.[17] By this he means that a lie told with the intention of bringing another person into erroneous belief makes the teller of the lie responsible for willing an evil against another person. For Augustine the most important indicator of truthfulness is the desire to avoid being a cause of error, a desire which springs from a commitment to make others share one's love of truth.

  If Augustine allows that some deception is compatible with the virtue of truthfulness, this raises all the more acutely the question of why he considers all lies to be sins. Augustine concedes that lies can be beneficial and told with the best intentions. But he cannot condone any lies. His first argument centers on the harm done to the integrity of the person who tells a lie, while the second is based on the type of community Christians have been called to form. The fullest development of the first argument is in a key passage from *On Lying*:

> But who will assert that a liar has integrity of mind? Consider that desire itself is rightly defined as an appetite of the mind by which any temporal things are pre-ferred to eternal goods. No one, therefore, can prove that it is sometimes right to lie, unless he could show that some eternal good can be gained by lying. But since a person departs from eternity insofar as he departs from truth, it is the height

of absurdity to say that someone can attain any good by departing from it. Now if there is any eternal good which truth does not comprise, it will not be a true good, and hence not good at all, because it will be false. As the mind is to be preferred to the body, so truth is to be preferred to the mind itself, so that the mind might not only love truth more than the body but even more than itself. Thus the mind will truly be more virtuous and more chaste when it fully enjoys the immutability of truth rather than its own mutability.[18]

Truth is at the center of the moral life because without it there can be no goodness, only our own delusions of what is good. Accordingly, when we start to disregard what we know or believe to be true in order to attain some good, we lose (or forfeit) the perspective that enables us to perceive things rightly and appreciate them for their own, divinely given beauty. Thus we engage in a spiraling descent into our own, private worlds, in which the true good becomes ever more difficult to discern, because we have committed ourselves to a false order of goods. Every action that embodies a preference of one's own standard of goodness reinforces this commitment and introduces that much more confusion into our purchase on reality.[19]

Such reasoning seems to subordinate others' needs and interests to a concern for one's own purity. And this is, in fact, what Augustine recommends, but not without an honest and searching inquiry into one's motives. Still, Augustine's absolute prohibition of lying sits uneasily with his virtue-based ethics. If the goal is to promote love of truth, perhaps there might be circumstances in which a lie would be the most suitable way to instill this love in another person. Moreover, an a priori rejection of every lie goes against the flexibility and context-sensitive nature of virtue ethics, which typically put good character before rule-following.

Augustine would point out that all genuine love is rightly ordered love. The order of love requires us to put love of our own soul above our concern for others' souls. This is because we cannot give what we do not have. If any approval of falsehood deforms our soul, then lying cannot become the means of helping others, for we would reduce our capacity to bestow love in our attempt to do good. In other words, to put the desire for another's welfare ahead of one's love for truth defeats the purpose, which is to share *true* goodness by giving ourselves in *true* love.

Augustine's second argument extends this reasoning and puts it in an explicitly Christian context. It is an argument from the nature or character of Christian witness, which is exemplified most fully in Scripture and which cannot tolerate any approval of lying. Augustine's reflections on the truthfulness of Scripture seem to have been occasioned by St. Jerome's interpretation of the second chapter of Galatians, where St. Paul relates his defiance of St. Peter's hypocrisy in acting as though it was necessary for Jewish Christians to observe the Jewish law. To soften the charge against Peter, Jerome contended that Paul had misrepresented Peter's actions in order to make his point about the non-necessity of Jewish observances more forcefully. Augustine moved the debate from exegetical grounds to a foundational issue of the relationship between faith and life: "If we once admit in that supreme authority even one polite lie, there will be nothing left of those books, because, whenever anyone finds anything difficult to practice or hard to believe, he will follow this most dangerous precedent and explain it as the idea or practice of a lying author."[20] Here Augustine stresses the deleterious effects on the moral lives of those who take Scripture as their final authority. Since it is impossible to tell when someone might consider lying justified, it would also be impossible to appeal to scriptural authority in exhortations to live a better life. Augustine is not ready to claim that he or any other church authority has the ability to read the minds of the authors and thereby discern which statements are meant to be taken as true and which are lies. And even if he did make this claim, then someone who disagreed with him and also claimed this ability could not be refuted, but only defeated. The basis of all religious authority would be arbitrary, because it would arise from an access to truth that is denied to all except those with ecclesiastical power.

Augustine turns his appeal to Scripture into a positive argument against lying in *On Lying*. There he points out that in the New Testament, "if you consider the life and conduct of the saints along with their deeds and words, . . . you will not find anything which might in any way serve as an example for lying."[21] The reason for this is that "since the teaching that leads to salvation consists partly of things to be believed and partly of things to be understood, it is impossible to reach understanding unless the things to be believed are first believed."[22] Christians not only believe teachings that can be known by reason, they also believe things that cannot be demonstrated, such as the Incarnation or the Resurrection of Christ. One can only understand these doctrines if one believes them without any doubt to be true.

Augustine's larger point is that Christians should, like the apostles, be examples of lives patterned on Scripture. As the words of Scripture are free of all lying, so should Christians live truthfully, without any misrepresentation of their religious beliefs. Augustine brings out both the dependence of the community on Scripture's truthfulness and the interdependence of Christians when he notes that "true doctrine" is not available all at once in its fullness, but "advances by means of human words and the symbols of corporeal sacraments."[23] Augustine seems to have set aside his earlier suspicion of signs in this acknowledgment that a mediating language is necessary for progress in understanding truth. With this recognition of the role of language comes a new emphasis on the communal character of knowledge. The words of Scripture enable Christians to shape their lives according to the truth, but these words do not operate in a vacuum. They become effective when members of the community manifest their truthful character by speaking only what they have conceived in their minds. Lying is, therefore, not just a betrayal of one's own integrity that can damage trust, it is also a betrayal of Scripture's authority, because the strength of scriptural witness depends on how authentically Christians live by it.

Truthfulness and Community

In his account of his own passage from infancy to boyhood, Augustine implies a strong correlation between learning to speak and becoming a participant in society: "Thus I learned to express my needs to the people among whom I lived, and they made their wishes known to me; and I waded deeper into the stormy world of human life."[24] He develops this point in the contemporaneous *On Christian Teaching*:

> Therefore just as all of these significations move men's minds in accordance with the consent of their societies, and because this consent varies, they move them differently, nor do men agree upon them because they have innate value, but they have a value because they are agreed upon. In the same way those signs which form the basis for a pernicious alliance with demons are of value only in accordance with the observations of the individual.[25]

To wish to communicate one's thoughts is natural to human beings, as is the use of signs to do so. We invent languages, various systems of communication, as means to accomplish this. But the use of these systems is not morally neutral; they embody the agreements about what is important to a particular society. The more Augustine the boy entered the linguistic culture of his society, the more strongly he allied himself with its attitudes and its priorities.

Robert Markus brings out the connection between learning a language and entering a society:

> But, of course, magicians and soothsayers do not make an agreement with demons and then go on to use the conventions agreed on. It must be the intention to enter such an association that lies at the roots of the conventions which hold it together. It is as if a person entered the "contract" with the demons in the very movement of his will towards the demons with which he associates himself. In this, these signs are like all "given," intentional signs: they are "the kind of thing which starts a motion towards what it signifies and, mediately, towards whomever [*sic*] employs it as a sign."[26]

As a signifying practice, language is the enactment of a pact among the users of that language. As Markus notes, there does not need to be—and there normally isn't—a previous agreement about the conventions the members of a society use. Rather, the conventions are already there, waiting for us, as we begin to use a community's language, and we unite ourselves more fully with the community as long as we continue to follow its linguistic conventions.

In the nineteenth book of the *City of God*, Augustine defines a people as "a community of a rational multitude which is associated by a communal concord of the things it loves."[27] The basis for a community is the agreement of its members with a scale of values. Therefore, the stronger the "concord" about what is most valuable, the stronger the community will be *qua* community. As we have seen, the intention to associate with others is embodied in the linguistic conventions of the community. We have also noted that, according to Augustine, a person's growth in linguistic proficiency is the primary means by which he or she becomes an active, participating member of a society. Although this may not be conducive to the individual's moral and spiritual well-being, especially if the society one is entering is demonic, the adoption of these conventions is an important indication for the society of the individual's allegiance to it. By making the community's language one's own, one joins wills with all the other members of that community. There are thus good social reasons to encourage linguistic competence and to reward those who are virtuosos in a particular language. One reason is that such people have taken the trouble to attain excellence in the language, and this excellence affirms the society's values. A deeper reason is that linguistic virtuosity reinforces the union of one's will to the communal concord. And not only one's own will, since the rhetorical power such excellence evinces also strengthens the hearers' (or readers') intention to unite themselves with the community's goals, even if they are not aware of this effect on them.

This pervasive, even insidious, influence of language in forming a community explains the importance of Scripture for Augustine. The conventions of scriptural language convey the intention to build a community centered on love of God and love of neighbor. Mark Jordan points out that the relationship between intention and signification is reciprocal:

> The act of grasping the semantic relation [of speaker to hearer] is part of the act of grasping the intention in the speaker's mind. In every case of an intentional sign, there *is* such an intention—natural signs are distinguished precisely by the absence of intention (*sine voluntate atque ullo appetitu significandi*, 2.1.2). The condition for interpreting the Scriptures is, then, a certain foreknowledge of what is intended in them. Lacking that foreknowledge, the interpreter cannot hope properly to grasp the semantic relation. Moreover, in learning about God, the interpreter is incorporated into the community of believers.[28] . . . Scriptural exege-

sis is thoroughly subordinated to the way-of-life found in the faithful community because the way-of-life embodies the intention behind the Scriptural signs.[29]

The necessity of reading the Scriptures as belonging to a community applies to all attempts at interpretation. We can only understand the point of a person's statement if we have some grasp of his culture and the values it maintains. If we wish to enter that person's world, then we must also unite our intention with his by allowing our minds to be shaped by his community's way of life.

The importance of scriptural interpretation derives from Scripture's status as the source of all true propositions for leading a genuinely good life, a life directed toward fulfillment in God.[30] On the one hand, we can only learn how to live truthfully if we already have the intention to love God and neighbor, an intention that we do not get from our own resources but receive from God. On the other hand, the bare intention is rarely sufficient for leading the way of life that Scripture prescribes and represents. We learn to make the intention of Scripture our own by entering more fully into the intentions of the scriptural authors and adopting the way of life they commend to us; as we imbue our minds with the language of Scripture and conform our actions to its values, we become participants in the will of God.

At this point, we can summarize the various ways in which Augustine discusses language. First, language is the expression of our natural capacity to communicate. As he puts it in his *Enchiridion*, "speech was given (*instituta*) to man, not that men might therewith deceive one another, but that one man might make known his thoughts to another."[31] The inarticulate cries of the infant become the imperious demands of the young child with the ability to formulate desires in words. Lying is a repudiation of this gift. Second, language refers to the particular forms humans use to communicate their thoughts, the different languages, such as Greek or Latin or Chinese. In order to make our thoughts known, we must attain a certain technical competence, learning to make the sounds that those around us will recognize as signifying our intentions. For Augustine, this second meaning of language is generally subsumed under the first as the means of translating thoughts into outward signs. Third, language is a human practice that unites people's wills. Although Augustine focuses on language as a moral practice, he also realizes that in the concrete, these three senses of the term are inseparable: the rational creature's capacity to use language has to be in some particular language, and this language is always already uniting wills around certain objects.

Accordingly, the virtue of truthfulness has three components. First, one's mind must have formed a true concept, an inner word that accurately reflects reality. This means that the mind's intention must be united with God, the source of all truth. Second, there is the translation of the voiceless inner word into an outer word that is part of a system of signification, a language. Care-lessness in this act of translation, in which we join concept with formulation by an act of consent, is the vice of opinion. Finally, we speak outwardly, shar-ing the outer words we have chosen with others in order to lead them to share the inner word that these words represent.

Truthfulness in the Earthly City

In this final section, we turn to Augustine's political thought, particularly in his *City of God*. Although there is a wide range of interpretations of Augus-tine's basic message in this work, the two most prominent schools of recent thought seem diametrically opposed on the question of whether he accorded any value to political institutions per se. Some read him as ultimately denying any positive value to political activity; at its best, the state will merely limit the harm that human beings wish to inflict on each other in their lust to domi-nate. Others have seen Augustine as a defender of the Roman empire, even to the point of setting Roman heroes as examples of virtue. If we apply Augus-tine's thought on truthfulness to this issue, we find that both sides have grasped an important dimension of Augustine's political thought, and that Augustine can recognize a positive role for political institutions, precisely as moral guides, without thereby compromising the necessity of grace for salva-tion.

Markus has given one of the most sophisticated and compelling arguments for Augustine's fundamental rejection of the idea that politics is a natural human good:

> In Augustine's mature view of society the purpose of political arrangements was to contain the disorder and the tensions inevitably present in any society of sin-ful men. The ingrained habits of self-centred impulse, the competitive and pos-sessive drives towards domination and exploitation, the pursuit of sectional in-terest rather than the "common good"—all that Augustine would have included in the category of the "private"—are inescapable, permanent features of human groups.[32]

According to Markus, and the majority of scholars who have written on this topic, for Augustine politics itself is thus a result of the fall, an art that arose in response to human vice and that would have had no place in paradise. This reading has clear support in Augustine's *City of God*:

> The fact is that the soul may appear to rule the body and the reason to govern the vicious elements in the most praiseworthy fashion; and yet if the soul and

reason do not serve God as God himself has commanded that he should be served, then they do not in any way exercise the right kind of rule over the body and the vicious propensities. For what kind of a mistress over the body and the vices can a mind be that is ignorant of the true God and is not subjected to his rule, but instead is prostituted to the corrupting influence of vicious demons? Thus the virtues which the mind imagines it possesses, by means of which it rules the body and the vicious elements, are themselves vices rather than virtues, if the mind does not bring them into relation with God in order to achieve anything whatsoever and to maintain that achievement. For although the virtues are reckoned by some people to be genuine and honourable when they are related only to themselves and are sought for no other end, even then they are puffed up and proud, and so are to be accounted vices rather than virtues.[33]

As we have seen, for Augustine the virtue of truthfulness depends on adherence to truth. It would seem, therefore, that he has little to say about any society that does not explicitly foster worship of the Christian God.

Yet Augustine does bestow high praise on some members of Roman society, precisely as Roman. Some interpreters have taken this to indicate that, contrary to appearances, Augustine does affirm true justice in secular polities. John von Heyking is a recent example of this school. Specifically, he points to Augustine's admiration of Regulus, a Roman consul and general who preferred to return to imprisonment, torture, and death rather than break his promise to Rome's enemies:

> Both Augustine's quotations of biblical texts and Cicero's definitions indicate that true glory is constituted by two necessary (but insufficient if taken singly) conditions: virtue and praise by a competent judge. Cicero failed to provide the true judge, and the force of Augustine's rhetoric suggests that failure to do so meant that the Romans loved human praise more than virtue. However, Augustine's allusion to the few who practiced virtue the true way (*vera via*), Regulus for example, means that a few actually loved virtue more than human praise even though they may have sought human praise for their virtue, because the common good is furthered when people praise virtue.[34]

Heyking quotes from *City of God* 5.19, where Augustine states that one "who loves glory, therefore, will either ascend to it by the true way (*vera via*), or strive for it by treachery and deceit, wishing to seem good even though he is not." However, if we read further in this paragraph, we find that "a truly good man" is one "who receives his virtues from the spirit of God." Moreover, going back to Augustine's encomium of Regulus we find a high virtue that rings hollow. Regulus was indeed the greatest example of virtue among men who were "the bravest and most distinguished" because they were "defenders of an earthly fatherland and of their gods—false gods, certainly; but they were not false worshipers, for they indeed kept their oaths most faithfully."[35] The falsity of their worship relegates their "true way" to the status of a means to an illusory fulfillment.

Augustine, then, clearly does not allow any beatific or salvific function to any institutions outside the Christian community. On the contrary, he not only brands their supposed virtues real vices, he also believes their ultimate ends are fundamentally demonic. There is thus some basis in Augustine for a sectarianism that would eschew all participation in secular society; even the smallest degree of cooperation seems a betrayal of genuine love of God, if our discourses themselves embody orientations to sets of values. But Augustine does not in fact endorse such a radical sectarianism. Rather than yielding to pessimism about the world, he shows confidence in the ability of Christians to take what is good in secular communities and their philosophies and make them contribute to salvation by integrating them into the context of Christian faith. In a famous passage in *On Christian Teaching*, Augustine interprets the Israelites' spoiling of the Egyptians as an allegory of the relationship of Christianity to non-Christian cultural achievements: "If those who are called philosophers, especially the Platonists, have said things which are indeed true and are well accommodated to our faith, they should not be feared; rather, what they have said should be taken from them as from unjust possessors and converted to our use."[36] Augustine goes on to say that these truths pertain not only to technical matters, but also include "some most useful precepts concerning morals" and "even some truths concerning the worship of one God."[37] The Scriptures contain all that is necessary for salvation, but this does not entail that Christians should ignore other sources of knowledge. Even if they are not, strictly speaking, necessary for living a full Christian life, non-Christian societies can and do furnish materials that promote adherence to God.

In the end, Augustine is optimistic about the resources of philosophy and secular culture, yet he holds that these resources are ultimately of no benefit to those who developed them. Augustine does regard the attainments of extra-Christian societies as genuinely good, yet powerless to use that good for its essential purpose, which is to lead its possessors to God. Augustine cannot grant that non-Christians were truly virtuous, but he can and does acknowledge in some of them a high degree of integrity that Christians would do well to emulate. Because citizens of the earthly city can serve as models for Christians, the members of the city of God have more than a merely negative stake in secular affairs. According to this view, Christians can legitimately demand a high level of integrity from others, both on the grounds that such integrity is beneficial to earthly societies and on the grounds that Christians have a rightful claim on all goodness, wherever it might be found.

As much as anyone, Augustine was aware of the limits on attaining virtue in this life. He also recognized in non-Christians, especially the philosophers, a common yearning for transcendent truth that is the precondition for genuine moral growth. Platonism represented the purest expression of the desire to leave one's own private interests behind and ascend to a sure and lasting experience of God as God is in Himself. However, as appreciative as he was of the truth in Platonism and despite his respect for their integrity in pursuit of the truth, he knew that their efforts were doomed to failure. They could not achieve a taste of the divine sweetness, because only God's grace can supply it. And the only source is Christ, who is the righteousness of God:

> This righteousness of God, which is the gift of grace regardless of merits, is unknown to those who wish to establish a righteousness of their own, and who have therefore not subjected themselves to the righteousness of God, which is Christ. It is in this righteousness that the great abundance of God's sweetness is found; and so it is said in the psalm, "Taste and see how sweet the Lord is" (Ps 34:8). This sweetness we do indeed taste during our pilgrimage; but we do not have our fill of it. Rather, we "hunger and thirst" (Matt 5:6) after it now, so that we may have our fill of it hereafter, when "we shall see Him as He is" (1 John 3:2). Then, what is written will be fulfilled: "I shall be satisfied when thy glory shall appear" (Ps 17:15). Thus, Christ perfects the great abundance of his sweetness for those who hope in Him.[38]

Both Christians and Platonists have a longing for the true God, and both use truthful means to make what progress is available in this life. But what separates them is even deeper than these bonds and all they imply. By receiving the grace of Christ, a Christian has the capacity to taste God's sweetness, whereas Platonists cannot. They might have a taste *for* God, but they can never, of themselves, have a taste *of* God. The difference in prepositions may seem slight, but for Augustine it is the difference between salvation and ultimate misery.

Conclusion

According to Augustine, there is no kind of creature more social than the human race.[39] God also created human beings with the power to share their minds through language. Misuse of this gift, especially by lying, necessarily weakens the bonds between the members of a society even as it undermines the integrity of the speaker. To sin against truth is not only morally wrong but also an offense against the foundation of society itself, namely the mutual trust on which we rely in pursuing any common goal. For Augustine, this means that lying can never be beneficial; there are no helpful lies, because

lying cannot encourage the trust on which we depend for lying to accomplish
its goal:

> Everyone who lies commits iniquity, and if anyone thinks that a lie may some-
> times be useful, he must think that iniquity is sometimes useful also. But no one
> who lies keeps faith concerning that about which he lies. For he wishes that the
> person to whom he lies should have that faith in him which he does not himself
> keep when he lies. But every violator of faith is iniquitous. Either iniquity is
> sometimes useful, which is impossible, or a lie is always useless.[40]

Although Augustine is here speaking especially of the church (and forcefully
reiterating his objection against Jerome's interpretation of Galatians), this argument applies to all communities, even pacts with demons. Because we all
necessarily belong to some community, there will have to be some degree of
trust, so every community will be healthier (in its own way) when its members are more truthful.

The ultimate criterion of a society is its end or goal, which is either love of
God to the point of despising self or love of self to the point of despising God.[41]
Thus, anyone whose life is not directed toward love of God does not have a correct ordering of loves and cannot be said to have any virtue, including truthfulness. Although this position might seem to entail denying any real moral
value to Roman heroes like Regulus, Augustine focuses instead on the greater
obligation to unity among Christians. He calls upon Christians to center their
attention on the language of Scripture, which can never lie and which gives the
means to live fully virtuous lives. This attention does not exclude searching for
truth in other cultures, which have also discovered important truths.

Augustine affirms both the integrity he finds in people outside the Christian faith and the truth, including truth about God, that is present in other cultures. As members of a larger community, Christians will not be sectarian or
isolationist but will take the truth wherever they find it, even as they witness
to Christian truth within their society. Moreover, as long as history continues,
Christians will belong to cultures that do not acknowledge the Christian God
and yet do have their own distinctive ideals. These ideals, lived with fidelity
and an openness to truth, are signs of hope that become a means of salvation
for all people.

Notes

1. *Conf.* 1.1.1, my translation.
2. See *Conf.* 11.29.39. Augustine longs to have his scattered desires gathered together so that he might attain peace.

3. See Leo Ferrari, "The Food of Truth in Augustine's *Confessions*," *Augustinian Studies* 9 (1978) 1–14.

4. *Conf.* 9.10.25, trans. Maria Boulding, *Augustine: The Confessions* (Hyde Park, NY: New City Press, 1997) 228–29.

5. See *On Christian Teaching* 1.4.4. Augustine's point here is that nothing should be loved for itself, closed off from God.

6. Augustine uses the verb *confluo*, "flow together," to refer to the goal of all loves in *On Christian Teaching* 1.26.27 and again at *Conf.* 11.29.39 as he prays that he might be melted by the fire of divine love and flow eventually into God.

7. See the final sentence of *Conf.* 7.17.23, where Augustine describes the result of his Platonic ascent as catching the fragrance of the divine life while being unable to share in the feast. In *The City of God* 21.24, Augustine reserves tasting the sweetness of God to those who have received grace.

8. See *Enchiridion* 22.

9. *The Teacher* 13.42, trans. J. H. S. Burleigh, in *Augustine: Earlier Writings* (Philadelphia: Westminster Press, 1953).

10. See *On Genesis against the Manichees* 2.4.5.

11. *On Lying* 3.3. All translations from this work are my own.

12. *Enchiridion* 18, trans. J. F. Shaw (Washington, DC: Regnery Gateway, 1961).

13. Thomas Aquinas, *Summa theologiae* II-II, q. 110, a. 2 (my translation).

14. Augustine excludes jokes from consideration in *On Lying* 2.2, and this has been taken as evidence that he did not include any jokes among lies. However, it is clear from *Expositions of the Psalms* 5.7 that he did understand some jokes as lies and counted them "not without vice," even though they had no deceptive intent.

15. *The Lord's Sermon on the Mount* 2.20.67.

16. *The Lord's Sermon on the Mount* 2.20.69.

17. *On Lying* 3.3: "Indeed, the fault (*culpa*) of someone who lies is the desire to deceive in stating his own mind, whether he deceives, that is when he is believed in stating a falsehood, or does not deceive, that is, either when he is not believed or when he states a truth (which he does not think true) with a will to deceive."

18. *On Lying* 7.10.

19. Gilbert C. Meilaender, *The Theory and Practice of Virtue* (Notre Dame, IN: University of Notre Dame Press, 1984) 17, makes the same point: "An ethic of virtue is dominated by the eye, by metaphors of sight and vision. To know what traits of character qualify as virtues we must *see* our world and human nature rightly. To *see* rightly, in turn, requires that we have the virtues. Virtue enhances *vision*; vice darkens and finally *blinds*."

20. Letter 28.3, in *Letters*, trans. Sr. Wilfrid Parsons (Washington, DC: The Catholic University of America Press, 1951).

21. *On Lying* 5.8.

22. *On Lying* 8.11.

23. *On Lying* 19.40.

24. *Confessions* 1.8.13 (trans. Boulding; see note 4).

25. *On Christian Teaching* 2.24.37. This translation from *On Christian Doctrine*, trans. D. W. Robertson, Jr. (Indianapolis: Bobbs-Merrill/Library of Liberal Arts, 1958). All quotations from this work are his translation.

26. Robert A. Markus, "Signs, Communication, and Communities in Augustine's *De doctrina christiana*," in *De Doctrina Christiana: A Classic of Western Culture* (eds. Duane W. H. Arnold and Pamela Bright; *Christianity and Judaism in Antiquity* 9; Notre Dame, IN: University of Notre Dame Press, 1995) 97–108: 100. The quotation in the last sentence is from Mark D. Jordan, "Words and Word: Incarnation and Signification in Augustine's *De doctrina christiana*," *Augustinian Studies* 11 (1980) 177–96: 186.

27. *The City of God* 19.24, trans. Henry Bettenson (Harmondsworth: Penguin, 1984).

28. Jordan, "Words and Word," 184.

29. *Ibid.* 185.

30. See *On Christian Teaching* 2.31.49: The rules of logic can be learned in secular schools, but "the truth of propositions is a matter to be discovered in the sacred books of the church."

31. *Enchiridion* 22.

32. Robert A. Markus, *Saeculum: History and Society in the Thought of St. Augustine* (rev. ed. Cambridge: Cambridge University Press, 1988) xviii. See also the carefully balanced discussion of this issue in chapter 4 of the same book. Nevertheless, Markus allows little, if any, positive role for politics: "If social life is natural, it is nevertheless, in the actual conditions of a politically organised community of sinful men, a burden, like a disease" (99).

33. *The City of God* 19.25, trans. Bettenson.

34. John von Heyking, *Augustine and Politics as Longing in the World* (University of Missouri Press, 2001) 157.

35. *The City of God* 1.24, trans. R. W. Dyson (Cambridge: Cambridge University Press, 1998).

36. *On Christian Teaching* 2.40.60.

37. *Ibid.*

38. *The City of God* 21.24, trans. Dyson.

39. *The City of God* 12.28.

40. *On Christian Teaching* 1.36.40.

41. See *The City of God* 14.28.

3

Friendship as Personal, Social, and Theological Virtue in Augustine

Kim Paffenroth

EVEN A CASUAL READER OF Augustine's *Confessions* would surely come away with the impression that Augustine valued his friendships highly, and this general impression is confirmed in scholarship, including Brown's magisterial work: "Augustine will never be alone . . . he formed a core of abiding friendships. . . . Augustine needed the constant response and reassurance of a circle of friends."[1] And lest one think this merely a typical attitude of an overwrought, sentimental soul, one need only look to Augustine's iciness toward his father and his callousness toward the mother of his son to see that Augustine did not bestow affection indiscriminately, generously, or evenly among the people in his life: his loves were quite particular.

But if Augustine's view of friendship is not sentimental, this particularity of friendship (*amicitia*) has proven much more troubling to some, who see such particularity as incompatible with Christian *agape* or *caritas*, the commanded love due to all others (even disagreeable fathers, inconvenient mistresses, and hostile theological opponents), not just to a select and enjoyable circle of congenial friends. Some have therefore simply ignored or denied this incompatibility and have equated Augustine's friendships with *caritas*, or made them inferior to it.[2] Far more accurate is the subtle analysis of Meilaender, who tries to describe the tension and dynamic between the particularity of friendship and the universality of Christian *caritas*: "Particular friendships are to school us in love; they are a sign and a call by which God draws us toward a love more universal in scope. Philia is transcended in caritas but not destroyed."[3] The two loves are related, but not identical, and while *caritas* may be superior in the sense of being the ultimate goal, friendship is clearly the more frequent and enjoyable experience (in this life).

Another way to look at it is to see the two loves as satisfying or responding to different parts of the human being:

> If friendship has both a metaphysical dimension—relation or reciprocity—and a psychological dimension—affection—then Augustine, in his mature thought, treated *christiana caritas* as the metaphysical dimension of friendship and equated it with fraternal charity. But he also held on to the affective dimension. . . . Augustine never made his ideas simple by ignoring his experience, and his experience taught him that friendship meant a good deal more than fraternal charity.[4]

Here the description is especially provocative: friendship "mean[s] a good deal *more than*" charity. Friendships guide and shape our lives more than the love we bestow on all, and as seen in Augustine's life, more even than familial or sexual love.

In my previous work on Augustine's idea of friendship, I focused on the Platonist and Ciceronian influences on his thought.[5] In this chapter I would like to reframe those historical observations around the ideas discussed in the previous paragraphs: that friendship is a school of virtue, and that different kinds of love may respond to different needs or parts of the human being. In this way I will be better able to show the different facets of friendship for Augustine—personal, social, and theological—and the rich and beautiful idea of friendship he has bequeathed us.

Friendship as a School of Virtue in Platonism and Augustine

In Platonism, friendship is fundamental to the education and improvement of human beings, so much so that it may be said to be a necessary part of human fulfillment: "There are many possible types of friendship in human experience. While some of these are deceptive, others are essential to education, to maturation, to the realization of knowledge and being."[6] In short, in a Platonist world, the advertising slogan of the U.S. Army ("Be all that you can be!") would apply to friendship as education, education practiced among dedicated friends. For Platonists, there are two related educational goals for friendship. The first is to wean one away from loving particulars to loving the Universal, as one comes to realize that what one loves in the friend is a reflection or image of the transcendent One or Beauty. A person is thereby taught to love Beauty, rather than particular (inferior) beautiful things, Virtue instead of individual (imperfect) virtuous acts. As beautiful and high-minded as this goal may be, its drawbacks are equally obvious:

Plato's view seems to suggest that it is not the friend but the form of beauty which inheres in the friend that is loved. And in that case, the friend would seem to be interchangeable with anyone else in whom beauty appears, for it is the same form which appears in many persons. But then has not the friend actually disappeared? To purchase universal love one has paid a high price indeed: the loss of all particular attachments.[7]

This is surely love or even passion, but not for the friend, who is only a pointer or vessel for some higher Being. In short, one loves particular people only so that one can learn not to love particular people.

Now consider Augustine's modification of such an idea: "He loves his friend truly who loves God in him—either because He is in him, or so that He might be in him."[8] If one were to end the quotation before the dash, one could have a purely Platonist idea here, and some seem to do just that, emphasizing the presence of God in the beloved as the essence of friendship for Augustine: "His friend was more than a mere man; God was in him, he was the surest place to find God."[9] But the second half of the quotation surely undermines such an interpretation. The presence of God in the friend is not the object of affection and longing (as the image of the Good in the friend is the object of love for Platonists); instead, it is a good—the highest good of all, of course—for which one rejoices if the friend already possesses it, or which one wishes the friend to have if he does not already. Here the love of the friend is real and not incidental or subservient to some higher Good; the love of the friend is central, and the longing or rejoicing for the presence of God is an expression of that love. On this point, Augustine adapts Platonist ideas more than he adopts them.

The second educational aspect of friendship for Platonists is one Augustine embraces more fully. In his early dialogue the *Soliloquies*, it seems that the main goal of friendship is to seek God together, and if friends fail to do so, then they are to be discarded:

Reason: But I ask you, why do you want those people whom you love to live, or more specifically, to live with you?

Augustine: So that together and in complete agreement we can search for ourselves and God. For in that way, whoever first makes a discovery can easily lead the others to it without difficulty.

R: But what if they do not want to search for these things?

A: I will convince them, so that they will want to.

R: But what if you are unable to do that, either because they have decided that these things are already found, or are impossible to find, or because they are hindered by cares and desires for other things?

A: I will teach them, and they me, as much as we can.

R: But what if their very presence keeps you from your search? Won't this trouble you, and if they cannot change, make you wish that they were not with you, rather than be like this?

A: I admit, it is as you say.

R: Therefore you do not desire their life or their presence for its own sake, but only in order to find wisdom?

A: I agree completely. . . .

. . . *A:* I love only wisdom for her own sake, and only for her sake do I want to have, and fear losing, other things, such as life, peace, friends. How can my love of that beauty have a limit? Not only do I not begrudge her to others, but I even seek many more who will pursue her with me, long for her with me, grasp her with me, and enjoy her with me, and they will be my friends even more, the more the love of her is shared among us.

R: That is just how lovers of wisdom ought to be.[10]

This is a huge admission from a man so passionately devoted to his friends, and while we must concede more agreement with Platonism here than on the previous point, we should also observe that this possibility—discarding friends who impede the quest for wisdom—remains just that for Augustine—a theoretical possibility. From Cassiciacum to his later life as a bishop, Augustine always relied on his friends in his quest to do what is right and find what is true: his reliance on the greater stability and innate virtue of Alypius is especially notable.[11] A solitary pursuit of wisdom was always a theoretical, never a real, possibility for Augustine: "Despite Augustine's admission, the impression remains that he could not imagine such a philosophical enquiry without the presence and participation of his friends. However intellectually he looked at this point in his life upon friendship, it had weathered the storms of doubt and conversion. . . . Whatever happens, he cannot imagine life without friends."[12] Wisdom is the goal of friendship and therefore the ultimate object of love, but the joy of pursuing wisdom is really only imaginable for Augustine if it is shared and thereby increased with friends. One is reminded of the saved in Dante's *Paradise*, who reflect God's light, and therefore love to shine and reflect on one another, for this only increases the light and love in God's kingdom (e.g., *Paradise* 5.103–20). Just as one's wish that God be in the friend is a sign that one loves the friend, one would also wish the friend to share in wisdom, as the end of the above quotation brings out rather graphically, almost scandalously, with Augustine seeking to "long," "grasp," and "enjoy" wisdom together with her other devotees.[13]

Augustine is thoroughly Platonist in his estimation that friendship is a profound transformation or education of oneself, an orientation toward higher and eternal things and away from the limitations of selfishness, carnality, and ephemerality. The Platonist idea of loving God in the friend does not quite fit Augustine's experience, however, for it too much abandons or discounts the particular love in favor of the universal love; Augustine sees the former as an education for the latter, but not an education that one should strive to set aside. Instead, he focuses on how the members of a community united by love of God and wisdom bring each other greater joy by their love for each other: "Augustine always held on to the human aspect of friendship, to human affection, to the *inclinatio*, to the *delectatio* added to *dilectio*."[14] Indeed, it is always a source of disappointment to me that Augustine has such a reputation as a judgmental scold, when he strives so vehemently to make the life of philosophy or faith more humane, more heartfelt, more joyful. God is the only ultimate object of desire, for only God can give the peace that satisfies all our heart's restlessness, but friends undeniably and quite rightly bring us greater delight as they help us pursue that desire and seek that peace together. Indeed, for Augustine and many of us, the soul's quest for God's peace may be possible only with the help and love of friends.

Cicero and Augustine on Friendship and Community

Perhaps the most explicit influence on Augustine's descriptions of friendship is Cicero.[15] Augustine quotes Cicero's definition of friendship three times with complete approval and agreement: "Now friendship may be thus defined: a complete accord on all subjects human and divine, joined with mutual good will and affection."[16] Although Augustine's discussion of the definition dwells on the meaning of "subjects human and divine," the two agree profoundly on the other elements of the definition—"complete accord, mutual good will, and affection." From Cicero we have this description right after his definition:

> Well, between men like these the advantages of friendship are almost more than I can say. To begin with, how can life be worth living, to use the words of Ennius, which lacks that repose which is to be found in the mutual good will of a friend? What can be more delightful than to have some one to whom you can say everything with the same absolute confidence as to yourself? Is not prosperity robbed of half its value if you have no one to share your joy? On the other hand, misfortunes would be hard to bear if there were not some one to feel them even more acutely than yourself. In a word, other objects of ambition serve for particular ends—riches for use, power for securing homage, office for reputation, pleasure for enjoyment, health for freedom from pain and the full use of the functions of the body. But friendship embraces innumerable advantages. Turn which way you please, you will find it at hand. It is everywhere; and yet never out

of place, never unwelcome. Fire and water themselves, to use a common expression, are not of more universal use than friendship. I am not now speaking of the common or modified form of it, though even that is a source of pleasure and profit, but of that true and complete friendship which existed between the select few who are known to fame. Such friendship enhances prosperity, and relieves adversity of its burden by halving and sharing it.[17]

From their agreement, good will, and affection, friends make any happiness more enjoyable, and any affliction more bearable.

Augustine's heartfelt description of his youthful friendships in *Confessions* is similar, though it focuses more on the positive, joyful experiences:

There were other things done in their company which more completely seized my mind: to talk and to laugh with them; to do friendly acts of service for one another; to read well-written books together; sometimes to tell jokes and sometimes to be serious; to disagree at times, but without hard feelings, just as a man does with himself; and to keep our many discussions pleasant by the very rarity of such differences; to teach things to the others and to learn from them; to long impatiently for those who were absent, and to receive with joy those joining us. These and similar expressions, proceeding from the hearts of those who loved and repaid their comrades' love, by way of countenance, tongue, eyes, and a thousand pleasing gestures, were like fuel to set our minds ablaze and to make but one out of many.[18]

Friends are not duplicates, but their similarities—together with the affection that makes them overlook their differences—make for a life of unity, peace, and pleasure. At the same time, even their dissimilarities or disagreements are a source of learning and pleasure. Friends criticize our flaws in ways enemies never could (for we simply ignore and disdain the criticism of enemies), thereby making us grow in ways we never could have on our own. Cicero underlines this with his bitter criticism of flattery: ". . . there can be nothing more utterly subversive of friendship than flattery, adulation, and base compliance."[19] And it comes from the biblical wisdom tradition as well: "Well meant are the wounds a friend inflicts, but profuse are the kisses of an enemy. . . . Iron sharpens iron, and one person sharpens the wits of another" (Prov 27:6, 17). It is the greatest perversion of his friendship that at the time Augustine discounted his friend's deathbed conversion, for such a dismissive attitude and inability to take criticism make the friend into an insignificant object of use and manipulation and not a true partner in love, trust, and *mutual* learning.[20]

For both Cicero and Augustine, friendship is a most healthy, pleasant, and necessary part of human life. It helps to eliminate, or at least minimize, brutality and sorrow in this world, while it increases the frequency and depth of the enjoyment we have in life. Friendship teaches its practitioners empathy, reciprocity, generosity, patience, honesty, sincerity, and loyalty. It provides a microcosm and constant reminder of the virtues and goals of all political life: "Life in a city-state was an education for virtue, a fully human life, the good life."[21] Both men even go so far as to say that only friendship ultimately makes life worth living, by building a community of mutual joy to overcome the darkness and pain of this imperfect (for Augustine, fallen) world. Such a beautiful but somber description of the value of friendship is given by Augustine near the end of his life: ". . . what consolation have we in this human society, so replete with mistaken notions and distressing anxieties, except the unfeigned faith and mutual affections of genuine, loyal friends?"[22]

As the Platonist-Augustinian friendship discussed above focused on the personal, individual virtue and education to be drawn from a loving community of friends, Cicero and Augustine focus on how the virtues (and shortcomings) of the individuals make up a community that is greater than the sum of its parts. Lonely and unhappy individuals come together to form a community that is neither lonely nor unhappy; they encourage each other's virtues as they discourage each other's vices and alleviate each other's sorrows. Friendship is the virtue that makes it possible for a society and its members to pursue—and, just as importantly, to enjoy—the other virtues.

Augustine's Loving Friends "in God": The Theological Meaning of Friendship

Augustine adopts a poetic image for his own experience of friendship: "Well has someone said of his friend that he is half his soul. For I thought that my soul and his were but one soul in two bodies."[23] He later applies a similar image to his love for his mother: "When I was bereft of such great consolation, my heart was wounded through and my life was as if ripped asunder. For out of her life and mine one life had been made."[24] A loved one not only complements one, but completes one; the love not only makes life enjoyable, it makes life fulfilling and meaningful. Two people loving each other are really one, and loving someone is losing and finding oneself, a self now freed and made whole by being given away and taken up in something more. And any great song, poem, or parable about love focuses on the paradoxes of it, celebrating it and being somewhat scared at how love can simultaneously bring such elation and fear, power and vulnerability, permanence and fragility. True friendship is, in short, one of the strongest experiences one can have of onself and another human being as the image of God,[25] simultaneous with one of the strongest experiences of oneself and the friend as vulnerable, fallen creatures. These two sides of the experience and of human nature, each so intensely and completely true, are what give friendship its overwhelming and transformative power, teaching and showing us who we really are.

But how do we each find our perfectly compatible friends? In a world of chance or fate, it would be by accident, or, at best, serendipity. In a world of karmic cycles, it would be the payback for some unremembered previous goodness, for which we could be appreciative, but hardly grateful. In a world of astrology or its rough modern equivalent, personal ads, we could try to manipulate, manufacture, or predict such compatibility. But in a world governed by a kind, loving God, there would be something much more beautiful going on:

> All men are to be loved equally. But since you cannot do good to all, you are to pay special regard to those who, by the accidents of time, or place, or circumstance, are brought into closer connection with you. . . . Just so among men, since you cannot consult for the good of them all, you must take the matter as decided for you by a sort of lot, according as each man happens for the time being to be more closely connected with you.[26]

I am such close friends with some of the other contributors to this volume because of a thousand unlikely "accidents of time, or place, or circumstance," but they are accidents for which I am most profoundly grateful to God: "Yet, of course, they are not accidents in another sense; they are the gift of God, and it is quite right that we should delight in the friends given us."[27] In a different way than the Platonists, loving friends points us to loving God when we realize that God has put them in our path. Friends are to be loved as gifts of God, and one of the highest gifts of all, even "a grace."[28] Loving a friend is loving a soul that we long for and that we long to do good for with no thought of return, but who nonetheless beautifully returns all our love and kindness. Friends are the people from whom you want nothing but their own good, but since loving and pleasing you *is* their good, they end up giving everything you need (though not necessarily everything you want, as we saw above with the criticism of friends).

This gratitude to God for the mysteriously providential gift of friends leads to Augustine's unique formulation that reverses the Platonist idea of loving the Good in the friend: "But blessed is the man who loves you, and his friend in you."[29] Augustine conceives of God as a third partner in any true friendship, as God gives the friends each other, and the friends love God together. An added and most important concept is that God makes permanent and eternal the necessarily temporary, human friendship: "For he alone loses no dear one to whom all are dear in him who is not lost."[30] Loved ones necessarily die and leave us distraught, but not in despair, for we know they are still alive and are now happier than we. But although their happiness is our highest wish and joy, a grieving human being needs more consolation, as Augustine himself finds at the death of his mother described in Book Nine of *Confessions*.[31] Such pain and loss require the assurance that not only is the loved one still alive and well, but that our special relationship with him or her will one day be enjoyed again in fullness and perfection. Augustine offers his vision of just such a re-union and the bliss it will eternally bring us: "[F]rom this life we shall pass into that other life, in which they [our friends in this life] shall be to us more beloved as they shall be better known, and in which our pleasure in loving them shall not be alloyed by any fear of separation."[32] The friends who in this life helped us find God will be given back to us by God for an eternity of joy,[33] just as Dante knows he will be with his Beatrice forever, and she will be more beautiful than ever she was in Florence.

To conclude with another comparison, it is as though Platonism provided the goal of friendship, Cicero gave the best description of its benefits and ef-fects, and Augustine added an almost sacramental element. This would help explain why, even though true friendship is the love between souls, for Au-gustine their physical presence is not therefore incidental, superfluous, or detrimental to the experience, any more than is the physical presence of a sacrament.[34] And like a sacrament, true friends mysteriously—in ways that defy our attempts to explain to others outside the relationship—bring us into an encounter with Christ, Wisdom, and God, the God who gave us our friends in the first place. A friendship in God is one that gratefully acknowledges and joyously celebrates the fact that God has given one the most precious gift of all—another soul to whom one gives oneself, in whom one finds oneself, and with whom one completes oneself in freedom and love.

Conclusion

Although usually more pleasant than love of enemy, friendship is not there-fore necessarily easier, as all of us know. Both kinds of love struggle with the limitations of the other person and of oneself: in love of enemy, we struggle to love people we don't like, while with friends, we struggle to love people we do. The former is certainly more difficult at first, but the latter often gets more difficult as time goes on: unlike an old shirt or wine, friends most definitely do not necessarily improve with age (though Cicero and we are right to hope that they do).[35] It is much like Ivan's admission in *The Brothers Karamazov* that the people near one are the most difficult to love,[36] for they inevitably change, disappoint, and even disgust. And when such change and disappoint-ment reaches the point of ending the friendship, the pain becomes almost un-bearable for Augustine:

> there is the much more bitter fear, that their friendship be changed into treach-ery, malice and baseness. And when such things do happen (and the more nu-merous our friends, the more often they happen) and the news is brought to our

ears, who, except one who has this experience, can be aware of the burning sorrow that ravages our hearts? Certainly we would rather hear that our friends were dead, although this also we could not hear without grief.[37]

There is a good reason why the story of Judas runs like a red thread through Christian theology, literature, folklore, and art: a hero being betrayed and destroyed by a friend is much more fascinating and meaningful than him being killed by an enemy.[38]

Enemies, on the other hand, can more easily be loved in the abstract (so long as they keep a respectable distance), for unlike one's friends, there are no emotional needs or expectations that enemies could fail to fulfill: enemies are in this way ironically and inconveniently much more reliable than friends. But if we take our commitment and loyalty seriously, we cannot simply "move on" and make new friends, or friendship would have no meaning beyond mere and temporary approval or convenience. And even when the friend and oneself are in perfect harmony and agreement, there is the related temptation to use the friend for one's own needs, to tyrannize and objectify the other person, the way Augustine seems to have done to his unnamed friend in Book Four of *Confessions*. Pride and selfishness pervert our loves as much as they create our hates, and neither friendship nor love of enemy is immune from these influences.

In either love of enemy or friendship, the difficulty is in treating the other person as a subject with whom one has a relationship, not as an object onto which one projects like or dislike, or from which one draws benefits or pleasures. In this way, the Platonist idea of friendship as loving the Good and Beautiful in the friend seems to objectify and discard the friend far too much—who needs an earthly, human friend when you can have the Real Thing?—and Augustine leaves this out of his idea of friendship. But unlike some Christians who reject friendship as incompatible with *caritas*, Augustine rightly understood that friendship provides a better school for virtue than love of enemies, because friends can more reliably be counted on to remind us that they are not objects. They inevitably do things to disappoint us, but still want our love; they change, and still ask us to adapt and accept them in their new state; they criticize, and expect us to respond. The love is constantly challenged and renewed from without as well as from within.

It is a rich and unique combination of ideas on friendship that Augustine put together and handed on to us, combining the Platonist idea that friends long for and seek together something beyond and above themselves, the Ciceronian description of how friendship makes tolerable and even enjoyable the limitations and weaknesses of this life, and his own Christian vision of

God as a third partner in every true friendship. Friendship therefore brings us closer to God (as in Platonism), allows us better to enjoy God's world (as in Cicero), and even gives us a way to experience God now, as we gratefully and joyfully live our relationships in Him. It will always be true that a human life or community built around such relationships will be truly blessed, and those that are not will be inhumane, incomplete, and base.

Notes

1. P. Brown, *Augustine of Hippo: A Biography* (Berkeley and Los Angeles: University of California Press, 1967) 61, 200–201. See the similar comments of J. J. O'Meara, *The Young Augustine: The Growth of St. Augustine's Mind up to His Conversion* (London: Longmans, Green and Co., 1954) 86. Thanks to my fellow contributors Robert P. Kennedy and Kevin L. Hughes for their comments on this essay.

2. Thus M. A. McNamara, *Friends and Friendship for Saint Augustine* (Staten Island, NY: Alba House, 1958), 236: "He saw it [friendship] always as a part of charity"; A. M. Fiske, "St. Augustine and Friendship," *Monastic Studies* 2 (1964) 127–35, esp. 135: "Friendship was the union of two souls, seeking the same goal, full of grace and *caritas*"; J. F. Monagle, "Friendship in St. Augustine's Biography," *Augustinian Studies* 2 (1971) 81–92, esp. 92: "Augustine . . . elevates the notion of friendship to a level of eminent distinction: Christian, fraternal charity."

3. G. C. Meilaender, *Friendship: A Study in Theological Ethics* (Notre Dame and London: University of Notre Dame Press, 1981) 17–18.

4. J. T. Lienhard, "Friendship in Paulinus of Nola and Augustine," *Augustiniana* 40 (1990) 279–96, quotation from p. 296.

5. K. Paffenroth, "God in the Friend, or the Friend in God? The Meaning of Friendship for Augustine," *Augustinian Heritage* 38 (1992) 123–36.

6. P. S. Bashor, "Plato and Aristotle on Friendship," *The Journal of Value Inquiry* 2 (1958) 269–80, quotation from p. 273.

7. Meilaender, *Friendship*, 12.

8. Sermon 336, cited without comment by McNamara, *Friends and Friendship*, 215; and Lienhard, "Friendship in Paulinus of Nola and Augustine," 292. The date of the sermon is unknown.

9. Fiske, "St. Augustine and Friendship," 135.

10. Augustine, *Soliloquies* (trans. K. Paffenroth; Hyde Park, NY: New City Press, 2000) 1.20, 22–23.

11. On their friendship, see Brown, *Augustine of Hippo*, 201.

12. B. P. McGuire, *Friendship and Community: The Monastic Experience 350–1250* (Kalamazoo, MI: Cistercian Publications, 1988) 50.

13. See my analysis of the passage in chapter 2 of *In Praise of Wisdom: Literary and Theological Reflections on Faith and Reason* (Harrisburg: Continuum, 2004).

14. Lienhard, "Friendship in Paulinus of Nola and Augustine," 296.

15. See McNamara, 236; Monagle, 81–82; Lienhard, 292–93. For a full treatment of all of Augustine's use of Cicero, see the thorough survey of H. Hagendahl, *Augustine and the Latin Classics* (Göteborg: Elanders, 1967) 479–588.

16. Cicero, *De Amicitia* 6; in *The Letters of Marcus Tullius Cicero, with His Treatises on Friendship and Old Age* (trans. by E. S. Shuckburgh; New York: P. F. Collier, 1909). Available online at http://www.fordham.edu/halsall/ancient/cicero-friendship.html. It is quoted by Augustine once in *Answer to the Skeptics* 3.6.13, and twice in Letter 258.

17. Cicero, *De Amicitia* 6.

18. *Conf.* 4.8.13. (trans. J. K. Ryan; New York: Image Books, 1960). All references to *Confessions* are to this translation.

19. Cicero, *De Amicitia* 25.

20. See James Wetzel, "Book Four: The Trappings of Woe," in *A Reader's Companion to Augustine's Confessions* (eds. K. Paffenroth and R. P. Kennedy; Louisville: Westminster John Knox Press, 2003).

21. R. A. Markus, *Saeculum: History and Society in the Theology of St. Augustine* (Cambridge, UK: Cambridge University Press, 1970) 73.

22. *City of God* (trans. H. Bettenson; New York: Penguin, 1984) 19.8. All references to *City of God* are to this translation.

23. *Conf.* 4.6.11.

24. *Conf.* 9.12.30.

25. Cf. J. F. Harvey, *Moral Theology of the* Confessions *of Saint Augustine* (Washington, DC: Catholic University of America Press, 1951) 37, "Thus the solution of the problem of human friendship lies in the integration of the love of man with the love of God. One loves his friend as the image of God."

26. *On Christian Doctrine* (Nicene and Post-Nicene Fathers, First Series, vol. II; New York: Scribners, 1958) 1.28, quoted in Meilaender, *Friendship*, 19.

27. Meilaender, *Friendship*, 20.

28. Lienhard, "Friendship in Paulinus of Nola and Augustine," 295; cf. Harvey, *Moral Theology*, 37, "It must not be forgotten that the goodness one loves in his friend comes from God and must be referred back to Him."

29. *Conf.* 4.9.14.

30. *Conf.* 4.9.14.

31. See my "Tears of Grief and Joy. *Confessions* Book 9: Chronological Sequence and Structure," *Augustinian Studies* 28 (1997) 141–54, as well as "Book Nine: The Emotional Heart of the *Confessions*," in *A Reader's Companion to Augustine's Confessions* (eds. K. Paffenroth and R. P. Kennedy; Louisville: Westminster John Knox Press, 2003).

32. Letter 92, in Nicene and Post-Nicene Fathers, First Series, vol. I (trans. J. G. Cunningham; Edinburgh: T. & T. Clark, 1886) available online at http://www.ccel.org/fathers2/. The letter is dated to 408.

33. Cf. Meilaender, *Friendship*, 18, "In referring back to God the friend whom God gives, we continually receive the friend back from God."

34. See Brown, *Augustine of Hippo*, 161, "A good Platonist, he might agree that the physical presence of the friend was a 'tiny thing': but he had the courage to admit how much he 'greatly craved' this 'tiny thing.'" Cf. Fiske, "St. Augustine and Friendship," 133–34.

35. Cicero, *De Amicitia*, 19, "For there should be no satiety in friendship, as there is in other things. The older the sweeter, as in wines that keep well."

36. At the beginning of Part 2, Book V, Chapter 4, "Rebellion."

37. *City of God* 19.8.

38. See my *Judas: Images of the Lost Disciple* (Louisville: Westminster John Knox Press, 2001).

4

Freedom Beyond Our Choosing:
Augustine on the Will and Its Objects

David C. Schindler

THE QUESTION CONCERNING freedom warrants the same response Augustine gave to the question concerning time: "I know well enough what it is, provided that nobody asks me; but if I am asked what it is and try to explain, I am baffled."[1] Servais Pinckaers has observed that, since it lies at the heart of any activity that belongs most intimately to us, we have a profound grasp of the meaning of freedom. But he adds, nevertheless, "[a]t the same time, freedom is what we know least, for no idea can encompass it, no piling up of concepts reveal it adequately."[2] Precisely because it is *freedom*, we have difficulty giving a single determinate account of it; the term gathers up quite a variety of experiences, events, and realities without for all that disappearing into pure equivocity. Common political discourse, however, tends to neglect the real mystery of freedom, and contents itself instead with a paltry share of a rich philosophical legacy, reducing the notion to the mere capacity to choose or determine oneself. What we debate in the political sphere is rarely whether this is an adequate conception of freedom, but most often if and to what extent the power to choose ought to be regulated, how to ensure this power to the greatest number of people, and what are the most effective means of multiplying options in order to increase this power.

Behind the view of freedom presupposed by such debates lies a particular conception of will, namely, as an essentially self-directing faculty that operates independently of any external factors, as well as of the other faculties constituting the human psyche. St. Augustine, who was called by Hannah Arendt the "first philosopher of the will,"[3] is typically credited with being the source of this view. In a well-regarded book on the subject, Albrecht Dihle claims that

"St. Augustine was, in fact, the inventor of our modern notion of the will."[4] In contrast to the major Greek thinkers who understood themselves to be giving a sufficient account of human activity through the interplay of reason and the passions, Augustine—for a number of reasons, including his own moral experience as depicted in the *Confessions*, the usage made of the technical term "voluntas" in Roman law, and developments in Trinitarian theology—recognized the need to appeal to an additional faculty. We act the way we do, not because our passions drive us or our reason apprehends what is best, but ultimately because of what we choose. "From St. Augustine's reflections," Dihle says, "emerged the concept of a human will, prior to and independent of the act of intellectual cognition, yet fundamentally different from sensual and irrational emotion."[5] The will is, in other words, the autonomous power of choice, and thus ultimately accountable only to itself.

Now, while this may be our modern concept of the will, I suggest that it is not an adequate description of Augustine's conception. In the essay that follows, I wish to challenge this description, both because it does not do justice to Augustine's full view, and also because, unless it is qualified, it yields an extremely problematic notion of freedom.[6] Augustine, I hope to show, far from being the original author of the conventional modern notion of freedom, offers resources for a significant alternative. Needless to say, there is no room in the present context for a systematic account of Augustine's views on the will and freedom, which in any event would lie beyond my competence. I intend, instead, to think through the philosophical implications of issues raised by the conventional notion of freedom, and in particular the role of choice in that view, in the light of insights from Augustine and texts from some of his commentators.

A Possible Interpretation and Its Consequences

Let us begin by sketching a plausible interpretation of Augustine's notion of free will. In Book III of *De libero arbitrio*, Augustine uses the example of a falling stone to illustrate the difference between a natural movement and a voluntary one. A stone is compelled by its nature to move downward. We cannot "blame" the stone for its action, Augustine remarks, without showing ourselves to be more senseless than the stone itself. But we *can* hold a human being responsible for his or her actions, and we can do so because human beings possess a will, which makes their action, in principle, not dictated by their nature, but voluntary. While Augustine does not deny that there is a movement that is natural to the will (an assertion that has vast implications, to be discussed later), he insists that the will is ultimately not *compelled* by its nature the way a stone is: it is free to follow its natural movement or not. The will acts, not by necessity, but by its own forces.

What is it that causes a person to choose one thing rather than another? To answer this question, we might wish to appeal to a reason, or to a desire, or to some other prompting of nature. But Augustine observes that, if the will has the power either to assent to or resist any desire or reason, there would have to be a further reason behind one's assent or refusal, that is, a further cause of the cause: "You are asking about the cause of the will itself," he explains to Evodius, his interlocutor, "Suppose I could find this cause? Wouldn't we then have to look for the cause of this cause? What limit will there be on this search?"[7] In order to avoid an infinite regression, he concludes, we have to consider the will to be, in some sense, a cause of itself, thus requiring no further cause to explain it in turn. It follows that, whatever else we may say to give an account of a particular human action, we must ultimately end with an appeal to the will as its original source.[8]

For Augustine, it would seem to be precisely the will's character as *causa sui* that makes it free. A stone is determined in its action by its nature; a will is determined (according to this interpretation) only by itself. While nature, desires, or reasons are things we cannot be said ultimately to be responsible for, the movement of our will is due to us alone. There is "nothing so completely in our power as the will itself," Augustine affirms, and adds that "since it is in our power, we are free with respect to it."[9] It thus appears that Augustine equates freedom with power, specifically, the power of determination. To say that we have free will would seem to mean nothing else but that we have the power to determine ourselves, and that this is what makes us responsible agents. Indeed, given Augustine's account just presented, we would be tempted to say that there is nothing that belongs to us more profoundly than our will, there is nothing more intimate to us than this freedom. Because there is nothing in heaven or on earth over which we have more control than that by which we have whatever control we have, what lies at the very core of our being is our power to choose, our free will. Augustine, on this view, would have anticipated by more than a thousand years Jean-Paul Sartre's assertion: "My freedom is not an added quality or a property of my nature; it is the very stuff of my being."[10]

Now, the reason for the subjunctive mode of these inferences is that this sketch represents a very partial interpretation of Augustine's notion of free will, and ignores a good deal of qualifying affirmations regarding freedom and the will not only in *De libero arbitrio*, but in Augustine's thought more generally. If I have sketched it thus, it is both because this view of freedom resonates quite clearly with our familiar modern notion (freedom as the ability to choose), and also because Augustine says enough along these lines to make it a possible way to interpret him. We know that it is possible, because it is actual: a translator of

De libero arbitrio, defining "libertarianism" as the claim that human beings have "metaphysical freedom," which he in turn defines as "the freedom to choose in a way that is not determined by anything outside my control," hails Augustine as "one of the great defenders of libertarianism; indeed, he was the first to articulate the view clearly."[11] The will, the translator continues, "is not determined by any external factors. Only the will can determine itself to choose."[12] This interpretation is echoed, moreover, in Alasdair MacIntyre, who affirms in his own explication of Augustine's position that "[t]he will, being anterior to reason, has at the most fundamental level no reason for its biddings."[13] MacIntyre draws on Dihle, who claims that the inspiration for Augustine's "discovery" of the will was in part the biblical notion of God as creator *ex nihilo*, a notion unknown to the Greeks. Just as God willed to create without prior cause, so too human beings will without prior cause.[14] This spontaneity of the will, which neither Plato nor Aristotle would have had the conceptual means to recognize, is precisely what stamps it as free.

But how is it possible to reconcile this spontaneity with Augustine's consistent affirmation of the will's having an intrinsic nature that inclines it—prior to any choice—to seek fulfillment in what it believes to be good? The passages from Augustine we discussed above, in which he lays emphasis on the spontaneity of choice, pertain in fact to a very specific aspect of the broader issue of the will, namely, the role of choice in the possibility of sin. We must keep in mind, as Mary Clark has pointed out, the limited scope of *De libero arbitrio*: it is not entitled *De libertate*,[15] nor, we might add, *De voluntate*. To derive an interpretation of Augustine primarily from this text, then, would be too limited.[16] What alternatives stand before us if we seek to take a broader view?

First, we must decide whether the will is ordered to the good in an a priori way. On the one hand, we could simply deny that the will has any intrinsic nature, but is essentially "self-creating." We will discuss the problems that arise from this direction of interpretation below. On the other hand, we could admit that the will is intrinsically ordered to the good. Doing so brings us to another crossroads for interpretation. We may affirm, on the one hand, that freedom means the ability to be determined by nothing but oneself, in which case we are free only when we *reject* the good to which the will is a priori determined. This path leads to the identification of sin and freedom, which follows the logic of the assumptions even as it defies common sense. Georg Kohler, for example, has forced Augustine into this direction: "The human will in its created character is free only to the extent that it says 'no' and thus becomes the origin of evil, and is in no way free if it remains related to God and the good."[17] On the other hand, we could refuse to identify freedom with the simple power to choose, and integrate that power within a fuller conception that affirms both the will's ordering to the good *and* its power to determine itself. Only this final possibility will do justice to Augustine's view. Before exploring what it entails, however, we will consider the problems that necessarily arise from a notion of the will as a *causa sui* to the exclusion of any external or prior determination, and therefore of any intrinsic ordering. Our analysis here will draw principally from Servais Pinckaers's *The Sources of Christian Ethics* and Iris Murdoch's *The Sovereignty of Good.*[18]

There are at least three problems that would arise if we interpret "self-determination" as meaning "not determined by another": this view fragments the integrity of the acting subject, it makes freedom arbitrary and thus an empty abstraction, and it evacuates the world of intrinsic value. The first problem has been brilliantly elaborated by Pinckaers, who criticizes this interpretation under the name of "freedom of indifference," and shows how it sets the distinct aspects of the human psychology in opposition to each other. According to Pinckaers, the classical Christian notion of the will understood prior determining factors as *intrinsic to* rather than as *intrusions upon* the will's proper activity. Thus, things such as the natural appetite for the good, or the necessity of certain bonds (not only between the will and the good, but also, for example, loyalties to an ideal, a person, a way of life, an institution, or a previous choice)[19] were included as constitutive of the will, and therefore of the freedom that is essential to it. Separating the will's own activity from those other factors that are, so to speak, naturally ingredients in it, entails a fragmentation of both the will and the integrity of soul.

The most fateful rupture entailed in the definition of freedom as the capacity to choose, according to Pinckaers, is the break between the will and reason. If choice is free precisely insofar as it is not determined by something outside of itself, then it finds its freedom only in independence from reason. Reason, after all, determines grounds for a choice, and, to that extent, would incline the will one way or another *prior* to its decision: "If freedom consisted in the ability to choose between the *yes* and the *no*, it would have to affirm itself primarily against reason, against the 'reasons' proposed for determining its choice and requiring of it a *yes*."[20] But the severance of will from an intrinsic relationship to reason has implications for both faculties: will becomes irrational or "arbitrary" in the modern sense, that is, freedom becomes in itself something wholly indeterminate; and reason, on the other hand, becomes rationalistic or mechanistic, that is, something which bears no intrinsic relation to freedom. Pinckaers concludes his analysis with a striking list of the various dichotomies that follow of necessity from the notion of freedom as pure self-determination: either freedom or law, either freedom or reason, either freedom or nature, either freedom or grace, either man was free or God, either subject or object, either freedom or sensibility, either my freedom or the freedom of others, either the individual or society.[21]

One of the immediate implications of the divorce between the will and reason is that choice becomes "arbitrary" by its very essence. What would give a particular choice weight is a determinate reason or natural inclination, something distinct from the simple power to choose and which bears on the will from outside of itself. If the will, by its nature, stands altogether outside the various possibilities that reason proposes or the movements that nature initiates, like a perfectly indifferent spectator unmoved by what it observes until it decides to move itself, its selection of any one of the possibilities will be itself purely unmotivated. The act of choosing will be a spontaneous eruption, a sheer volitional "positing," inaccessible to the mind (both that of an outside observer and that of the agent him- or herself), because it is altogether without reason. But in this case, freedom is an empty notion. Lacking any determination, it lacks all content.

In one of the essays from *The Sovereignty of Good*, Murdoch attacks just such an "inflated and yet empty concept of the will,"[22] and we ought to notice that it is inflated for precisely the same reason that it is empty. If freedom is not determined by anything outside of itself, then there is nothing to which it can be subordinated. But there is equally in this case nothing that would give it an intrinsic quality or character. Freedom as choice means freedom as an isolated abstraction, a ghost cut off from all that would fill it out and make it concrete. Echoing from a different perspective what we saw in Pinckaers, Murdoch shows what this notion of freedom entails for our conception of the person:

> Reason and rule represent a sort of impersonal tyranny in relation to which however the personal will represents perfect freedom. The machinery is relentless, but until the moment of choice the agent is outside the machinery. Morality resides at the point of action. What I am "objectively" is not under my control; logic and observers decide that. What I am "subjectively" is a foot-loose, solitary, substanceless will. Personality dwindles to a point of pure will.[23]

If freedom consists simply in the power to choose, it can bear no positive account of its essential character without losing precisely to that extent its freedom. "If the will is to be totally free," Murdoch explains (taking "free" here to mean "not determined by an other"), "the world it moves in must be devoid of normative characteristics, so that morality can reside entirely in the pointer of pure choice."[24] Viewing the will as pure power of choosing leads to what Murdoch calls "a fictitious sense of freedom: I may as well toss a coin."[25]

But it is not only the will that becomes empty under this notion; the world, too, loses any substance of its own in relation to this personality "dwindled to a point of pure will." The way the world manifests itself to us is in a profound sense mediated by our concept of the will. As the scholastics used to say, that which is received is received in the mode of the recipient. If the will is in some respect the locus of our relation to the world as persons, then the nature of the will will bring itself to bear on that relation, and therefore on the term of that relation. The question is, then, How does the objective correlate of the will, understood as pure self-determination, appear? If self-determination strictly excludes any determination by an other, then the object of the will, that which stands outside of the will, can have no bearing whatsoever on the will. It can make no claim on the will that is not automatically trumped at the will's discretion, and so presents itself to the will only as a function of the will's choice. In other words, that which stands before the pure power of self-determination, insofar as that power cannot be intrinsically determined by anything outside of itself, can only be a function of that power. It cannot be good; it can only be "optional." Seen from within the horizon established by freedom as the power to choose, the world in general is reduced to a series of options, none of which can be any more compelling than any other for the simple reason that none can be compelling at all.

Let us consider more carefully why something that is purely optional cannot, strictly speaking, be intrinsically good. The distinction between *uti* and *frui*, which Augustine draws in the well-known passages at the beginning of *De doctrina christiana*,[26] calls our attention to what specifically characterizes goodness in its most proper sense: to say that something is a good is to say that it is an *end*, that wherein the will's activity comes to rest. For Augustine, we *enjoy* a good precisely because it presents itself as an end: "to enjoy something is to cling to it with love for its own sake."[27] By contrast, those things that we will other than in the mode of enjoyment (i.e., all relative or instrumental goods [*uti*]), are willed ultimately for the sake of those things willed for themselves alone. Recalling this same point in *De trinitate*, Augustine states: "For we enjoy things known, in which things themselves the will finds delight for their own sake, and so reposes; but we use those things, which we refer to some other thing which we are to enjoy."[28] But if this is the case, then unless there exists some good that is good in an absolute sense, that is, good in itself, as an ultimate end, there can be no goods even in a relative sense. Without some ultimate end, the will has no place to come to rest.

Now, as Aristotle says, an end is not something that comes simply at the end of an activity, but in fact also precedes the activity insofar as the activity is initiated for the sake of its end.[29] An end that came only at the end would be an accident rather than a *telos*. In this respect, the end, to be an end, must be prior to the activity that brings it about, and its capacity to determine that activity is in fact dependent on this priority. For something to be good, that is, for something to be an *end*, it must, so to speak, determine the act that achieves it before that act determines the end. In this respect, a will cannot will a good except insofar as it is determined by that good prior to its act. But if we define the will precisely as the power of self-determination (i.e., in the sense that excludes determination by an other), then the will can in fact will nothing good. We might say that, precisely to the extent that it is exclusively self-determining, the will *usurps* all priority from its object, and therefore undermines the possibility of its relating to that object as to a good.

Those who would defend a view of freedom as self-determination might object that this view does not exclude determination by an other in every respect, but simply from the act of choosing: "I *freely choose* what I take to be good, but then I allow myself to be determined by the good I have chosen." The question is to what extent this "allowing oneself" continues to be a free act of the will. Insofar as it does, and will is understood to be pure self-determination, it continues to usurp the good character of the "good." Insofar as it does not, then the will, as pure self-determination, is no longer essentially involved in the adherence to the good. But if the will is not involved, then on this view neither is the person, because as we saw above, a notion of will as pure self-determination necessarily entails the identification of the person with this will. In short, then, the will so-conceived cannot will a good, even one that it has chosen: either the will remains, and the good-character of the good is eliminated, or the good remains, and the freedom of the will is eliminated.

But it is not altogether correct to say that the will, understood in this sense, cannot will a good as good. In reality, it is impossible for an act of will, as act, to be without an end. The de facto good is whatever determines the act, and if the will is essentially self-determining, then the end of the will in its operation is the will itself. The will, as power to choose, necessarily makes itself ultimate in each of its choices. Such a will can have no true end outside of itself; each of its choices becomes instrumental relative to this end. But relative goods derive their goodness from the end to which they are relative. On the one hand, this therefore means, as Murdoch shows, that the will itself becomes the source of all goodness: "The centre of this type of post-Kantian moral philosophy is the notion of the will as the creator of value. Values which were previously in some sense inscribed in the heavens and guaranteed by God collapse into the human will. There is no transcendent reality. The idea of the good remains indefinable and empty so that human choice may fill it."[30] On the other hand, however, because the will lacks all intrinsic determination, it possesses in fact no goodness with which to fill the idea of the good. In its sheer power, it is impotent to do anything but reflect its emptiness into the world. Its intrinsic emptiness is, as it were, logically contagious. Making all values contingent upon choice does not magnify the power of the human ego, as it might seem to at first glance, but dissolves the substance of both world and ego into the empty abstraction of freedom. It would be illuminating, here, to compare the transformation of the objects of choice from goods into options within the abstract self-relation of freedom to Marx's analysis of the transformation of commodities into abstract exchange-values within the essentially unlimited circulation of capital: "instead of simply representing relations of commodities, it enters now, so to say, into private relations with itself."[31]

The final result of identifying freedom with the power to choose is nihilism, as Nietzsche describes it in *The Will to Power*: "What does nihilism mean? *That the highest values devaluate themselves.* The aim is lacking; 'why?' finds no answer."[32] A genuine aim requires a genuine end, something that offers a response to the question "why?" But a genuine end, as we have seen, must in some respect move me prior to my choosing of it. Goodness or value presents itself phenomenologically as attraction, and attraction is the action upon me of an external object, the intimate "tugging" on me of something other than myself. But such attraction loses any force to the extent that I identify myself with my will as the power to choose. If there is no possibility of profound attraction, then even if there did exist things in the world—things of genuine value—they could never be perceived as such, because to be experienced as good would require intruding upon and supplanting the end that the will makes of itself. If to be merely an "option" means that a thing makes no claim whatsoever on the will before the will makes a claim on it, then, from what we have just seen, one way to characterize nihilism would be to say that the world appears as nothing but a set of options; and defining the will as the power to choose allows the world to appear in no other way.

In reaction to the problems we have been exploring, we may be inclined to think that the only alternative is to eliminate the notion of choice or self-determination from our understanding of the will, and thus that we can keep from drowning in nihilism only by clinging to the planks of some form of determinism. Either way, it would seem, we insist on freedom at the risk of nihilism, or we insist that there are things that must be imposed on the will from without, things concerning which the will is simply not free. But neither of these alternatives adequately expresses Augustine's view. When Augustine elaborated the will's apparently sovereign power of choice in his relatively early work, *De libero arbitrio*, he did so explicitly within the context of an affirmation of the will's being ordered by its nature to the supreme Good, God. Moreover, while he laid increasing emphasis on the will's being determined from outside of itself in his later writings and especially in debate with the Pelagians, he never surrendered his insistence on the will's free power to choose.[33] *Prima facie*, these two affirmations seem to stand in great tension, if not outright contradiction. If Augustine did not see them as mutually exclusive, it can only be because he was operating with a notion of freedom significantly different from the one we tend to presume.

Freedom, Love, and Goodness

There can be no question in the present context of elaborating a full account of Augustine's notion of freedom, or tracing the different shades of emphasis as the notion evolved within the different contexts of his writing. We will, instead, engage his thought specifically for light on this question: In what respect and to what extent is the will determined from within, that is, by itself, and to what extent is the will determined from without, that is, by an other, in its normal operation? Exploring the structure of the will's operation will in turn open up insight into the meaning of freedom.

The first essential characteristic of the will worth recalling here is what we might call its "transparency": the will, for Augustine, is essentially *intentional*, that is, not so much a thing closed in on itself, as a relation to what is other than itself. In *De duabus animabus*, Augustine defines the will as a "movement of the soul" (*animi motus*),[34] and he specifies the possible types of movement in the *City of God*: the will is either the soul's movement to acquire a good, to preserve a good that has been acquired, to avoid an evil, or to reject an evil that is being suffered.[35] Now, as we can see, what characterizes the movement in each case is a good under a particular modality, either as good per se or as the negation of an evil. James Wetzel is therefore correct to affirm that "[w]henever we act, Augustine would contend, we act under some representation of the good,"[36] an affirmation that can be denied only by denying either that the will is a movement or that a movement has some destination. But to say that the will acts under a representation of the good means that its own movement begins, not first in itself, but in the good that it represents to itself. In this, Augustine's view accords with that of Aristotle, for whom "the first mover of [our action] is the object of desire."[37] In other words, if the act of will is a motion, that motion is generated at least in part by something other than the will, namely, by its object. Augustine's comparison of the will's natural movement to a stone's weight (*pondus*) illustrates this point beautifully: we tend to think of weight as an intrinsic property of a body, while in fact this property is unintelligible merely in itself, but can be understood only as the attraction or pull of another body.[38] Similarly, however self-moving the will appears to be, its motion is likewise explicable only by reference to some attraction.

It is not an accident that Augustine uses the image of the "weight" to reveal the nature not only of the will, but also of love.[39] Indeed, Augustine goes so far as to *identify* the will with love,[40] and he can do so because, as Gilson shows, he understands love, like the will, as "by definition, a natural tendency toward a certain good."[41] In other words, love is not just one of the various possible activities of the will, as we might think insofar as we take the will to be an indifferent power of choice, but it brings to light the very essence of the will.

Now, viewing the will as love immediately expands our conception of its operation. Love is not the abstract activity of "sheer willing," but in fact involves all of the human faculties required to perceive, be moved by, pursue, attain, enjoy, and adhere to goodness: namely, the senses, the will, the passions, and the intelligence. In this respect, whatever enables the will to achieve its own acts enters *intrinsically* into its operation rather than intruding upon it from the outside. While the will preserves its own activity, that activity is always mediated by the other faculties, even as it gathers these up and directs them. As Gilson puts it,

> The action of the will upon the human being as a whole is accomplished through the mediation of the images and ideas that it uses. In Augustine's psychology, the will is not the "originator" of the representations, but it is the power that "couples" with them. In other words, it is the will that either applies our faculties of sensation, imagination, and thought to their own acts, or turns these faculties away from them; hence the dominant influence that the will exercises by taking up all of the human being's activities into the direction of its dominant love.[42]

In the same vein, Arendt explains that Augustine calls the will "love" because both are essentially a "coupling, binding agent."[43] Understood as love, she continues, the will operates not as a separate faculty in itself, but "in its function within the mind as a whole, where all single faculties—memory, intellect, and will—are 'mutually referred to each other.'"[44] In short, seeing the will as love leads us to consider it not as an autonomous power, but as a distinct faculty through which the whole human being operates: the will, in this case, is as receptive as it is spontaneous, acting in response to and in conjunction with the activities of the other faculties, because it acts in response to a perceived good.

Before facing the obvious objections to viewing the will as essentially a love for the good, it is worthwhile to take note of the path it opens through the dichotomies entailed by the problematic view of freedom sketched at the outset. As we saw there, to the extent that freedom means exclusive self-determination, I can be truly free only in a world devoid of intrinsic value, wherein nothing makes any particular claim on me, so that the act of choosing finally reduces to an explosion of random spontaneity. Since the world does, in fact, contain determinate goods, my freedom would in this case come to expression *only* in my rejection of these goods. By contrast, if we acknowledge that the will is essentially love, such that it fulfills itself *as* will, and comes to its proper flourishing in the attainment of what is good, then being determined by an external object—that is, the good—represents no compromise of freedom but in fact one of its crucial preconditions.

We tend to assume that freedom is opposed to necessity of any sort. If the will is viewed as love, however, it is not opposed to all forms of necessity, but

only a particular form, namely, coercion.[45] What is the difference between coercion and the sort of necessity that would be harmonious with freedom? In
the former, the will is forced in an extrinsic sense to move in a direction contrary to itself. However, as Augustine repeatedly observes, it is possible for the
will to be compelled by something other than itself, but in a "non-coercive"
way. If the will is compelled by something that is genuinely good, it has the capacity actively to appropriate that external determination to itself, so that it is
in this case compelled as much by itself, by its own inner nature, as it is by the
good.[46] Augustine calls this active, inward appropriation *delight* or *enjoyment*
(*delectatio*). Such delight is, indeed, a form of necessity—as he puts it, "we
necessarily act according to that which most delights us"[47]—but it is a form
distinct from coercion insofar as it does not run contrary to the will's own
willing: "What is more absurd," asks Augustine, "than to say that someone unwillingly wills the good?"[48] It is, then, precisely delight that marks the difference between being slavishly determined by another and being freely determined by an other.[49] Indeed, as Juan Pegueroles has put it, *delectatio* is the
"moving principle of the will."[50] But if it is the case that delight is a free necessity, then we already begin to see how freedom could increase rather than
decrease in the presence of things that delight, that is, things of intrinsic value.
For the greater the presence of the good, the stronger the love for it; the
stronger the love, the stronger and more complete the will, and therefore, the
fuller the freedom.

But more can be said on this score. To insist on the *self*-determining character of the will tends to presuppose an opposition between freedom and dependence. This opposition, however, turns out to be an illusion. The reason
one offers for rejecting the claim an intrinsic good makes upon us is that the
dependence on this good seems to imply a curtailment of our self-dependence
or freedom. But if it is the case that the will, insofar as it is motivated at all, always acts under the representation of some good, the will cannot in fact escape from some external determination. What this implies, then, is that the di-
chotomy between freedom and dependence is a false one. Indeed, because
every act of the will is determined in some respect by something outside of itself, having a human will necessarily means being, at every moment, in a state
of dependence. To will is always to bind ourselves: the real question is therefore not whether we choose to be free or to be dependent, but rather whether
we choose to bind ourselves to what enslaves or to what liberates.

Augustine's view on this point is unequivocally clear, and remained essentially the same from the beginning of his writings to the end. It is possible to
lay out his view in five simple points. First, as human beings, we cannot live
without willing, and therefore loving: "What is this? Are you supposed to stop
loving? Impossible! Motionless, dead, abominable, miserable: that is what you

would be if you loved nothing."[51] Second, it is impossible to will without seeking happiness: "[D]o you think that there is anyone who does not in every way will and desire a happy life?"[52] Third, we cannot, therefore, will without binding ourselves to something outside of ourselves: "Whether he will or no, a man is necessarily a slave to the things by means of which he seeks to be happy."[53] Fourth, to the extent that we bind ourselves to what is "lower" than us (i.e., purely material things), we compromise our freedom, thus pledging ourselves to a "voluntary abandonment of highest being, and toil among inferior beings which is not voluntary."[54] As an illustration of this insight, we might think of the richly suggestive figure of Caliban in *The Tempest*, a living embodiment of the rudimentary passions, who, though confessing abject servitude to his captors, in fact leads them at will by the nose. And finally, we come into possession of freedom, by contrast, by binding ourselves to what is truly good in itself: "This is our freedom, when we are subject to the truth," which is "not merely one good among others; it is the highest good, the good that makes us happy."[55]

Once we acknowledge that freedom does not exclude dependence, but rather presupposes a dependence of a particular sort, it is no longer possible to identify freedom simply with the power to choose. Indeed, this power becomes relativized, in a manner we have to discuss, insofar as freedom, in Augustine's view, implies the sort of attachment that excludes certain choices. Thus, in describing freedom in its most perfect sense—eschatological freedom—Augustine claims that those in heaven, having lost the capacity to sin—i.e., to make certain choices—are not only happier, but are specifically *freer*: "Now the fact that they will be unable to delight in sin does not entail that they will have no free will. In fact, the will will be the freer in that it is freed from delight in sin and immovably fixed in a delight in not sinning."[56] The difference between Augustine's view and the conventional modern one rings out particularly clearly in his description of the state of freedom as being "immovably fixed." We can make no sense of this passage if we identify freedom, in a negative sense, with "having options open." Instead, we must begin to consider a more positive conception of freedom—for example, as the "power to abide in the good," which Augustine describes at the end of *De vera religione*.[57] But how to understand this more positive view, and what role it preserves for choice, will have to be unfolded, which we can do by considering some objections.

Specifically, two often-cited and related difficulties spring up immediately from this analysis. On the one hand, if the will is ordered to the good in such a way that it is inwardly strengthened precisely to the extent that it is determined from without, then have we simply eliminated any room at all for something like "self-determination" in the functioning of the will? What would be the difference, in this case, between a human being with a will naturally ordered to the good, and a creature that reacted passively and automatically to the presence of the good, its acts being exhaustively a function of whatever natural inclination or reason dominated at any given moment? Aware of this difficulty, there are some commentators that point to Augustine's earlier work on free choice as an insight into freedom that he compromised, if not altogether abandoned, in his debate with the Pelagians in which he laid so much emphasis on the supreme determining power of the external order of grace.[58] But Augustine himself was aware of this objection, and yet it never shook his conviction about the will's natural ordination to the good. On the other hand, if the will is naturally ordered to the good, how can we explain the possibility of what is evidently an actuality, namely, that the will can choose things that are not good, and even, strangely, things it *knows* are not good? Augustine himself accounts for the existence of evil in a world brought into being by a perfectly good Creator through an appeal to the existence of free will.[59] Doesn't this imply an understanding of will, not as love of the good, but as essentially the capacity to choose, which is precisely the understanding that proved problematic in our earlier analysis? How—to put the question again—can we reconcile this view of the will with its being naturally ordered to the good?

Consent as Co-act

We will need to find an answer to the first difficulty in order to be able to respond fruitfully to the second. If it is the case that this first difficulty stems, once again, from the apparent dilemma—*either* will as pure self-determination, *or* will as pure determination by another—we can resolve it if we can find some way to reject the opposition it implies. Augustine overcomes a version of this dilemma in his working out of the encounter of grace and human freedom in the debate with the Pelagians, and the essence of his response turns on the notion of *consent* (*con-sentire*, to "perceive with an other"), an act that so to speak weaves together the work of two agents into one: "To consent to the calling of God or to refuse it belongs to our own will: which, so far from conflicting with the text *What hast thou which thou hast not received?*, does even confirm it. For the soul cannot receive and possess the gift there spoken of but by consenting. *What* the soul is to possess, *what* it is to receive, pertains to God: the receiving and possessing, necessarily to him who receives and possesses."[60] As this passage affirms, consent is something that one *gives*, i.e., it is therefore an act that originates from the consentor; and yet the very same act is somehow *received* from God, and therefore originates from a source beyond the consentor. As Wetzel concisely puts it, "consent is a gift."[61] By appealing to this notion, Augustine intends, in other words, to describe an act that is wholly due to God, and yet in such a way that human agency is not short-circuited. Cardinal Bellarmine characterizes the operation of grace as an act for which both God and man are wholly responsible: "there is nothing of ours that is not God's, nor anything of God's that is not ours. God does the *whole* and man does the *whole*."[62]

I propose that the notion of consent that Augustine here introduces opens up a way to overcome the dilemma at the heart of the problem of freedom, not only in relation to the divine activity of grace, but analogously in relation to the activity of the good upon the will in its normal operation.[63] If the will always operates under the representation of some good, we may say that each of its acts is not the *ex nihilo* creation of values, but always an act of consent to something that precedes it. In this case, as we shall see, we avoid determinism insofar as we affirm the spontaneous agency of the will, but we also avoid nihilism insofar as we understand that agency precisely as the "letting be" of the good's own activity. In this way, the notion of consent allows a complex view of the will's activity, which will prove fruitful for our understanding of freedom. Let us therefore consider in more detail the structure of the act of consent.

The first thing we can say about the act of consent is that it is in every case a *response*. I can consent only *to* something, and that "something" must be present to elicit my act, and therefore must precede it. There is, thus, no such thing as a purely spontaneous act of consent. Furthermore, the content of the act of consent is given by the object of that act rather than by the consenting subject. Consent doesn't invent, it receives. Receptivity constitutes the very essence of the act. At the same time, however, this sort of receptivity is active rather than passive. A dead will can be manipulated, but it cannot give its consent. For that, a kind of spontaneity is required, in order that the determinate content presented not be imposed from without, but instead actively embraced from within. There is consent, then, only where there is genuinely free and spontaneous agency, even if—or, better, precisely *because*—the character of this agency is receptive.

Now, the suggestion that consent should be essential to any act we would recognize as free does not seem like a revelation: we hear it affirmed quite regularly in normal political discourse. The real bite of the notion makes itself felt only when we are careful to distinguish Augustine's notion from the conventional one. We are accustomed to think of consent in terms of the notion of free choice we discussed at the outset: whenever something is presented to me, I am free to decide whether to accept or reject it, which means that my will stands in a state of indifference or "neutrality" before the present good, and whether I consent or not depends wholly upon my choice, my power of self-determination. As powerful as the attraction of the good might be, as compelling as the reason to choose it might be, it is my will that ultimately stamps it with a "yea" or "nay," and my will may be informed by motives, but it is in no way controlled by them. If I thus claim to be free, it is because I affirm that there remains in me a faculty independent of both my desires and my intellect, and that it is to this faculty that the final word in my activities is reserved.[64]

But such a view returns us to our earlier difficulties: it implies that the movement of the will is from first to last self-originated, and it thus becomes once again a purely arbitrary, and therefore empty, act. To avoid these difficulties, however, we do not have to eliminate a moment of consent or choice from the will's relation to the good. Instead, we need only deny that this moment is a separate and "self-enclosed" act, possessing its own logic, which is defined by the autonomous agent as its sole source. In Augustine's view, consent is not something the will does alone, but is essentially a "co-act," that is, a single act that is constituted by two irreducibly distinct "agencies," namely, the good's activity of determination and the will's spontaneous act of allowing itself to be determined. While these activities are different from one another, they are nevertheless inseparable; indeed, they are in some respect identical within the single act of "letting be." It is impossible, within this single act, to determine precisely where one agency ends and the other begins, and it is likewise impossible to say that the two agencies ever merge together in a way that would confuse their distinction.[65]

As paradoxical as such a "co-act" may at first appear, examples are not difficult to find. Let us consider the act of teaching. Teaching is never simply an acting *on* a passive student from the outside (as teachers experience, with frustration, every day), but is by its very essence a "co-acting": the student is not taught, does not learn, except through active participation, through the intense and demanding activity of attending to what is being said and receiving it. This activity is not a self-enclosed activity that is secondarily added to the first activity of teaching, but is rather the inward reception of an external determination. Not being added from without, this reception is in fact an *integral part* of the giving, such that the teaching could not be said to occur without it. Thus, there is no teaching without learning. But the contrary is even more obviously true: there is no learning without teaching. Indeed, even if teaching is dependent on the active reception of the learner, it has a certain priority over this activity, since it is what initiates the learning. Thus, there is (1) a mutual dependence between the two activities, which is (2) nevertheless *asymmetrical*, since the teaching gives rise to the capacity to learn, which in turn allows the capacity to teach, even if (3) this asymmetry does not in any way imply chronological succession: clearly, learning cannot come chronologically *after* teaching because the act of teaching includes this responsive act within its own act. Indeed, it is possible to say that the act is something the student is *wholly* responsible for, just as it is possible to say the responsibility rests entirely with the teacher. Here we have two distinct agencies dependent upon one another for the occurrence of a single event.

That there exists an analogy between the act of consent/being-determined and the act of learning/teaching should be evident. The various dilemmas we have encountered up to this point have all cropped up because of an assumption that the activity of the will to determine itself and the determining activity of the will's object, the good, have to be two separate activities if they are to be distinct at all, and that we can subsequently overcome the problems of their separation only by reductively absorbing one into the other. Taking our cue from Augustine's notion of consent as a single act constituted by two distinct activities, however, we can propose an alternative: the act of the will is nothing other than the actualization of the good, a participation in its determining activity. It is, so to speak, a spontaneous "letting be" of the determination of the good, which is not a separate activity added on to the good's determination, but is nevertheless a distinct element in that good's actual determining of the will and thus its own completion as goodness. If this is the case, it becomes impossible to think of the will as a sovereign power of choice standing as a self-enclosed indifference over and above the good of its objects. Insofar as the power of the will lies in its consent, which is always an act *shared* by the will and some good, then, on its own, the will is impotent. It is the very essence of the will to be involved in the good's presentation of itself as good, such that the will actively fulfills itself in *allowing* the good to determine it.

There are three things to note in this mutual play between the will and the good. First of all, according to this view, "will power" is a gift. The will's own impetus arises, not first from the will itself, but from the good to which the will consents: "For the strength of our will to anything is proportionate to the certainty of our knowledge of its goodness, and the ardor of our delight in it."[66] Second, for Augustine, as we have already observed, when the will enjoys or takes delight in an object that is other than itself, it is not "coerced" by, but inwardly appropriates, the object's extrinsic determination. In other words, the will receives its own power from the good insofar as it, through its own most intimate inward movement, joins the extrinsically determining act of the good—not as one thing added to another, but as an intrinsic part of a single whole—and thus makes this act its own. Third, it is a discrete act of consent that effects this appropriation. We can, and indeed *must*, speak of free choice in this context, insofar as the joining of the will and the good would not occur without a real spontaneity on the part of the will, a spontaneity that can, in principle, be lacking as we shall see. But it would miss the point to think of the will as the indifferent capacity to choose between alternatives. Rather, it would in this case best be understood as original and active participation in goodness. In this sense, the will would receive its meaning always in relation to some good, even while not being thereby forced to surrender its own spontaneous agency. The spontaneous agency it retains, however, is never simply a random "happening," but is always initiated by the provocative presence of some good.

We return, then, to the passage from Augustine cited above: there is nothing our will possesses that it has not received—i.e., the will's own act "begins," as it were, in the goodness of its object and in this sense the movement of the will belongs to the object. And yet the will does not receive this act except through its own spontaneous act of consent—i.e., the movement of the will cannot be simply reduced to the attraction of the good.

Freedom as Original Participation in Goodness

If consent represents the essential act of the will, then freedom is best viewed as original participation in goodness. To see what we have gained by this conception, we may consider how it serves to recover those things we typically associate with freedom—namely, choice, the possibility of evil, self-determination, surprise or spontaneity, and even a kind of autonomy—but within a conception that avoids their potential problems because it radically transforms their meaning.

First, while it is true that Augustine does not identify freedom with the capacity to choose, his view does not diminish, but in fact amplifies its importance. For Plotinus, the will contributes nothing to the mind's apprehension of the good;[67] for Augustine, by contrast, the soul's relation to the good is deficient without the will's choosing of it. But this choice is not a power that the will "lords over" the good in its freedom. Quite to the contrary, it is a demand that the good imposes on the will. We are called upon to choose the good, and invest ourselves in our choice, precisely *in order to* be free. The importance of this choice in Augustine's view of freedom, and its contrast to the conventional notion, perhaps come to light best in the drama that forms the climax of the *Confessions*, Book VIII: Augustine experiences a lack of freedom, not because his options are too limited, but in a sense because they are not sufficiently limited. There is a residual disorder in his soul, by virtue of which he finds himself incapable of being fully attracted to what he knows is fully good. He cannot, as it were, will what he wills, or in other words: he cannot give full, single-hearted consent: "The one necessary condition, which meant not only going but at once arriving there, was to have the will to go—provided only that the will was strong and unqualified, not the turning and twisting first this way, then that, of a will half-wounded, struggling with one part rising up and the other part falling down."[68] His capacity to choose, in this case, is indeed his freedom, but that capacity is the ability to consent with the whole of his being to the good that demands to lay hold of him. Without his consent, the good is merely good in itself, and not good for him, i.e., it does not in fact claim him.[69] And yet it is nothing but the claim that the good makes on him that enables his choice. Freedom of choice is here coincident with the compelling nature of the good. The freedom that we would possess, in short, *demands* that we choose, and it is the good itself that gives us the power to make the choice.

Moreover, viewing the determining action of the good as a "co-act" shared by the will and the good allows us to accommodate the possibility of sin without surrendering the will's natural ordering to the good. Without entering into all of the complexities of the debate surrounding this question,[70] we have at least the principle of a coherent interpretation of Augustine's view. It is well-known that Augustine appeals to evil as proof of the existence of free will. But in the *City of God*, he affirms that it is also evidence of the will's being ordered to the good, since, otherwise, evil would not be bad: "That is why the *choice* of evil is an impressive proof that the *nature* is good."[71] Those who believe they can explain the possibility of sin simply by saying that the will is "free," i.e., capable of choosing between indifferent alternatives, are therefore mistaken. They do not solve, but in fact exacerbate the problem: if goodness is not an inherent quality of nature, then evil loses its meaning; if nature is good, then the will is separate from the good in all of its acts precisely to the extent that it is "independent" of nature. The problem, in this case, becomes not to explain how sin is possible, but how anything *other* than sin is possible.

On the other hand, those who insist on the will's natural ordering to the good are at a loss to explain the possibility of sin *only insofar as they reduce the will's activity to the good's determination*. In this case, we would have to find some "objective" cause of evil in nature, and in the end would be unable to avoid implicating God. But if we understand the good's acting upon the will as in every instance a "co-act," and therefore as an act that requires the responsive contribution of the will's own agency, then we have a source of responsibility, which is nevertheless *not* a "reified choice" or the simple addition of a new causality. As Augustine says, an evil will "has no cause."[72] To "explain" it, he introduces the notion of "deficient" causality (i.e., the failure of a positive cause), a term that makes sense only in the context of the co-act of consent. The choice of evil is not, in its essence, a spontaneous act of the will, insofar as such spontaneity occurs only through the co-agency of the good. Instead, the choice of evil is a lack of the spontaneity that receptive adherence to the good requires. At the root of any choice of evil there is thus a half-hearted willing. This is not to say, of course, that such a choice will not be perhaps filled with an intensity that overwhelms the person who makes it; it is just that this intensity, being merely self-propelled, will be the intensity of only "half" of a person, rather than the integral "gathering up" of the personality that genuine consent implies.[73] If the good's determination involves consent, then, we can say that sin is a *result* of freedom without making it the *expression* of freedom: because the reception of the good requires my contribution, and thus my freedom, I can fail it; but if freedom means active participation in the good, then in not receiving the good I am surrendering, rather than fulfilling, my freedom. Gilson offers a characteristically pithy statement of this insight: "man is free, and by his own choice he does evil, but not by that which makes his choice free."[74]

Further, the view of freedom as original participation in the good also enables us to recover a notion of self-determination in our understanding of the will, while avoiding the emptiness necessarily implied in the conventional understanding. There is no act of will that is not determined by some good, and yet that good does not determine the will unless the will shares in the determining activity. In other words, the good does not determine the will unless the will is *also* self-determining. We can recall, here, Augustine's struggle in the *Confessions*: he suffered from an impotence to determine himself precisely because he was unable to receive in a profound way the determining power of the good. Aquinas clarifies what lies implicit in Augustine, by distinguishing between first and second causes: the will causes its own movement without being the *first* cause of this movement.[75] To put it another way, the will determines itself *only within* the comprehensive determination of the good. The problem with the conventional notion is therefore not that it insists on self-determination in its understanding of the will, but that it assumes that self-determination means *not* being determined by another. If *consent* describes the proper activity of the will, by contrast, self-determination will both require being determined by another and it will in turn be required by it. Instead of the opposition between the self and the other that Pinckaers described, then, we get a recasting of the powerful paradox we saw above: the more *spontaneously* the will involves itself in the determination, the more profoundly it is determined by the good acting upon it. And the converse is also true: the more compellingly the good offers itself to the will, the more free or self-determining the will becomes in its reception. The two activities are not in competition, but instead co-operate in the one act of being determined through consent, and so they increase in tandem.[76]

If the will does, then, possess a spontaneity and self-causality in its reception of the good, are its choices determined by its reasons for choosing? The best answer is both yes and no. Clearly, there is an ultimate inexplicability in the choice of evil as such, insofar as such choices have no positive cause, and, as Augustine says, "What is not anything, cannot be known."[77] But it would seem that *good* choices are wholly explicable in terms of the determination of the good chosen. According to Wetzel, if we admit the slightest spontaneity into the will's operation distinct from the good's determination, human action becomes opaque as a rule: "The theory of will as the power of choice, informed by but independent of desire, makes every action to some degree unintelligible, for if the theory were true, no action would ever be sufficiently explained by its motives." It is this insight that leads him to make the radical claim that, for Augustine, "[t]here is no faculty of will, distinct from desire, which we can use to determine our actions."[78] But Wetzel's concern here is justified only insofar as we concede the conventional notion of choice as a purely spontaneous, and therefore unmotivated, act. Making this concession in turn forces us to adopt a deterministic understanding of human action in order to preserve its intelligibility.

If we view choice, by contrast, as consent and therefore conceive freedom as original participation in goodness, a third alternative presents itself: all human action becomes, to some degree, a *surprise*, without for all that being utterly arbitrary and without motivation. Interior to the good's determination is the will's spontaneous consent, which co-enables its actualization. The consent brings the good into being in a particular form, here and now, in a way that cannot be determined beforehand merely on the basis of the good alone. In this respect, there is a certain gratuity or "whylessness," something that transcends explanation, in every act of the will. But this gratuity does not make the act random or irrational, because the entire content of the act is nevertheless determinate, insofar as the act of the will is not the addition of new content, but the letting be of a good.[79] Thus, we are in fact led to see the good, not simply as an object of the will, but more comprehensively as an event that includes the will's consent within its own being. The *gratuitous* consent, in other words, is a *necessary* part of its own nature. Because the essence of choice is consent, i.e., an indispensable causality that nevertheless adds nothing from the outside, it can be *wholly* motivated without thereby being reduced to the determination of the good that motivates it. In this sense, sufficient reasons can be given for an act that has taken place, but at the same time, we do not have to infer that the action was therefore an automatic result of those reasons, and that it would necessarily occur again or in the same way if the same reasons were present.

Augustine illustrates this unpredictability with a consideration of two identical men facing the same situation, who nonetheless make different choices.[80] He also tells the story of twins who, despite the very same constitution, exhibit different behavior, and he suggests that the only explanation is a difference in the use of the will.[81] Finally, in *City of God* 12.21, Augustine affirms that human freedom is a genuine novelty (*novitas*) which is not blind chance, but is harmonious with the providential ordering of the world. Interpreting this passage, Arendt observes that, while everything else in the world was created in the sense of being given a beginning (*principium*), the human being was created *as* a beginning (*initium*), that is, as a relatively absolute reflection of God's own absoluteness.[82] In short, since freedom is a participation in the goodness of being, there is something of the gratuity or "whylessness" of creation at the heart of every act of the will.

The final, and perhaps most surprising, implication of this view of freedom that we will mention is that it allows us to say that there is a certain sense in which freedom of the will *can* in fact be understood as autonomous, or independent of external determination. It is surprising because this was the sense of freedom we ruled out at the beginning as incoherent. But we did so, then, in the light of a view of the will as independent of the good. If the will is separate from the good, its being undetermined by what is other than itself would necessarily imply the nihilism we spoke of above. If, by contrast, freedom is understood precisely as original participation in the good, then it shares in the character of the good in which it participates. As we have seen, according to Augustine, there are two types of good, namely, *uti* and *frui*. The former represents things that are good for the sake of something else, the latter, things that are good in and of themselves, simply for their own sake. Being good for their own sake, these latter do not need to be referred beyond themselves for their value. Indeed, we may call such goods "gratuitous," insofar as our attempt to explain the reason for their goodness finally comes to a rest in the things themselves: in the end, they are good because they *are*. Now, if it is the case, as we saw above, that for Augustine the will becomes the slave of that in which it seeks its happiness, the "use" of goods subordinates us to, and thus makes us in some respect the servant of, that for which they are used. But intrinsic goods have a value beyond their use. Our "enjoyment" of them therefore likewise places us beyond instrumentality; it makes us free. By adhering to what is good *in* itself, and inwardly participating in it, the will is no more determined by something outside of itself than is the good in which it shares. The *freedom* of this good thus becomes the will's own freedom.

It is crucial to see, however, that this "not being determined by another" is *not* indeterminate and empty of all content, but is, to the contrary, perfectly full of content. What distinguishes freedom here from external determination is not the negating of the other, but the positive affirmation of relation with what is other, namely, the good. Augustine describes the ultimate, eschatological freedom as being "filled with all good."[83] It is, in other words, a kind of saturation of determination, as opposed to the mere open possibility of receiving determination. Here, our reflections connect on the one hand with Yves Simone's helpful notion of "superdetermination," a kind of boundless potency, which he offers in the place of "indeterminacy" as the distinguishing feature of true freedom,[84] as well as with the more general cultural observations of Josef Pieper and Hugo Rahner on the free enjoyment of that which transcends mere usefulness, that is, the leisure and play which are indispensable to genuine human life.[85]

We saw earlier that, since the will is dependent in some sense in all of its acts, it finds freedom to the extent that it makes itself dependent on what is truly good, and these last reflections show why this is the case: the will shares in the goodness of that to which it binds itself. This notion has two implications worth noticing. First of all, the degree of the freedom that the will finds is proportionate to the "absoluteness" of the good to which it binds itself. In other words, it is precisely the *intrinsic* nature of the goodness of the will's object that liberates it. But a good of this sort, however much it may be an object of the will's free choice, can never be merely a function of that choice (i.e., it can never be merely an "option"), precisely to the extent that its goodness is something to be enjoyed rather than used, to the extent that it is an intrinsic or absolute good, rather than an instrumental one. While we tend to think of having freedom only with respect to those things under our control, it is in fact the case that our freedom is dependent on things having a goodness beyond our choosing, beyond our capacity to decide about them. For Augustine, if everything were completely under our control, we would have no freedom: this is just the "flip side" of his description of perfect freedom as the state of being "immovably fixed" in the good.

The second point to notice is that it is only such a conception that allows us to think of freedom, not just as a means to achieve what we take to be good, but already as being itself something intrinsically good. Earlier, we saw that the conception of freedom as pure, and therefore empty, choice is the subjective correlate of a world without value. If we start, by contrast, with the affirmation of intrinsic, "non-optional" goodness, we arrive, in turn, at a notion of freedom as possessing a value within itself, as being a state to be enjoyed, rather than merely an instrument by which to seek enjoyment. The view of freedom as indeterminate possibility is tied to an instrumentalist conception of freedom insofar as both view the relationship to goodness in an extrinsic manner: freedom thus conceived is something that can be, and perhaps ought to be, *used* to attain what is good, but simply in itself it is empty. Liberal and conservative debates over freedom tend to remain stuck on this point: both take for granted a view of freedom as an instrument, but while liberals insist that we ought to be left in control of this instrument (the so-called "negative" view of freedom—"freedom from"), conservatives argue that we should be obliged to use this instrument to make particular choices (the so-called "positive" view of freedom—"freedom for"). But Augustine has a different view.

The possibility that we associate with freedom is not indeterminate possibility, but rather the possibility that springs from actuality.[86] The *power* to adhere to the good arises from our attachment to it; the greater the actuality, the greater the possibility.

It is this view that allows Augustine to attach an absolute value to freedom, to regard it not only as a *means* to the enjoyment of what is good, but as an *object* of enjoyment itself.[87] In Gilson's words, "man is truly free when he acts in such a way that the object of his delight is freedom itself."[88] It is also why Augustine identifies freedom with joy:[89] not that we need freedom in order to find joy, but that freedom and joy are ultimately the same thing insofar as both are the possession of the good. In *De diversis quaestionibus*, 83.35.2, Augustine affirms that to love eternal things is to become eternal. Analogously, we could say that to love free things—i.e., things of intrinsic goodness, whose value transcends the use that can be made of them—is to become free. Indeed, in the end, we are saying the same thing.

Freedom and Beauty

The mention of joy, intrinsic goodness, and love leads us to Augustine's notion of beauty. While this rich notion exceeds the present context, a brief observation on the relationship between freedom and beauty makes a fitting conclusion, if only because it sets into striking relief the difference between Augustine's view of freedom and the conventional one. I suggest that beauty ties together the various elements that constitute genuine freedom, to such an extent that, according to the logic of Augustine's view, a world without beauty will be a world without freedom. As Emmanuel Chapman has shown, beauty represents, for Augustine, the proper object of love.[90] It does so because beauty is what elicits delight, and indeed, delight of a certain type, namely, an essentially *contemplative* joy. Now, for Augustine, the joy brought by beauty serves to integrate the human faculties. A will that intrumentalizes its objects as mere options entails, as we saw, a fragmented psychology, wherein the human faculties work not only independently of, but even in opposition to, one another. Because beauty, by contrast, connects the intellectual apprehension of an object with the delight it affords, and thus weds the true and the good, the experience of beauty joins together the distinct activities of the spiritual faculties, both the intellect and will, into a single act.[91]

Moreover, joy in beauty is specifically *contemplative* precisely because it rests in a good perceived as an end in itself and thus in a certain respect absolute. As Chapman puts it, "Beauty is seen and loved for its own sake, and in this sense can be called absolute."[92] But it is precisely the absolute nature of the goodness beauty presents that, on the one hand, lifts us beyond the merely useful, and, on the other hand, enables a whole-hearted consent. In other words, it is by being absolute that beauty makes freedom possible. If freedom is original participation in intrinsic goodness, beauty is the invitation to freedom, because it is the radiation of a goodness beyond our immediate control. If we wish to encapsulate this Augustinian insight into freedom in a nutshell, we could say that freedom is the fruit of beauty.

We have thus come quite far from the conventional notion. If freedom is choice, then the political order, insofar as it wishes to promote freedom, must seek as far as possible to multiply options. But if freedom is original participation in intrinsic goodness, then the simple multiplication of options undermines freedom. If freedom is choice, then the affirmation of things as *intrinsically* good, as having a value independent of any will and therefore as making a claim on the will, is a threat to freedom because it establishes a limit to power. The conception we developed from Augustine, however, dissociates freedom from power or the capacity to control. Freedom is *dependent* on the existence of things of intrinsic value. A world of mere options is a world without the possibility of freedom. There can be no freedom except in the presence of goods that are precisely "non-negotiable," insofar as what is utterly "negotiable" (*neg-otium*, the negation of leisure or enjoyment of things for their own sake) is stripped of any intrinsic value. A political order, then, does not protect freedom by refusing to commit itself to substantive goods, but in fact must so commit itself in order to ensure freedom. To cultivate freedom, a political order must present goods, not indifferently as possible objects of choice, but compellingly as things worthy of being loved precisely because they possess a goodness over which we have no control. In other words, because they are, before all else, things of beauty.

"Late have I loved thee, o beauty, so ancient and so new: late have I loved thee" (*Conf.* 10.27.38). Augustine is here describing something essential to the aesthetic experience: our love for beauty *always* comes "late," because beauty moves us before we can move ourselves. And this is just why beauty, more than any expansion of choices, sets us free.

Notes

1. Augustine, *Confessions* (= *Conf.*) 11.14 (trans. R. S. Pine-Coffin; New York: Penguin Books, 1961) 264. All citations of the *Confessions* in the present essay are from this translation.

2. Servais Pinckaers, O.P., *The Sources of Christian Ethics* (trans. Sr. Mary Thomas Noble, O.P. Washington, DC: The Catholic University of America Press, 1995) 328.

3. Hannah Arendt, *The Life of the Mind*, vol. 2: *Willing* (New York: Harcourt Brace Jovanovich, 1978) 84–110.

4. Albrecht Dihle, *The Theory of Will in Classical Antiquity* (Berkeley: University of California Press, 1982) 144.

5. Dihle, *Theory of Will*, 127.

6. The criticism presented in this essay owes much to James Wetzel, *Augustine and the Limits of Virtue* (Cambridge: Cambridge University Press, 1992), a book brought to my attention by Michael Hanby. Where my proposal differs from Wetzel's will be indicated when appropriate.

7. Augustine, *De libero arbitrio* (= *De lib.*) 3.17, *On Free Choice of the Will* (trans. Thomas Williams; Indianapolis: Hackett Publishing Company, 1993) 104. All citations of *De lib.* in the present essay are from this translation.

8. See Karl Ubl, "Verantwortlichkeit und autonomes Handeln: zur Entwicklung zweier Freiheitsbegriffe von Augustinus bis Thomas von Aquino," *Freiburger Zeitschrift für Philosophie und Theologie* 46.1–2 (1999) 79–114, esp. 86.

9. *De lib.* 3.3.

10. Quoted, without indication of source, in Pinckaers, *Christian Ethics*, 332. Claude Romano explicates Sartre's view of freedom as a logical working-out of Augustine's notion: see "La liberté sartrienne, ou le rêve d'Adam," *Archives de Philosophie* 63 (2000) 468–93.

11. Thomas Williams, "Introduction" to *On Free Choice of the Will*, xi.

12. Williams, "Introduction," xii.

13. Alasdair MacIntyre, *Whose Justice? Which Rationality?* (Notre Dame: University of Notre Dame Press, 1988) 156.

14. Dihle, *Theory of Will*, 127.

15. Mary Clark, *Augustine, Philosopher of Freedom* (New York: Desclee Company, 1958) 149.

16. T. D. J. Chappell, *Aristotle and Augustine on Freedom: Two Theories of Freedom, Voluntary Action and Akrasia* (New York: St. Martin's Press, 1995), argues that when Augustine appears to give the will the role of wholly autonomous activity, which has been emphasized by Brown, Dihle, MacIntyre, Thonnard, and others, he is in fact not talking about the will per se, but only the "bad will." The will in its proper activity, he claims, is hardly autonomous.

17. Georg Kohler, "Selbstbezug, Selbsttranszendenz und die Nichtigkeit der Freiheit: Zur augustinischen Theorie des Bösen in *De civitate Dei* XII," *Studia Philosophica* 52 (1993) 67–79, quotation from 78.

18. Iris Murdoch, *The Sovereignty of Good* (London: Routledge and Kegan Paul, 1970).

19. Pinckaers, *Christian Ethics*, 340.

20. Pinckaers, *Christian Ethics*, 340.

21. Pinckaers, *Christian Ethics*, 350–51.

22. Murdoch, *Sovereignty of Good*, 76.

23. Murdoch, *Sovereignty of Good*, 16.

24. Murdoch, *Sovereignty of Good*, 42

25. Murdoch, *Sovereignty of Good*, 91.

26. Augustine, *De doctrina christiana* (= *De doct.*), 1.3; *On Christian Doctrine* (trans. D. W. Robertson, Jr. New York: Macmillan Publishing Company, 1958).

27. AugustineI, *De doct.* 1.4.

28. Augustine, *De trinitate* (= *De trin.*) 10.10, 13.

29. See Aristotle, *Physics*, 2, 8, 199a10, and *Parts of Animals*, 639b15.

30. Murdoch, *Sovereignty of Good*, 80.

31. Karl Marx, *Capital*, vol. I, in *The Marx-Engels Reader* (ed. Robert C. Tucker; 2nd ed. New York: W.W. Norton & Company, 1978) 335.

32. Friedrich Nietzsche, *The Will to Power* (trans. Walter Kaufmann and R. J. Hollingdale; New York: Vintage Books, 1967) 9.

33. See Jose Antonio Galindo, "La libertad como autodeterminación en san Agustín," *Augustinus* 35 (1990) 299–320, esp. 300–01. In evidence of this point, Mary Clark, *Augustine*, 98–101, cites numerous passages from Augustine's later writings.

34. Augustine, *De Duabus Animabus*, 10.14.

35. Augustine, *De civitate dei* (= *De civ.*) 14.6 (trans. Henry Bettenson; New York: Penguin Books, 1984) 556. All citations from *De civ.* will be from this translation.

36. Wetzel, *Augustine and the Limits of Virtue*, 8.

37. Aristotle, *De Anima*, 3, 10, 433b12.

38. *De lib.*, 3.1: "This movement of the will [i.e., its natural movement] is similar to the downward movement of a stone in that it belongs to the will just as that downward movement belongs to the stone."

39. See *Conf.* 13.9.10; cf. *De civ.* 11.28.

40. *De civ.* 14.7: "And so a rightly directed will is love in a good sense and a perverted will is love in a bad sense. Therefore a love which strains after the possession of the loved object is desire; and the love which possesses and enjoys that object is joy."

41. Étienne Gilson, *Introduction à l'étude de Saint Augustin* (Paris: Librairie Philosophique J. Vrin, 1949) 175. On the connection between love and the will in Augustine, see ibid., 170–77, and Arendt, *Life of the Mind*, 102–04.

42. Gilson, *Introduction*, 174, n.2.

43. Arendt, *Life of the Mind*, 102.

44. Arendt, *Life of the Mind*, 104.

45. Juan Pegueroles offers an excellent account of the difference between coercion, which is not free, and the sort of necessity that is quite compatible with freedom, in "Libertad como posibilidad, libertad como necesidad. Juliano y San Agustín," *Espíritu* 36 (1987) 109–24, esp. 110–11.

46. Galindo, "La libertad," 307, expresses a similar point through the paradox that a free act that is ordered to the good is "*necessary* with respect to the *act*, but *free* with respect to the internal *mode* in which this act is carried out." But Galindo seems to overlook the real paradox of Augustine's idea insofar as he articulates the act by *separating* what is free from what is necessary, claiming, in the end, that "An internally necessary desire of the free will is a contradiction" (Galindo, "La libertad," 311). Augustine, by contrast, insists that the desire is *both* necessary and free.

47. Augustine, *Expositio epistolae ad Galatas*, 49.

48. Augustine, *Contra Iulianum opus imperfectum*, 101.

49. See John Burnaby, *Amor Dei: A Study of the Religion of St. Augustine* (London: Hodder & Stoughton, 1947) 232–34.

50. Pegueroles, "Libertad," 119.

51. Augustine, *De bono viduitatis*, 21.26, quoted in Gilson, *Introduction*, 175.

52. *De lib.* 1.14.

53. Augustine, *De vera religione* [= *De ver.*] 38.69; *Of True Religion* (trans. J. H. S. Burleigh; Chicago: Henry Regnery Company, 1964) 66. All citations of *De ver.* will be from this translation.

54. *De ver.* 40.76.

55. *De lib.* 2.13, 15.

56. *De civ.* 22.30.

57. *De ver.* 54.113. Articulating this positive sense of freedom is one of the primary aims of Mary Clark's book, *Augustine: Philosopher of Freedom*. See also Battista Mondin, "L'Antropologia Cristiana di S. Agostino," *Sapienza* 54/1 (2001) 3–16, esp. 11. Susan Wolff has more recently offered a strong defense of a positive view of freedom as intrinsically bound to the True and the Good, in her acclaimed book *Freedom Within Reason* (Oxford: Oxford University Press, 1990). She does so, not in reference to Augustine, but on its own terms.

58. See, for example, Wetzel's discussion of Gerard O'Daly and John Rist, whom he charges with being unable to "imagine that being determined to respond to the good was a form of freedom, irreducible to either liberty of indifference or freedom from constraint" (Wetzel, *Augustine and the Limits of Virtue*, 221).

59. See, e.g., *De ver.* 14.27.

60. Augustine, *De spiritu et littera*, 60.

61. Wetzel, *Augustine and the Limits of Virtue*, 166.

62. Cardinal Bellarmine, *De Justificatione*, v. 5, cited in Burnaby, *Amor Dei*, 239.

63. Ultimately, the analogy depends on the theological context—the relations of the persons of the Trinity, Mary's consent, and the relation of the two natures of Christ in the one person—which becomes increasingly evident the further one enters into the problematic. On the importance of the theological horizon for Augustine's treatment of philosophical issues, see, for example, Michael Hanby, *Augustine and Modernity* (London: Routledge, 2003) 72–105.

64. Charles Kahn, "Discovering the Will: From Aristotle to Augustine," in *The Question of Ecclecticism: Studies in Later Greek Philosophy*, ed. J. M. Dillion and A. A. Cook (Berkeley: University of California Press, 1988) 234–59, esp. 247, identifies consent as the locus of freedom in Aquinas's psychology, but does not sufficiently differentiate it from the Stoic notion of assent, which exhibits the same problems as the conventional notion we have been elaborating. For a fuller treatment of the difficulties of the Stoic view, see Hanby, *Augustine and Modernity*, 93–105.

65. Hanby, *Augustine and Modernity*, 82.

66. Augustine, *De peccatorum meritis et remissione*, 2.26.

67. Plotinus, *Ennead* 6.8.6.

68. *Conf.* 8.8.19.

69. On this point, see Clark, *Augustine*, 139.

70. On the various issues implied in an ontological conception of evil in comparison to the more modern, "voluntaristic" conception, see Herbert Rommel, *Zum Begriff des Bösen bei Augustinus und Kant* (Frankfurt am Main: Pater Lang GmbH, 1997). The classic studies on evil in Augustine are G. Philips, *La raison d'être du mal d'après S. Augustine* (Louvain: Editions du Museum Lessianum, 1927), and R. Jolivet, *Le problème du mal d'après S. Augustine* (Paris: G. Beauchesne, 1936).

71. *De civ.* 11.17.

72. *De civ.* 12.6.

73. In *Physics*, 7, 1, 241b25–242a16, Aristotle makes a brilliant argument that a self-mover can never move itself as a whole, and that the only way for a thing to move itself as a whole is to be moved by another.

74. Gilson, *Introduction*, 318.

75. Thomas Aquinas, *Summa Theologica* (trans. Fathers of the English Dominican Province; vol. 1; Reprinted by Christian Classics; New York: Benziger Brothers, 1981) 1, 83, 1 ad3: "Free-will is the cause of its own movement, because by his free-will man moves himself to act. But it does not of necessity belong to liberty that what is free should be the first cause of itself, as neither for one thing to be cause of another need it be the first cause."

76. In giving an account of the source of faith and meritorious works, Augustine likewise says at the very end of his life that "faith itself is found among God's gifts, which are given *through the same Spirit. Both therefore are ours*, because of our will's free choice, and yet both are given, through the Spirit of faith and love" (*Retractiones*, 1.23, cited in Burnaby, *Amor Dei*, 230).

77. *De lib.* 2.20.

78. Wetzel, *Augustine and the Limits of Virtue*, 8.

79. Burnaby makes the same claim about God's act of creation, which (as Albrecht Dihle has claimed) is the horizon within which Augustine developed his own notion of will. *Creatio ex nihilo* is by definition "unmotivated," and yet at the same time it is not arbitrary precisely because it is *good*: see Burnaby, *Amor Dei*, 165–66.

80. *De civ.* 12.6.

81. *De civ.* 5.2.

82. Arendt, *Life of the Mind*, 109–10. Arendt, however, connects this assertion by Augustine too quickly with Kant's notion of spontaneity. But their views are in fact worlds apart, insofar as Kant would have no room in his philosophy for the truly and necessarily *receptive* spontaneity that we have seen is the key to Augustine's notion of freedom.

83. *De civ.* 22.30.

84. We, however, have a crucial difference with Simone on this point: while he makes "superdetermination," the abundance of actuality that gives the will its freedom, something that resides in the will itself (" . . . it is in the will that we find the energy [i.e., the superdeterminate actuality] which the object lacks" [Simone, *Freedom of Choice* (ed. Peter Wolff; New York: Fordham University Press, 1969) 150]), we insist that the will has this character only in the actual possession of something intrinsically good. What is at stake in this difference is the question to what extent freedom is essentially relational,

and to what extent the will is always structurally receptive in its spontaneity. On this point, the passage from Maritain that Simone appeals to in this context offers more support for our position than for his: "For [the will] pours out upon that particular good, of itself wholly incapable of determining it, the superabundant determination it receives from its necessary object, good as such" (Maritain, *A Preface to Metaphysics: Seven Lectures in Being* [New York: Sheed and Ward, 1948] 103).

85. See Hugo Rahner, *Man at Play* (trans. Brian Battershaw and Edward Quinn; New York: Herder and Herder, 1972), and Josef Pieper, *Leisure as the Basis of Culture* (trans. Alexander Dru; New York: Random House, 1963).

86. Pegueroles, "Libertad," 122, refers to free choice, *liberum arbitrium*, as the "potential" to be free, and *libertas* as the *act* of *being free*.

87. See *De ver.* 48.93: "He who delights in liberty seeks to be free from the love of mutable things."

88. Gilson, *Introduction*, 211.

89. See Augustine, *Enchiridion*, 30, "This is what constitutes true freedom: joy experienced in doing what is right," cited in Clark, *Augustine*, 125.

90. Emmanuel Chapman, *Saint Augustine's Philosophy of Beauty* (New York: Sheed & Ward, 1939) 1–12. On beauty as the proper object of love, see *Conf.* 4.13.20; *De Musica* 6.13. Augustine also says that goodness is the sole object of love (*De trin.* 8.3). There need be no difficulties in reconciling these assertions, as Chapman argues, *Philosophy of Beauty*, 102, n.1.

91. Francisco Weismann describes Augustine's view of freedom as the joining together of the activities of desiring and reasoning: "La libertad como busqueda de la verdad en el joven Agustín," *Filosofía y Teología* (1990) 65–73, esp. 69.

92. Chapman, *Philosophy of Beauty*, 49.

Part II

AUGUSTINE'S THEORY AND CRITIQUE OF POLITICS

5

Between the Two Cities:
Political Action in Augustine of Hippo

Robert Dodaro, O.S.A.

To suggest that Augustine of Hippo engaged in "political activism" is to invite the charge of anachronism. Yet no historian would deny that, following the Constantinian revolution and, even more clearly, the Theodosian settlement of the fourth century, bishops in late antiquity sought to enhance their political power with respect to the Roman Empire.[1] The questions that historians pose today concern more precise definitions of the aims (and therefore motives), chronologies, strategies, successes, and failures surrounding the relationships between bishops and the structures of political power from the time of the emperors Constantine to Justinian. Augustine of Hippo offers only one, in some respects hardly typical, example of an African bishop at the turn of the fifth century who used his office in order to stake out political and social claims on behalf of the church and its teachings. A comprehensive evaluation of his political activism should take into consideration a host of initiatives, most notably the following. First, the broad-ranging criticisms of Roman political history, public officials, and political and social institutions, that he registered in the *City of God*, but also in his *Confessions* and in a number of his sermons, particularly those preached in conjunction with the feast-days of Christian martyrs. Second, his involvement with the "bishop's tribunal" (*audientia episcopalis, episcopale iudicium*), a legal forum in which fourth- and fifth-century Catholic bishops in local churches throughout the Roman Empire presided over a judicial arbitration of mostly civil cases such as those concerned with small claims, property, and inheritance.[2] And finally, his efforts to seek imperial sanctions against the Donatist church, the Manichean sect, and the Pelagian movement.[3]

Although additional factors could be added to this list, it suffices to demonstrate that discussion and evaluation of Augustine's political activism in its widest sense requires consideration of his various modes of engagement in public affairs. A comprehensive treatment of the question lies, therefore, beyond the scope of this chapter. Instead, an examination of Augustine's efforts to mitigate the severity with which political institutions and public officials of his day treated members of his congregation may reveal something about the purposes and strategies behind this engagement.

Augustine's Political Activism

An exchange of letters between Augustine and a high-ranking imperial official makes this point clear. Macedonius was a Catholic who, as imperial vicar for Africa, was charged with the administration of justice in the civil diocese of Africa, excepting Proconsular Africa, and was, therefore, one of the most powerful Catholics in the imperial administration of Africa.[4] Macedonius regarded Augustine as a friend and a spiritual father, but objected to the bishop's requests for clemency on behalf of criminals condemned to death. In his letter, the vicar told Augustine that bishops should not intervene in cases involving the death penalty because such intercession "had nothing to do with religion."[5] Augustine wrote and explained in response that insofar as society needs laws and penalties in order to function justly, it also requires that the Gospel be preached against excesses of cruelty which promote injustice and deter the reform of criminals. He thus insisted that bishops were fulfilling their pastoral office by interceding with civil officials on behalf of clemency for the condemned.[6]

In this letter, Augustine made it clear indirectly that he did not regard the political sphere as lying beyond the church's mission. Bishops had an obligation to preach the Gospel even within the political realm. This is a different sort of claim, however, than to plead for an episcopal right to exercise power within the Empire. In Augustine's view, bishops seek to evangelize the political process without intending to shift institutional power from magistrates to themselves. Augustine's political activism should be distinguished, moreover, from political dissidence, especially when the latter involves violence against public officials or against the Empire. Political activism, aimed as it is at mitigating some of the injustices associated with public institutions, processes, and policies, implies almost by definition an underlying respect for the authority and legitimacy of the public sphere (*res publica*). In Augustine's case, this respect need not be considered as absolute, nor as an uncritical allegiance, but his attitude manifests a bias in favor of a given, civil authority at a fundamental level.

For Augustine, there are theological principles that support this position. First, he recognized a divine order behind the civil authority. By this understanding—which he believed was authorized by the scriptures as at Romans 13—legitimately established civil officials ought to be obeyed unless they command one to violate God's law.[7] Augustine had the Christian martyrs in mind when he formulated this principle, and while it allows in theory for the possibility of a nonviolent, conscientious, civil disobedience outside of martyrdom, it is not easy to imagine cases in which he would have thought its application justifiable. In no case could it be extended as a principle to justify armed insurrection or violence against persons, property, or public institutions.

A second theological principle supporting Augustine's rejection of political dissidence is framed, along with the first, in *Sermon* 302, preached on the feast-day of St. Laurence. As mentioned above, Augustine's sermons for the feastdays of Christian martyrs frequently provided him with occasions for criticizing the political and social institutions of his day. He often did this by sketching in these sermons a vision of civic virtues such as justice, piety, and the love and forgiveness of enemies that he believed constitute the essence of a Christian society. In *Sermon* 302, he praised the martyred deacon as an example to Christians of the nonviolent resistance that Christ taught as a more effective alternative than violent, civil insurrection at combatting social and political injustice. Augustine preached this sermon shortly following an incident at Hippo in which members of his congregation took part in the assasination of an imperial official who was accused of some form of corruption. Possibly he was a customs officer guilty of levying unlawful and oppressive duties on goods arriving in the port. In the sermon, Augustine reminded his hearers of St. Paul's admonition at Romans 13:1 that there is an established government, a political order, to which Christians, along with other members of society, are held accountable. Even in a society as unjust as that of the Roman Empire, there are laws and penalties that can be applied against corrupt public officials. By taking the law into their own hands, members of his congregation failed to follow the example of Christ and of St. Laurence, both of whom resisted injustice on the part of public officials by nonviolent means. In doing so, they witnessed to a higher justice and to the enjoyment of a higher good than could ever be achieved through the attainment of political or military power. Augustine made it clear in this sermon that what he most feared in political dissidence was its capacity to corrupt the desires of Christians to live justly into a form of envy aimed at possessing and exercising the same corrupting power that those in public office possess. If Christians truly desire to create a more just society, they should first renounce the desire to become like their enemies by renouncing the use of violence. Christ and the martyrs testify that the only efficacious way to reform political society is to oppose injustice through nonviolence.

Augustine as Advocate

Given the generally oppressive social and political atmosphere and conditions of the late Roman Empire, the social injustices that lured Augustine into political activity were surprisingly numerous and varied in kind, and include—in addition to capital punishment and criminal justice—slavery, the right of sanctuary, and the protection of other civil rights among the populace at large.

We have already touched upon Augustine's occasional intercession for clemency on behalf of criminals, including those condemned to death.[8] In addition to the letter written to Macedonius on this subject, Augustine also wrote to Donatus, the proconsul of Africa with responsibility for governing the Roman province that included both Carthage and Hippo Regius, and urged him to avoid capital punishment in dealing with Donatists.[9] The proconsul had been ordered to crack down on members of the outlawed sect within the province.[10] Augustine anticipated that Donatus would apply the death penalty in cases of murder, implored him not to do so, and warned him that if he intended to carry out executions, Catholics would refuse to cooperate with the imperial prosecution of Donatists for murder, even if it meant that the latter would then feel free to kill Catholics with impunity. He urged the governor not to allow the lapse of public security that would occur in such a case.

His warning to the imperial proconsul, himself a Catholic, was consisent with the position outlined in *Sermon* 302: nonviolent resistance offers the only truly efficacious means of rectifying injustice; violent means, when pursued, only increase the violence. By putting to death Donatists guilty of violence against Catholics, imperial officials would only create martyrs for the Donatist cause and incite them to further violence. Catholics would resist Donatist violence within the means afforded by the law; however, they would not cooperate with an imperial policy which was itself unwise, because that policy could never lead to the reconciliation of the two religious communities. By standing up to the proconsul in this way, Augustine, in effect, threatened a Catholic boycott of the imperial tribunals.[11] He had calculated the costs of his policy to his own community and was prepared that it should pay them, tragic as such an outcome would be. He had himself once narrowly escaped a Donatist ambush earlier in his episcopal career. Later, in 411, he witnessed the vicious murder of one of his own priests, Restitutus, and, consistent with the policy he outlined earlier in his letter to Donatus, he wrote to the new imperial proconsul, Apringius, and asked that the death penalty not be applied to the Donatist murderers.[12]

Augustine's political advocacy on behalf of penal reform also led him to a strong, vocal opposition to the use of torture either during interrogation of persons suspected of criminal acts, or as punishment for those convicted of crimes.[13] He expressed his opposition to torture directly through letters to imperial officials. In a letter to an imperial military commander, Flavius Marcellinus, Augustine praised his efforts to extract a confession from those accused of murdering Restitutus without the use of the more brutal forms of torture which were conventionally employed by the courts.[14] In another incident, a group of pagan residents at Calama (65 km. southwest of Hippo Regius) attacked and burned the bishop's church during anti-Christian rioting in 408 and killed a member of the congregation. Afterwards, Nectarius, a former imperial official, implored Augustine to intercede with imperial officials so that pagans accused of the violence would not be tortured during investigation of the crimes nor executed upon conviction.[15] Augustine responded immediately that mercy should be shown to those involved in the incident so that they should not pay for what they did with their lives, nor should torture be employed as a means of securing confessions from the accused.[16] He wrote to Nectarius that he would intercede with imperial officials to ask that they employ penalties far less harsh than capital punishment or torture in order to guarantee that such episodes of violence were not repeated. He asked Nectarius to communicate with him at once if he learned that torture was being applied in the matter.[17]

Augustine's letter to Macedonius lays out some criteria for the treatment of lawbreakers that the bishop believed should characterize a Christian approach to justice. Criminals deserve to be loved and pitied because they are human beings. Judges and public officials, like bishops, are thus bound to criminals in a "human fellowship." Society ought, therefore, to seek their reform, not their destruction.[18] Augustine acknowledged that political communities engage in a just and necessary activity when they threaten sanctions against those who violate just laws. In doing this, they seek to promote the good not only of the innocent, but of the guilty who must be deterred from acting unlawfully. Yet he explained that moral conversion is often a slow process, one that can require a deep compassion even for recidivists who do not respond positively to punishments inflicted after a first offense. Augustine sympathized with the plight of imperial officials concerned with the prevention of crime: human beings lack the patience required in order to wait until some criminals abandon their evil ways. But he insisted that God, who does not lack this patience, provides a model which human beings ought to strive to imitate. Penal reform, as discussed in this letter, offered Augustine an ideal issue through which to observe the ways in which the political process and the church's mission of evangelization closely paralleled each other. Both imperial officials and Christian pastors desire the reform of criminals, but oftentimes neither the Empire nor the church knows how to bring this about. His letter to Macedonius makes clear his view that, in their present circumstances, both the church and the political community still need to search out new and more efficacious processes for encouraging moral conversion among their respective members. Augustine does not offer any clear solutions to the problem, but he underlines the principle that, while penal institutions are necessary in order to deter human beings from breaking the law, such institutions and penalties ought to be evaluated on the basis of a demonstrated capacity to promote true conversion of life. This conversion will not be realized in institutions or processes that subject human beings to destructive forms of violence.

Beyond the issue of criminal justice, slavery offers an additional, rich context for examining Augustine's political activity. Slavery was subject to regulation under Roman law. When they judged it practical to do so, African bishops, including Augustine, sought to institute reforms to the practice of slavery in order to limit its growth and mitigate its harmful effects. Augustine's friend and biographer, Possidius, reminds us that Augustine frequently drew from his church's treasury in order to purchase the freedom of slaves.[19] Moreover, on one occasion, while he was absent from Hippo, some members of his congregation stormed a ship and freed over 100 slaves held captive there.[20] But Augustine's efforts to reduce the evil of slavery were not restricted to acts of charity, nor, as he indicated in *Sermon* 302, did he believe that the use of force would ultimately foster social justice. Instead, his approach was highly rational. He was well aware that the economic conditions of Roman Africa at this time were so dismal, and taxes so intolerably high, that many people were better off living in the relative security of slavery than they would be as free citizens reduced to penury.[21] Much social improvement, however, could be procured if a number of the unlawful excesses of the slave industry were curbed. Two years before his death, Augustine wrote a memorandum to Alypius, who was on his way to Italy, and asked his friend and fellow bishop to urge the emperor to order greater publicity and enforcement of a number of laws prohibiting the kidnapping and sale of persons into slavery.[22] This unlawful practice had by then reached oppressive proportions in the coastal area immediately surrounding Hippo. Augustine included in his memorandum a copy of an edict promulgated some years earlier by the Emperor Honorius that strictly forbade such excesses. Alypius had received training in the legal profession earlier in his life and once served in the imperial civil service in Rome as an assessor for the Italian treasury; thus, he knew his way around the imperial bureaucracy.[23] Augustine advised him to pass through Rome and verify the accuracy of the law against a copy of the text before presenting himself at the imperial court at Ravenna. Once there, he should plead not only that this and other laws prohibiting unlawful activities by slave traders and their organized criminal partners be well-published and more effectively enforced, but that the penalties attached to such crimes be reduced from the nearly lethal beatings with whips

tipped with lead which the existing laws prescribed. Augustine asked for the reduction in penalties so that he, his fellow bishops, and imperial officials would
be more inclined to seek prosecutions of such criminal activity than they
would under the present law, because the latter most assuredly involved sen-
tencing the slave-traders to a gruesome death.[24]

Besides seeking, thus, to persuade the emperor to deter criminal violators
of the slave laws from profiteering in the absence of law enforcement in the region, Augustine also sought to improve his own knowledge of the complicated
Roman laws concerning slavery. He did so in conjunction with his responsibility as a bishop to arbitrate civil suits that were regularly brought before
him. Again, Possidius informs us that Augustine spent long periods of his
mornings receiving litigants in audience and issuing juridically binding judgments on the issues presented to him.[25] In conjunction with this activity, Augustine frequently sought advice from a legal expert, Eustochius. This man
may have worked closely with Augustine as an adviser on legal matters before
moving to another locale.[26] At one point, Augustine wrote a letter to him asking for detailed information on Roman law concerning the temporary leasing
of persons into slavery, a form of indentured servitude in which fathers would
typically lease their children as slaves for a fixed period of time in order to
raise money needed to pay off serious debts. Although the practice was law-
ful, it led to abuses that were increasingly difficult to prevent, because in order
to do so, one had to be closely familiar with a complex Roman legal code concerning slavery. When cases involving the legal status of such children arrived
before Augustine's tribunal, he was strictly bound to decide them on the basis
of Roman law which, while it could be tempered at times by the gentleness of
the Gospel, could not be substituted by it.[27] As a result of this legal requirement, Augustine endeavored both to study Roman slave law in its exhausting
detail and to call upon the services of a professional legal expert. He thus
hoped that by mastering the legislation in question, he would find loopholes
through which he could free children who would otherwise remain slaves,
possibly for life.[28]

I mention Augustine's involvement with the "bishop's tribunal" at this point
because both his relationship with Eustochius, the professional legal expert
(*iurisperitus*), and his own considerable efforts to understand Roman law in
its enormous complexity, represent aspects of the bishop's pastoral ministry
that especially equipped him for his interventions with imperial officials on
matters concerning slavery and other social questions. Although he was not
formally trained in Roman law, Augustine understood that the reform of political institutions demanded a high degree of familiarity with the law and political institutions. His association with Eustochius hints at how much Augustine devoted to pursuing this activity: the quality of involvement in legal

activity that he sought for himself; the time devoted to study and consultation over the law; the labor dedicated to the preparation of petitions and memoranda on legal matters; the travel required on his part to and from the provincial capital at Carthage and, on the part of his emissaries, to and from the imperial court at Ravenna; and, finally, the not insignificant financial expenses incurred in support of this activity.

Turning now to Augustine's active support of the right of sanctuary, one is perhaps struck by how much of his political activism is largely focused on the defense of persons accused or convicted of crimes. In considering this fact, one ought to keep in mind how easy it was in Augustine's day for poorer members of society to be criminalized on account of inequities introduced and maintained through political structures, such as the unjust and oppressive distribution of the tax burden. Among those seeking sanctuary in churches during the fifth century was a growing number of persons who were sought by imperial officials on charges related to financial debt. Increased imperial expenditures during the late fourth and early fifth centuries, combined with the corruption of public officials, led to the imposition of more exorbitant and excessive taxes that were strongly felt in Africa, as elsewhere.[29] As a result, modest landowners and merchants who were not wealthy but who normally would have enjoyed a modicum of financial security, now faced mounting debts and criminalization. The assassination of the unidentified imperial official mentioned in Augustine's *Sermon* 302 expresses the explosive tensions that his own people felt over this tax burden. Temporary sanctuary in churches offered debtors time to meet their obligations (often with the assistance of the bishops) before being arrested and subjected to judicial procedures, which frequently involved torture. We know of one occasion in which Augustine granted sanctuary to a lay member of his congregation, Fascius, when the latter found himself facing just such tax-related financial difficulties and the threat of official persecution which accompanied them.[30]

On another occasion, Faventius, a tenant farmer (*conductor*) on a large estate at Paratianus, near Hippo, took sanctuary in Augustine's church after he was accused of wrongdoing by the wealthy landowner. When he slipped out of the church one evening for dinner, he was arrested by Florentinus, an officer attached to the military governor of Africa (*comes Africae*), and was held incommunicado at an undisclosed location. Florentinus acted unlawfully, however, when he transported the unfortunate Faventius outside the city. Augustine wrote to Cresconius, the officer in charge of the coastal customs police and asked him to search for Faventius.[31] On the next day it was determined where the accused was being held, and Augustine dispatched Caelestinus, one of his priests, to go and speak with him. When Florentinus would not allow this, Augustine wrote to him on the day after and demanded that he show respect for the imperial law regarding the holding of prisoners awaiting trial, a copy of which he enclosed with the letter.[32] Augustine explained to the military official that he wanted the case tried locally, as the law required. But Florentinus instead sent Faventius to the Numidian provincial capital at Constantine (Cirta) where he would be forced to appear before the tribunal of the provincial governor (*consularis*), Generosus. Augustine realized that the dangers facing Faventius were now increasing. He might be subjected to torture in order to force a confession. Moreover, the landowner who had brought the criminal accusation against the tenant farmer might now use his wealth to influence the governor should the latter decide to hear the case. As a result, an innocent man could be condemned to harsh penalties over an incident which might be more quickly and felicitously resolved were it adjudicated at Hippo. Augustine immediately wrote to the governor and asked him to receive the local bishop, Fortunatus, in audience and to allow him to appeal on Augustine's behalf so that the case against Faventius would be sent back to Hippo, its proper jurisdiction, in accord with imperial law.[33] In a separate letter to the bishop of Constantine, Augustine explained the entire history of the case and asked the bishop to intervene on his behalf with the governor.[34]

His defense of Faventius illustrates the extension and complexity involved in this form of advocacy. To be successful, Augustine had to know the relevant imperial laws and be able to argue them convincingly against public officials who were empowered to enforce them in the provinces. Moreover, he had to deal simultaneously with several levels of administration—imperial, provincial, and municipal—as well as with complicated questions concerned with negotiating boundaries between political, legal, and military jurisdictions. Should he have been successful in persuading the provincial governor to remand Faventius to Hippo for trial, he would then have had to use his legal and personal skills in order to persuade the local authorities to settle the matter without recourse to torture, and to allow the accused sufficient time to prepare his case. All of this activity had to be undertaken against the backdrop of the enormous influence wielded by the plaintiff with his wealthy estate. The case also illustrates that side of political activism consisting in defense of the civil rights of the poor. Faventius had the right (*ius*), guaranteed by imperial law, to be tried in Hippo should he have so wished. He also had the right to a thirty-day period to prepare his case or to reach a settlement with the plaintiff and the authorities. Augustine sought to defend these rights by arguing and pleading with imperial officials, both military and political, at both the local and provincial levels, against whatever pressures or financial inducements the wealthy landowner in question was capable of applying.

An observer of Augustine the bishop also notes an addtional, striking feature of his political activity. This is the extent to which he carried on this activity in strict collaboration with other bishops, such as Alypius, bishop of Thagaste and a lifelong friend, and Fortunatus, the bishop of Constantine; with his own clergy, such as the priest Caelestinus who, at some personal risk, attempted unsuccessfully to speak with Faventius while the latter was being held illegally by Florentinus; and with laypeople, such as Eustochius, the legal expert who advised Augustine on slave law and, presumably, on other questions of law. Reading Augustine's correspondance leaves one with the clear impression of an African church capable, against almost all the odds, of undertaking an extremely limited level of coordinated political activity in support of social justice. Furthermore, one ought not lose sight of the cooperation in this endeavor offered to Augustine by a number of public officials, some of whom were also members of the church. Macedonius and Flavius Marcellinus have already been mentioned as imperial officials with whom Augustine cultivated warm, personal relations. He thanked Marcellinus, in particular, for the clemency granted to the Donatist murderers of Restitutus. One should also not fail to remember Augustine's close relationship with Boniface, the *comes* or military commander of Africa, or the cordial acquaintance he struck near the end of his life with Darius, a high-ranking military officer sent to Africa to end a rebellion affecting Boniface and imperial troops, and to negotiate a peace with the Vandal forces who were advancing across Roman Africa. In both these efforts, Darius was apparently successful at the time, and Augustine wrote to him: "It is a matter for greater glory to eliminate wars with diplomacy rather than human beings with weaponry (*uerbo . . . ferro*), and to seek and maintain peace by peace, and not by war."[35]

Episcopal Councils

While the contributions of individual Christians to the promotion of justice and peace in fifth-century Africa should not be minimized, one of the most important ecclesial structures at the heart of this political activity is found in the episcopal councils. Early church councils normally treated doctrinal and disciplinary matters arising in the course of the bishops' pastoral work, questions concerning the Catholic faith and regulations for the clergy. Yet on a number of occasions, the African bishops took advantage of the opportunities and strength of their common gathering to apply delicate, diplomatic pressure to the imperial court in order to redress social and political injustices occurring within Roman Africa. It would be difficult to find another region in the Catholic church of the early fifth century in which episcopal councils were as efficiently organized as they were in Africa during the years 393–411. Evidently, the driving force behind the organization of the African bishops' councils was the need for the bishops to meet frequently in order to coordinate their efforts in response to the challenges of Donatism, a crisis which came to a head in Africa during these years. However, the experience of gathering in order to reflect and legislate at a collegial level on a regular basis and over a number of years clearly seems to have emboldened the bishops to use the council as a format for addressing the imperial administration with a united voice, one that was respectful without being timid, and for seeking reforms that would contribute to the formation of a more just society while asserting at the same time the legitimate role of the church in fostering justice.

In June 401, bishops who were gathered for a synod at Carthage decided to send representatives to the Italian churches to speak with bishops there about ecclesiastical manumission. This practice, which had been instituted by imperial edict, authorized Catholic bishops to witness in their churches declarations by which slave owners formally emancipated one or more of their slaves. As a result of this action, the freed slaves would automatically gain Roman citizenship in addition to freedom. Once the African bishops ascertained that the practice was working in the Italian church and that it was feasible as well in Africa, they approved a resolution in another synod held during September of that same year to dispatch episcopal delegates to the imperial court in order to petition the Emperor Honorius to allow the same practice in the African church.[36] Apparently imperial authorization was granted, and the practice was initiated. Augustine witnessed a small number of manumissions.[37]

African episcopal councils in which Augustine took part pursued other political issues in addition to slavery. With the increase in the numbers of people seeking sanctuary from tax collectors, Roman emperors, beginning in 392 C.E., banned delinquent taxpayers from the possibility of temporary sanctuary in churches.[38] In 399, the Council of Carthage petitioned the emperor to reverse this decision and not to prohibit sanctuary in churches for any reason whatsoever.[39] It was not, however, until twenty years later in 419 that the Emperors Honorius and Theodosius II recognized an inviolable right of sanctuary. Their edict ordered the arrest and severe punishment of imperial officials who forcibly seized sanctuary seekers.[40]

Yet another example of political advocacy on the part of the African bishops' councils concerned the institution of *defensores ciuitatum*, imperial officials whose function it was to protect rights guaranteed to all citizens by imperial law. The *defensor ciuitatis*, one of whom was, in theory, appointed for each city, held the specific responsibility of protecting the poorer classes who were hardly able to understand the rights that a series of imperial laws and edicts had guaranteed them. The meager property that these poorer landowners and merchants possessed was under constant threat of confiscation from corrupt government officials and from wealthier private citizens.[41] The *defensor ciuitatis* was empowered both to explain to common people the rights that Roman laws guaranteed them and to intervene with other imperial officials in order to protect the rights of the lower classes against the interests of the wealthy and the dishonest. In *Sermon* 302, Augustine implies that if there had been a *defensor* in place at Hippo, poorer merchants and other common people might have been able to avoid the exploitation wrought by the corrupt public official, and the violence which ensued might have been avoided.[42] In September 401, during the same Council of Carthage in which the African bishops petitioned the emperor to allow ecclesiastical manumission in the African provinces, they also appealed to the emperor to provide a *defensor* for each African city in order, they said, "to alleviate the suffering of the poor."[43] Six years later, in 407, the Emperor Honorius issued an edict in which he ordered that the local bishop and clergy, along with the high-ranking citizens (*honestiores*) of each city, should elect the *defensor*.[44] It may have been that, by including the clergy among the electors, the emperor was responding in part to pressure from the African bishops (as that exhibited at the Council of Carthage in 401) to select as *defensores* citizens who could remain impartial to their more powerful peers.

Augustine's precise role in encouraging the African bishops' councils to take on this kind of political advocacy on behalf of the poor of Africa cannot be determined directly from the official acts of the African councils in our possession, nor from other sources. However, throughout his episcopate, Augustine exercised leadership among the African bishops, and his relationship to the presiding bishop, Aurelius of Carthage, was one of closest collaboration. He was frequently called upon by the other bishops to speak on their behalf, and he was one of seven episcopal delegates chosen to represent the Catholic church in the Conference of 411 held in common with the Donatist hierarchy. It is generally supposed by scholars that his role in the episcopal synods of Carthage was of paramount importance. At the same time, we should remember that the nature of an episcopal synod requires that it act as a united body, one in which the participation of particular bishops is of less importance than the collective, collegial spirit and activity of all the bishops present in the synod. Hence, we need not observe Augustine acting in a leadership position within the council in order to associate him with this new and significant form of episcopal political activism.

Conclusion

Regarding Augustine's aims and strategies in engaging the political process of his day, one could say that he is respectful, but not complacent or passive, toward the existing political order. He supports the rule of law in theory and in practice, and he often seeks to make the existing laws better known by public officials and the populace at large and to see them enforced by application of humane penalties which are, however, capable of deterring criminal activity. Augustine is not programmatic where political activism is concerned. Although his approach to this activity is theologically principled, he does not seek to implement a particular political plan. His activity responds to particular social ills as they arise among people for whose pastoral care he feels responsible. At the same time, he strives for a high degree of expertise in dealing with public officials. Whether he is seeking advice from an expert in Roman law, making recommendations for the appointment of a qualified *defensor* for his city, or choosing an episcopal emissary to represent him at the imperial court, he consistently attempts to ensure that his efforts to mitigate violence and injustice are supported by the most competent people he can recruit. Thus, he understands that political advocacy requires an orchestration of ordained church ministers and laypeople who perform tasks proper to their state of life, talents, and professional training. A great deal of the work characterizing this advocacy consists in chancery activity. Letters and memoranda have to be written, research in municipal and imperial archives has to be undertaken, law codes have to be procured, read, and copied. Legal and philosophical arguments have to be composed, attention has to be paid to clarity of thought and style. In line with this point, political activism is joined to political criticism. Augustine not only intervenes with public officials in order to modify their policies or procedures, he invites them to examine with him the roots of social and political ills. In this way, too, political activity becomes an intellectual activity, a theological conversation about God, Christ, and the nature of the public good.

Notes

1. On the question in general, see, for example, P. Brown, *Power and Persuasion in Late Antiquity. Towards a Christian Empire* (Madison: University of Wisconsin Press, 1992); R. Lizzi, *Il potere episcopale nell'Oriente Romano. Rappresentazione ideologica e realtà politica, IV–V sec. d.C.* (Rome: Edizioni dell'ateneo, 1987); T. Barnes, "Religion and Society in the Age of Theodosius," in *Grace, Politics, and Desire: Essays on Augustine* (ed. H. Meynell; Calgary : University of Calgary Press, 1990) 157–74; E. Rebillard and C. Sotinel, eds., *L'évêque dans la cité du Ier au Ve siècle. Image et autorité. Actes de la table ronde organisée par l'Istituto patristico Augustinianum et l'École française de Rome, 1er et 2 décembre 1995* (Rome: École française de Rome, 1998).

2. See C. Munier, "Audientia episcopalis," *Augustinus-Lexikon*, vol. 1 (ed. C. Mayer; Basel: Schwabe & Co., 1986–1994) c. 511–15; K. Raikas, "St Augustine on Juridical Duties: Some Aspects of the Episcopal Office in Late Antiquity," in *Collectanea*

Augustiniana, vol. 1, *Augustine: Second Founder of the Faith* (eds. J. Schnaubelt and F. Van Fleteren; New York: Peter Lang, 1990) 467–83; G. Vismara, *La giurisdizione civile dei vescovi, secoli I-IX* (Milan: Dott. A. Giuffrè, 1995); J. C. Lamoreaux, "Episcopal Courts in Late Antiquity," *Journal of Early Christian Studies* 3:2 (1995) 143–67; R. Dodaro, "Church and State," *Augustine through the Ages: An Encyclopedia* (ed. A. Fitzgerald; Grand Rapids: Eerdmans, 1999) 176–84, esp. 176–78.

3. See, for example, J. P. Burns, "Augustine's Role in the Imperial Action against Pelagius," *Journal of Theological Studies*, n. s. 30 (1979) 67–83.

4. See J. R. Martindale, *The Prosopography of the Late Roman Empire*, vol. 2, A.D. 395–527 (Cambridge: Cambridge University Press, 1980) 697, s.v. Macedonius 3; *Prosopographie chrétienne du Bas-Empire*, vol. 1, *Prosopographie de l'Afrique chrétienne, AD 303–533* (ed. A. Mandouze; Paris : Éditions du CNRS, 1982) 659–61, s.v. Macedonius 2. See also F. Morgenstern, *Die Briefpartner des Augustinus von Hippo. Prosopographische, sozial- und ideologie-geschichtliche Untersuchungen* (Bochum: Universitätsverlag Dr. N. Brockmeyer, 1993) 107–8.

5. See Augustine, *ep.* 152.2 (Macedonius to Augustine). Abbreviations for Augustine's works are those found in *Augustinus-Lexikon*, vol. 2 (ed. C. Mayer; Basel: Schwabe & Co., 1996) xi–xxiv. English translation of this and many other letters cited in this essay, along with explanatory historical notes on their contents can be found in E. M. Atkins and R. J. Dodaro, eds., *Augustine: Political Writings* (Cambridge: Cambridge University Press, 2001).

6. See Augustine, *ep.* 153.16–17.

7. See Augustine, *s.* 62.8.

8. See Augustine, *ep.* 100, 133, 134, 139, 151, 153, 155.11; *en. Ps.* 50. See also Possidius, *Vita Augustini* 20.

9. See Augustine, *ep.* 100. Augustine wrote the letter in autumn-winter 408–409. See Mandouze, *Prosopographie*, 309–10, s.v. Donatus 24.

10. See *Codex Theodosianus* 16.5.44 (24 November 408).

11. N. McLynn, "Augustine's Roman Empire," in *History, Apocalypse and the Secular Imagination: New Essays on Augustine's* City of God (eds. M. Vessey, K. Pollman, and A. D. Fitzgerald, O.S.A; Bowling Green, OH: Philosophy Documentation Center [= *Augustinian Studies* 30:2] 1999) 29–44, dates Augustine's letter to the proconsul to sometime soon after August 408, but prior to the publication of the aforementioned edict on 24 November. McLynn points to the last third of the letter in which Augustine "invites the governor to issue an edict to show the Donatists that the laws against them are still in force," and argues that it would represent an "apparent redundancy" if Augustine's letter had been written after the publication of the imperial edict in question (McLynn, 38–39). McLynn thus concludes that Augustine's discussion of sanctions against the Donastists in this letter is hypothetical and contingent upon the proconsul's decision to move against the sect. As further support for this conclusion, he notes that Augustine carries on his discussion of sanctions in the conditional mood, and that his tone in addressing Donatus is characterized by "tortuously indirect politeness" (McLynn, 38–39). The earlier dating of Augustine's letter allows McLynn to argue that it has been "misunderstood" by scholars, and that the bishop's "purpose in writing Donatus is not to offer fatherly advice but to pump continuously

for information" as to whether, in the wake of the recent fall of Stilicho, existing imperial laws against the Donatists are still to be applied (McLynn, 38–39). If McLynn is correct in his reasoning, the force of Augustine's opposition to the death penalty for Donastists and his threatened "boycott" of judicial procedures against them as stated in this letter is substantially diminished. However, I am not persuaded by his arguments either to assume that Augustine lacks reason to fear a genuine intention on the part of the proconsul to apply the death penalty against the Donatists, or to conclude from the bishop's use of the conditional that his tone in addressing the proconsul lacks sternness, although he is clearly respectful. See Augustine, *ep.* 100.2 (CSEL 34/2.537). English translation of this letter can be found in Atkins and Dodaro, *Augustine: Political Writings*, 134–36.

12. See Augustine, *ep.* 134. See also Augustine, *ep.* 133 and 139, concerning the same incident.

13. See Augustine, *ep.* 133.2–3, 91.9, 104.1; *ciu.* 19.6.

14. See Augustine, *ep.* 133.2. See also Mandouze, *Prosopographie*, 67–78, s.v. Flauius Marcellinus; and M. Moreau, "Le dossier Marcellinus dans la Correspondance d'Augustin," *Recherches augustiniennes* 9 (1973) 5–181.

15. See Augustine, *ep.* 90 (Nectarius to Augustine). The Catholic church at Calama was governed by its bishop, Possidius, a friend of Augustine and his first biographer. It remains unclear to historians why Nectarius forwarded his appeal to Augustine.

16. See Augustine, *ep.* 91.9; cf. *ep.* 104.1, which concerns the same case.

17. See Augustine, *ep.* 104.1, 16, 17. Concerning the exchange of correspondence between Augustine and Nectarius, see especially H. Huisman, *Augustins' Briefwisseling met Nectarius. Inleideing, tekxt, vertaling, commentaar* (Amsterdam: J. Babeliowski, 1956). On Augustine's conception of criminal justice and reform in the context of the episode at Calama, see R. Dodaro, "Augustine's Secular City," in *Augustine and His Critics* (eds. R. Dodaro and G. Lawless; London: Routledge, 2000) 231–59.

18. See Augustine, *ep.* 153.3. For further discussion of this letter in the context of Augustine's views concerning criminal justice, see O. O'Donovan and J. Lockwood O'Donovan, eds., *From Irenaeus to Grotius: a Sourcebook in Christian Political Thought, 100–1625* (Grand Rapids: Eerdmans, 1999) 107–108; R. Dodaro, "Augustine of Hippo Between the Secular City and the City of God," in *Augustinus Afer. Saint Augustin: africanité et universalité. Actes du colloque international, Alger-Annaba, 1–7 avril 2001* (eds. P.-Y. Fux, J.-M. Roessli, O. Wermelinger; Fribourg: Universitätsverlag, 2003).

19. See Possidius, *Vita Augustini* 24. The best available edition is that of A. A. R. Bastiaensen, ed., *Vita di Cipriano, Vita di Ambrogio, Vita di Agostino* (Rome: Fondazione Lorenzo Valla, 1975). For a superb English translation, see T. F. X. Noble and T. Head, eds., *Soldiers of Christ. Saints and Saints Lives from Late Antiquity and the Early Middle Ages* (University Park: Pennsylvania State University Press, 1995).

20. See Augustine, *ep.* 10*.7. Asterisks appearing following the enumeration of Augustine's letters refer to the new series of his letters that was discovered by Johannes Divjak in the municipal libraries of Marseilles and Paris and published in 1981 in CSEL 88.

21. See Augustine, *s.* 21.6, 356.3–7; *en. Ps.* 99.7. For this reason, many freed slaves entered monasteries. See Augustine, *en. Ps.* 103.3.16; *op. mon.* 22.25.

22. See Augustine, *ep.* 10*.2–8.

23. This, at least, was Augustine's judgment of him. See Augustine, *conf.* 6.10.16. See also Mandouze, *Prosopographie,* 53–65, s.v. Alypius, on p. 53; and E. Feldmann, A. Schindler, and O. Wermelinger, "Alypius," *Augustinus-Lexikon,* vol. 1 (ed. C. Mayer; Basel: Schwabe & Co., 1986–1994) c. 245–67, esp. c. 246.

24. See Augustine, *ep.* 10*.4.

25. See Possidius, *Vita Augustini* 19. Cf. Augustine, *ep.* 48.1, 139.3, 213.5; *en. Ps.* 118.24.3; *s.* 340; *op. mon.* 29.37; *uera rel.* 58. Studies on *audientia episcopalis* are cited above, note 2.

26. The best explanation of the role of Eustochius is offered at various points in an article by C. Lepelley, "Liberté, colonat et esclavage d'après la Lettre 24*: la jurisdiction épiscopale «de liberali causa»," in *Les lettres de saint Augustin découvertes par Johannes Divjak* (Paris: Études augustiniennes, 1983) 329–42.

27. See *Codex Theodosianus* 3.1.8; cf. Augustine, *ep.* 83, 8*.1, 9*.4, 10*.4, 24*. See the studies on *audientia episcopalis* cited above, note 2. The critical edition of the Theodosian Code and of the Sirmondian Constitutions (cf. below, note 40) is found in *Theodosii libri XVI cum Constitutionibus Sirmondianis et Leges Novellae ad Theodosianum pertinentes* (eds. T. Mommsen and P. M. Meyer; Berlin: Weidmann, 1904–5; reprinted Dublin and Zurich: Weidmann, 1970). They are translated in *The Theodosian Code and Novels and the Sirmondian Constitutions* (trans. C. Pharr; New York: Greenwood Press, 1952).

28. The tone and content of Augustine's *ep.* 24* justify this inference.

29. For a brief and dated but still useful introduction to the tax burden, see A. H. M. Jones, *The Later Roman Empire 284–602,* vol. 1 (Oxford: Basil Blackwell, 1964) 462–69. For more recent, in-depth treatments, see P. A. Brunt, *Roman Imperial Themes* (Oxford: Clarendon Press, 1990; reissued 1999); R. Delmaire, "Cités et fiscalités au Bas-Empire. A propos du rôdes curiales dans la levée des impôts," in *La fin de la cité antique et le début de la cité médiévale de la fin du III siècle à l'avènement de Charlemagne* (ed. C. Lepelley; Bari: Edipuglia, 1996) 59–70; W. Liebeschütz, "Cities, Taxes and Accomodation of the Barbarians: The Theories of Duliat and Goffart," in *Kingdoms of the Empire. The Integration of the Barbarians in Late Antiquity* (ed. W. Pohl; Leiden: Brill, 1997) 136–51.

30. See Augustine, *ep.* 268. See Mandouze, *Prosopographie,* 381, s.v. Fascius.

31. See Augustine, *ep.* 113.

32. See Augustine, *ep.* 114; cf. *Codex Theodosianus* 9.3.6 (30 December 380) and 9.2.6 (21 January 409).

33. See Augustine, *ep.* 116. See Martindale, *Prosopography,* 501, s.v. Generosus 1; Mandouze, *Prosopographie,* 532–33, s.v. Generosus 1. G. Folliet, "L'affare Faventius. Examen du dossier (Augustin, Epist. 113–116)," *Revue des Études augustiniennes* 30 (1984) 240–50, argues convincingly along the lines of Lenain de Tillemont that the events recorded in this correspondance can not be dated with more precision than to sometime between 409–423, and not to somewhere between 399–401 as suggested by the *Prosopographie chrétienne.*

34. See Augustine, *ep.* 115.

35. See Augustine, *ep.* 229.2.

36. See *Registri ecclesiae Carthaginiensis excerpta*, canon 64 (= CCL 149.198) and canon 82 (= CCL 149.204).

37. See Augustine, *s.* 21.6, 356.3–7; *en. Ps.* 99.7. On ecclesiastical manumission in general, see F. Fabbrini, *La manumissio in ecclesia* (Milan: Dott. A. Giuffrè, 1965).

38. The original law can be found in the *Codex Theodosianus* 9.45.1, dated 18 October 392.

39. See *Registri ecclesiae Carthaginiensis excerpta*, canon 56 (=CCL 149.193–194).

40. For this edict, see the *Constitutiones Sirmondianae* 13. For critical edition and English translation, see above, note 27.

41. See the explanation for the duties of the *defensor ciuitatis* given in the *Codex Justinianus* 1.55.4 (a constitution dated 385 C.E.). See also Dodaro, "Church and State," 179.

42. See Augustine, *s.* 302.17; cf. *ep.* 22*.2. See also C. Lepelley, "Le patronat épiscopal aux I^{ve} et Ve siècles: continuités et ruptures avec le patronat classique," in E. Rebillard and C. Sotinel, eds., *L'évêque dans la citè*, 17–33, esp. 27–32; F. Jacques, "Le défenseur de cité d'après la Lettre 22* de saint Augustin," *Revue des Études augustiniennes* 32 (1986) 56–73.

43. See *Registri ecclesiae Carthaginiensis excerpta*, canon 75 (= CCL 149.202).

44. See *Codex Justinianus* 1.55.8.

6

Democracy and Its Demons

Michael Hanby

Religion and Imperial Rhetoric

"I WOULD THEREFORE HAVE OUR adversaries consider the possibility that to rejoice in the extent of empire is not a characteristic of good men."[1] Those at the onset of each new war who predictably invoke Augustine's name as the father of Christian just-war theory rarely give equal credence to his warnings about "patriotism" and the fabulous and civil theologies that provoke and sustain it.[2] Yet within this broader critique, even just wars are shown to play a sinister "religious" function, enjoining "demonic" sacrifice and furthering the worship of imperial power. In this chapter, I will first consider this critique and the "liturgical" function of just war within the civil theology of empire, and I will then suggest how this critical aspect of Augustine's thoughts on war, and not the traditional reductive appropriation of his thought, best serves a church in search of faithful responses to war and state violence.

The Christian and Augustinian conviction that we are created in the image and likeness of the God who is a Trinity results in some basic axioms that are repeated in different forms throughout the Augustinian *corpus*.[3] Divine simplicity and the ultimate convertibility of beauty, goodness, and truth in God's triune being mean for us that love and knowledge are inextricable, that we cannot but desire happiness and that we therefore inevitably act, individually and socially, in pursuit of what we love.[4] This axiom makes worship the basic form of human action and rules out a purely secular politics or a religiously indifferent political realm, an important point for the critique to follow.[5] The fundamental question for Augustine is never *whether* God will be worshipped, but *which* god will be worshipped. And the objects of our love and devotion famously become the ground for distinguishing between the heavenly and earthly city, though this distinction is only eschatologically reliable.[6] Similarly, and as a consequence of the inevitability of desire, we cannot but desire happiness, and since perfect happiness is inconceivable without internal and external peace we cannot but seek peace in all our actions, including war. Here again, the question is not whether peace, but *what kind* of peace.

> For every man is in quest of peace, even in waging war, whereas no one is in quest of war when making peace. In fact, even when men wish a present state of peace to be disturbed they do so not because they hate peace, but because they desire the present peace to be exchanged for one that suits their wishes. Thus their desire is not that there should not be peace but that it should be the kind of peace they wish for. . . .

> For even the wicked whey they go to war do so to defend the peace of their own people, and desire to make all men their own people, if they can, so that all men and all things might be subservient to one master. And how could that happen, *unless they should consent to a peace of his dictation either through love or through fear.*[7]

The final remark is particularly crucial, as it signals the means by which imperial power sustains itself. In Augustine's moral psychology, all passions, even contrary passions, are forms of will or desire, so what appear to be contrary forms of motivation each appeal differently to the *libido dominandi*.[8] In his "genealogical" criticism of Rome's *libido dominandi* in the early books of *De Civ.*, Augustine had exposed both love and fear as integral to the effectiveness of Roman power, anticipating Rousseau's later observation that the power of a state which rules by fear alone is limited by its capacity for physical coercion.[9] In Rome's early history, when Sallust says "justice and morality prevailed among [the Romans] by nature as much as by law," Augustine argues that it was fear of threat from the Carthaginians, spared in the interim between the Punic Wars, that ensured the preservation of a "high standard of moral conduct."[10] That is, Rome owes both its peace and its virtue to its enemies.[11] Hence Roman civic virtue originates, "not from the love of justice, but the fear that peace was unreliable while Carthage still stood," and we know from Augustine's anti-Pelagian arguments (and from Plato) that virtue rooted in fear rather than a love of the good is not really virtue at all.[12] When the pressure from Carthage was relaxed, "the country gradually changed, from the height of excellence to the depth of depravity."[13] The victory over Alba, also a descendent of Aeneas and, thus, "a monstrous crime of a war between allies and within families," is not recalled in Roman annals with sorrow and lament, but is renamed as "glory" and met with much popular acclaim, spurring the city on to greater triumphs and seducing it with the future promise of "hollow victories."[14]

The observation says something about the nature of empire that anticipates contemporary analyses of this question. To recognize a city as "an organization of rational people united in common agreement on the objects of their love" and imperial power as sustained both by fear and encouragement, is to recognize that imperial sovereignty is not antithetical to "democratic" processes and opinions.[15] To the contrary, in contrast to "modern European conceptions of sovereignty which consigned political power to a transcendent realm and thus estranged and alienated the sources of power from society," it is immanent democratic sovereignty that *most perfectly* realizes the form of empire.[16] This is because sovereign imperial power, while still a police power, is not an externality, but rather is internal to an ever-expansive totality that knows no "outside." Imperial powers desire to "make all men their own people," and yet it takes *both* the fear of "outsiders" and the forces of law *and* the promotion of desirable goods to achieve this feat.[17] Augustine's observations imply, in other words, that "empire is formed not on the basis of force itself but on the basis of the capacity to present force as being in the service of right and peace. . . . The first task of Empire, then, is to enlarge the realm of the consensuses that support its own power."[18]

If an empire is sustained not merely by force but by consensus, and if a people is an order of love, then the maintenance of empire requires a rhetoric whose purpose is to "delight and move" its subjects in a common desire constitutive of the body politic.[19] Augustine's analysis of imperial power thus becomes a critique of the organs of imperial discipline which manufacture and enforce that desire, flowing quite naturally into criticism of Roman civil religion and its counterpart, the fabulous theology of the stage.[20] "By this means [the human leaders] bound [people] tighter, as it were, to the citizen community, so that they might bring them under control and keep them there by the same technique."[21] Ontological tragedy, transcendental violence projected onto being by both cult and stage, then underwrites human tragedy and violence committed in the name of imperial glory.

> To mitigate the disgust caused by such tragedies, and to inflame the ardour for this abominable warfare, the malign devils (whom the Romans thought of as gods and the proper objects of worship and veneration) decided to show themselves to men as fighting among themselves, so that the natural affection between citizens should not shrink to imitate such battles, but that the gods' example might rather excuse the crimes of men.[22]

While I do not mean to suggest that the "political" and the "religious" constitute two distinct realms or kinds of activity—indeed I am arguing just the opposite—it is nevertheless heuristically useful to distinguish between them in order to see the multifarious functions of this rhetorico-political apparatus. The first of these is to provide political legitimacy to imperial power, and *De Civ.* provides numerous examples. One such instance is the famous encounter recorded by Cicero between Alexander the Great and the pirate. When asked by Alexander of his idea in infesting the sea the pirate responds, "the same as yours in infesting the earth! But because I do it with a tiny craft, I'm called a pirate: because you have a might navy, you're called an emperor."[23] The point is not merely that empire is brigandage on a larger scale, though Augustine does emphasize that empires are formed by a history of conquest, winning over demoralized recruits, acquiring territory, establishing bases, and subduing peoples.[24] Rather the point is that such activity allows some pirates to claim legitimacy over others, to arrogate to themselves titles that conceal the tragic and sinful character of this history, titles "conferred on them in the eyes of the world, not by the renouncing of aggression but by the attainment of impunity."[25] Alexander therefore *needs* the pirate. The pirate's existence legitimizes the emperor's power of protection; the emperor's power to brand the pirate helps to conceal the extent of his own brigandage.[26]

Latent in the emperor's dependence is a dynamic that is both politically and theologically crucial. This dynamic is repeated, in both these aspects, in a second example from the empire's rhetorico-political apparatus: its use of just war.

> The increase of empire was assisted by the wickedness of those against whom just wars were waged. The empire would have been small indeed if neighbouring peoples had been peaceable, had always acted with justice and had never provoked attack by any wrong-doing. In that case, human affairs would have been in a happier state; all kingdoms would have been small and would have rejoiced in concord with their neighbors. There would have been a multitude of kingdoms in the world, as there are multitudes of homes in our cities.[27]

The justice of any particular action is not at issue here. Augustine even seems to grant the Romans their just wars.[28] Rather, the issue is twofold: the function of just-war rhetoric and whether "it is a characteristic of good men" to rejoice in the glory of the empire, that is, whether a "patriotic" interpretation of Roman history is morally and theologically adequate. "Just wars" play a pernicious role here, providing a rhetorical function similar to the branding of the pirate. They enlist support for legitimate action and they conceal a history of violence, disguising the lamentable fact that "the Roman Empire could not have been increased so far and wide, and Roman glory could not have been spread, except by continual wars following one upon another."[29] As Alexander needs the pirate, so too imperial reach and glory need unjust enemies, who occasion and legitimate the expansion of imperial power. Love of the earthly *patria*, elicited by a noble and glorious history of "just" and therefore legitimate conquest, entails within it a love of the very "foreign injustice" that occasions such conflict. (Christ, for Augustine, is the true *patria*.)[30] As an order of love that binds its members into a social body, this desire is intrinsically "religious"; so much so that Augustine mockingly suggests elevating "foreign injustice" to the pantheon of official deities.[31]

> So if it was by waging wars that were just, not impious and unjust, that the Romans were able to acquire so vast an empire, surely they should worship the Injustice of others as a kind of goddess? For we observe how much help 'she' has given towards the extension of the Empire by making others wrong-doers, so that the Romans should have enemies to fight in a just cause and so increase Rome's power. Why should not Injustice be a goddess—at least the Injustice of foreign nations—if Panic and Pallor and Fever earned a place among Roman gods? With the support of these two Goddesses, 'Foreign Injustice' and Victory, the Empire grew, even when Jupiter took a holiday. Injustice stirred up the causes of war; Victory brought the war to its happy conclusion.[32]

Augustine clearly thinks that this civil religion is malignant. "It is a wicked prayer to ask to have someone to hate or fear, that he may be someone to conquer." Yet to understand just how this prayer is wicked we must digress to explore this dynamic of dependence in more detail before then contrasting this religion and its sacrificial order with the sacrifice of Christ.

The End of Sacrifice

We can best understand this dynamic if we first consider it from a first-person perspective, a move warranted by the macrocosmic/microcosmic isomorphism between the soul and the city and displayed at various points throughout the *Confessions* and in the relationship between that text and the *City of God*.[33] Nietzsche's great complaint against the claims of (especially Christian) virtue was that it is reactive: "it secretly celebrates as its occasion a prior evil; it lives out of what it opposes."[34] Augustine anticipates this criticism. Early in his career, in *De Libero Arbitrio*, he had consigned virtue to the position of an intermediate good, subordinate to the love of love itself.[35] He carries through on that argument, in his criticism of pagan moral philosophy in *De Civ.* XIX, agonizing the virtues and making temptation, and thus involuntary sin, integral to justice and prudence.[36] Inasmuch as an "external" world of injustice provides the occasion for our justice, or an "internal" world of temptation the occasion for our prudence, one can almost conclude that virtue, while a great good, is a lamentable good whose necessity is nevertheless cause for weeping.

In *Confessions* III, Augustine ponders the subtle attraction of stage plays, how we are willingly manipulated to take pleasure in the spectacle of a sorrow that we would not wish upon ourselves. While the sorrow itself is an object of enjoyment, the pleasure it brings cannot be intelligibly derived from our own misery if love (whether *caritas* or *cupiditas*) has some perceived good as its formal object.[37] This forces Augustine to search for the good which the spectator loves and enjoys, and he makes a distinction between the sorrow felt at our own sufferings—misery—and that felt at the suffering of another, which he calls pity. Noting that the spectator is not moved to help the fictitious sufferer, he poses a rhetorical question: "May it be that whereas no one wants to be miserable, there is real pleasure in pitying others—and we love their sorrows because without them we would have nothing to pity?" The implied answer is that we often secretly love the misfortunes of others as an occasion for the exercise of our own apparent goodness; though "apparent" is a key qualifier since "my" genuine good entails "internal" and "external peace," and is therefore a social good incompatible with the love of another's suffering.[38] The true object of our love in this case is our own apparent advantage, fueled by that suffering. Augustine's interpretation of this phenomenon mirrors his self-diagnosis in the pear tree episode, where he recognizes his theft as a perverse imitation of divine power. His compassion in this instance is a perverse and self-deceived imitation of divine compassion, distinguished both in kind and magnitude from God who is "more incorruptibly compassionate because no sorrow can reach to wound you."[39]

In contrast to Augustine's pity, which depends upon a privation as an instrument of distorted self-love, God's generosity is eternal and impassible, and therefore precedes all privation.[40] The same eternal generosity that sustains creation's existence before and after the fall is manifest visibly and temporally in the incarnation, which proceeds from this generosity.[41] As Henri de Lubac puts it, "[G]race is not more necessary to us, basically, than it was to Adam. . . . Properly speaking, it does not lead us further, but it comes to seek us further away—and further down."[42] The Fall simply extends the need for grace's reach into the darkness of the abyss.[43] Consequently, Augustine denies that the Son must die to appease the wrath of the Father and concludes that "the Father loved us also before, not only before the Son died for us, but before He created the world."[44] Christ's passion, in other words, does not issue from and therefore validate a prior privation, but originates from and manifests the inner life of God.[45] It does not satisfy an infinite offense, but expresses an infinite generosity, giving itself even to the point of solidarity with us in our death, returning the gift in newness of life, and thereby revealing the ineffable love between the Father and the Son.[46] Participation in Christ, in his condescension and self-donation, makes faith and hope in the resurrection the ground of a genuine compassion that does not celebrate a prior privation, though we shall have to consider how this occurs.[47] The soul possessed of this compassion is one doubly transfigured: first, because the objects and causes of that compassion have been changed, "*today* I have more pity for the sinner getting enjoyment from his sin than when he suffers torment from the loss of pleasure which is ultimately destructive"; second, because compassion itself becomes lamentable and is thus freed of its dialectical dependence on evil, "the sorrow I feel . . . gives me no pleasure."[48]

Like Augustine in the theater reveling in his own pity, the empire's celebration of glory, underwritten by "just war," also revels in a privation—the goddess "foreign injustice" Augustine's mythic exemplification of the projection of ontological tragedy. We are now in a better position to see both the theological consequences of this worship and its political ramifications. These consequences come to light in a contrast between the imperial ideology of just wars in the excerpt from *De Civ.* IV.15 and the wise man compelled to fight them in *De Civ.* XIX.7.

> But the wise man, they say, will wage just wars. Surely, if he remembers that he is a human being, he will lament the fact that he is faced with the necessity of waging just wars; for if they were not just, he would not have to engage in them, and consequently there would be no wars for a wise man. For it is the injustice of the opposing side that lays on the wise man the duty of waging wars; and this injustice is assuredly to be deplored by a human being, since it is the injustice of human beings, even though no necessity for war should arise from it. And so everyone who reflects with sorrow on such grievous evils, in all their horror and cruelty, must acknowledge the misery of them. And yet a man who experiences such evils, or even thinks about them, without heartfelt grief, is assuredly in a far more pitiable condition, if he thinks himself happy simply because he has lost all human feeling.[49]

The rhetorical shift between the two passages, from the *iusta bella* in book IV to *sapiens,* is significant. The invocation of the "wise man" is an invitation to recollection. If he *remembers* that he is a human being—which suggests that we risk forgetting and in some sense ceasing to be human—then he will recognize that the events which provoke his justice are incompatible with his own interests and his own goodness.[50] Even more significant, however, is the relation between justice and wisdom. For Augustine justice, "that virtue which assigns to everyone his due," necessarily falls within *sapientia* for two reasons. First, true justice is finally impossible for Augustine without true worship—without the charity which participates in the divine generosity, defeating the devil with justice rather than power.[51] Second, this worship takes place in Christ, who, joining creature and Creator, humanity and divinity, is both our *scientia* of temporal things and our *sapientia* of eternal things, an exemplar whose beauty elicits our desire and transforms it in conformity with his infinite giving.[52] The juxtaposition of the true wise man and the imperial stance is a contrast between the true justice of the heavenly city and the simulacrum of the earthly, which "takes a man away from the true God and subjects him to unclean demons."[53] The appeal to the *sapiens* is, implicitly, a christological appeal.

Augustine's imaginary interlocutor insists that "the Imperial City has been at pains to impose on conquered peoples not only her yoke but her language also, as a bond of peace and fellowship."[54] Earlier, Augustine had appealed to the goddess injustice and to a tragic if not criminal history to deflate the imperial conceits about its own justice. Here too, he appeals subversively to an ignoble history.

> True; but think of the cost of this achievement! Consider the scale of those wars, with all that slaughter of human beings, all the blood that was shed! Those wars are now past history; and yet the misery of these evils has not yet ended. For although there has been, and still is, no lack of enemies among foreign nations, yet the very extent of Empire has given rise to wars of a worse kind.[55]

The rhetoric of imperial glory is historically perverse, an indication that Rome has forgotten its own humanity, partly because it forgets the humanity of its enemies. But that observation does not do sufficient justice to the extent of Augustine's criticism. In denying Rome its noble history, Augustine implicitly denies a conception of progress that would grant a providential purpose to evil, a conception that entails a perverse sacrificial economy.

The voices of empire must transmute the war dead into victims and death into noble sacrifice in order to sustain this optimism. They must assuage their grief at the soldier's death, and enlist further victims for the cause, by making him heroic, by consoling themselves that his courage was expended for a great cause or a better future. Evil thus becomes a dialectical moment in the realization of empire, a moment that calls forth its victims' blood in exchange for "glory."

This dialectical logic is finally Manichean. By opposing evil and goodness in this way, it sees evil not as a privation, but as a "substance" that is the antithesis of goodness. This logic thus grants evil a providential role and a rationale by making it intrinsic to the realization of the "higher synthesis" of the good in the form of a "noble cause" or a "better future." This logic thus makes evil the occasion for sacrificial celebration integral to the maintenance of empire. We already saw how imperial power requires the collaboration of both the stage and the civic apparatus in order to claim both the fear and devotion of its citizens and thus to sustain its power. Augustine also suggests that it is imperial power itself that is the real object of devotion, regardless of whether this devotion is motivated by fear or encouragement. This is partly because

Augustine recognizes that the putative object of this devotion, being false, is ultimately nothing, but also because no passion could motivate us if it were not a form of intelligible love, a point crucial to his critique of pagan moral psychology in book XIV.[56] Even the fear cultivated and manipulated by imperial rhetoric is a form of worship. Such fear is useful to the empire because it preys upon the very form of self-love of which empire itself is an expression.

On the one hand, this fear prompts the manufacture of self-deception in the form of heroic glory, lasting security, and other devices of false immortality, thereby inciting devotion to the power that demands sacrifice in blood in exchange for staving off ultimate loss. On the other hand, fear wields this penultimate power only because it preys upon the self-love of disordered souls who have elevated bare survival to the place of the highest good in an attempt to deny the inevitability of death. The result is a sort of willful self-deception, bordering on madness. At least that is how Augustine understands those Roman refugees fleeing to Carthage, who in a desire to "return to normal" after the sack of 410, crowded the theaters, while "nations in the East were bewailing your catastrophe."[57] The tragedy here is that it is precisely this form of deception, this denial of death, that insulates those souls from the gratuity that exceeds death. There is a certain irony to this, as James O'Donnell notes.[58] While it is commonplace to dismiss Augustine's heavenly city as otherworldly, idealistic, and utopian, it is Augustine's eschatological hope, his refusal to let death define the bounds of reality, that allows him to confront with honesty the quite real miseries of this life and thus to unmask the reciprocal relation between the earthly city's lust for domination and the fear that holds this city in its grip.[59] It is Augustine, refusing the deceptions of imperial conceit, who is the realist.

These deceptions do not end here, however. Although this sacrificial logic pretends to combat evil with goodness, it actually fails to take seriously *either* goodness *or* evil, and this is true of both its theology and its "liturgy." A God who has an opposite is not God, but a finite object. Evil that actually exists has meaning, and is therefore a rational component of "goodness." Reflecting this metaphysical confusion, the liturgical embodiment of this theology trivializes life by rationalizing its loss. It banalizes death by giving it a positive upshot. This logic is thus neither truly celebratory nor truly mournful, though this claim requires that we think of both joy and grief as more than mere psychological categories. This rhetoric therefore neither truly appreciates lives generously given nor mourns those criminally lost, but sacrifices both to the progressive teleology of empire. In place of a genuine response this logic instead abortively inaugurates an "aberrated mourning" and "a counsel of hopelessness that extols Messianic hope" which perversely celebrate their own sublime occasion.[60] Truly this is "to lose all human feeling."[61]

Let us return to Jesus' death, which overcomes this demonic sacrifice with an original generosity and denies tragedy and death any ontological purchase. As we have seen, Augustine denies a propitiatory understanding of the atonement on grounds that the love manifested by the incarnation precedes any privation. This generosity, this solidarity with humanity in its suffering, extends to death, our deepest alienation—even death on a cross.[62] In virtue of this solidarity, perhaps, we can say that Christ's death was "necessary." To become human in a world that has estranged itself from God is to die; to become human as divine love is to invite gratuitous hatred and rejection.[63] But in another, equally profound, sense, Jesus' death is utterly pointless. He dies *innocently*, not to appease the wrath of the Father, but the wrath of the mob.[64] This insistence on Jesus' innocence denies his persecutors any rationale that would make Judas the true hero of the story. The Son's condescension to human form, Jesus' humble willingness to lay down his life and his resurrection to new life, are pointless in a second sense as well. These acts of self-donation are not resolved in a "higher synthesis." They do not underwrite human violence, but reject it. They terminate in a loving union with humanity that affirms creation's original, objective goodness and refuses the death that would rob it of this goodness, restoring creation to union with God even in the depths of hell. It is this restoration of creation as creation, this refusal to relinquish God's original order and plan, this expression of the love God has for his creation before the foundation of the world, that leads Augustine to conclude that God conquers the devil, rescues us from death, not by power, but by justice.[65]

Christ's passion and resurrection do not therefore give "meaning" to death; they bring forth new life from the nothingness of death. The resurrection is thus not a "greater good" that gives death purpose and implicitly validates the animosity of Jesus' persecutors. Jesus' death would be a crime were it not for the sanction of law; as it is, it is worse than a crime. It is a deed so scandalous, so arbitrary, so pointless, so devoid of being and meaning and light, that it shakes the earth and blots out the sun.[66] Yet this scandal, and Jesus' willingness to endure it, also confirms the "great price" God originally set upon his good creation. God patiently endures this animosity, binding himself in the Son to humanity in the meaningless moment of its deepest rejection of him, and he restores humanity, in spite of this rejection, to the love between the Father and the Son in the resurrection. Jesus does not give meaning to death in his "sacrifice": he reveals its nothingness and the emptiness at the heart of the power that inflicts it. And he can do this because God, who does not even have nonbeing for an opposite, whose internal differentiation in the relationship between lover and beloved is itself God and greater than the difference between God and creation or between God and nothing, is not only its recipient, but as the one who lays down his life, the priest, as the one whose life is laid down, the victim, giving himself not only to his friends, but to his enemies.[67] "Father, forgive them, for they know not what they do."[68]

Christians are united to Christ in his "sacrifice," indeed become this sacrifice, through charity, by participating, through worship that transforms our desire and therefore our being, in Christ's generous humility.[69] Since "the devil was overcome, not by the power of God, but by his justice," this humility, a self-giving refusal to celebrate power, is integral to the definition of justice.[70] Hence Christian participation in this sacrifice entails an analogous refusal, an analogous humility, indeed a certain mourning—"the sacrifice of a broken spirit"—that refuses falsely to glorify its own power or the evil which occasions its virtue.[71] Charity again becomes the ground of genuine virtue, but only because humility and forgiveness becomes the *modus operandi* of the heavenly city: for these counter privations with a generosity that refuses to celebrate the privation. This charity thus takes more seriously *both* the profundity of "sacrificial" donation *and* the emptiness and alienation of privation, and it institutes a mode of celebration that is both truly grateful *and* truly mournful, and more the latter for being the former.[72] As a practical matter, this virtue requires a *confessio* that relinquishes the conceits of temporal glory and refuses the empire's subtle celebration of death through blood sacrifice.

The juxtaposition between the wise man's *humilitas* and the *praesumptio* of the empire reflects this refusal. Just as Christ's body, the church, meets the humility of its head and master with "the sacrifice of a broken heart," the just in Christ mourn the losses of war all the more for the fact that they were occasioned by injustice which by definition *cannot* be rationalized. Deprived of the myths that justify their power and thus the incentives to accumulate it, just warriors and just people refuse to celebrate their power. They fight war with horror, perhaps even with penance, for they know what demons call forth their "justice." They know that any further advantage attained as a result of their conquest, far from serving a greater good, likely stores up wrath for another day. Therefore they do not celebrate their history as a progression of noble triumphs to be marked by military parades; they lament this kind of "progress" as a fall to be marked by penitential processions. A just people recognizes the horrific cost of war, for they have no prior need, fueled by a history of conquest, to make war appear sanitary and uncostly, and they have contemplated that the price of fighting justly might even be surrender or defeat.

The wise man, therefore, far from granting license for war, stands as the alternative to imperial justice. Furthermore, since a wise people is one that refuses to celebrate its power, it is less likely to acquire it, and is therefore a people for whom the question of just war need not very often arise. In other words, the very qualities that make Christians just warriors also make them unfit to fight. According to Hardt and Negri, "renewed interest in and effectiveness of the concept of *bellum justum*, or 'just war'" is a symptom of the contemporary reemergence of empire. Two significant features of their analysis tend to comport with Augustine's view. "On the one hand, war is reduced to the status of police action, and on the other, the new power that can legitimately exercise ethical functions through war is *sacralized*."[73] As we have now seen, Augustine's critique of the imperial use of just war is part of a much larger critique of the empire's sacral order. To the conservative *literati* who retreated to a retrenched position after the attack of 410, the critique comes as a direct rebuke. To the Christians, "lingering in a hundred ways on the fringe of paganism, with pagan relatives, pagan neighbours, loyalties to their city that could only be expressed by pagan ceremonies," the critique comes as a call to self-examination.[74] One could only hope that it would have the same effect on the contemporary church, which once again confronts a hostile sacral order.

Empire Strikes Back

How might the church appropriate this line of criticism in our own day, both as an exercise in self-examination and as a challenge to contemporary imperial power? The first step is to agree that contemporary American power has an imperial quality. I use this description not to be polemical a priori, and not simply because America alone is capable of projecting military force to all corners of the globe at once, but because the constellation of institutional forces which constitute this power is too complex simply to go by the designation "state" understood in Hobbesian fashion as a centralized consolidation of sovereignty. As Hardt and Negri contend, the current constitution of empire is premised on "a discontinuous form of sovereignty" in which "center and margins seem continually to be shifting positions."[75]

These shifts can nevertheless be plotted. First, empire operates through juridical structures that internalize the external. This is visible both in the U.N. mediation of an essentially American constitutional structure and through the more perfect union of capital and political power given juridical structure again by GATT, the IMF, WTO, and so forth, though frequent American self-exemption from the jurisdiction of these legitimating organs demonstrates the paradox of sovereign power: "that it is both outside and inside the juridical order," founding its power on what it excludes.[76] The loss of an "outside" to imperial sovereignty thus corresponds to the loss of an "outside" to the world market, as American consumer goods help forge the sacramental bond of a new (and false) catholicity and bind the members of this body to the contractual mechanism that accompanies those goods and the police mechanisms that enforce the contract.[77]

This first movement entails three subsequent moments: a moment of liberal inclusion, an apparent affirmation of difference, and a subsequent regulation and management of the domesticated differences by imperial command structures operating, like Alexander in the encounter with the pirate, with the luxury of a normative backdrop.[78] This is perhaps more true of American imperialism than the older, European variety which "held the other at a subordinated distance, permitting its otherness, even while subordinating it for the sake of an exploitation of human and natural resources."[79] In the American variant, the subordination and exploitation continue, but these now marginal differences are more perfectly "liberated" by tolerance for the service of capital.[80]

In a second "movement," the new internality created in these moments becomes the basis for "universal" values to which custodians of imperial power can then appeal in policing disturbances, values that transcend the now privatized differences of class or creed. Just as we saw earlier that the need for consensus is integral to the maintenance of imperial power, so here this sovereignty is not inconsistent with a certain multilateralism. Just as democracy more fully realizes imperial power, eliminating the external, so too does it more fully realize itself in a certain multilateral dialogue between the imperial organs—economic, governmental, and other communications media—who continually call each other into being.[81]

Third and finally, this process of internalization, this dialectic of inclusion and policing, conspire to make "omnicrisis" the motive force of empire.[82] Omnicrisis differs from the dialectic between a transcendental Self and "Other" who delimits sovereignty with sovereignty, though, as we shall see, it is still rhetorically useful to invoke that memory. Rather, omnicrisis locates the perpetual problem *within* the scope of imperial ambition and thus indicates the form of its solution. Like Alexander's pirate, the "Other" is now internalized and transformed into a problem of management much like the pluralities welcomed in the first moment, provoking "wars" of infinite magnitude and duration on poverty, recession, drugs, and terrorism. Each of these enemies is internal, since empire recognizes no externality, yet each defies local placement, and therefore ultimate victory or defeat, thus providing an infinite supply of fuel to imperial power.

Omnicrisis creates (and reflects) fear, which Augustine diagnosed as necessary for the empire to maintain power over its subjects. Both this motive and the positive motive of love or encouragement were induced by a rhetoric of legitimation itself sustained by a rhetorico-political edifice comprised of government, the civic religious cult, and the stage. A similar edifice, a military-entertainment complex that covertly celebrates the perpetual emergency, is visible in our own case.[83] Each wing of this edifice calls forth the other. Negatively, omnicrisis and thus fear are promoted through the news cycle by media organs with a financial stake in the poignancy and drama of the constant crisis. Dramatic musical scores, graphics, and provocative headlines accompany a steady rhythm of urgent news to sustain and cultivate the anxiety and tension. The anxiety and tension then further underwrite the consolidation of power, even as these same media organs ostensibly (though rarely enough) criticize that power. This negative rhetoric is accompanied by a positive, universalist rhetoric of "responsibility," "freedom," "patriotism," and, importantly, "sacrifice." These themes are endlessly promoted through film—Steven Spielberg's *Saving Private Ryan* comes to mind—advertisements, and the strange commingling of the military with a celebrity and sports culture.[84] One need only watch a Super Bowl to see all of these facets of the military-entertainment complex working in concert.

Our earlier analysis of the *City of God* showed the religious effect of this sort of rhetoric. Inasmuch as the empire itself, as the guarantor of eternal values, is the object of worship in these rituals, they inevitably inflame the *libido dominandi* from which empire is built.[85] But this occurs in part by creating a perverse dependence on the evil which elicits the empire's sacrificial victims. Does this dynamic apply to the contemporary scene?

At the center of American civil religion is the ubiquitous flag. Carolyn Marvin and David Ingle have argued that it is the flag's function to bind the nation together through blood sacrifice.[86] As an object, it is to be treated with the utmost reverence: "it must not touch the ground, it must hang in proper alignment, it must not be lower than other flags, it must appear in the place of honor on the right, it much not be used as a receptacle or covering."[87] This is because of the "sacramental" quality the nation invests in it. "For having flown in a particular lived battle or touched the casket of the remembered deceased," a specific flag becomes a holy relic, communicating the "real-presence" of those united in it.[88] Conversely, "if all members of a single military unit die in combat, the regimental colors are retired, for the flag dies when the group dies."[89] Hence to violate or desecrate the flag is to desecrate those who died for it. This is because "the flag is treated both as a living being and as the sacred embodiment of a dead one," the centerpiece of a mystical union formed through blood sacrifice.[90]

The flag embodies not only the memory of sacrificial victims, but a historical narrative of national glory that makes the deaths of those slaughtered in the nation's war sacrificial. At this point we may ask whether in fact the goddess of foreign injustice is not once again dispensing her "blessings." The usefulness of the pre-imperial dialectic, particularly the lessons provided by the Second World War, is illuminating here. This war is not to be understood as the European Civil War, the shame of a failed Christendom, the perilous consequence

of technocratic society or the moment at which the paganism briefly inter-
rupted by Christianity reconsolidated its forces with Christian complicity—all
possibilities that might provoke sober and penitential reflection. Rather Hitler,
as the eternal anti-type, the problem to which we are forever the solution, provides the occasion of our self-celebration, and every aspiring tyrant becomes a
Hitler.[91] (Modern and postmodern aesthetics that make sublime terror transcendental only aid and abet these political tendencies.) This explains the recent surge in films centered on World War II and cable television channels devoted to endless reruns of war documentaries and film from the Nuremburg
rallies. It explains why American Holocaust museums wage grotesque bidding
wars for the last remaining barracks from Auschwitz-Birkenau, a spectacle that
led Gillian Rose to conclude, "The Holocaust has become a civil religion in the
United States," with Auschwitz as "the anti-city of the American political community."[92] We remain locked in a counter-identification and therefore dependent on our enemies for our greatness. "Evil is real, and it must be opposed."[93]
Of course if evil is "*real*" and *can* be opposed, then God is not,[94] for we are back
in a Manichean world of ontological tragedy.

Within the view of ourselves underwritten by this counter-identification,
unfortunate deviations from the path of progress—the Middle Passage, the
Monroe Doctrine—become mere dialectical moments in the triumphant
march that occasion greater self-celebration for having been overcome. Even
those historical moments that should provoke lament serve to justify the
power that produced them.[95] Moral and human tragedy becomes the occasion
for celebrating our own greatness. The aftermath to the horror of September
11 provides a sobering example.

> In the brave sacrifice of soldiers, the fierce brotherhood of firefighters and the
> bravery and generosity of ordinary citizens, we have glimpsed what a new cul-
> ture of responsibility could look like. We want to be a nation that serves goals
> larger than self. We have been offered a unique opportunity, and we must not let
> this moment pass.[96]

Absent from the celebration of this sacrifice or the passage "to goals larger
than self" is the remorseful admission that "the very breadth of Empire has
produced wars of a worse kind"; instead there is only the optimism of imperial hubris.[97] But we have seen that this optimism flourishes by loving the privation that it claims to deplore and banalizing the self-donation it claims to
celebrate. The very syntax of this rhetoric belies this logic. "We have been offered a unique opportunity." One is tempted to ask, "Offered by whom?"[98]

Augustine challenges imperial hubris, the inability of power to mourn its
own failures, with a monumental act of Christian imagination that confronts
the powerful with the limits and self-deception inherent in their might and

with the void at the heart of their commitment to it. It is here, and not merely in the permission he allegedly grants to fight just wars, that Augustine is most relevant to our predicament today. His real import lies first, in his unmasking of the rhetorico-liturgical apparatus of the *libido dominandi*, and second, in his exposure of its sacrificial logic.

It would take an act of imagination no less bold for the church to make full use of these criticisms in our own time. Beyond resisting the urge to bless each new war as just, it would mean naming the economy of sacrifice that organizes imperial power as an economy of love for a god that is ultimately death. It would mean denying that this power is indeed secular, despite its claims to institute and protect the neutral space of religious freedom. This space is religious through and through; it channels our activities and claims our devotion, and it is not one which Christians can either easily inhabit or realistically escape. Yet it behooves both Christians and "secular" power alike to name more clearly the gods to which this power sacrifices and the liturgical apparatus which elicits these offerings. Practically speaking, this would require the church to refuse to lend its liturgy to color guards and to remove the flag from its premises, especially in time of war. It would mean denying the president's right to pronounce priestly blessings or to enlist God in the cause. It would mean declining the temptation to dispense false comfort by rationalizing human loss as noble sacrifice and the victims as heroes, not because those who give their lives for others are not genuinely courageous or virtuous, but because such descriptions are incompatible with the true sacrifice of Christ and the true nature of these virtues. It does them more honor to say, in a sense, that they died for no good reason at all.

Imperial power must give death meaning, make it rational and heroic. In so doing, it makes death useful. This power cannot say that its victims die for nothing, which is to say that imperial power can neither truly mourn nor truly celebrate acts of charitable self-donation. For genuine grief and genuine celebration would deprive this power of the engine for its own accumulation. By contrast, a genuine Augustinian imagination would encourage this grief by treating the occasion for American justice as an occasion for mourning and penance, confronting ourselves with demands for the restitution of historic wrongs and divestment of imperial advantages, and refusing to situate human horror within the teleology of empire whose capacity to elicit sacrifices depends upon banalizing them. Christian hope contains a proper lament, a confession that partakes of the humility which is hope's source and end. It is not therapy by other means, and it refuses the consoling rhetoric that trivializes suffering and forestalls any reflection beyond that designed to congratulate ourselves.

To recognize the centrality of confession to the genuine sacrifice of a broken heart is to recall that the *City of God* speaks different messages to different audiences. To the empire, Augustine offers a word of judgment even as he praises the genuine goods the empire tragically pursues. To those who would identify themselves as citizens of that other city, he extends a call to self-examination, to sort out the claims made upon our affections and our complicity in the distortion and disorder of the earthly city.[99] A church that would follow Augustine's lead would follow suit, announcing God's judgment on the earthly city, the Word of the Cross, even while confessing that the border dividing the two cities runs through our own souls.

Notes

1. Augustine, *Concerning the City of God against the Pagans*, trans. Henry Bettenson (London: Penguin, 1984), IV.15. Hereafter I will designate *City of God* by its Latin abbreviation, *De Civ.*, and cite it by book and chapter.

2. I am skeptical of attempts to place Augustine at the font of the just-war tradition and to the extent that he *can* be located there, I have questions about the exegetical, christological, and ontological adequacy of his reflections. For instance, *c. Faust,* XXII.70 arguably strains itself explaining Jesus' rebuke of Peter—for wielding the sword without proper authority—and chapter 76 employs a tenuous distinction between inner intent and outward act to interiorize the command to turn the other cheek. Yet in *ep.* 138, Christ himself undermines the distinction, transgressing the literal sense of the command by offering his life for his enemies. It is unclear just how Christ's example relates to those who are compelled by charity to act opposite Christ on the basis of the same distinction. For a survey of the Augustinian texts dealing with these questions, see David A. Lenihan, "The Just War Theory in the Work of Saint Augustine," *Augustinian Studies* 19 (1988), 37–70. While I am sympathetic with an argument for an Augustinian pacifism, it fails to fully convince. For a more nuanced, though still problematic example of the alternative view, see Paul Ramsey, "Just War According to St. Augustine," in *Just War Theory*, ed. Jean Bethke Elshtain (New York: New York University Press, 1992), 21–22. On the question of compatibility between Augustine's endorsement of coercion and his ontology, see John Milbank, *Theology and Social Theory* (Oxford: Blackwell, 1990), 417–23.

I am also skeptical that any modern war can satisfy either *ad bellum* or *in bello* criteria. Can modern states, premised both historically and conceptually on the privatization and policing of the church, meet the condition of legitimate authority according to theological criteria? (I'm indebted to Darrell Cole for this point.) Can wars fought against a largely faceless –ism stand a reasonable chance of success? How would we know when this success is ever achieved? How can the criteria of proportionality ever be fulfilled when the conditions for that fulfillment lie in a nonexistent future? Can one invoke proportionality when one warring nation's strength is so superior that it leaves an enemy effectively defenseless and thus unable to conduct war by just means? Or put differently, can a just war be one in which the strength of one side deprives the other of

the means for fighting justly? Must we make a virtue of the often vicious history of conquest, consumption, and production that have produced the military's capacity to use
discriminate force?

   3. Augustine, *De Trin.*, VIII.4.6–6.9; IX.10.15, XIII.4.7; *De Civ.*, XIX.1, 12. I do not
intend to suggest that the mind's "resemblance" to the Trinity is the basis of the *imago
dei*; indeed Augustine explicitly denies this. Our similarity to God occurs within the
context of an infinitely greater dissimilarity which, paradoxically, is the basis of the
likeness. Rather we are in the image of God when our love and knowledge coincide in
the Son as image of the Father, in whom knowledge and love perfectly coincide (*De
Trin.*, XIV.4). Since we are the *imago dei* in the Son, through the love of the Holy
Spirit, the image ultimately finds its completion in Christ's Body, thus confirming the
conclusion of *De Civ.* XIX.5 that the life of the saints is inherently social, repairing our
natural sociality rent asunder in Adam. See Henri De Lubac, *Catholicism: Christ and
the Common Destiny of Man*, trans. Lancelot Sheppard (San Francisco: Ignatius Press,
1988), 25–47. Rowan Williams, "*Sapientia* and the Trinity: Reflections on the *De
Trinitate*," *Collectanea Augustiniana*, ed. B. Bruning et al. (Leuven: Leuven University
Press, 1990), 317–32; Lewis Ayres, "Remember that You Are Catholic" (serm.52.2):
Augustine on the Unity of the Triune God," *Journal of Early Christian Studies* 8:1
(2000), 39–82.

   4. See Augustine, *De Trin.*, IX.5.8, and Michael Hanby, *Augustine and Modernity*
(London: Routledge, 2003), chs. 2 and 3.

   5. See Augustine, *De Trin.*, I.8.17, XIV.12.15.

   6. Augustine, *De Civ.*, XIX.24. Augustine retains, albeit in dramatically altered
form, something of the Platonic isomorphism between soul and city, with the *Confessions* giving first-person expression to the same dynamics of misdirected desire that
the *City of God* unveils on a social scale. Consequently, while objective rites such as
baptism mark a necessary (though not sufficient) condition for citizenship in the
heavenly city, the line demarcating the two cities runs not simply between agents but
through them. Rhetorically, then, the *City of God* arrives to a Christian audience as
both a reassurance and a call to self-examination. The rhetorical effect among hostile
pagans was undoubtedly quite different.

   7. Augustine, *De Civ.*, XIX.12, emphasis mine. See also *De Civ.*, III.10.

   8. Augustine, *De Civ.*, XIV.6.

   9. Rousseau, *The Social Contract* (London: Penguin, 1968), 52ff.

   10. Augustine, *De Civ.*, II.17, citing Sallust, *Catalina*, 9.1

   11. Augustine, *De Civ.*, II.18, III.10.

   12. Augustine, *De Civ.*, II.18. The passage continues, ". . . and that is why Nascia resisted the annihilation of Carthage, so that wickedness should be restrained by fear,
immorality checked, and the high standard of moral conduct preserved."

   13. Augustine, *De Civ.*, citing Sallust, *Catalina*, 5.9.

   14. Augustine, *De Civ.*, III.15

   15. Augustine, *De Civ.*, XIX.24.

   16. Michael Hardt and Antonio Negri, *Empire* (Cambridge: Harvard University
Press, 2000), 164.

   17. Augustine, *De Civ.*, XIX.12.

18. Hardt and Negri, *Empire*, 16. One can invert Hardt's and Negri's point and say that the empire's need for legitimacy is susceptible to Augustine's definition of a city insofar as "consensus" requires appeal to certain goods.

19. Augustine, *De Doc. Ch.*, IV.12. Augustine takes over this formulation from Cicero to describe Christian rhetoric. For more on the theological importance of Christian rhetoric, see Carol Harrison, "The rhetoric of scripture and preaching: Classical decadence or Christian aesthetic?" in Robert Dodaro and George Lawless (eds), *Augustine and His Critics: Essays in honour of Gerald Bonner* (London: Routledge, 2000), 214–30.

20. On the integral relation between civil and fabulous theology, see *De Civ.* VI.8. "Anyone who intelligently examines the futile obscenities of both will conclude that both are fabulous; anyone who observes that stage shows closely related to 'fabulous' theology are included in the festivals of the gods of the city and in the civic religious cult, will recognize that both theologies are, in fact, civil." See also Robert Dodaro OSA, "Pirates or Superpowers: Reading Augustine in a Hall of Mirrors," *New Blackfriars* 72.845 (January, 1991), 9–19. "Augustine, however, paid far more attention to the linguistic and social communications techniques at work in the politicization process than do modern just-war theorists and the bishops and theologians whom the theorists influence. He realized that Roman society was founded upon an extreme patriotism, a love for the *patria* above all else, which was promoted by means of Roman education, folklore, literature, civil religion and theatre. . . . In Book IV he set out to criticize the received 'history' of Roman imperial expansion. As a former teacher of rhetoric, Augustine was well aware that history was treated as a branch of rhetoric. He put his readers on notice that he intended to read Roman history critically, exposing all the rhetorical 'hidden persuaders' with which that history was normally composed." Interestingly, Dodaro's article was written during the Gulf War arguments over just war, and anticipates many of the concerns of this essay.

21. Augustine, *De Civ.*, IV.32.

22. Augustine, *De Civ.*, II.25. Chapter 27 continues, "These scandalous and slanderous stories about the gods, those disgraceful actions attributed to them, infamous and outrageous if really committed, still more infamous and outrageous if invented, all those were presented to the eyes and ears of the public for the instruction of the whole community."

23. Augustine, *De Civ.*, IV.4.

24. Augustine, *De Civ.*, IV.4.

25. Augustine, *De Civ.*, IV.4. The recognition that imperial power works by acquiring impunity comports with Agamben's understanding of the paradox of sovereign power: "that it is both outside and inside the juridical order," founding itself on its capacity to name itself the exception to that order. See Giorgio Agamben, *Homo Sacer: Sovereign Power and Bare Life*, trans. Daniel Heller Roazen (Stanford: Stanford University Press, 1995), 16.

26. I am grateful to Robert Dodaro for illuminating this passage. In private correspondence he writes, "Augustine argues that the emperor needs the pirate's lesser injustice in order to conceal his own greater injustice. By labeling the pirate as such, the emperor assumes the guise of a legitimate political authority. He is able to posit this

legitimacy only because he can focus popular disapproval on the pirate. The emperor knows that, provided he can make his accusations against the pirate stick in the minds of his audience, the far greater scale of his own injustices can effectively be hidden from view. The emperor's primary rhetorical activity is not in directly defending himself, but in labeling his enemy as a 'pirate'. This is of course meant to be inflammatory, but at a more fundamental level, the emperor's intention is also to de-legitimize his opponent by constituting him an outlaw, and therefore, different from himself. He can achieve this rhetorical feat only because the complexity of the political, social, economic communication and legal structures which conceal his injustices is greater, more powerful than the pirate's. The pirate's rejoinder challenges the emperor's rhetoric not solely or primarily by pointing out the moral symmetry which exists between them, but by exposing the rhetorical sleight-of-hand by which the emperor conceals the greater scale of his own injustices. ('I have one ship . . . you have many ships')." One should hesitate, however, in drawing overly extravagant conclusions from this symmetry. "[I]f piracy as a concept is going to hold any real meaning . . . it must stand out in some dramatic way within the politics assumed in that narrative over against other, considerably less unjust regimes. Otherwise, all shipping and commerce is simply indiscriminate piracy. If that is the case then the term 'pirate' and its cognates are voided of the meaning we understand them to hold. Augustine can not have it both ways (and I don't think he wants to.) If all kingdoms are really just sophisticated piracies, then there is no piracy and no pirates. Augustine may want to argue that all kings are in some ways pirates, but I think he would allow that this is not the same thing as saying that there is no difference except in scale between kingdoms and pirate bands. I therefore think that his use of the image of the emperor (*imperator*), as opposed to king (*rex*) at *De civ*.4,4 is intentional, and ought to cause us to reflect on the nature of empire (*imperium*) as opposed to kingdom (*regnum*)." See also Dodaro, "Pirates or Superpowers," 14–17.

27. Augustine, *De Civ.*, IV.15.

28. Augustine continues that "to make war and to extend the realm by crushing other peoples, is good fortune in the eyes of the wicked; to the good, it is necessity." I have altered the Bettenson translation slightly, omitting the adjective "stern" before necessity, which seemed gratuitous. "*Proinde belligerare et perdomitiis gentibus dilatare regnum malis uideter felicitas, bonis necessitas.*" Augustine, *De Civ*, IV.15, CCSL XLVII, 111.

29. Augustine, *De Civ.*, III.10.

30. Augustine, *Confessions*, VII.21.

31. One must be careful in using the term "religious" to describe an abstract, a priori phenomenon existing "hypostatically" prior to distinct religious communities. As William Cavanaugh has shown, this use of the word corresponds to the modern invention of the "religious" as a distinct sphere and type of activity subject to the police power of the modern state that is allegedly religiously neutral. My use of the word draws upon the older sense of *religio* as a virtue and a binding discipline, a species of justice, and it occurs, at any rate, from within the context of Christian and Augustinian claims about the inevitability of worship stemming from the nature of the *imago dei*. See Cavanaugh, "A Fire Strong Enough to Consume the House: The 'Wars of Religion' and the Rise of the State," in *Modern Theology* 11:4 (October, 1995), 397–419.

32. Augustine, *De Civ.*, IV.15.

33. Compare the following dynamics. "Because my will was perverse it changed to lust, and lust yielded to become habit, and habit not resisted became necessity" (*Conf.* VIII.5). "I cannot refrain from speaking about the city of this world, a city which aims at dominion, which holds nations in enslavement, but is itself dominated by the very lust for domination" (*De Civ.*, I, pref.).

34. See Milbank, "Can Morality Be Christian?" in *The Word Made Strange: Theology, Language, Culture* (Oxford: Blackwell, 1997), 221. "Friedrich Nietzsche saw a ground for still further suspicions: for if these prior evils have not yet recognized themselves as such, but are only named evil by the supposed good which resists them, then are they not simply even in the case of the presence of human agency, spontaneous natural manifestations of energy, knowing no vindictiveness? Whereas, to the contrary, if virtue takes its starting point in a threatened position, and one must concede that to be threatened is something bad, generating fear, insecurity, self-enclosure and so forth—something morally bad, not just a non-moral evil—then virtue is bound to begin with envy, spite, pettiness, priggishness, and self-righteousness, *however* seemingly good its cause."

35. Augustine, *De Lib.*, I.13.

36. Augustine, *De Civ.* XIX.4. See James Wetzel, *Augustine and the Limits of Virtue* (Cambridge: Cambridge University Press, 1990), 98–111.

37. I disagree with those who think Augustine's understanding of will makes it intelligible to will evil for its own sake, that is, that sin doesn't entail an intellectual error. Both the mutual entailment of intellect and will in Augustine's understanding of the *mens* and the role of *delectatio* in action militate against that conclusion, as does the *Confessions'* repeated references to blindness as a consequence of sin. In the pear tree episode, where Augustine allegedly displays such an account, Augustine interrogates the object of his own delight, that is, what *seems* good to him. It turns out to be his own power, the *mistaken* sense that he can be omnipotent.

38. See Augustine, *De Civ.*, XV.5. "A man's possession of goodness is in no way diminished by the arrival, or the continuance, of a sharer in it; indeed, goodness is a possession enjoyed more widely by the united affection of partners in that possession in proportion to the harmony that exists among them. In fact, anyone who refuses to enjoy this possession in partnership will not enjoy it at all; and he will find that he possesses it in ampler measure in proportion to his ability to love his partner in it."

39. Augustine, *Conf.*, III.2.

40. "Distorted" is a crucial term here. *De Civ.*, XIX.14, "Now God, our master, teaches two chief precepts, love of God and love of neighbour; and in them man finds three objects for his love: God, himself, and his neighbour; and a man who loves God is not wrong in loving himself." See also *De Trin.*, XIV.14.18.

41. Augustine, *De Trin.*, XIII.10.13, "For what was so necessary for the building of our hope, and for freeing the minds of mortals cast down by the condition of mortality itself, than that it should be demonstrated to us at how great a price God rated us, and how greatly he loved us?"

42. Henri de Lubac, S.J., *Augustinianism and Modern Theology*, 48–49.

43. Perhaps this is why Augustine often refers to Christ, whose saving work consists partly in his exemplary function, as healing salve (*collyrio*) for the eye. See Augustine,

Conf., VII.10. For an extended discussion see James O'Donnell, *Augustine Confessions Commentary,* vol. II (Oxford: Clarendon Press, 1992), 410–11. For Jesus as *exemplum,* see *De Trin.*, IV.3.6.

44. Augustine, *De Trin.*, XIII.11.15.

45. God's "responsiveness" to our need, a description employing temporal categories, also needs to be qualified in light of the difference between time and eternity. In the contingency of time, *we* experience this grace (to the extent we can experience it *as* grace) as responsive. Yet our language here must be qualified, just as Aquinas qualifies the inadequacy of our "composite" way of speaking. Even God's "internal" receptivity must be understood as active, namely the activity of electing "us in him before the foundation of the world" (Eph. 1.4). This means, as Balthasar notes, that "the first idea of what man is already bears the determining mark of the Trinitarian economy." (Balthasar, *Mysterium Paschale,* 12.)

46. Augustine, *De Trin.*, VI.10.12. "For in that Trinity is the supreme source of all things, and the most perfect beauty, and the most blessed delight. Those three, therefore, both seem to be mutually determined to each other and infinite in themselves . . . So both each are in each, and all in each, and each in all, and all in all, and all are one."

47. Milbank, "Can Morality be Christian?" 232, n. 23, writes, "This is not to say that there cannot be exemplary treatments of the complexity of non-reactive charity . . . [U]nder faith and charity one can once again speak of diverse virtues—truthfulness, fidelity and so forth—yet their character is transformed. For example in charity there is an *essential* patience which respects our ontological distance from God, a distance we rejoice in as it alone gives God to us. Hence the patience of faith is not in a sulk, is not putting up with anything. However, it is precisely this patience which, in the fallen world, can put up with *everything*."

48. Augustine, *Conf.*, III.2.

49. Augustine, *De Civ.*, XIX.7.

50. Augustine, *De Civ.*, XV.5.

51. Augustine, *De Trin.*, XIII.13.17, "But since the devil, by the fault of his own perversity, was made a lover of power, and a forsaker and assailant of justice, it pleased God, that in order to rescue man from the grasp of the devil, the devil should be conquered, not by power, but by justice, and that also men, imitating Christ, should seek to conquer the devil by justice not by power."

52. Augustine, *De Civ.*, XIX.25; *De Trin.*, XII.19.24 (citing Col.2.1–3). "Therefore Christ is our knowledge (*scientia*) and the same Christ is also our wisdom (*sapientia*). He himself implants in us faith concerning temporal things; He himself shows forth the truth concerning eternal things. Through him we reach on to himself: we stretch through knowledge to wisdom; yet we do not withdraw from one and the same Christ 'in whom are hidden all the treasures of wisdom and knowledge.'"

53. Augustine, *De Civ.*, XIX.21.

54. Augustine, *De Civ.*, XIX.7.

55. Augustine, *De Civ.*, XIX.7.

56. See Augustine, *De Civ.*, XIV.6–10; Wetzel, *Augustine and the Limits of Virtue,* 101.

57. Augustine, *De Civ.*, III.33.

58. James J. O'Donnell, "Augustine: Christianity and Society, The Critique of Ideology (1)," http://ccat.sas.upenn.edu/jod/twayne/aug3.html, 18.

59. See Augustine, *De Civ.*, I.9–11. Despite the polemical tone of *De Civ.*, Augustine does not suggest ultimately that death is small or should not be feared. This temporal life is a great good and its loss a genuine loss. He does not champion the "hero's death" which is problematic partly because the hero can be persuaded to overcome fear with sacrifice in exchange for glory. This reluctance is obvious in *Jo. eu. tr.*, 123.5, where Augustine says of Peter's impending crucifixion, "For indeed loosed from the body, he wished to be with Christ, but if it were possible, he ardently desired eternal life apart from the distress of death. And unwillingly he was led to this distress, but willingly he was led away from it. Unwillingly he came to it, but willingly he overcame it. And he left behind this feeling of weakness by which no one wishes to die, so exceedingly natural that not even old age could take it away from the blessed Peter . . ." The difference consists in precisely *which goods* are taken to be eternal, and which virtues are appropriate to those goods. The saint overcomes fear with humility; the hero, with deception and pride. See Augustine, *Tractates on the Gospel of John*, trans. John W. Rettig, Fathers of the Church 92 (Washington: Catholic University Press, 1995), 80. I want to thank Robert Dodaro for his reflections with me on the *timor mortis* in Augustine and the difference between saintly and heroic death. See also D.X. Burt, O.S.A. "Augustine on the Authentic Approach to Death," *Augustinianum* 28 (1988), 527–63; Carole Straw, "Timor Mortis," in *Augustine Through the Ages: An Encyclopedia*, ed. Alan D. Fitzgerald, O.S.A. (Grand Rapids: Eerdmans, 1999), 838–42.

60. The phrases are Gillian Rose's, and they come from her critique of postmodern philosophy, which she describes as "despairing rationalism without reason." Yet it is a perfect fit for the sacrificial logic of imperial power, thus perhaps affirming the thesis of Jameson, Hardt and Negri, Nicholas Boyle, and others, that "these gestures risk enforcing imperial power rather than challenging it," (Hardt and Negri, *Empire*, 217). Rose, *Mourning Becomes the Law: Philosophy and Representation* (Cambridge: Cambridge University Press, 1996), 69–70, 11.

61. Augustine, *De Civ.*, XIX.7.

62. Phil. 2.8

63. The "perhaps" is crucial, because such a formulation can lead to thorny problems. It would seem to depend on taking human nature as a pre-given datum to which the Son then unites himself, rather than seeing the hypostatic union as paradigmatic of what it means to be human. In the latter case, Christ's death would be by no means "necessary." One could perhaps avoid this by saying that to become incarnate in a world under sin, is necessarily to die because it is to invite the world's wrath.

64. Augustine, *De Trin.*, XIII.11.15, "And what is meant by 'being reconciled by the death of his Son? Was it indeed so, that when the Father was wroth with us, He saw the death of His Son for us, and was appeased toward us? Was then His Son already so far appeased toward us, that He even deigned to die for us; while the Father was still in his wrath, that except His Son died for us He would not be appeased? Pray, unless the Father had been already appeased, would he have delivered up His own Son, not sparing Him for us? Does not this opinion seem contrary to that? In the one, the Son dies for us, and the Father is reconciled to us by His death; in the other, as though the Father

first loved us, He Himself on our account does not spare the Son. He himself for us delivers Him up to death. But I see that the Father loved us before, not only before the Son died for us, but before He created the world. . . . Therefore together both the Father and the Son, and the Spirit of both, work all things equally and harmoniously; yet we are justified in the blood of Christ, and we are reconciled to God by the death of his Son."

65. Augustine, *De Trin.*, XIII.13.17.

66. Matt. 27.51, Luke 23.45. As John Milbank has observed (in a forthcoming article "Christ the Exception"), Jesus almost appears in the end to have been crucified by accident. Pilate's decision appears obscure, as he is at once condemning Jesus to death and washing his hands of the matter, and Jesus is passed back and forth, with the Sanhedrin turning him over to Pilate, Pilate passing him to Herod and Herod returning the gesture, before finally delivering him to the mob who appropriates a Roman legal apparatus that had found no fault with him. It is partly this that I mean by arbitrary, but also the Augustinian sense that there can be no good and rational reason for sin when viewed from the perspective of justice.

67. Augustine, *De Civ.*, X.6.

68. Luke, 23.34. See Augustine, *ep.* 138. Augustine portrays Christ's suffering as both refusing evil *and* graciously giving, though there is perhaps some ambivalence in the counsel to refer this patience "rather to the disposition of the heart than to the act which appears exteriorly." On the one hand, it is this distinction that typically underwrites Christian participation in war: if the injunction to turn the other cheek requires merely an inward disposition, it makes possible contrary outward actions (see *c. Faust.*, XXII.76). In this case, however, the inward disposition of patience justifies Christ's transgression of the literal sense of his own commandment in the outward act of self-donation. Augustine, *Letters*, trans. Wilfrid Parsons, S.N.D, Fathers of the Church 20 (Washington, DC: Catholic University Press, 1953). "This is clearly shown in the case of the Lord Christ Himself, a unique model of patience, who was struck on the fact and answered: 'If I have spoken evil, give testimony to the evil, but if well, why strikest me thou?' If we look at the words literally, He obviously did not fulfill His own precept, for He did not offer His other cheek to the striker; on the contrary, He forbade the one who did it to augment the wrong, yet He came prepared not only to be struck on the face, but even to die on the cross for those from whom He suffered these wrongs, and when He hung on the cross He prayed for them: 'Father, forgive them, for they know not what they do.'"

69. Augustine, *De Civ.*, X.6. To have one's desires transformed, moved by the beauty of Christ as exemplar, is to participate in the gift of the Spirit, the love between the Father and the Son. Hence imitation is always already participation, and since God's love is convertible in God's simplicity with God's being, a transformation of desire is ultimately a movement in being.

70. Augustine, *De Trin.*, XIII.13.17, PL 42, 1026. "*Non autem diabolus potentia dei, sed justitia superandus fuit.*"

71. Augustine, *De Trin.*, X.5, Ps. 51.18.

72. Wetzel, *Augustine and the Limits of Virtue*, 109, asks, "Why does one sort of wisdom [Stoic] exclude grief and the other embrace it? A correct but misleading answer would be to say that Augustine has given up the possibility of perfect beatitude for this

life, and so a grieving wisdom would not mar the perfection of Christian beatitude as it would Stoic beatitude. The answer misleads because it fails to address the source of wisdom's grief. . . . When the Christian saint grieves, it is not for the loss of material well-being, but for personal failures of vision and love, for having robbed creation of its creator, for having usurped God's dominion."

73. Hardt and Negri, *Empire*, 16, emphasis mine. They note some significant changes in the contemporary application. "Far from merely repeating ancient or medieval notions, however, today's concept presents some truly fundamental innovations. Just war is no longer in any sense an activity of defense or resistance, as it was, for example in the Christian tradition from Saint Augustine to the scholastics of the Counter-Reformation, as a necessity of the "worldly city" to guarantee its own survival. It has become an activity that is justified in itself. Two distinct elements are combined in this concept of just war: first, the legitimacy of the military apparatus insofar as it is ethically grounded, and second, the effectiveness of military action to achieve the desired order and peace. The synthesis of these two elements may indeed be a key factor determining the foundation and the new tradition of Empire. Today the enemy, just like war itself, comes to be at once banalized (reduced to an object of routine police repression) and absolutized (as the Enemy, an absolute threat to the ethical order)."

74. Peter Brown, *Augustine of Hippo: A Biography* (London: Faber and Faber, 1967), 313.

75. Hardt and Negri, *Empire*, 39.

76. Agamben, *Homo Sacer: Sovereign Power and Bare Life*, 16.

77. See William T. Cavanaugh, "The City: Beyond Secular Parodies," in *Radical Orthodoxy: A New Theology*, ed. John Milbank, Catherine Pickstock and Graham Ward (London: Routledge, 1999), 190–98.

78. While Hardt and Negri identify these moments, they are not the first to do so. See Hardt and Negri, *Empire*, 198–99. See Cavanaugh, "The City: Beyond Secular Parodies," 190–98; Talal Asad, *Genealogies of Religion: Discipline and Reasons of Power in Christianity and Islam* (Baltimore: Johns Hopkins, 1993), 205–6.

79. John Milbank, "Sovereignty, Empire, Capital and Terror," delivered at the Forum on Imperialism and Terror, University of Virginia, October 1, 2001, 3.

80. See Nicholas Boyle, *Who Are We Now? Christian Humanism and the Global Market from Hegel to Heaney* (Edinburgh: T & T Clark, 1998), 28. "In the language of Thatcherism people, that is—workers—must be flexible or unemployed. They must not be tied to a place, but prepared to move to follow employment. They must not be tied to time, but prepared to work all hours and days of the week, especially Sundays. It follows that they must not be tied to any particular group of people or community: that they have families, even, is of no social significance in the market, except as distracting from their flexibility. Above all they must expect to retrain, to work to satisfy quite different needs several times in their working life. They are in short to be dismembered, reduced to a series of functions that they exercise in accordance with no principle of continuity of their own choosing but only with the demands of the market." And this, arguably, is the good news. In the new corporate "colonies" of the Third World, this dismemberment occurs without the apparent benefits of the reverse side of this economic identity, that of "consumer."

81. Consider this exchange on the January 8, 2002 edition of PBS's the *Newshour,* between journalist Robert Kaplan and Margaret Warner. Each assumes that American policing of the global community is normative, and the exchange ends with Warner giving Kaplan the opportunity to invite U.S. action. See http://www.pbs.org/new-shour/international/jan-jun02/kaplan.html.

> KAPLAN: "The Islamic world needs to undergo the equivalent of what Christendom went through during the protestant reformation. That's what happened in certain places."
> WARNER: "Explain what you mean by that."
> KAPLAN: "It needs to reinvent religion for a modern mass society where religion can co-exist without too much contradiction, with a modern mass society. And the best example of that is what has been happening in Turkey over the last few decades. You have had Islamic parties working within Turkey's democracy and because of that they've had to make deals and back. . . . In back rooms, sleazy compromises, but that process has led to a moderation of that Islamic intensity because the very act of making these deals with secular forces, you know, leads to a change. . . . Leads. . . . It leads to an adaptation of Islam. You know, if there is a Protestant style reformation going on, it's going on in Turkey. It needs to happen in more places."
> WARNER: "But you're saying that kind of essentially political process can affect the evolution of a religion?"
> KAPLAN: "Yes, I think ultimately political Islam must die because political Judaism, political Christianity is all bad. When religion becomes politicized it leads to militancy and a kind of, you know, a rigid self-righteousness. So the idea is to return Islam to being a great religion out of politics to the degree it can be."
> WARNER: "So if the United States is facing all this, what should it be looking for in these countries? What kind of regimes are best able to at least create the space in which this can happen?"

82. See Hardt and Negri, *Empire,* 190, for a discussion of "omnicrisis." President Bush's remarks on the eve of what appears to be an intensification of the war with Iraq does little to refute this view. George W. Bush, "State of the Union 2003," *New York Times,* (January 29, 2003), A12. "The threat is new. America's duty is familiar. Once again this nation and our friends are all that stands between a world at peace, and a world of chaos and constant alarm. Once again, we are called to defend the safety of our own people, and the hopes of all mankind. And we accept this responsibility."

83. I owe this term to my colleague Louis Hamilton.

84. In the climactic scene of *Private Ryan,* a film framed by an illuminated flag waving above a war cemetery in France where an elderly Private Ryan has gathered with several generations of his family, the platoon captain who has incurred mortal wounds to rescue the young Ryan, lies on a bridge under heavy fire. Speaking ostensibly to Ryan, he looks into the camera and whispers to the audience to "be worthy." We, the generations, are left with Ryan at the cemetery at the end of the film to ponder our worthiness.

85. George W. Bush, "State of the Union 2002," *New York Times,* (January 30, 2002), A22. "America will lead by defending liberty and justice because they are right and true

and unchanging for all people everywhere. No nation owns these aspirations, and no nation is exempt from them. We have no intention of imposing our culture, but America will always stand firm for the nonnegotiable demands of human dignity: the rule of law, limits on the power of the state, respect for women, private property, free speech, equal justice, and religious tolerance."

86. See Carolyn Marvin and David W. Ingle, *Blood Sacrifice and the Nation: Totem Rituals and the American Flag* (Cambridge: Cambridge University Press, 1999), 63. "The flag symbolizes the sacrificed body of the citizen. This label has meaning only in reference to the group that defines it, the nation. Blood sacrifice links the citizen to the nation. It is a ritual in the most profound sense, for it creates the nation from the flesh of its citizens. The flag is the sign and agent of the nation formed in blood sacrifice." While I have found Marvin's and Ingle's analysis of the particular rituals comprising American flag worship useful for this portion of the argument, their Durkheimian approach suffers fundamental weaknesses, particularly with respect to Christianity which claims to institute an alternative economy. (Think of the role of Cain/Abel and Romulus/Remus in *De Civ.* XV.5ff.) They impose a formal, transcendental structure on the dynamics of historic groups, while failing to acknowledge the contingent and metaphysical character of their own theoretical apparatus or the historic debts they owe to a perverse form of Christianity. They then re-inscribe all historic communities with the sacrificial economy characteristic of modern politics, thus reinforcing that politics while claiming to diagnose it. Meanwhile, in making positivist assertions such as "The fundamental primitive process that transforms individual bodies into social ones is sacrifice" (13) or "to join an enduring group is to commit to a system of organized violence" (66), they never provide an account of "natural kinds" necessary to sustain the intelligibility of "violence" nor consider that "individual bodies," considered as such, might not be prior to "social bodies." So while I largely agree with them that the "violent blood-sacrifice creates nation-state unity" (12), my grounds for agreeing are theological and historical, not sociological, and therefore, not positivist and transcendental. For a thorough demolition of this method, see John Milbank, *Theology and Social Theory: Beyond Secular Reason,* (London: Blackwell, 1990), 51–74.

87. Marvin and Ingle, *Blood Sacrifice and the Nation*, 80.

88. Marvin and Ingle, *Blood Sacrifice and the Nation*, 43. Marvin and Ingle give numerous examples, such as this excerpt from a televised encounter between the author and a Philadelphia city councilman. The councilman: "When a Gold Star mother . . . gets that flag, you have to watch them. You have to watch what they do with that flag; they cradle it like they do a baby, and them, it's a symbol of that son, and when you burn that flag, you're taking another shot at her son, a son whom she'll never see again. It's more than just a flag, it's a baby, that's what it is."

89. Marvin and Ingle, *Blood Sacrifice and the Nation*, 44.

90. Ibid., 31. Marvin and Ingle, *Blood Sacrifice*, 80, record MacArthur's words to the graduates of West Point. "The long grey line has never failed us. Were you to do so, a million ghosts in olive drab, in brown khaki, in blue and grey, would rise from their white crosses, thundering those magic words: Duty, honor, country."

91. Bush, "State of the Union 2003," A12. "Throughout the twentieth century, small groups of men seized control of great nations and built armies and arsenals and set out

to dominate the weak and intimidate the world. In each case, their ambitions of cruelty and murder had no limit. In each case, the ambitions of Hitlerism, militarism, and communism were defeated by the will of free peoples, by the strength of great alliances, and by the might of the United States of America. Now, in this century, the ideology of power and domination has appeared again. . . ."

92. Rose, *Mourning Becomes the Law*, 30. See 42–54 for a devastating critique of Spielberg's *Schindler's List* as symptomatic of this phenomenon. Rose served for several years as a consultant to the Polish Commission for the Future of Auschwitz.

93. George Bush, "The State of the Union 2002," A22.

94. The hypostasization of evil is undoubtedly a function of liberal democracy's inability to articulate substantive common goods.

95. Of course this obscures the role of that power in bringing about those atrocities. "Free labor," for instance, as the solution to slavery obscures the role that Lockean conceptions of property play in making the slave trade possible.

96. George W. Bush, "The State of the Union 2002," A22. Bush continues, "None of us would ever wish the evil that was done on September 11, yet after America was attacked, it was as if our entire country looked into a mirror and saw our better selves." One would hope that this event might have caused us to see more in the mirror than just that.

97. Augustine, *De Civ.*, XIX.7.

98. In a world in which "evil is real" and must be opposed, it is difficult not to conclude that it is not the goddess foreign injustice, incarnate in the malice of our enemies who offers the opportunities. The repeated language in these speeches of "being called by history" to act does not relieve this concern.

99. Augustine, *De Civ.*, I.10.

7

Local Politics: The Political Place of the Household in Augustine's *City of God*

Kevin L. Hughes[1]

M UCH INK HAS BEEN SPILLED over several generations of scholarship about what Augustine's political theory is. Is politics the realm of "confession," as P. D. Bathory suggests?[2] Or is Augustine a "political realist" who holds little hope for the transformation of the coercive power of politics? Is Augustine the forerunner of the classical liberal "naked public square," the neutral meeting ground for interests religious and profane?[3] Most of these readings presuppose that what Augustine articulates in the *City of God* is a political theory of state and society, or something of the sort. While I do not deny that Augustine has something to say about the proper conduct of political officers and institutions,[4] I think that there is a potential mistake in taking his arguments only at such a grand scale. The mistake is both theoretical and practical. Theoretically, it is not at all clear that "political theory" as it is usually construed had any appeal or meaning to Augustine—forms of government, for example, do not seem to occupy him all that much, and when he does in fact turn to them, he is as inclined to see Athenian democracy and Babylonian tyranny as comparable forms of a "res publica" as he is to distinguish Roman virtue from tyrannical vice. So, if Augustine has a political theory, it is of a different sort than we expect. Several of the chapters in this book are devoted to this theoretical issue.

It is the practical mistake that I wish to consider here. When I have taught texts in political theory to undergraduates, I have been struck by both the facility with which they discuss matters of freedom and rights and the degree to which they find such issues utterly irrelevant. When reading Adam Smith and Marx, for example, students find talk about free markets and labor rather interesting to discuss, but with little or no impact upon the practical conduct of their life. Insofar as these texts are "political theory," they are removed from most students' concerns, since politics does not seem to be a sphere of choice. Many of my students, for example, do not vote, because they perceive themselves to have little or no impact upon the political process. In a world dominated by global media, the significance of a single vote does not seem to have an impact upon them. Politics, rather than being the pursuit of social life as such, is a separate sphere of action having to do with governance, and they find this sphere to be outside their concerns for most of the time. In other words, politics is currently something to be informed about and to comment upon, rather than something to be done. So to take Augustine's concern to be "political theory" is for students to perhaps make it more interesting than theology (!), but it is also to remove it concretely from any practical effect on their lives.

This is a misuse of any work of political theory, but it is especially misguided as a way to read Augustine. The impact of Augustine's *magnum opus et arduum* is first and perhaps best felt not at the level of constitutional theory or of world history and the governance of empires, but on a much smaller, humbler scale, within what Augustine calls the "beginning or component" (*initium sive particula*) of any city—the household. The *City of God* is addressed fundamentally to the philosophical question, "How shall I live?" Or, better, the properly political question, "How shall we live?" Such questions must be addressed within the immediate context of one's life and circumstances. They require, therefore, attention to the immediate social context of family and household. It is at this level, before all others, that the work is political.

In treating the household as the fundamental political unit, Augustine is in company with Aristotle and classical political theory. Where Augustine departs from Aristotle is in defining the city or commonwealth *theologically*, by the degree to which a community is able to or fails to love God. The thrust of this chapter is twofold. First, I intend to argue for a recovery of the notion of the household/family as a political sphere of some creativity and freedom— an argument shared by many ancient thinkers. Consequently, however, I wish to suggest that such a robust household politics is possible, at least in circumstances like our own, only through something like Augustine's *theological* reading of political identity.

The Political Household (1): Aristotle and Classical Thought

To say that the household was the fundamental unit of the *polis* is at least as old as Aristotle, more than seven hundred years before Augustine wrote. Aristotle, in *Politics* Book I, offers a genealogy of the *polis*: The household is fundamental, but not self-sufficient, so households band together to form villages, and eventually villages congeal into the *polis*, which for Aristotle represented the first *complete* political unit (i.e., the unit large enough to be self-sufficient).[5] As he sets out in the *Politics* to explore the nature of political leadership, he begins by exploring the qualities of household management. "The household is the partnership constituted by nature for [the needs of] daily life" (I.2, 1252b), and it requires skill in "mastery (of slaves), marital rule, and parental rule" (I.3, 1253b). In addition, says Aristotle, there are some who say household management requires "business expertise" (I.3, 1253b), but this is a claim he wishes to investigate. The household manager must have facility in "acquiring possessions," (I.4, 1253b), and these include matters of trade and currency, but there is a risk attendant to such skills. (Our word "economy" is derived from the Greek word for "house.") With the invention of currency, wealth becomes an unlimited asset (1257a), and household managers could easily be led into thinking that their necessary economic skills should be devoted to the acquisition of wealth itself, what Aristotle calls "business expertise." "So some hold that this [business expertise] is the work of expertise in household management, and they proceed on the supposition that they should either preserve or increase without limit their property in money" (I.9.15, 1257b). Such confusion is to be expected, he says, since knowledge of economic matters is the tool both for wealth acquisition and household management.[6] However, Aristotle scorns those who are so confused—they are interested with merely living, not with living well (I.9.16, 1257b). The unlimited pursuit of wealth is simply the pursuit of survival run amok; the household manager pursues only as much wealth as will contribute to the flourishing—the "living well"—of his household. Said another way, Aristotle's criterion for good household management is that it "gives more serious attention to human beings than to inanimate possessions" (I.13.1, 1250b), in which possessions are put to the purpose of human well-being.

Aristotle thus sees the household as a community that can and should be "serious about living well,"[7] but the flourishing life of a household can easily be subverted by an inordinate attachment to wealth or possessions. And it is only once he has presented these options on the scale of household management that Aristotle feels free to proceed to discuss the traditional political question of the best regime. The implication seems clear—the fundamental political opportunities and dangers are already present within the microcosmic project of managing a household. The household, like the *polis* of which it is a part, can either be a community of flourishing life, in which all possessions are directed in the proper scale to that end, or it can slavishly or endlessly pursue wealth at the expense of other virtues.[8]

Aristotle's insight more than likely influenced Augustine indirectly, as it was carried into the philosophical schools of the Hellenistic world. The Stoics—a more proximate influence on St. Augustine—root social and political life in the marriage of a man and woman. For Cicero, "the origin of society is in the joining of man and woman, next in children, then in a single household, all things held in common; this is the foundation of the city and, so to speak, the seed-bed of the commonwealth (*seminarium rei publicae*)."[9] In Stoic terms, this ascending social scale was rooted in the natural desires of the human person—the natural instinct of self-preservation extends to or "appropriates" the preservation of family, friends, cities, and even humanity as a whole.[10]

Augustine inherits this rich tradition of reflection on the household from the Hellenistic world. Aristotle and the Stoics agree that the household is a basic building block of the city, and it therefore has a fundamental role in the formation of citizens. However, set in the context of Augustine's theological vision in the *City of God*, traditional teaching on the household will take on a new sense and create the possibility not just for formation, but for resistance.

The Political Household (2): Augustine's *City of God*

Augustine seems to take over the Stoic vision in the *City of God*, but in his hands it takes a slightly different shape:

> Now God our master, teaches two chief precepts, love of God and love of neighbor; and in them a man finds three objects for his love: God, himself, and his neighbor; and a man who loves God is not wrong in loving himself. It follows therefore that he will be concerned also that his neighbor should love God, since he is told to love his neighbor as himself; and the same is true of his concern for his wife, his children, for the members of his household, and for all other men, so far as possible. . . . For this reason he will be at peace, as far as lies in him, with all men, in that peace among men, that ordered harmony; and the basis of this order is the observance of two rules: first, to do no harm to anyone, and, secondly, to help everyone whenever possible.[11]

Augustine shares the vision of social and political life that begins from wife, children, and household, but he has already given this Stoic argument a theological turn: the foundational relationship is not the instinct to self-preservation, but the love of God, and it is that love which applies to oneself and one's neighbor by appropriation. One loves oneself as a gift of the Creator, and one loves one's neighbor for the very same reason.

The principal sphere of the exercise of this appropriated love is one's household, since "obviously, both in the order of nature and in the framework of human society, he has easier and more immediate contact with them; he can exercise his concern for them."[12] The household is a manageable sphere for the exercise of concern; practically speaking, one can only express care for people who are within reach. But the household is not a private sphere, different in kind from the world of politics; it, too, is an "ordered harmony about the giving and obeying of orders."[13] The household is a domain of command and obedience, just like the city or the empire.

When Augustine speaks of a harmony of giving and obeying orders, he has a very specific model in mind. The classical Roman family is led by the *paterfamilias*, the father whose authority is final. Household politics occur when "the husband gives orders to the wife, parents to children, masters to servants," and when "wives obey husbands, the children obey their parents, the servants their masters."[14] As many have noted, Augustine is strikingly non-revolutionary in his sense of the impact of Christian faith upon the institutional structures of the family: the household still is under the headship of the *paterfamilias*, who still may and should correct those under his authority, by force if necessary. And those under his authority include not only family members, but also slaves. In this, Augustine is very much a man of the Empire, and he could invoke the New Testament here as well[15]; the structures of the household persist.

In fact, on the first reading Augustine's teaching on the household may not seem at all novel or interesting; he seems simply to rehearse the classical Aristotelian and Stoic insights:

> Now a man's house (*domus*) ought to be the beginning, or rather a small component part (*initium sive particular debet esse civitatis*) of the city, and every beginning is directed to (*referatur ad*) some end of its own kind, and every component part is directed to the completeness of the whole of which it forms a part. The implication is quite apparent, that domestic peace is directed toward (*referatur ad*) the peace of the city—that is, the ordered harmony of those who live together in a house in the matter of giving and obeying orders is directed toward the ordered harmony concerning authority and obedience obtaining among citizens. Consequently, it is fitting that the father of a household should take his rules from the law of the city and govern his household in such a way that fits with the peace of the city.[16]

This seems rather straightforward and analytical, and in this passage Augustine sounds most like a political philosopher. So straightforward is it that one might be tempted to understand it as referring to the relationship, say, between the way I run my household and the form of governance in Media, Pennsylvania or the United States. And so, in incautious moments, perhaps, do some seem to take it.[17]

In this view, it is not at all surprising that Augustine does not consider paternal authority, coercive force, and slavery to be elements alien to a household set upon the love of God. Here the household takes the laws of the city of Rome and, as one scholar puts it, "superimposes another meaning"[18] on these structures and relationships. The impact of Christian faith in the household seems to be above all a question of attitude: one can be a slaveholder, but one must be a good slaveholder. In this account, Augustine does seem a bit like an apologist for the status quo.

However, Augustine interrupts his treatment of the household to spend quite a bit of time on the issue of slavery in particular, which might suggest that there is more of an argument to be made than appears at first sight. Instead of arguing for the conventional qualities of traditional Roman structures and customs, Augustine builds a *theological* argument for slavery (which suggests that he might think it needs one). That theological argument may leave us unsatisfied. We see slavery and patriarchal dominion themselves as disordered and so we attribute them to the *libido dominandi*; for Augustine, slavery and authority could be used rightly if rightly ordered, and are abused, not used, by the *libido dominandi*. But if we find the argument unsettling, we should at least see what sort of argument it is. His arguments for slavery and coercive force are built upon his theological assessment of the human condition as fallen, not on a particular understanding of custom or culture. In the "order of nature,"[19] says Augustine, humans were created to have dominion over the nonrational elements of creation. Slavery—the subjection of human persons to the dominion of other humans—is not natural, but mandated as a recompense of sinners. As long as the heavenly city lives on pilgrimage, humanity remains in its fractured and wounded state, and so slavery remains as a fitting institution.[20] Like it or not, this argument for slavery is theologically rooted in Augustine's anthropology, and therefore, it can stand independent of particular customs or regimes. Likewise, the paternal use of coercive force is required to eliminate threats to the peace of the household through disobedience. It is considered remedial, ". . . for the benefit of the offender, intended to readjust him to the domestic peace from which he had broken away."[21] Augustine argues here (as elsewhere in sermons and letters) that a father would fail in his responsibilities if he did not act to restrain his son from sin or punish a sin already committed. These structures for Augustine are given in Scripture and are legitimate and often necessary avenues for the performance of charity.[22]

That Augustine takes pains to construct these arguments theologically suggests that the structures of the household, despite appearances, may potentially be less conventional than they seem.[23] Such a shift in perspective is possible when one comes to terms with Augustine's assessment of the relationship between the household and the city, the *ciuitas*.

Ciuitas and *Domus* in Augustine's Theological Politics

Ciuitas in Augustine's careful usage in the book refers to the communities ordered by either love of God or love of self: "Two loves built two cities—the earthly city built by love of self to the point of disregard for God; the heavenly city built by the love of God to the point of disregard for self."[24] These two cities are intermingled as long as the Heavenly City lives on pilgrimage here in this earthly life. *Ciuitas* has become a theological designation, no longer designating any particular geopolitical regime, large or small; rather, it designates each of the two communities into which all humanity is divided. In this light, the particular geographical and political structures and institutions that conventionally designate a "city" or an "empire" are understood in Augustinian terms as representative of a deeper cultural and theological identity, not constitutive of it. Borrowing Marxist terms, we might say that "Rome" itself—its political institutions, etc.—is the "superstructure" that expresses the "base" of the distorted love that constitutes the earthly city. Rome is a "city" only insofar as its regime is typical and representative of that (worldwide) community that loves itself to the point of disregard for God. This worldwide community of self-love generates institutions and structures that aim to protect and perpetuate earthly, temporal goods. The heavenly city makes use of these, since it requires temporal peace "until this mortal state for which that kind of peace is essential, passes away,"[25] but it always does so *ad hoc*. The pilgrim contingent of the Heavenly City lives "a life of captivity in this earthly city as in a foreign land."

Ciuitas is thus in the *City of God* first and foremost a theological term, and it is only subsequently applied to particular arrangements in Rome or Athens or Babylon for the earthly city, and, in a provisional sense, to the church for the heavenly city. So much is fundamental to the understanding of the *City of God* at all, and of Book Nineteen in particular. But this terminology must be applied consistently; when Augustine refers in *City of God* 19.16 to the "laws" or "rules" that the householder adopts from his city, it is not so much a function of where the household is found geographically, but rather of what the household loves. In other words, the "ordered harmony concerning the giving and obeying of orders" is, for citizens of the Heavenly City, a harmony ordered to the love of God; for earthly citizens, it is a "harmony" ordered by the love of domination (*libido dominandi*).

Indeed, it is in the ordering to charity that these relationships are distinguished from those in the households of earthly citizens: "But in the household of the just man who lives by faith and who is still on pilgrimage, far from that Heavenly City, even those who give orders are the servants of those whom they appear to command."[26] Their proper ordering to the love of God transfigures household relationships, such that leadership becomes service (even slavery) undertaken in love. All in a household are equal with respect to the worship of God and distinguished only in their proper roles and responsibilities in the maintenance of domestic peace.[27] Household positions become offices *pro tempore*; they engage the officeholder, but do not define him or her. Households therefore become first and foremost communities for the exercise of concern (*consulere*) and right worship (*colere ad Deum*); only secondarily are they structured for the maintenance of temporal peace. The two relations are formally distinct, although they are never found in isolation: the son is always fellow pilgrim and subordinate son, and the proper exercise of his life as a pilgrim in the household is in the role of subordinate son. But such roles are finally contingent, not ultimate.[28] The household, as Williams says, becomes a "'laboratory of the spirit,' a place for the maturation of souls (the soul of the ruler as well as the ruled),"[29] wherein all learn the practice of charity.

"Household" (*domus*) thus has a more empirical sense for Augustine, without the theological metonymy that unites the earthly city and Rome, for example. While he will sometimes refer to the church as the *domus Dei*, this seems in context to be more explicitly metaphorical in practice, and his treatment of the *domus* in Book Nineteen seems to be rooted soundly in the empirical and the mundane. O'Donovan notices that the *domus* has a certain concrete exemplarity in *City of God* 19.16–17, and from this he makes a "reasonable inference" that Augustine "thinks of a Christian household as achieving a concrete form in a way that a Christian city does not."[30] If this is so, perhaps it is because Augustine imagines that charity is more possible in that community with which "both in the order of nature and in the framework of society he has easier and more immediate contact."[31] But Augustine goes on to say that the peace obtained in this concrete household form "is directed to the peace of the city." So the household is never an isolated unit; it always stands in some relation to the larger set of social relations called the "city."[32] The household is thus connected to a community of faith, but this community "calls out citizens from all nations and so collects a society of aliens, speaking all languages."[33] While it is potentially alien to its next-door neighbor, the household of faith finds fellowship in a universal, multicultural community.

Civic Relations: The Household on Pilgrimage

If my sense of Augustine's consistent theological use of *ciuitas* is right, then the supposedly analytic passage at the end of *City of God* 19.16 about the household taking its laws from the city of which it is a part must refer to the ways in which particular households point toward the theological communities of ordered or disordered loves. In the contrast that follows at the beginning of

City of God 19.17, Augustine draws out a very grammatically nuanced comparison between an earthly and a heavenly household and the ends toward which they are directed. The peace of an earthly citizen's household, says Augustine, can only be aimed or directed toward (*sectatur*) the "earthly peace which comes from the affairs and benefits of the earthly city," *as an end*, while the household of the heavenly citizen looks forward to (*exspectat*) the eternal [affairs and benefits] promised to the Heavenly City in the future.[34] In the mean time, the pilgrim Heavenly City makes use of (*utitur*) earthly affairs and temporal things *as means* to its proper eternal end. The earthly household has a foreshortened scope, precisely because it is part of a city whose end is constricted to temporal things. The household of faith, on the other hand, is part of the Heavenly City and is directed toward an eternal destiny.

The net effect of this rather tedious reading of a few lines of text is that one must imagine that, if I live at 221B Baker Street, I may very well be a citizen of a different *ciuitas* than the resident of 221A, which means the *lex ciuitatis*, the laws of the city by which I run my household might be radically other than that of my neighbor. Although the structure of authority may appear the same, our households may be as different in orientation as "the love of self to the point of disregard for God" and the "love of God to the point of disregard for self." For Augustine, this difference outweighs any and all similarities of structure or custom we neighbors may share.

The household of faith is part of a different city, a different culture, in a sense. Its activities with reference to the temporal goods of life may overlap with its neighbors, but only in the way that households in rural America and rural Korea might overlap in the raising of canines. Both share in the activities of housing, feeding, and tending to the needs of dogs, but to radically different ends: for one household, such care is intended toward companionship; for the other, toward a good meal. The same means are deployed to different ends. To live as part of the Heavenly City, then, is to live "what we may call a life of captivity in this earthly city as in a foreign land." However, the life of captivity cannot lend itself simply to a isolationist siege mentality within the household of faith; the cities (and their concrete parts, households) share the mortal condition of life here and now, so they must preserve harmony between themselves "in things that are relevant to it." And, for the most part, this means that the household of faith remains integrally engaged with the regime under which it lives, since the earthly city of which the latter is an expression is constituted by the pursuit of things relevant to the mortal condition. The difference remains that the earthly goods are ends in themselves to the earthly city, while they are only means to the household of faith. And because the former city is doomed to failure in the end, the relationship between them remains *ad hoc*.

Such *ad hoc* arrangements are always undertaken with care. It is worth noting that as soon as Augustine has given an argument for the cooperative relationship of the two cities, he immediately adds words of caution:

> But this earthly city had wise men of its own that are rejected by holy teaching. Either led astray by their own speculation or deluded by demons, these thinkers came to believe that there are many gods to be won over for human affairs, and that they have, as it were, different departments with different delegated responsibilities.[35]

He goes on to discuss the ways in which Roman life is soaked in the pagan pantheon: the body is divided up among different deities for the head, the neck, and so on; the mind is divvied up among gods of lust, anger, potential, education; social life is dispersed among gods of flocks, grain, forests, money, marriage, birth, fertility, and so on. To these holy teachings opposes the singular worship of the one true God.

This passage revisits briefly what Augustine has discussed in great detail in Book Four, where he paints a rococo portrait of paganism, where supersaturating details and flourish of deity after deity overburden the picture to such a point where it collapses into restless incoherence.[36] Augustine points out in Book Four that philosophers and politicians preserve the pagan system among the people in full knowledge of its incoherence, since "by this means they bound them tighter, as it were, to the citizen community, so that they might bring them under control and keep them there by the same technique."[37] Pagan religion survives and thrives in Rome by the conspiracy of the demonic forces it invokes and pragmatic imperialist politicians as a means of social control. In revisiting this argument in Book Nineteen in his discussion of the relationship between the two cities, Augustine seems to make the earlier argument more pointed: Roman culture is not simply a public ritual activity, a spectacle of civic unity, a matter of public, as opposed to private, life; rather, it has colonized the imagination, spreading and settling in the most intimate and the most mundane details of human life. The activity of the household of faith within such a context must be handled with caution and prudence, since the walls of the household are permeable and prone to these colonizing powers.

The household of faith, then, is both the spirit's laboratory and its safe house. First, it is a sphere of social relations that is of sufficiently manageable proportions that it can teach its members the practice of charity.[38] Members of the household of faith learn how the love of God is appropriated to the love of neighbor, how leadership is properly service, how all humans share equality in worshiping the true God, and so on. But precisely as such a sphere in which charity can be learned, the household becomes a safe house, a refuge from a culture whose ethos is established by the passion for glory, the *libido dominandi*, the worship of false gods, or any other such distortions of love.[39] Such an *ethos* colonizes the Roman imagination and settles throughout Roman private life, so the household must be vigilant in its pursuit of the laws of its true city, the Heavenly City.

In the end, Augustine's formal resemblance to Aristotelian or Stoic notions of the relationship of household to city may obscure important differences between them. Aristotle's household remains integrally connected to the city of which it is a part. It is from within that place of integral connection that the Aristotelian householder must take up his concern for "living well." This task, however, is made considerably more difficult if one were to be integrally and inexorably connected with a city and a culture that have lost the distinction between living and living well. In such a situation, one would require the dialectical and protreptic exercise of the philosophy to resist the influence of such a city, and one would find one's household permanently hobbled, unable to seek its proper end in the *polis*. One might imagine a philosophical household within the Aristotelian regime, but such a household would seem to carry within it a sense of tragic incompleteness.

Augustine's theological understanding of the city as constituted theologically—transnationally and transculturally—by the ordering of loves, enables the household within that city to imagine the world otherwise, to see the possibilities disclosed by an eschatological orientation toward the "Heavenly City," in which one can participate proleptically and imperfectly now. Augustine's household of faith is already participant and member of a city that seeks its proper end in the worship (*latreia*) of the one true God. For Augustine, it is the Roman regime, not the household, that is tragically incomplete, an expression of the earthly city destined to fall short of its desired end. While both Aristotle and Augustine retrieve a strong sense of the household as a vital political community—a sphere of freedom within which a social body can make free choices to live well—Augustine's household of faith offers the possibility and even the promise of participation and wholeness in a city of peace, even in the midst of a hostile culture.

Household Politics and Household Economy: Sketching Some Implications

Since I began with the practical concern of teaching Augustine to students as more than an interesting period piece, it may be worthwhile to consider briefly the practical effects of Augustine's vision of the politics of the household. It is difficult for us to "have ears to hear" Augustine (or Aristotle) in our contemporary world, since it seems that we have lost the sense that the household is a political unit. Rather than conceiving of the family as a constructive, productive experiment in a way of shared life, we tend to conceive of the household as the private horizon of consumption. "The modern household," says Wendell Berry, "is the place where the consumptive couple do their consuming. Nothing productive is done there. Such work as is done there is done at the expense of the resident couple of family, and to the profit of suppliers of energy and household technology. For entertainment, the inmates consume televisions or purchase other consumable diversion elsewhere."[40] The reduction of the household to a community of shared consumption comes in the wake of globalization, where "The world has become less divided, but more disparate."[41] As people find themselves farther and farther removed from the production of resources and material upon which they are dependent, and as they simultaneously are alienated from their own productive labor as it is siphoned into the globalized information economy, consumption seems to be the only remaining realm of freedom within the household. We establish ourselves through what we buy. As a local convenience store's recent campaign says, "My choice, my Wawa." In other words, "I establish my capacity to choose through the sandwich I purchase at the local Wawa."

But such a vision of the household has eerie resonance with Augustine's vision of the Roman household colonized by the Roman imperial pagan ideology. If Augustine saw the areas of private life, such as sex, as colonized by the various deities of the hymen, of penetration, etc.,[42] we see sexuality colonized by soft-core marketing of Victoria's Secret and contraceptive patches. If the care of children was crowded with Vaticanus (the god of babies' cries), Levana (the goddess of holding babies), and Cunina (the goddess of cradles),[43] our own nurseries overflow with Playtex baby bottles, Similac formula, and Baby Bjorn baby carrier—all name brands which become identified with their function. Such insights are hardly new and earth shattering, nor are they unique to cranky counter-cultural Christians. Don DeLillo's novel *White Noise* sees the sacral quality of consumer culture, but he seems to be at once amused and enthralled by it.

DeLillo's slightly absurdist portrait of American culture in the throes of late capitalism is strikingly religious (or "pseudo-religious," as some of my more devout students prefer me to say) and, although it is now more than fifteen years old, remarkably descriptive of our current climate. (Indeed, one suspects that the excesses of the dot.com nineties have made some dimensions of the portrait seem less absurd!)

The protagonist, Jack Gladney, an apparently successful but insecure and anxious academic at a small midwestern college, narrates the novel. Jack has been married three times before, and his fourth wife, Babette, has been mar-

ried and divorced twice. They assemble the children from these several marriages under one roof to make their family, a group which they try carefully to
forge and craft into a cohesive whole. Family life in late modernity is already
something new, a pastiche that requires creativity and improvisation to hold
together at all.

By narrating Jack's family through the daily and weekly grind, DeLillo's
novel shines light on the situation of the family—whatever it is—in the context of late modernity. Such illumination occasionally arises in the form of explicit commentary by Jack. After a humorous volley of misquotes, half-truths,
and rumors passed around the family on a Friday TV night, Jack muses,

> The family is the cradle of the world's misinformation. There must be something
> in family life that generates factual error. Overcloseness, the noise and the heat
> of being. Perhaps something even deeper, like the need to survive. Murray says
> we are fragile creatures surrounded by a world of hostile facts. Facts threaten our
> happiness and security. The deeper we delve into the nature of things, the looser
> our structure may seem to become. The family process works toward sealing off
> the world. . . . The family is strongest where objective reality is most likely to be
> misinterpreted.[44]

There is an intimate connection between worldview and the shape of the family. Jack suggests that the family is in the business of a sort of therapeutic misinformation, precisely because the state of the world is violent. "Fragile creatures" take refuge from "a world of hostile facts" in the family, engaging in a
collective fantasy that insulates them from the hostility of the real. Of course,
the center of this collective fantasy in the late modern/postmodern world is
the television, which fills the background throughout the novel with com-
mercials and factoids: "There are forms of vertigo that do not include spin-
ning . . . and other trends that could dramatically impact your portfolio. . . .
Toyota Celica."[45] The family in *White Noise* has become a community of sheer
consumption, pursuing an illusory stability, power, and control through robust consumerism.

The supermarket thus becomes an American analogue to a Tibetan temple:
it "recharges us spiritually . . . prepares us, it's a gate or a pathway."[46] Emerging from the supermarket, Jack and Babette feel renewed, almost reborn:

> It seemed to me that Babette and I, in the mass and variety of our purchases, in
> the sheer plenitude those crowded bags suggested, the weight and size and num-
> ber, the familiar package designs and vivid lettering, the giant sizes, the family
> bargain packs with Day-Glo sale stickers, in the sense of replenishment we felt,
> the sense of well-being, the security and contentment these products brought to
> some snug home in our souls—it seemed we had achieved a fullness of being

that is not known to people who need less, expect less, who plan their lives around lonely walks in the evening.[47]

Not only the act of consuming, but the products themselves and even their market-driven packaging become markers of tranquility, of "fullness of being," which nourish the consuming family in a way that exceeds the traditional life of simplicity. Consumerism has become the spiritual practice, the religious worship, of the late-capitalist household. The novel's religious sense of this pursuit expands in a scene that portrays a mall-shopping binge into a liturgy of consumption.

Jack, who has created a professional persona as a mysterious and foreboding scholar of Hitler Studies, runs into a colleague off campus. Seeing Jack out of his usual uniform of academic robes and dark glasses, the colleague is bemused and sees Jack as "harmless" and "indistinct." His psychic defenses devastated, Jack is put "in the mood to shop." His family accompanies him into the mall,

> puzzled but excited by my desire to buy. When I could not decide between two shirts, they encouraged me to buy both. . . . The two girls scouted ahead, spotting things they thought I might want or need, running back to get me, to clutch my arms, plead with me to follow. They were my guides to endless well-being. People swarmed through the boutiques and gourmet shops. Organ music rose from the great court. We smelled chocolate, popcorn, cologne; we smelled rugs and furs, hanging salamis and deathly vinyl. My family gloried in the event. I was one of them, shopping at last. . . . I began to grow in value and self-regard. I filled myself out, found new aspects of myself, located a person I'd forgotten existed. Brightness settled around me. . . . We drove home in silence. We went to our respective rooms, wishing to be alone.[48]

Empowered by this ritual feast of consumerism in its organ-filled cathedral, Jack returns home with his family in silence. Shopping becomes an ecstatic exercise in transcendence that resolves itself into a holy silence.

When I read this text with students, they smile at the humor, but it is a knowing smile; they recognize themselves in passages like these, magnified, perhaps, but not altered, by DeLillo's ironic narrative. *White Noise* puts its finger on the pulse of the family in postmodernity: faced with the overwhelming hostility of the world, the family becomes a refuge but, as such, it takes refuge only in the misinformation, the illusion of happiness that the TV both represents and conveys. Households in late modernity become vehicles of consumption. They are colonized precisely by the "world of hostile facts" from which they wish to retreat.

In such a context, the "household of faith" is still possible, but the challenge is significant. Consumption and exchange are necessary transactions for the household to tend to "the things pertaining to mortal life," but, at the same time, they are soaked with the consumerist ideology that DeLillo so blithely illuminates. The household of faith will have to be careful stewards of its consumption, therefore, if it is to resist the infiltration of consumerism. For Wendell Berry, the "reformation of our private or household economies" begins here: "What we must do is use well the considerable power we have as consumers: the power of choice. We can choose to buy or not to buy, and we can choose what to buy."[49] Consuming well is more difficult than it may seem, however, since it requires an imaginative recovery of a wider horizon of choice than marketing economies produce. Whereas consumer choice usually reduces to "Pick any of these options, from A through Z," consuming well will require being open to the choice *not* to pick any of the above.[50]

Beyond such strategic consumption, however, the household can cultivate new habits of production, so that the home becomes more than a consumptive space. Household politics involves a household economy, and an economy is properly a balance of production and consumption. The power of the household to produce seems to be obscured by the exigencies of suburban consumer life, and yet for Nicholas Boyle it is vital to the recovery of what he calls "Christian humanism." "To think of ourselves purely as consumer is to misread fundamentally the most important social developments of the last hundred years. We are . . . producers too, and this fact is systematically kept from our minds by 'the market' itself and by its intellectual fellow-travelers."[51] Berry, too, recommends that a married couple "makes around itself a household economy that involves the work of both wife and husband, that gives them a measure of economic independence and self-protection, a measure of self-employment, a measure of freedom, as well as a common ground and a common satisfaction."[52] In other words, such practices of production cultivate within the household a sense of independence from the colonizing culture of consumerism while at the same time nurturing habits of charity within the household, since, as Berry says elsewhere, "the right scale in work gives power to affection. . . . An adequate local culture, among other things, keeps work within the reach of love."[53]

In sum, the household of faith in the *pax Americana* will need creatively to reimagine its practices of production and consumption, because the dominant ethos in the culture of globalization is consumerist. As DeLillo suggests, such an ethos carries within it a "theology," an account or worldview which, I am suggesting, is incompatible with the habits and practices of Christian life. Household politics must therefore include home economics, for it is these practices that can enable the household both to engage with this earthly city in those matters relevant to the condition of mortal life and to resist the colonization of the imagination by the idolatry of consumerism. As I hope is apparent, I do not intend to suggest that the form of the household as Augustine discusses it—with the authoritative *paterfamilias* as the disseminator of commands—is the proper form for the school of charity. At least in the *City of God*, Augustine seems to approve of the Roman paterfamilial structure not because authority is properly invested in the male as father, but rather because some structure of authority, some sphere of command and obedience, is necessary for social life in the world of sin. The *paterfamilias* seemed to him to fit these constraints. If we live in a world that does not quite know what (if any) models remain for family structure, the household of faith today may embrace some plurality in the ways the sphere of command and obedience is ordered.

My argument has been both simpler and more radical. I am arguing merely *that* the household be considered as a school of charity, in whatever form. In other words, what Augustine offers us is a vigorous notion of the household as a viable arena for the formation and support of persons in the love of God and neighbor. This is a simple notion, but its consequences for the practices of everyday life may be more profound. Such a notion will require the household to adopt strategies of resistance to the cultural forms of consumerism that structure and constrain Western life, including family life. The family must be, as Williams says, a "laboratory of the spirit," an environment protected from arbitrary influence and thus enabled to cultivate spiritual habits of charity. Such habits will inform and constrain subsidiary habits of consumption and production—those things necessary for household management, as Aristotle would say—or "those things necessary for earthly peace," in a more Augustinian frame. It is in this way that the household of faith, on pilgrimage in the twenty-first century as it was in the fifth, may "know only one God who is worthy of worship and who alone is due the service which the Greeks call *latreia*."[54]

Notes

1. This essay is the fruit of many long conversations over coffee about the *City of God* with my friend and colleague Thomas W. Smith, who has been both critical sounding board for this argument and model of the householder it aims to portray. My deepest thanks to him. I will refer to what has become a standard edition of the *City of God*: *Sancti Aurelii Augustini, de Civitate Dei* (eds. B. Dombart and A. Kalb; *Corpus Christianorum, Series Latina*, vols. 47-48; Turnhout: Brepols, 1954), hereafter DCD. The translation is taken from *Concerning the City of God against the Pagans* (trans. Henry Bettenson; New York: Penguin, 1984), unless otherwise noted.

2. P. D. Bathory, *Political Theory as Public Confession: The Social and Political Thought of St. Augustine of Hippo* (New Brunswick, NJ: Transaction Books, 1981).

3. While the term "naked public square" is that of Richard John Neuhaus, *The Naked Public Square* (2nd ed. Grand Rapids: Eerdmans, 1996), the term fits well Robert Markus's discussion of Augustine in *Saeculum: History and Society in the The-*

ology of St. Augustine (Cambridge: Cambridge University Press, 1970; rev. ed. 1988).

4. For the best reading of the political implications of the *City of God* on a larger scale, see Rowan Williams, "Politics and the Soul: A Reading of the *City of God*," *Milltown Studies* 19:20 (1987) 55-72; Oliver O'Donovan, "Augustine's *City of God* XIX and Western Political Thought," *Dionysius* XI (December 1987) 89–110; Thomas W. Smith, "The Glory and Tragedy of Politics," in this volume.

5. ". . . the partnership that is most authoritative of all and embraces all the others does so particularly, and aims at the most authoritative good of all. This is what is called the city," Aristotle, *The Politics* (trans. Carnes Lord; Chicago: University of Chicago Press, 1984) I.1, 1252a5. See also 1252b, 28-30. All translations will be taken from the Lord edition.

6. Aristotle, *Politics*, 1257a. "For possessions serve the same use, though not in the same respect, but in the one case the end is increase, in the other something else."

7. Note that this seems to contradict Hannah Arendt's claims about the nature of the "private life" of the household versus the free public realm of politics in Greek political philosophy. See *The Human Condition* (Chicago: University of Chicago Press, 1958) 28-30. Also see Paul A. Rahe, "The Primacy of Politics in Ancient Greece," *American Historical Review* 89 (1984) 265–93.

8. Cf. I.9.16-17: ". . . since that desire of theirs is without limit, they also desire what is productive of unlimited things. . . . For as gratification consists in excess, they seek the sort that is productive of the excess characteristic of gratification; and if they are unable to supply it through expertise in commerce, they attempt this in some other fashion, using each sort of capacity in a way not according to nature."

9. Cicero, *de Officiis*, Loeb Classical Library (Cambridge: Harvard University Press, 1975) 1.17.54.

10. According to C. J. de Vogel, this doctrine is widely found among the Stoics, but may have roots in Theophrastus and Aristotle. See C. J. de Vogel, *Greek Philosophy*, 3 vols. (Leiden: E.J. Brill, 1953–1959) vol. 3, 127ff.

11. DCD 19.14: "*Iam uero quia duo praecipua praecepta, hoc est dilectionem Dei et dilectionem proximi, docet magister Deus, in quibus tria inuenit homo quae diligat, Deum, se ipsum, et proximum, atque ille in se diligendo non errat, qui Deum diligit: consequense est, ut etiam proximo ad diligendum Deum consulat, quem iubetur sicut se ipsum diligere (sic uxori, sic filiis, sic domesticis, sic ceteris quibus potuerit hominibus), et ad hoc sibi a proximo, si forte indiget, consuli uelit; ac per hoc erit pacatus, quantum in ipso est, omni homini pace hominum, id est ordinata concordia, cuius hic ordo est, primum ut nulli noceat, deinde ut etiam prosit cui potuerit.*"

12. DCD 19.14, ". . . *ad eos quippe habet oportuniorem facilioremque aditum consulendi, uel naturae ordine uel ipsius societatis humanae.*"

13. DCD 19.14, ". . . *ordinata imperandi oboediendique concordia cohabitantium . . .*"

14. DCD. 19.14, "*Imperant enim, qui consulunt; sicut uir uxori, parentes filiis, domini seruis. Oboediunt autem quibus consulitur; sicut mulieres maritis, filii parentibus, serui dominis.*"

15. E.g., Ephesians 5:21-6:9; Colossians 3:18-4:1; 1 Timothy 6:1–2.

16. DCD 19.16, "*Quia igitur hominis domus initium sive particula debet esse civitatis, omne autem initium ad aliquem sui generis finem et omnis pars ad universis, cuius pars est,*"

integritatem refertur; satis apparet esse, ut ordinata imperandi obeoediendique concordia cohabitantium referatur ad ordinatam imperandi oboediendique concordiam civium. Ita fit, ut ex lege civitatis praecepta sumere patrem familias oporteat, quibus domum suam sic regat, ut si paci adeomodata civitatis." Translation is that of Bettenson with the exception of "*referatur,*" which B. renders as "contributes."

17. See, e.g., Rowan Williams's comment in the context of a discussion of educational policy: R. Williams, *Lost Icons: Reflections on Cultural Bereavement* (Edinburgh: T. & T. Clark, 2000) 50. This stands in tension with his sensitive treatment of the issue in "Politics and the Soul," 62–64.

18. O'Donovan, "Augustine's *City of God* XIX," 104. O'Donovan's argument presents a stronger case for Augustine's vision of the household than the one I present here, but it does not seem quite strong enough to say that one "superimposes another meaning" on customary relationships. Augustine's rationale for slavery is itself given theologically.

19. DCD 19.15, "*Hoc naturalis ordo praescribit. . . . Rationalem factum ad imaginem suam noluit nisi inrationalibus dominari.*"

20. DCD 19.15–16.

21. DCD 19.16: "*. . . pro eius qui corripitur utilitate, ut paci unde dissiluerat coaptetur.*"

22. Indeed, we rightly congratulate ourselves for seeing the injustice of slavery, but often, in a globalized society, we fail to realize how much of our quality of life is built upon the slave or near-slave labor of third world labor markets. So perhaps we have not eliminated such institutions or relations from the functioning order of our households; we have just removed them to a distance that puts them beyond our contact and so beyond the "exercise of our concern" (*aditus consulendi*, cf. DCD 19.14).

23. In other words, the paterfamilial structure is practically efficient, but not necessarily essential to the pursuit of the proper end—the education in charity of the members of the household. The non-negotiable seems to be the necessity for broken human persons to be formed under some kind of authority. But Augustine is as prone to criticize the conventions of familial authority as he is to support them (cf. *Confessions* Book One), so one might leave open the possibility, in an admittedly revisionist fashion, of authorizing other structures of familial authority with Augustinian principles. See my brief comments at the end of this chapter for more on this.

24. DCD 14.28: "*Fecerunt itaque ciuitates duas amores duo, terrenam scilicet amor sui usque ad contemtum Dei, caelestem uero amor Dei usque ad contemtum sui.*" Translation mine.

25. DCD 19.17, "*. . . donec ipsa, cui talis pax necessaria est, mortalitas transeat.*"

26. DCD 19.14, "*Sed in domo iusti uiuentis ex fide et adhuc ab illa caelesti ciuitate peregrinantis etiam qui imperant seruiunt eis, quibus uidentur imperare.*"

27. DCD 19.16, "*Quocirca etiamsi habuerunt seruos iusti patres nostri, sic administrabant domesticam pacem, ut secundum haec temporalia bona filiorum sortem a seruorum condicione distinguerunt.*" This reference to "these temporal goods" should be taken to apply more broadly than inheritance, as some have done. See Brent D. Shaw, "The Family in Late Antiquity: The Experience of Augustine," *Past and Present* 115 (May 1987) 3–51, esp. 11; *sed contra*, DCD 19.13 for Augustine's broader understanding of temporal goods.

28. So, I think, O'Donovan is only partly right to see that Augustine's vision falls "considerably short of what is meant if we speak of the 'transformation' of cultural institutions." See Oliver O'Donovan, "Augustine's *City of God*," 104. While the authority structure appears to be the same, it is fundamentally changed, or, as Rowan Greer says, "transfigured": Rowan Greer, *Broken Lights and Mended Lives: Theology and Common Life in the Early Church* (University Park: Pennsylvania State University Press, 1986) 116.

29. Williams, "Politics and the Soul," 64.

30. Oliver O'Donovan, "Augustine's *City of God* XIX," 104.

31. DCD 19.14, "... *ad eos quippe habet opportuniorem facilioremque aditum consulendi.*"

32. In this way, Augustine echoes Aristotle, since the peace of the household, as a unit that cannot be self-sufficient, could only refer to that social unit that can, the city.

33. DCD 19.17, "*Haec ergo caelestis ciuitas dum peregrinatur in terra ex omnibus gentibus ciues euocat atque in omnibus linguis peregrinam colligit societatem, non curans quidquid in moribus legibus institutisque diuersum est . . .*"

34. In other words, these terms (*sectatur, exspectat*) at the beginning of 19.17 are to be taken as specifications of the term "*referatur*" in the preceding paragraph at the end of 19.16. The earthly household "is aimed" toward its larger whole; the heavenly city "awaits" its larger whole. Both are directed toward ends, but the mode of direction or intention is different for each.

35. DCD 19.17, "*Verum quia terrena ciuitas habuit quosdam suos sapientes, quos diuina improbat disciplina, qui uel suspicati uel decepti a daemonibus crederent multos deos conciliandos esse rebus humanis atque ad eorum diuersa quodam modo officia diuersa subdita pertinere . . .*" (translation mine).

36. DCD 4.8-34. In 4.16 he notes that the altar to the goddess Quies, Tranquility, is outside the city gates and thus not a national shrine. He wonders, "Was this an indication of a restless spirit? Or did it rather signify that whoever continued to worship that mob of demons—plainly they are not gods—cannot have that rest to which the true Physician summons him, saying, 'Learn from me, for I am gentle and humble of heart'" (*Vtrum indicium fuit animi inquieti, an potius ita signficatum est, qui illam turbam colere perseruaret non plane deorum, sed daemoniorum, eum quietum habere non posse? Ad quam uocat uerus medicus dicens:* discite a me, quoniam mitis sum et humilis corde, et inuenientis requiem animabus uestris). Translation mine.

37. DCD 4.32, "... *hoc modo eos ciuili societati uelut aptius adligantes, quo similiter subditos possiderent.*"

38. The same holds true for Augustine's vision of monastic community, as the Rule of St. Augustine suggests. See the chapter by Thomas Martin, OSA in this volume for further discussion of this theme.

39. In fact, Augustine would suggest that these several possibilities are all reducible to the same root, false worship.

40. Wendell Berry, "Feminism, the Body and the Machine," in *What Are People For?* (New York: North Point Press, 1990) 179–96, this quotation on 180.

41. Nicholas Boyle, *Who Are We Now? Christian Humanism and the Global Market from Hegel to Heaney* (Notre Dame: University of Notre Dame Press, 1998) 4.

42. DCD 6.9.

43. DCD 4.11.

44. Don Delillo, *White Noise. Penguin Great Books of the 20th Century* (New York: Penguin Books, 1999) 81-82.

45. Delillo, *White Noise*, 56, 61, 148.

46. DeLillo, *White Noise. Penguin Great Books of the 20th Century* (New York: Penguin Books, 1999) 37.

47. DeLillo, *White Noise*, 20.

48. DeLillo, *White Noise*, 84.

49. Wendell Berry, "Conservation Is Good Work," in *Sex, Economy, Freedom, and Community* (New York: Pantheon Books, 1993) 27–43. This quotation on p. 40.

50. Among consumer choices that my students have found puzzling or ridiculous—and thus in some sense beyond the horizon of their imaginations—are not eating meat, not getting cable or satellite TV, not buying a car, not buying fast food, not buying shoes made in China.

51. Nicholas Boyle, *Who Are We Now?*, 4.

52. Wendell Berry, "Feminism, the Body, and the Machine," in *What Are People For?* (New York: North Point Press, 1990) 178–96. This quotation on p. 180.

53. Wendell Berry, "Out of Your Car, Off Your Horse," in *Sex, Economy, Freedom, and Community*, 21-26, this quotation on p. 24.

54. DCD 19.17, "*caelestis autem ciuitas <cum> unum Deum solum colendum nosset eique tantum modo serviendum servitute illa, quae Graece latreia dicitur et non nisi debetur.*" Translation mine.

8

Augustine and the Politics of Monasticism

Thomas F. Martin, O.S.A.

W ITHOUT A DOUBT, THE MATURE Augustine's political thinking never oper-
ated within the specific boundaries that mark and define the scope of
contemporary political theory. His understanding of the organization and
governance of human society was explored and expressed in the context of a
deep and explicitly religious conviction: that the only true and real community is the *civitas Dei*. Anything short of that graced heavenly community
must be understood, judged, and directed in its light. In turn, this religious
conviction cannot be understood apart from what was a long-standing ancient assumption about the city: " . . . *dans l'Ántiquité il n'y a pas de cité sans
culte. La cité est une réalité politico-religieuse.*"[1] In the ancient world, there was
always a soteriological dimension to political life. This is most clear in pagan
reaction against the sacking of Rome in 410: they saw the catastrophe not in
socio-political, but rather socio-religious terms. No one critiqued imperial
military, economic, or foreign-affairs policies: what was at stake was cult.

Without persistent reference to this framework guiding Augustine's thinking, it is impossible to assess properly either the content or the intent of his
political thought. Thus Augustine gives all forms of human community a theological referent. They cannot be viewed apart from the Christ-event:

> the fundamental role played by Christ sets Augustine's political thought apart
> from the classical tradition. Augustine believed with orthodox Christianity that
> Christ was fully human; therefore he was able to exemplify a just human life,
> which consisted in love of God and neighbour. Yet the incarnation meant that
> Christ was also the unique instrument of grace by which God assisted human
> beings in living justly.[2]

This Christ-centered framework of understanding has substantive content that gives an Augustinian vision of human community its specific contours. It is thoroughly biblical in its makeup, including many biblical concepts. Humans are made "for community." The first human community was indeed paradisiacal. Adam and Eve's disobedience, original sin, breaks not just individuals, but human community itself. Sinfulness is the constant experience as well as persistent threat of every human community. The only remedy for humanity is Christ, a remedy already brought about but not yet totally experienced. Even present-day "Christ-communities" remain remedial and transient; true community is an eschatological hope. Although some commentators have and continue to label this Augustinian "political" vision pessimistic, such an analysis often fails to recognize its specific theological framework and intent: it is a determined and hopeful effort to ground human community in what Augustine believes to be its only salvation and guarantee, Jesus Christ. Apparent pessimism is in fact a deliberate and strategic effort on his part to point humanity toward its only true realization. Thus, "Augustinian politics" are pastoral-ascetical-spiritual in their scope and intention, designed to aid and assist a present pilgrim community toward its true homeland "when God will be all in all" (*ut sit Deus omnia in omnibus*; 1 Cor 15:28).[3]

Perhaps this immediately suggests an at best limited and at worst hollow value to Augustine's political thinking. It represents, does it not, a now-discarded and long-obsolete model of theocracy? However, anyone familiar with the thought of Augustine instinctively realizes that he is not to be so easily or summarily dismissed. The fact is that he was not only an astute observer of human behavior, including the political kind; and not only does he offer even to the nontheologian a challenging insight into the make-up, demands, and possibilities of the *vita socialis*. But precisely because his voice has been so prominent within Western historical and cultural traditions with deep political implications stemming from this presence, the need to appreciate and evaluate the original content and actual intention of that voice remains perennial. And in fact, theocracy for Augustine is not really an earthly possibility: it is only achievable in the hereafter. Augustine remained very chary of any claims that even the ecclesial earthly community was the unambiguous realization or finished embodiment of God's own community.

Further, the fact that one can identify specific historical initiatives taken by Augustine laden with political impact and precedent (one need only think of the ever-controversial Donatist question), invites continued analysis and reflection on the nature of Augustine's political thought, its application in practice, and its impact upon history, especially as sustained research and study continues on the nature of Christianity's presence in that world now referred to as Late Antiquity. One such historical initiative by Augustine that has potential for offering such insight is his monastic enterprise. Here we not only have Augustine offering ample theoretical explanation concerning the nature of an organized social community (the monastery), but we also have ample practical documentation of its realization in practice. Robert Markus has already noted the importance of Augustine's monastic choice of the city over the desert.[4] This decision for "urban monasticism" was deliberate, making possible for "the city" a provocative yet functional model for what community can be and can achieve. Augustine's monasticism offers the potential for a rich and often overlooked resource for better understanding his political thinking in practice: the concrete precepts and matter-of-fact comments he has left behind regarding the organization and actual living out of the monastic life *in community*. These are above all (though not exclusively) to be found in his charter for monastic living, the *Praeceptum* (or *Rule of St. Augustine*). Does Augustine's "politics of monasticism" offer us insight regarding his political thinking? That is the question underlying this exploration.

A Monastic Dossier

Before proceeding it should be noted that the latter half of the twentieth century saw a revival of serious study of the texts associated with Augustinian monasticism. Most notable among this scholarship is the two-volume study of L. Verheijen.[5] His careful philological, thematic, and historical analysis remains, to date, the most comprehensive and definitive study of that text that is the centerpiece of Augustinian monasticism, the *Rule of Saint Augustine*. This text has a complex manuscript history, coming down in both a masculine and a feminine form and, especially in the Middle Ages, being combined with a variety of other texts associated with the Augustinian monastic tradition. Further complicating this history is the fact that Augustine never tells us that he wrote a *Rule*. The attribution comes from the Abbot Eugippius of Lucullanum, some one hundred years after Augustine's death.[6] Verheijen's exhaustive and careful study led him to conclude that the text is authentically Augustine's and that the masculine version has textual priority. Verheijen proposed that Augustine wrote it on the occasion of his move from the "garden monastery" (see below) to the bishop's residence in Hippo Regius where he established a monastery of clerics. This would place its composition shortly before the year 400. In an effort to refocus a manuscript tradition that had become even more confused by a series of accumulated labels for the various versions and combinations of the *Rule* that had developed down through the centuries, he proposed that the original text be referred to as the *Praeceptum*. He took this title from the first line of the document: "*Haec sunt quae ut obseruetis praecipimus in monasterio constituti*—these are the things which we prescribe you who have been established in the monastery to observe" (*Praeceptum* 1.1).[7]

This foundational text is complemented by a series of other texts that complete the Augustinian monastic dossier:[8]

> We live here with you, and we live here for you (*vobiscum hic vivimus et propter vos vivimus*); and my intention and wish is that we may live with you in Christ's presence forever. I think our way of life is plain for you to see (*ante oculos vestros*); so that I too may perhaps make bold to say what the apostle said, though I can't of course be compared with him: "Be imitators of me, as I too am of Christ." (1 Cor 4:16)

> I brought nothing with me; I came to this Church with only the clothes I was wearing at the time. And because what I was planning was to be in a monastery with the brothers, Father Valerius of blessed memory [the Bishop who "drafted" and ordained Augustine], having learned of my purpose and desire, gave me that garden plot where the monastery now is. I began to gather together brothers of good will, my companions in poverty, having nothing just like me, and imitating me. Just as I had sold my slender poor man's property and distributed the proceeds to the poor, so those who wished to stay with me did the same, so that we might live on what we had in common. But what would be our really great and profitable common estate was God himself (*magnum et uberrimum praedium ipse Deus*).

> I arrived at the episcopate. I saw that the bishop is under the necessity of showing hospitable kindness to all visitors and travelers; indeed if a bishop didn't do that he would be said to be lacking in humanity. But if this custom was transferred to the monastery it would not be fitting. And that's why I wanted to have a monastery of clergy in this bishop's residence. This then is how we live; nobody in our company is allowed to have any private property (*habere aliquid proprium*). But perhaps some do; nobody's allowed to; if any do have it, they are doing what is not allowed. But I have a good opinion of my brothers, and believing the best of them, I have always refrained from making any inquiries because to make such inquiries would, so it seemed to me, indicate I had a low opinion of them. I knew, you see, and I still know, that all who were living with me knew about our purpose (*propositum nostrum*), knew about the law governing our life together (*legem vitae nostrae*). (*s.* 355. 1–2)[9]

These late-in-life comments not only give us a brief autobiographical account of Augustine's monastic history, but they also make absolutely clear the public nature of his monastic endeavor. From the original garden plot within the church compound, to the nearby episcopal residence turned into a clergy monastery, the monastic life style Augustine undertook was neither remote nor hidden away. It was "plain for all to see." "We live here for you," and his usage of 1 Cor. 4:16 highlight a deliberate effort to be conspicuous. This is also confirmed by the text of the *Praeceptum*, where reference is frequently made to the monastic community's public *visibility*.[10] And perhaps this should come as no surprise, since the guiding scriptural source for both the lay and the clerical community came from the portrayal of the first Christian community in the Book of Acts and the impact they had on all of the city of Jerusalem in those days immediately following the Resurrection: "Now the multitude of believers had one soul and heart, and none of them said that what they possessed was their own, but they had all things in common. And the apostles were testifying with great power to the resurrection of the Lord Jesus; and great grace was upon them" (Acts 4:32, see s.356.1).[11] It is precisely this high visibility that suggests the potential "political intentions" tied to Augustine's monastic endeavors.

However, did Augustine's concern for such "visibility" reflect actual reality? We have two explicit indications that it did, aided by implicit evidence as well. In *Letter 78*, written in 404 and addressed to the entire Christian community of Hippo Regius—clergy, monks, and laity—Augustine publicly confronts a public scandal between a priest of his monastery named Boniface and one of its younger members. Boniface had accused the young monk Spes of a grave offense against chastity and Spes replied by protesting his innocence and claiming Boniface was, in fact, the guilty party. The scandal quickly became known to the entire community and Augustine openly addressed the question, fearing not only the distress this was causing the faithful, but equally the potential damage to the monastery's reputation. His late-in-life *Sermons* 355–356, dated to 425–426, likewise confront a monastery scandal that quickly became public: one of the priests of the monastery, Januarius, had died and left a will. This was a clear violation of their monastic commitment to place all possessions in common and "call nothing one's own" (see *Praeceptum* 1.1). The incident quickly became a source of gossip and scandal and Augustine felt compelled to confront the matter openly. Both incidents and Augustine's reporting of them provide abundant material for insight into the complex relationship that existed between the monastic community of Augustine and the larger Christian and civic community of Hippo Regius. For the purpose of this study they simply make clear that Augustine's concern that the monastic community model what true community could and should be— "we live here for you"—was neither an abstract concern nor a simply theoretical ideal. His monastic community was highly visible and so potentially influential for good or for bad. This also finds implicit verification in the number of times Augustine manifests concern that the monastery community's imperfections not be used as an excuse for the wider community's moral laxity (see, e.g. *en. Ps.* 99.9–13; 132.4; *s.* 73A.3).

Practically speaking, what kind of modeling of community was available to Augustine's monastic community that could be of "political" value for the larger Roman African community that surrounded this Augustinian monastery? The *Praeceptum* suggests a variety of communal practices and behaviors, some of them reflective of classic Roman values, others certainly subversive by traditional Roman standards. At the end of the *Praeceptum*, Augustine proposes that this little work serve the monastic community as a kind of mirror: "that you may see yourselves in this little book as in a mirror—*ut autem vos in hoc libello tamquam in speculo possisitis inspicere*" (8.2). Augustine is drawing upon James 1:23–25 and frequently throughout his preaching draws upon this use of the mirror image to highlight a need for Christian dedication to transformation: "with solicitous care let us cleanse our appearance, lest we be ashamed when we once again look in the mirror—*cura sollicita detergamus, ne rursus inspecto speculo erubescamus*" (*s.* 301A.1). As Augustine often presents this image, it is obvious that what he has in mind is no ordinary mirror, since in it we see not only what we are now, but also what we can and ought to be through God's call and grace. It may be suggested that just as texts like the *Praeceptum* and most especially the Scriptures serve this mirror function, so likewise Augustine expects the monastic community to be mirror and model for the larger community: "let not your clothing attract attention, nor seek to please by your garments but by your behavior—*non sit notabilis habitus vester, nec affectetis vestibus placere sed moribus*" (*Praeceptum*, 4.1). The very fact that they model a way of life, in fact a *vita socialis—placere moribus—* and that this example is *notabilis* places the monastic community in a privileged role that is not without political implications.

Reipublicae Salus

In some remarks of 411/412 to the cultured though non-Christian Volousianus, Augustine offers a description of and prescription for "political health," *reipublicae salus*:[12]

> Herein is the praiseworthy security of the state (*laudabilis reipublicae salus*), for the best city is erected and safeguarded (*conditur et custoditur optime civitas*) on no other foundation than the bond of faith and unbreakable concord (*vinculo fidei, firmaeque concordiae*). This happens when the common good (*bonum commune*) is loved, when God is the highest and truest good, and when people love each other most sincerely because they love one another for the sake of Him (*propter illum*) from whom the spirit of their love they cannot hide. (*ep.* 137.5.17)[13]

When *fides*, *concordia*, and *bonum commune* are present, these virtues guarantee the security of the *civitas*: "*conditur et custoditur optime civitas*." Thus *firmitas virtutum* (see *ep.* 137.5.20) becomes, for Augustine, the only reliable guarantee of the *civitas* (keeping always in mind that "city" here means "the state" or "the commonwealth"), a challenge to those who mistakenly see Christianity as undermining it: "*qui propterea putant, vel putari volunt christianam doctrinam utilitate non convenire reipublicae*" (*ep.* 137.5.20). The fact is, Augustine argues, the Christian community alone offers the possibility for an authentic realization of *fides, concordia,* and *bonum commune*. As the monastic community shines forth for all to see, it offers a direct and practical witness of these virtues. Thus a profile of the community envisioned in the *Praeceptum* offers ample evidence that these virtues are at the heart of Augustine's envisioning of the communal monastic endeavor, enabling the monastic community to offer a challenging and compelling model of *reipublicae salus*.

Fides

> *Et profecto ita est ut id habendum sit antiquissimum et Deo proximum, quod sit optimum.* (Cicero, *De legibus* 2.40)
> *Unde autem sciunt illi quid sit fides, cuius primum et maximum officium est, ut in verum credatur Deum?* (*de Civ.* 4.20)
> "The Romans liked to consider themselves the people of *fides*."[14]

Augustine's choice of the term *fides* was undoubtedly deliberate and strategic. The Romans had a tradition of veneration for the goddess *Fides* and her temple played an important role in both religious and civic life. In Augustine's Christian world it had become a profoundly rich and foundationally important religious and theological word: *Iustus autem ex fide vivit* (Rom 1:17; Hab 2:4). Undoubtedly, the monastic community is a model of *fides Christi*, and this is not without social consequences. The monastic community bridges two worlds. Their vocation is to give forth the good odor of Christ by the pleasing fragrance of their exemplary living: "*bono Christi odore de bona conversatione flagrantes*" (*Praeceptum* 8.1; see 2 Cor 2:15). This odor is an unmistakable affirmation that the witness of the monastic community is "in the public domain." (*Conversatio*, "lifestyle" is a "public" word for Augustine: "*conscientia tua coram Deo, conversatio tua coram fratre tuo*," *s.* 47.11; see e.g., *s.* 264.5; *bon.vid.* 22.27. It immediately calls to mind *fama*: see e.g. *epp.* 48.4; 65.2.) The Pauline text that provides the basis for this monastic admonition occurs frequently in Augustine and is used by him to insist on the ultimately Christological and spiritual nature of all Christian witness. He speaks eloquently of Cyprian's martyrdom being a *bonus odor*: "*docendo de Christo, vivendo in Christo, moriendo pro Christo*" (*s.* 313C.2). What appeared to the public eye as humiliating defeat by execution was in fact salvific Christological witnessing. It was a manifestation of faith though this could only be so perceived in faith.

Elsewhere he talks of the *bonus odor Christi* as *odor cordi nostro* (*s.* 28.2), perceptible only by one's *olfactum interius* (*s.*159.4), *olfactum autem noster homo interior* (*s. Dolbeau* 6 [23B].5). Thus the witness of the community, the *odor Christi*, is indeed public, yet its perception requires, in this case, not the eyes of faith but the "nose of faith"! This "fragrance" is spiritual, indeed a *magnum sacramentum* (*s.* 273.5), leaving no doubt that we have entered into the sphere of mystery and grace, as well as that of spiritual perception.

The witness of this monastic community accordingly operates out of and speaks to the sphere of faith and grace, and it is only with a *spiritual* sense that the monastic community can be so seen and allowed to impact. There is a profound call here to redirect one's discernment regarding the nature and purpose of the example that is being offered by the monastic community: politics here is inseparable from *spirituality*! In that sense the political slogan undergirding the *fides* of this community is *sursum cor* (*Praeceptum* 2.6). This liturgical-Eucharistic acclamation is both a manifestation of and a commitment to the *fides Christi* that is at the origin and heart of the monastic community.

The Romans traditionally held up the *viri boni* of its perceived golden age (think only of the characters who make up Cicero's dialogues) as models of *fides*—manifestations of ideal citizenship and authentic patriotism. In the *Praeceptum* it is now the *uir sanctus* (4.5) who takes on this obligation. Men such as these no longer look to Rome, but rather to the model community of the first Christians in Jerusalem and their witness of community: *anima una et cor unum in Deum* (1.2; see Acts 4:32a). The Jerusalem community is one founded from faith and in faith:

> What happened in the case of many saints called to be joint heirs of Christ by the "adoption of children" (Eph 1:5), when one faith and one hope and one love (*una fides et una spes et una caritas*) made them of "one heart and one soul" toward God (*anima una et cor unum in Deum*, see Acts 4:32) is especially effective in making us understand that the one and same nature of the Father and the Son—the nature, if it may be so expressed, of Godhead—is such that the Father and the Son who are one, inseparably one and eternally one, are not two gods but one God. (*ep.* 238.2.13)[15]

The text cited from Acts 4:32 is a constitutive text for Augustine's thinking concerning monastic community in particular and ecclesial community in general: *anima una et cor unum in Deum.* Augustine has actually amended the Acts texts with "*in Deum*" to leave no doubt regarding the theocentric nature of this community, generated by faith in the risen Jesus, witnessing that same faith before all Jerusalem. In the passage just cited from Letter 238 to the Arian Pascentius, it is virtually in passing that Augustine makes evident the link between the oneness of that community in faith (joined here and regularly with hope and love), and the oneness of the Father and the Son.

In an early comment, still in his first stages as a Christian thinker, Augustine already associates the oneness of friendship with a religious dimension, in fact drawing upon Cicero for his authority: "For friendship has been rightly and with just reverence defined as 'agreement on things human and divine combined with goodwill and love.'"[16] For the mature Augustine, the union and unity implied in the Roman expression of *fides*, that civic ideal which blossoms into *amicitia et consensio*, is elevated to an even loftier spiritual plane, grounded in and linked to the very life of the Trinitarian God. Christian *fides* that finds public expression in *"anima una et cor unum in Deum"* guarantees lasting *amicitia* and genuine *consensio*,[17] giving rise to an authentic *societas*:

> Then again others have chosen to leave behind all secular ambitions and worldly conduct (*relicta omni spe saeculari et omni actione terrena*), and betake themselves to a community of holy people, to that life in common (*in societatem sanctorum, in communem illam vitam*) where no one claims anything as private property (*aliquid proprium*) but all goods are common to all (*sed sunt illis omnia communia*), and there is among them but one mind, one heart directed to God (*est illis anima una et cor unum in Deum*). (*en. ps.* 83.4)[18]

Augustine's horizon here transcends any earthly community, though a truly holy community will seek and long for such unity and love.

Despite the spiritual nature of this ideal that has abandoned all *spes saecularis* and *actio terrena*, there is no doubt that the *omnia communia* was profoundly tangible and so provocatively visible: *"non dicit aliquis aliquid proprium"* demanded outward manifestation. In a transformative way, faith intrudes upon all "secular and worldly goods" (*omnia communia*), lifting this community up and so purifying them that they might become "in *Deum*." The monastic community offers concrete witness of *vita fidei*.[19]

Concordia

> *Ita brevi multitude dispersa atque vaga, concordia civitas facta erat.* (Cicero, *De rep.* 1.39, quoted by Augustine in *ep.* 138.2.10)
>
> *Et quae harmonia a musicis dicitur in cantu, ea est in civitate concordia, artissimum atque optimum omni in re publica vinculum incolumitatis, eaque sine iustitia nullo pacto esse potest.* (Cicero, *De rep.* 2.69)
>
> *. . . huius enim templum simul omnes et singuli templa sumus, quia et omnium concordiam et singulos inhabitare dignatur; non in omnibus quam in singulis maior, quoniam nec mole distenditur nec partitione minuitur.* (*de Civ.* 10.3)
>
> *. . . ita etiam terrena civitas, quae non vivit ex fide, terrenam pacem appetit in eoque defigit imperandi oboediendique concordiam civium, ut sit eis de rebus ad mortalem vitam pertinentibus humanarum quaedam compositio, voluntatum.* (*de Civ.* 19.17)

Though Cicero's attempt to preserve the republic by proposing the *Concordia Ordinum* ultimately failed, the ideal and personification of *concordia* did not pass from Roman public or religious imagination. Tiberius' re-dedication of a new *Templum Corcordia* on 16 January 10 C.E. gave visible witness to its at least propagandistic importance for imperial policy, though barely beneath the surface of the term lurked underlying tension: "to proclaim *concordia* was to acknowledge that opposition existed."[20] Augustine's own choice of the term once again presupposes his awareness that the Roman understanding of *concordia* was pregnant with historical and political meaning. Of its nature it came to take on a conservative meaning.[21] That is, the desired *concordia* was understood to be between already established orders and privileged classes: it was by no means a *concordia universalis*. When the *Praeceptum* admonishes the monastic community to live together "in concord"—"*omnes ergo unanimiter et concorditer vivite*" (1.8)—Augustine has certainly in mind a notion of *concordia* that far transcends the Roman ideal. One way that the lofty and angelic ideals that manifest the *fides* of this community will be manifest will be by its *concordia* realized in a strikingly concrete way, a verification of the inner sincerity of its *fides*. This visibility in turn can be viewed *politically*, since it models a new ideal of community.

One of the most striking aspects of the *Praeceptum* that runs throughout the course of the entire text is, on the one hand, the diversity of its community's make-up and, on the other hand, the challenges and demands this places upon *concordia*. Living side by side are rich and poor, literate and illiterate, well-bred and low-born. Conservative Roman society had a deep-seated and profoundly intransigent sense of caste. Social order implied clear boundaries between the classes and a host of titles circulated freely to maintain that order and distinction: *vir clarissimus, vir egregius, vir eminentissimus, vir perfectissimus, senior, iunior, liberti, patres, classicus, curiales, equites, gentes minores, honestiores, humiliores, nobiles, novus homo, optimas, patricius, plebs, servi*, etc. Such titles privileged status, guaranteed distinction, and preserved differences.[22] Augustine and Monnica reflect such class distinctions over the question of marriage recounted by Augustine in the *Confessions*. Monnica's arranged marriage for Augustine with a girl from a distinguished family contrasts sharply with his common-law partner who apparently came from a lower social class and so was considered "unmarriageable."[23] By the time Augustine organized his monastic community and written them a rule of life all that had changed. Now it is precisely the transcending of such social barriers that gives this community its provocative public face. Thus this community is made up of "*qui aliquid habebant in saeculo*" (1.4), and "*qui non habebant [in saeculo]*" (1.5); those who are "*ex paupertate*" and those who are "*de parentum divitum dignitate*"; those "*qui infirmi sunt ex pristine consuetu-*

dine" and those "*quos facit alia consuetudo fortiores*"; those "*qui venerunt ex moribus delicatioribus*" as well as "[*qui*] *de humillima saeculi paupertate venerunt.*" One could hardly imagine such extreme ends of the social classes actually rubbing shoulders together under a single roof. The *Praeceptum* makes it clear that reciprocal interaction was not necessarily easy: "Nor should they put their nose in the air because they associate with people they did not dare approach in the world. Instead they should lift up their heart, and not pursue hollow worldly concerns."[24]

If the poor were tempted to take advantage of these new relationships, the rich were equally tempted: "And those who seemed to be something in the world ought not to look down upon their brothers who have come to this holy society from poverty" (*sed rursus etiam illi qui aliquid esse videbantur in saeculo non habeant fastidio fratres suos qui ad illam sanctam societatem ex paupertate venerunt*; 1.7). As already noted, to speak of *concordia* was to acknowledge conflict.

Interestingly, the tensions created by such social distances being bridged were not to be resolved by a leveling, one size to fit all: "The same is not to be given to all, because all do not have the same strength; rather each one is to be given according to their need" (*non aequaliter omnibus, quia non aequaliter valetis omnes, sed potius unicuique sicut cuique opus fuerit*; 1.3).

Here Augustine draws upon the religious authority of the Book of Acts and its portrayal of the first Christians in Jerusalem: "For thus you read in the Acts of the Apostles that 'everything was held in common and distribution was made to each once according to their need'" (*sic enim legitis in Actibus Apostolorum, quia "erant illis omnia communia et distribuebatur unicuique sicut cuique opus erat*; 1.3). *Omnia communia*, the great classic ideal, is both affirmed and transposed:

Those Romans had a republic (*rem publicam*) richly endowed with all resources (*opulentissimam atque ditissimam*) (and "republic" means "state of the people," "state of the country," "commonwealth") (*rem populi, rem patriae, rem communem*), while they themselves lived in poverty in their own homes (*in suis domibus pauperes erant*). So much so that one of them, who had already been consul twice, was dismissed from the senate by the censor's ban, because it was discovered that he had ten pounds of silver plate. Such was the poverty of men whose triumphs enriched the public treasury. It is a far nobler resolution (*excellentiore proposito*) that leads Christians (*omnes christiani*) to regard their riches as belonging to all (*qui diuitias suas communes faciunt*), according to the principle described in the Acts of Apostles; by which everything is shared out according to individual need, no one claims anything as his private property, and everything belongs to the common stock (*ut distribuatur unicuique, sicut cuique opus est, et nemo dicat aliquid proprium, sed sint illis omnia communia*). But Christians must understand that this gives them no ground for self-conceit (*iactantia*), since they do this to attain the fellowship of the angels (*id faciendo pro obtinenda societate angelorum*), while the Roman worthies did much the same to preserve Roman glory (*pro conseruanda gloria romanorum*).[25]

Nonne omnes christiani, qui excellentiore proposito diuitias suas communes faciunt—theirs is a "far nobler resolution," precisely because it is not for the sake of *gloria Romanorum*, but for attaining that *societas angelorum*, a divine citizenship that is embodied in the ideal of *anima una et cor unum in Deum*. The "proud" sacrifices made by the Romans for the sake of the *res publica*, the *res populi*, the *res patriae*, the *res communis* are both humbled (*ueteris hominis terrena desideria mortificantes*) and surpassed (*spiritalis uitae nouitate flagrantes*):

> And so mortifying now the earthly desires of the old man, and burning with the newness of the spiritual life (*ueteris hominis terrena desideria mortificantes, et spiritalis uitae nouitate flagrantes*), as the Lord had enjoined in the Gospel, they sold all that they had, and laid the price of their goods before the feet of the Apostles, in order that the latter might distribute them to everyone according to need; and living together in the concord of Christian love (*uiuentesque in christiana dilectione concorditer*), they did not call anything their own, but all things were common to them, and they were one soul and heart directed towards God. (*cat. rud.* 23.42)[26]

Viventes in Christiana dilectione concorditer—a commitment to a more radical *concordia* is underway in Augustine's monastic community; on the one hand more radical in its demands, on the other hand, directed beyond this world to a city that does not pass away.

However, the *Praeceptum* evidences that the demands of *concordia* were never effortless and, in fact, often painful. One of the striking manifestations of *concordia* involves what might be called the "monastic court" outlined above all in chapter 4 of the *Praeceptum*. Augustine outlines here a multi-stage process for dealing with monastic offenses.[27] It begins with private fraternal *admonitio* (4.8), proceeds to a small group *correptio*, followed-up by a reporting to the *praepositus* (4.9) who only then intervenes, and if necessary can bring the matter *coram omnibus*. At this stage it is the *praepositus* who imposes judgment and sentence, *arbitrium* and *emendatoria vindicta*. Refusal on the part of the individual leads to what may be called "monastic exile": "If he refuses to submit to punishment even if he is determined not to leave, expel him from your society" (*quam si ferre recusauerit, etiam si ipse non abscesserit, de vestra societate proiciatur*; 4.9).[28] However, such drastic measures are carefully conditioned by proper intention: "Even this is not an act of cruelty but of mercy: to prevent the contagion of his life from infecting more people" (*non enim et hoc fit crudeliter, sed misericorditer, ne contagione pestifera plurimos perdat*; 4.9). It is interesting to note the application of a medicinal, therapeutic metaphor to describe the drastic action: *ne contagione pestifera plurimos perdat*. The health of both the community and the individual are the driving force behind such action, a point Augustine has already insisted upon in bringing the individual to accountability:

> If your brother had a bodily wound which he wished to conceal for fear of surgery, would not your silence be cruel and your disclosure merciful? Your obligation to reveal the matter is, therefore, all the greater in order to stem the more harmful affection in the heart (*si enim frater tuus vulnus haberet in corpore, quod vellet occultare, cum timet sanari [secari], nonne crudeliter abs te sileretur et misericorditer indicaretur? Quanto ergo potius eum debet manifestare, ne perniciosius putrescat in corde?* 4.8)

In this *societas*, medicinal rather than punitive justice prevails, a concern that is found repeatedly in Augustine, most notably in his opposition to capital punishment on the basis of its finality, precluding conversion.

While Augustine has a clear sense of what justice demands in the form of punishment (and by modern standards harsh-sounding because of its assumption of physical pain needing to be inflicted),[29] he is always insistent, even in these cases of justice's medicinal application, on the need for reprimanding in such a way as to persuade the evil doer to repentance and reform of life. This holds equally for offenses against each other in this community. These private matters between two people require the same medicinal intention: *ex ipso ore proferre medicamenta, unde fact sunt vulnera* (6.2). Augustine explicitly links *salus* and *concordia*, both necessary for the *ordering* of the human body as well as the body politic:

> The peace of the body is a tempering of the component parts in duly ordered proportion (*ordinata temperatura partium*); the peace of the irrational soul is a duly ordered repose of the appetites (*ordinata requies appetitionum*); the peace of the rational soul is the duly ordered agreement of cognition and action (*ordinata cognitionis actionisque consensio*). The peace of body and soul is the duly ordered life and health of a living creature (*ordinata uita et salus animantis*); peace between the mortal human and God is an ordered obedience, in faith, in subjection to an everlasting law (*ordinata in fide sub aeterna lege oboedientia*); peace between humans is an ordered concord (*ordinata concordia*); the peace of a home is the ordered agreement among those who live together, giving and obeying orders (*ordinata imperandi atque oboediendi concordia cohabitantium*); the peace of the city is the ordered agreement among those who live together, giving and obeying orders (*ordinata imperandi atque oboediendi concordia ciuium*); the peace of the Heavenly City is a perfectly ordered and perfectly harmonious fellowship in the

enjoyment of God, and a mutual fellowship in God (*ordinatissima et concordis-sima societas fruendi Deo et inuicem in Deo*); the peace of all things is the tranquility of order (*pax omnium rerum tranquillitas ordinis*). (*de Civ.* 19.13)[30]

The justice of punishment, even to the point of expulsion, as well as the demands of mutual forgiveness are both directed toward that ideal of *salus concordiae* (see *de Civ.* 5.11), whose antithesis is embodied in so much of Roman history:

> But as for the objects of that people's love—both in the earliest times and in subsequent periods—and the morality of that people as it proceeded to bloody strife of parties and then to the social and civil wars, and corrupted and disrupted that very unity which is, as it were, the health of a people (*ipsam concordiam, quae salus est quodam modo populi*)—for all this we have the witness of history; and I have had a great deal to say about it in my preceding books. (*de Civ.* 19.24)

The monastic community offers Augustine's Roman world an alternative vision of the make-up and realization of *concordia salutis*.[31]

Bonum Commune

> *Quid est res publica nisi res populi? res ergo communis, res utique civitatis.*
>   (Cicero, *De rep.* 1.39)
> *Necesse est secundum eandem naturam omnium utilitatem esse com-munem.* (Cicero, *De of.* 3.27)

Where the *Praeceptum* is perhaps most striking in its presentation of the guiding ideals of this *sacra societas* is in regards to the relationship between individual and communal striving. Augustine proposes here a model of community in which the notion of the common good reigns supreme, yet he does so in a way that permits the uniqueness of each individual in both personal constitution and history to be attended to and respected. There can be no doubt that Augustine is deeply aware that the notion of the common good, the *bonum commune*, the *res communis*, represents some of the highest aspirations of the Roman political tradition:

> Herein is natural science (*physica*), since all the causes of all natures are found in God, the Creator; herein is ethics (*ethica*), since the good and honorable life is formed in no other way than by loving what ought to be loved as it ought to be loved, that is, God and our neighbor; herein is logic (*logica*), since there is no other truth and light for the rational mind than God; herein is the praiseworthy security of the state, for the best city is erected and safeguarded on no other

foundation than the bond of faith and unbreakable concord. This happens when the common good is loved. (*ep.* 137.5)[32]

We have already seen a text from the *City of God* which affirms the importance of the *common good* and yet provocatively places its greatest realization not in Rome, but in post-resurrection Jerusalem. Strikingly, this insistence upon the *res communis* builds upon and presupposes a care and concern for individual need. This is clear in a text already cited: ". . . by which everything is shared out according to individual need" (*ut distribuatur unicuique, sicut cuique opus est*; *de Civ.* 5.18). *Ut distribuatur unicuique, sicut cuique opus est* marks the *Praeceptum* from the outset as a document which does not erase the individual, reducing the single members of the monastic community to one common and perhaps bland denominator. Thus there is concern for individual background and health that allows for the personalization of diet, clothing, bedding, cleanliness, and health care (see 3.1ff.; 5.1ff.), and even temperament must be taken into consideration (see 6.2).

The *Praeceptum* makes clear that this was a source of tension and contention but this was not to be resolved by a leveling principle. Rather it made only more evident the need for a conversion of one's desires and intentions. This reaches a culmination in chapter 5, where Augustine lays out a demanding yet sensitive articulation of the struggles between the communal and the private:

> In this way, let no one work for himself alone, but all your work shall be for the common purpose, done with greater zeal and more concentrated effort than if each one worked for his private purpose. The Scriptures tell us: "Love is not self-seeking." We understand this to mean: the common good takes precedence over the individual good, the individual good yields to the common good. Here again, you will know the extent of your progress as you enlarge your concern for the common interest instead of your own private interest; enduring love will govern all matters pertaining to the fleeting necessities of life. (*ita sane, ut nullus sibi aliquid operetur, sed omnia opera vestra in commune fiant, maiori studio et frequentiori alacritate, quam si vobis singuli propria faceretis. Caritas enim, de quo scriptum est quod "non quaerat sua sunt," sic intellegitur, quia communia propiis, non propria communibus anteponit. Et ideo, quanto amplius rem communem quam propria vestra curaveritis, tanto vos amplius profecisse noveritis; ut in omnibus quibus utitur transitura necessitas, superemineat, quae permanet, caritas.*) (5.2)[33]

The tension is clear between *communia* and *propria*. The scriptural guide for these tensions, Augustine takes from 1 Cor 13:5: "*non quaerat quae sua sunt.*" This citation is a foundational monastic text for Augustine, but just as clearly the hallmark of true Christian dedication: "*non sua quaerentes, sed quae iesu Christi.*"[34]

Paradoxically, seeking what is Christ Jesus' both fulfills and transcends the self and inscribes one into that true city of happiness:

> All those who have no taste but for the things of this earth (*omnes qui terrena sapient*), all who prize earthly happiness above God, and all who seek their own ends (*omnes qui sua quaerunt*), not those of Jesus Christ, belong to that city whose mystical name is Babylon, the city that has the devil as its king (*ad unam illam ciuitatem pertinent, quae dicitur babylonia mystice, et habet regem diabolum*). (*en. ps.* 61.6)

"*Sua quaerentes*" does indeed have "political implications," as it becomes the hallmark of a perverse and sinful patriotism associated with that city called Babylon, and that kingdom whose ruler is called *diabolum* (a.k.a. *princeps huius mundi, princeps peccatorum, princeps daemoniorum, princeps impiae civitatis*).[35] "*Sua quaerentes*" functions virtually interchangeably with the notion of "*propria*" or "*privatus*," as is clear in the following comments to a community of monks other than his own:

> If, however, a person is converted to this life from poverty (*ex paupertate*), let him not consider that he is doing merely what he used to do, if, turning from the love of increasing his own private fortune, however little (*si ab amore vel augendae quantulaecumque rei priuatae*), and no longer seeking what things are his own but rather those of Jesus Christ (*iam non quaerens quae sua sunt, sed quae iesu christi*), he has devoted himself to the charity of common life (*ad communis uitae . . . caritatem*), intending to live in companionship (*in eorum societate*) with those who have one heart and one soul directed towards God, so that no one calls anything his own (*proprium*) but all things are held in common (*sed sint illis omnia communia*). (*op. mon.* 25.32)[36]

Turning aside from one's own interests involves an intense and difficult respect and protection of the private interests and needs of others.

Augustine's clear concern that individual needs be addressed and respected on the part of the monastic community places an even more acute responsibility upon the individual to seek to "lift up the heart" (*sursum cor*) to the higher ideal of *omnia communia*. In a paradoxical reversal, it seems that the very attention to the personal and individual awakens the possibility of transcending the personal and individual. The *amplius profecisse* in the just-cited passage of the *Praeceptum* is a statement of growth and progress in holiness, and it is precisely in the ongoing movement from the *propria* to the *res communis* that holiness can be "measured." It ultimately distinguishes two radically opposed "citizenships":

> These two loves—of which one is holy, the other unclean, one social (*socialis*), the other private (*priuatus*), one taking thought for the common good (*communi*

utilitati) because of the companionship of the heavenly community, the other putting even what is common at its own personal disposal (*etiam rem communem in potestatem propriam*) because of its lordly arrogance; one of them God's subject, the other God's rival, one of them calm, the other turbulent, one peaceable, the other rebellious; one of them setting more store by the truth than by the praises of those who stray from it, the other greedy for praise by whatever means; one friendly, the other jealous, one of them wanting for its neighbor what it wants for itself, the other wanting to subject its neighbor to itself; one of them exercising authority over its neighbor for its neighbor's good, the other for its own—these two loves were first manifested in the angels, one in the good, the other in the bad, and then distinguished the two cities, one of the just, the other of the wicked, founded in the human race under the wonderful and inexpressible providence of God as he administers and directs everything he has created. (Gen. *lit.* 11.15.20)[37]

This tension or, perhaps even better, antithesis between the *proprium/privatum* and the *res communis/omnis communia* forces and demands a choice of love and the consequences of that choice. Speaking in another context but with insight into the seamless garment that is the choice of one's love, Augustine insists that "love cannot be separated":

it is by loving that one becomes a member of Christ, becomes through love incorporated into the body of Christ; and there will be the one Christ loving himself . . . when therefore you love a member of Christ, you're loving Christ, you're loving the Son of God; when you love Christ, you're loving the Son of God, when you love the Son of God you love the Father. Love can never be separated (*non potest ergo separari dilectio*). Choose for yourself what you love and the rest will follow. (*ep. Io. tr.* 10.3)

Love the *proprium/privatum* and "the rest will follow." The monastic community is called upon to offer a visible example of what that choice of the *res communis* involves as well as an assurance that such a choice does not extinguish the individual, but instead promises that the collective life is the only salvation for the individual, uplifting and transforming him or her.

Leadership

It is clear in the *Praeceptum* that the community as a whole has shared responsibility for the lofty and demanding task of its welfare and well-being. Yet there is an equally clear assertion of the special importance of spiritual leadership in this community. In fact the *Praeceptum* makes clear that there were two levels of leadership, that of the *praepositus* and that of the *presbyterum*.

Although silent on many details, Augustine vividly describes how one is to lead in this community:

> The one who is over the community should not consider himself content by dominating forcefully but rather by serving lovingly. Let him have place of honor before you, but in fear before God let him be prostrate at your feet. . . . And although both may be necessary, nonetheless let him seek more to be loved by you rather than feared (*ipse vero qui vobis praeest, non se existimet postestate dominantem, sed caritate servientem felicem. Honore coram vobis praelatus sit uobis, timore coram Deo substratus sit pedibus vestris. . . . Et quamuis utrumque sit necessarium, tamen plus a vobis amari appetat quam timeri*) (7.3)

There is no indication of term of office or exact manner of selection regarding these positions of authority, but what is clear is that it is an office of love.

In fact, it is paternal love that sets the tone for the monastic leadership envisioned in the *Praeceptum*. Augustine, throughout his writings, frequently turns to the image of a father's love. It was a love he thought about much, both from his experience with his own father Patricius and from his tender love of his own deeply cherished son, Adeodatus. It is a complex love since it demands both tenderness and severity, correction as well as encouragement. Not infrequently will he turn to the example of fatherly love: "If you scold, love inwardly. When you're admonishing, coaxing, correcting, punishing: love and do what you will. A father indeed does not hate his son, yet when it is necessary he must apply the paddle; pain is inflicted so that health may be protected" (*s.* 163B.3). What is important to note is that the "*praeesse*" of this authority is always meant to be a *prodesse*, a "being for": "One who is in charge of people, must first understand that he is their servant" (*debet enim, qui praeest populo, prius intellegere se seruum esse multorum; s.* 340A.1); "I desire to be of service to the church rather than in authority over it" (*non tam praeesse quam prodesse desidero; ep.* 134.1). The purpose of authority with its care and responsibility for the community (the *praepositus* must always keep in mind the following: "*semper cogitans Deo se pro vobis redditurum esse rationem,*" *Praeceptum* 7.3), makes that office dangerous rather than prestigious, and makes the obedience owed a form of love: "Your being obedient is a way of being merciful not only to yourselves, but also towards him, whose higher position places him in greater danger" (*unde vos magis oboediendo, non solum vestri, verum etiam ipsius miseremini, quia inter vos, quanto in loco superiore, tanto in periculo maiore versatur; Praeceptum* 7.4). In turn authority is exercised as a form of mercy: "God's mercy knows under whose eyes I tremble like this, that I am led on by the duty of love (*officio dilectionis nos ducito*) to say these things to you, and that I am driven by the dread I feel, knowing that I am going to have to give an account to the Lord himself for you all (*ipsi*

domino rationem de omnibus reddituros; s. 114B.16). The monastic community not only offers a compelling model of the *vita socialis*, it also provides a
striking witness to a new understanding of leadership and authority, where
governance is founded on and is an expression of love.

Conclusion: The Politics of Grace

... *non sicut servi sub lege, sed sicut liberi sub gratia constituti* (*Praeceptum* 8.1).

The visibility (*notabilis*) of Augustine's monastic community offered it a privileged opportunity, but equally a demanding responsibility for a deliberate and
particular witness of *vita socialis*. When one takes into account the rich and never
tranquil Roman political tradition, the polemics ignited by the sack of Rome (by
its very intensity suggesting long-smouldering pagan-Christian tensions), and
the vision of a new ideal of kingdom, city, and community inscribed within
the pages of the New Testament, that insistence upon monastic visibility can
suggest a "political agenda"—we live here *propter vos*. Yet what is most original about this "new community" and marks a radical departure from Roman
civic models is that this is a community *sub gratia*, "under grace." Its foundation and source is the Christ-event. Peter Brown notes a change in "social
imagination" underway during the Patristic period.[38] There can be no doubt
that the monastic community offered a model for a "new imagining" of the
possibilities of the *vita socialis*. However, this *imagination* itself demanded a
new way of seeing, a graced *contemplatio*,[39] that made demands upon both the
monastic community and their *scrutatores* (*s.* 355.2). There is a great emphasis in the *Praeceptum* on how the monastic community *sees* itself and a constant call for a transformation of vision,[40] but we know from Augustine himself that there was an equally great awareness and desire that others *see* them,
though this too demanded a transformation of vision:[41] "For ourselves, our
conscience suffices; for you our reputation ought to be shining, not sullied"
(*propter nos, conscientia nostra sufficit nobis: propter vos, fama nostra non pol-
lui, sed pollere debet in vobis; s.* 355.1). The monastic community offered an
evangelical and faith-generated witness to what might be called "a republic of
grace,"[42] a model of *reipublicae salus* founded upon a Christ-centered and
graced understanding of *fides, concordia,* and *bonum commune,* foundational
components of such *salus* and the first fruits of "the possibility of a new social
identity."[43] Interestingly, however, the example offered is never claimed to be
utopian, as the *Praeceptum* ends with a recognition of imperfection, *deesse*
(8.2), and throughout makes it obvious that this monastic community is far
from perfect. The monastic community ought not to be viewed as a model

that has arrived at its final destination. This is a community still *peregrinans*, still *in via*. Nonetheless, the monastic community does witness to the "art of the possible,"[44] what can be done while still on pilgrimage. This "possible" was indeed demanding and lofty, was often threatened and compromised, was ever directed toward its eschatological fulfillment, but nonetheless offered in the present moment promise and hope, witness and example, consolation and comfort, but also challenge and demand for embracing and giving expression to a new vision of community, one that has still only begun to unfold. "The city remains which gave birth to us carnally. Thank God! Would that it would be spiritually born and with you would make its way to eternity" (*manet civitas quae nos carnaliter genuit. Deo gratias. Utinam et spiritualiter generetur, et vobiscum transeat ad aeternitatem*; s. 105.9).

Notes

1. Goulven Madec, "*Le De civitate Dei* comme *De vera religione*," in *Interiorità e intenzionalità nel "De civitate Dei" di Sant'Agostino*. Atti del III° Seminario Internazionale del Centro di Studi Agostiniani di Perugia. A cura di Remo Piccolomini (Rome: Institutum Patristicum "Augustinianum," 1991) 7.

2. E. M. Atkins and R. J. Dodaro, "Introduction," in *Augustine: Political Writings* (Cambridge Texts in the History of Political Thought; Cambridge: Cambridge University Press, 2001) xv.

3. See *Io. eu. tr.* 83.3; *en. Ps.* 84.10; 101.2.10; *s.* 55.4; *de Civ.* 14.28; 18.49; 19.15, 20; 22.30.

4. Robert Markus, *The End of Ancient Christianity* (Cambridge: Cambridge University Press, 1990) 157–77.

5. *La Règle de saint Augustin* (Paris: Études Augustiniennes, 1967). See also George Lawless, O.S.A., *Augustine of Hippo and His Monastic Rule* (Oxford: Clarendon Press, 1987).

6. For a helpful and succinct summary of the complex history of the Augustinian Rule, see G. Lawless, "Regula," in *Augustine through the Ages: An Encyclopedia* (ed. Allan D. Fitzgerald, O.S.A. Grand Rapids, MI: William B. Eerdmans Publishing Company, 1999) 707–9.

7. See now N. Cipriani, "La precettistica antica e la regola monastica di s. Agostino," *Augustinianum* 39.2 (1999) 365–80.

8. See *Letter 243* to Laetus, *Sermons 355–356*, and the *Exposition of Psalm 132 (133)*.

9. Translation has been adapted from Augustine, *Sermons* III/10 (trans. E. Hill; *The Works of Saint Augustine: A Translation for the 21st Century* [hereafter WSA]; Hyde Park, NY: New City Press, 1995) 165–66.

10. In this regard, see my "'An Abundant Supply of Discourse': Augustine and the Rhetoric of Monasticism," *The Downside Review* 116, no. 402 (January 1999) 7–25.

11. On the importance of this text in early Christianity, see Pier Cesare Bori, *Chiesa Primitiva: L'immagine della comunità delle origini—Atti 2,42–47; 4,32–37—nella storia della chiesa antica* (Brescia: Paideia Editrice, 1974).

12. See Serge Lancel, *Saint Augustine* (trans. Antonia Nevill; London: SCM Press, 2002) 395; see also Luc Verheijen, O.S.A., "La Règle de saint Augustin et l'éthique classique," in *Nouvelle Approche de la Règle de saint Augustin* (Bégrolles en Mauges: Abbaye de Bellefontaine, 1980) 243–47.

13. The translation is adapted from Saint Augustine, *Letters, Volume III, 131–164* (trans. Sister Wilfrid Parsons, S.N.D. The Fathers of the Church, A New Translation, Vol. 20 [hereafter FC]; Washington, DC: The Catholic University of America Press, 1953) 34.

14. Arnaldo Momigliano, "Religion in Athens, Rome, and Jerusalem," in *On Pagans, Jews, and Christians* (Hanover, NH: Wesleyan University Press, 1987) 76. I have relied on Momigliano for what follows on Roman *fides*.

15. Adapted from FC 32, 197–98.

16. Cicero, *de Amicitia*, 20: *amicitia rectissime atque sanctissime definita est rerum humanorum et divinorum cum benevolentia et caritate consensio.* Quoted in *c. Acad.* 3.6 (see also *ep.* 258.1): St. Augustine, *Against the Academics* (trans. and annotated by John J. O'Meara; *Ancient Christian Writers*, vol. 12 [hereafter, ACW]; Westminster, MD: The Newman Press, 1950) 112. Regarding the relationship between Cicero and Augustine see Maurice Testard, *Saint Augustin et Cicéron* (Paris: Études Augustiniennes, 1958), updated in *Augustinus-Lexicon* (ed. C. Mayer; Basel: Schwabe & Co., 1985–), "Cicero," 913–30. Regarding Augustine, friendship and God, see his classic comments in *conf.* 4.4.7ff, and the chapter by Kim Paffenroth in this volume.

17. Human *amicitia* is grounded in Trinitarian *amicitia*: "*Spiritus ergo sanctus commune aliquid est patris et filii, quidquid illud est, aut ipsa communio consubstantialis et coaeterna; quae si amicitia convenienter dici potest, dicatur, sed aptius dicitur caritas; et haec quoque substantia quia deus substantia et deus caritas sicut scriptum est*" (*trin.* 6.5).

18. Augustine, *Exposition of the Psalms* (trans. and notes by Maria Boulding, O.S.B.) WSA III/18, 188.

19. Regarding *vita fidei* see, e.g. *Io. eu. tr.* 19.9; 22.12.

20. See Barbara Levick in *Tiberius the Politician* (New York: Routledge, 1976) 86.

21. See M. Cary and H. H. Scullard, *A History of Rome: Down to the Reign of Constantine* (3rd ed. London: Macmillan, 1975) 247.

22. Regarding the importance of title and status, see Peter Brown, *Poverty and Leadership in Late Antiquity* (The Menahem Stern Jerusalem Lectures; Hanover, NH: University Press of New England, 2002) esp. 52–54.

23. See *conf.* 6.15.25.

24. *nec erigant cervicem, quia sociantur eis ad quos foris accdere non audebant, sed sursum cor habeant et terrena vana non quaerant, ne incipient esse monasteria divitibus utilia, non pauperibus, si divites illic humiliantur et pauperes illic inflator* (1.6). In this instance I have drawn upon G. Lawless's translation of the *Praeceptum* in his *Augustine of Hippo and His Monastic Rule*, 83.

25. *de Civ.* 5.18. The translation has been adapted from Augustine, *Concerning the City of God against the Pagans* (trans. Henry Bettenson; New York: Penguin Books, 1972) 210–11.

26. Translation adapted from St. Augustine, *The First Catechetical Instruction—De Catechizandis Rudibus* (trans. Joseph P. Christopher; ACW 2; Westminster, MD: The Newman Bookshop, 1946) 74.

27. See Ghislain Lafont, O.S.B., "Fraternal Correction in the Augustinian Community: A Confrontation Between the Praeceptum, IV, 6–9 and Matthew 18:15–17," *Word and Spirit* 10 (1988) 87–91; Luc Verheijen, O.S.A., "Expulsion, excommunication, degradation," in *Nouvelle Approche de la Règle de saint Augustin*, 322–46.

28. I have drawn upon Lawless's translation of the *Praeceptum* here.

29. See, e.g., *ss.* 83.8; 163B.3; 211.1.

30. Augustine often links "health" and "concord": see also *de Civ.* 5.11; *Io. eu. tr.* 14.10; *ss.* 277.4; 305A.8.

31. Certainly "expulsion" was not considered by Augustine an "ordinary" means of resolving difficulty. He speaks of someone's friend (*amicus*) offering scandal: "*Iam iste scandalum est. Amicus est, quid facturus es? Oculus est, manus est: 'Amputa, et proice abs te*" (Matt 18:8). *Quid est, 'Amputa, et proice abs te,? Noli consentire. Hog significant, 'Amputa, et proice abs te,'" noli consentire. Membra enim nostra in corpore nostro consensione faciunt unitatem, consensione vivunt, consensione invicem conectuuntur. Ubi dissensio, ibi morbum aut vulnus. Ergo membrum tuus est: diliges eum. Sed scandalizat te: 'Amputa eum, et proice abs te.' Noli consentere; averte ilum ab auribus tuis, forte correctus rediet*" (*s.* 81.4.). Note this "medicinal" approach to understanding and maintaining community unity!

32. See FC 20, 33–34.

33. See Lawless, 95.

34. See Luc Verheijen, O.S.A., "La charité ne cherche pas ses propres interest," in *Nouvelle Approche de la Règle de saint Augustin: II. Chemin vers la vie heureuse* (Louvain: Institut Historique Augustinien, 1988) 220–89.

35. See *Io. eu. tr.* 3.13; *en. ps.* 84.4; *s.* 112A.3; *de Civ.* 18.51.

36. St. Augustine, "The Work of Religious" (trans. Sister Mary Sarah Muldowney, S.S.J. in *Saint Augustine: Treatises on Various Subjects*; FC 16; New York: The Fathers of the Church, 1952).

37. The translation is adapted from WSA I/13, 439–40.

38. P. Brown, *Poverty and Leadership in the Later Roman Empire*, 6.

39. "*Quae licet utrique, id est actioni et contemplationi, sit necessaria, maxime tamen contemplatio perspectionem sibi vindicat veritatis*" (*de Civ.* 8.4); "*Contemplatio quippe merces est fidei, cui mercedi per fidem corda mundantur, sicut scriptum est: mundans fide corda eorum*" (*trin.* 1.8).

40. Visual verbs and nouns occur more than twenty times in the *Praeceptum*.

41. See, for example, his comments in *en. ps.* 99.8–13.

42. "*Recte igitur significat isaac, per repromissionem natus, filios gratiae, cives civitatis liberae, socios pacis aeternae, ubi sit non amor propriae ac priuatae quodam modo voluntatis, sed communi eodem que inmutabili bono gaudens atque ex multis unum cor faciens, id est perfecte concors oboedientia caritatis*" (*de Civ.* 15.3).

43. Markus, *The End of Ancient Christianity*, 81.

44. See Dodaro and Atkins, "Introduction," in *Augustine: Political Writings*, xxvi.

9

The Glory and Tragedy of Politics

Thomas W. Smith

W HAT ARE THE POLITICAL implications of Augustine's thought? Two approaches prevail in the contemporary literature. In one, Augustine ruins politics. In the other, he saves it.

For those in the anti-Augustine camp, the tradition known as "Political Augustinianism" stresses the strong presence of sin in human affairs and the necessity of salvation. This tradition also emphasizes an ultimate dimension to public life as the place where salvation is worked out. Yet while Political Augustinianism tends to infuse politics with this spiritual meaning, it despairs of redeeming social life through political action because of the effects of sin. Consequently some external spiritual force is required to assure the morality that public life requires. Thus Political Augustinianism insists on a close connection between politics and the Church, such as that advocated by Gregory the Great, Innocent III, or Giles of Rome. This endorses a homogenizing politico-religious orthodoxy. Moreover, its moralistic politics leads to the kind of intolerance and sectarian violence associated with the Crusades, the Inquisition, or early modern religious wars.[1]

Others have more to add. In one line of criticism, Augustine's otherworldliness undermines the conditions for civic virtue and political life generally.[2] Another tradition of modern philosophy argues that Augustinian Christianity bifurcates human experience into a schizophrenia-producing dualism. The belief in a perfect world beyond the here and now is one of several unappealing alternatives: a projection—a conservative, epiphenomenal justification for the economic powers that be, and an opiate that lulls the masses into complacency; unlikely wishful thinking; an expression of impotent resentment; or an immature longing to return to the womb. Thus Augustinian Christianity undermines the possibilities for critiques of established practices and for a flourishing life. If we are to ameliorate the conditions of human life and seek social justice here and now, Augustine's influence must be cast off.

However, others insist that Augustine saves politics. Augustine's "political realism" emphasizes the reality of evil, "which threatens the human community on every level."[3] This sense of the tragic limits of politics imbues people with a sober practical wisdom that eschews the kind of utopian ideologies that were so destructive in the twentieth century.[4] Some say that Augustine's articulation of the interaction of the two cities allowed him to take a "theologically neutral" attitude toward politics. Thus he advocates a politics that is relative, restricted, and autonomous within its designated area.[5] Augustine denies the classical contention that the state has the capacity to cultivate virtue.[6] Arising due to sin, politics is a "remedial institution."[7] It cannot create anything morally good but can be helpful for maintaining peace.[8] One implication is that Augustine paves the way for liberalism.[9] In effect, by opposing a politics of ultimate meaning, Augustine saves politics from "Political Augustinianism."

Yet this is a bewildering situation. Does Augustine foster theocracy, sectarian intolerance, and violence? Or does he pave the way for a limited state, political neutrality, and tolerance?

Interpretive Approaches

I will turn to the *City of God* to explore the political implications of Augustine's thought.[10] Yet how should we approach that intimidating book? Our interpretive framework will color what we take from it. For instance, the different interpretations I outlined above share a common hermeneutic. Specifically, they assume that Augustine intends to articulate a general systematic teaching about the nature of politics in the *City of God*. Thus they assume that Augustine's work is theoretical, in the sense of aiming at a disinterested, universally applicable account. However, approaching the *City of God* as if it were a treatise that sets forth conclusions overlooks its rhetorical, pedagogical, and indeed, spiritual dimensions.

The *City of God* is not a theoretical treatise aiming to clarify the nature of politics. Augustine's goal is practical: to offer a hymn of praise that glorifies the City of God.[11] At the very opening of the book, Augustine says his purpose is to illuminate the "most glorious City of God" (*gloriosissimam civitatem dei*). Mark Vessey comments,

The writer's purpose, following the psalmist, is to hymn the One City. Thus there is no mention of the 'other city' that exists only as a shadow, though its members are already numbered among the 'impious' who 'prefer their own gods.' Likewise, the apologetic project of the earlier books [i.e., Books I–X], while fully integrated in the syntax of the sentence (*civitatem dei . . . defendere . . . suscepi*), is rhetorically subordinate to the constructive project of the later ones, which stands at the front of the announcement. . . . Even by the standards of Augustine's own Ciceronianism, this is an unusually as well as magnificently suspenseful sentence. And that of course is its point, or, to speak more appropriately, his intention. While grammatical, rhetorical, and rhythmic *cursus* pull the reader in different directions, he or she holds fast in expectation to the direct object of the sentence, mentioned at its outset, "the most glorious City of God."[12]

But Augustine's praise has a pedagogical and pastoral dimension. Augustine defines glory as "clear knowledge together with praise."[13] *Gloria* is related to or derived from *clara*, which has the connotation of shining, bright, famous. Augustine's pastoral, pedagogical care is manifest in his effort to make more clearly known the shining attractiveness of the City of God to his readers so they will turn their lives around to recognize and praise it themselves. The pedagogical dimension of the book can be expressed in the following way. Augustine seeks to reorient his readers' loves; specifically, Augustine exhorts his reader to love divine rather than human glory. The *City of God* is a spiritual exercise intended to transform conventional notions of what is properly glorified.[14] Augustine seeks to educate his readers' desires and so their sense of what is worthy of worship. This pedagogy has far-reaching implications. Augustine believes that once one's life is transformed by love of God, all one's other loves will be transformed as well. This transformation will be reflected in the different way one relates to created goods, including one's politics. Thus the political dimension of the *City of God* is reflected above all in the way Augustine works toward a new conception of political practice that would comport with the standards of the City of God.

Augustine's pedagogy takes into account the prior commitments of his audience. The two cities are created by two loves, and these loves determine what each city glorifies; the City of God glories in the Lord, while the City of Man looks for glory from human beings (14.28). Thus Augustine's pedagogy proceeds through a critical examination of the Roman love of glory. Augustine shows that this love of human glory does not satisfy Romans the way they want it to. The desire for glory restrains their worst impulses, but its attendant spirit of competition and self-assertion undermines the condition for the flourishing, glorious community Romans desire.[15] For Augustine, classical culture cannot realize the life it seeks. Understanding how the Roman Empire's successes are paradoxically the cause of its failure allows Augustine's readers to wonder

whether the standards of the City of God—which seem foolish from the perspective of conventional notions of success—are really wise.

However, Augustine must also take into account the way the love of human
glory obscures divine glory. The *City of God* is a book of praise, but it takes seriously the difficulty of praising adequately from the perspective of its audience's commitments. For Augustine, the pursuit of conventional success veils
the course of the City of God through history. Augustine delegitimates Rome's
claim to success, for its approach to human life obscures the City of God. This
critique of human glory unveils the glory of the City of God. The City of God
can emerge out of Rome's shadow when we see the way Rome fails to achieve
what it promises.

Considered from the perspective of a lover of divine glory, the City of Man
is a mere shadow of the City of God insofar as it pursues a life that is a pale
imitation of the glory, felicity, and peace of the City of God.[16] In fact, the status of the City of Man as a just community is questionable insofar as the love
of human glory that binds it together also tends toward domination and fragmentation (19.21). However, the City of God lies in shadow if we adopt the
perspective of a lover of human glory. The City of Man seeks power, security,
territory, and wealth; the City of God seeks service, surrender, and spiritual
pilgrimage. From the perspective of the City of Man, the City of God is hidden in shadow, for it is always threatened, insecure, powerless, and homeless,
seeking goods that are risky and not physically manifest.[17] So one problem
with glorifying the City of God is that of vision: we will seek fulfillment in the
places where we think we will find it. If we look for fulfillment in human glory,
the standards of the City of God will make no sense. The Roman Empire
seems so massively successful that, by contrast, the glory of the City of God is
obscure. Thus Augustine's pedagogy aims to give his readers new eyes with
which to see. In modern terms, he presents a hermeneutical framework with
which to reinterpret what counts as human success and fulfillment. Indeed,
this hermeneutical framework demands a reorientation that would employ
fundamentally different standards for what would count as a central event in
human history. For Augustine, the rise and fall of empires are of secondary
importance for human happiness (5.18). Rather, the most important events
are those in salvation history, wherein God reveals the way to the fullness of
life. For Augustine, salvation history lies in shadow if we view history with eyes
accustomed to seeking success in the conventional sense.[18]

In this sense, Augustine's pedagogy simply recapitulates his notion of the
pedagogy of divine providence. Human beings generally believe that the kind
of success the City of Man pursues offers the greatest promise in this life for
peace, happiness, and security. But for Augustine, genuine hope for human
happiness is obscured by that very history. The hope that the City of God of-

fers lies in the shadow cast by the City of Man and the longings for human glory and worldly success that bring that city forth. Thus Augustine's spiritual hermeneutic recycles historical material from the ancient historians to give them new meaning.[19] For him, the history of the City of Man does not tell the tale of the triumph of human power and glory. Showing how and why the City of Man fails on its own terms dissipates the shadow cast by its "success," unveiling the City of God.

Be Careful What You Wish For: The Ironic Consequences of Classical Culture

The immediate reason Augustine writes the *City of God* is to argue against the charge that the Empire's adoption of Christianity as its official religion is responsible for the sack of Rome in 410 CE. The first ten books are polemical, devoted to showing how worshiping pagan gods is useless for securing the goods either of this life (Books 1–5), or the next (Books 6–10). The polemic is straightforward at first. But soon Augustine turns to the question of worship itself, in effect asking his readers, "What do you put at the center of your life? What are the fruits of this?" For Augustine, the Roman gods are worshiped not out of love or piety, but to ensure a stable enjoyment of goods such as wealth, prosperity, health, power, and honor. In this sense, the object of worship is not the gods, but rather a certain notion of success. Augustine looks at this notion from two perspectives. First, he devotes himself specifically to pagan theology. Second, he critically examines the Roman love of glory. In both cases he argues that the worship of earthly goods ruins them.

For Augustine, while the Roman gods are worshiped to assure the Empire of peaceful enjoyment of the world's goods, the fruit of this worship is a proliferation of gods and the dissipation and deception of mortals. Not only do the Roman gods fail to protect Romans and their allies (e.g., 3.20), but the pursuit of Roman success fosters an imperial expansion that leads the Empire to continual war.[20] So while the gods are worshiped to assure Rome of a peaceful enjoyment of external goods, that worship results in a profound restlessness, discontent, and war:

> Is it reasonable, is it sensible, to boast of the extent and grandeur of empire, when you cannot show that men lived in happiness as they passed their lives amid the horrors of war, amid the shedding of men's blood—whether the blood of enemies or fellow-citizens—under the shadow of fear and amid the terror of ruthless ambition? The only joy to be attained had the fragile brilliance of glass, a joy outweighed by the fear that it may be shattered in a moment. (4.4)[21]

For Augustine, worshiping this kind of success leads to fragmentation and dissipation, reflected in the proliferation of the pantheon. Anxious to protect
their goods and acquire still more, the Romans increased the size of their pantheon. This process includes the tendency to deify mortals (18.54). For Augustine worshiping gods for the sake of securing success had the paradoxical
effect of thinning out the worship itself. For Augustine, every theology presupposes an anthropology. The frantic search for a secure, peaceful enjoyment
of the world's goods led the Romans to dissipation and fragmentation, both
in their theology and in their humanity.

Augustine further points out that the whole process is fueled by a kind of
necessary self-deception. A large part of Augustine's polemic in the first ten
books of the *City of God* is devoted to showing the way pagan philosophers
can see through the gods of the poets and politicians, yet are in the position
of having to lie about them to protect the civic virtue the gods uphold.[22]

For Augustine, the object of Roman worship was not the gods, but the gifts
they promised to bestow. Yet if the pursuit of these goods did not yield happiness, Augustine concludes, perhaps we are led to wonder whether happiness
is coextensive with the divine itself. If so, it becomes wisdom to worship not
worldly success, but the god who is capable of bestowing genuine felicity.[23] For
Augustine, the ironic consequences of Roman worship should lead us to worship not the gifts but the giver.[24] At the end of this consideration of Roman
worship, Augustine points out that his pedagogy merely reflects the pedagogy
of divine providence. Whenever people stray from true worship, divine providence brings them back through the failure of their worship to secure what
they desired (4.34).

The treatment of worship paves the way for a consideration of the Roman
love of glory, which also produces ironic contradictions. The argument contains many twists and turns, but its thesis is simple: Romans love glory above
all. Yet their love of glory ironically ruins their chances of enjoying it.

For Augustine, the Roman Empire is a decisive improvement on ancient
eastern kingdoms which he believes were based on a lust for domination.[25]
The cause of Roman success is the kind of choices the Romans made, ani-
mated as they were by love of glory (5.1).[26] So the ancient Romans

> were greedy for praise, generous with their money, and aimed at vast renown and
> honorable riches. They were passionately devoted to glory; it was for this that
> they desired to live, for this they did not hesitate to die. This unbounded passion
> for glory, above all else, checked their other appetites. They felt it would be
> shameful for their country to be enslaved, but glorious for her to have dominion
> and empire; and so they set their hearts first on making her free, then on mak-
> ing her sovereign. (5.12)

Since God instituted an order of secondary causes in which people will in some broad fashion achieve what they strive for, Augustine holds that God gave the empire to the Romans because of their quasi-virtue (5.8–12, 15). The Romans got what they deserved.

Augustine thinks Rome is a great empire, full of a kind of virtue and glory. The love of praise provides a kind of spur to moral excellence because its ambition for greatness and fear of shame checks vice (5.14). Thus, contrary to what one might expect in a book devoted to a polemical defense of Christianity against Rome, the *City of God* is full of praise for Rome and her "marvelous achievements, which were, no doubt, praiseworthy and glorious" (5.12).[27] In fact, Augustine thinks that his fellow Christians ought to be spurred on by such examples, feeling "the prick of shame" (5.18) if they do not display the kind of qualities the Romans did in their pursuit of earthly glory.[28]

Augustine's praise is exuberant, but his criticisms attend them. Appealing to virtue in an honor-loving culture is inherently conservative, in the sense of preserving the status quo. In such a context, a particular appeal to "virtue" means "what respectable people imply when they speak about the qualities human beings require in order to be successful in this society." Since honor is merely a pointer to virtue, any culture's mode of giving honor is always an attempt to foster its own conception of human excellence. Thus the pursuit of honor is bounded by relatively specific normative expectations that are, by the definition of honor, socially constructed. Social relations in a culture devoted to honor are evaluative and competitive. In such a context social norms are reinforced by rewarding certain actions with praise or rewards and punishing other by assigning blame or shame. But this means that if virtue is seen as a means for achieving public glory and political power, then it becomes a virtue not to rise above common opinion. The pursuit of glory issues in a smug complacency that impedes the kind of dynamic critique every culture requires to be just. Struggling for public recognition may entail slavishly buying into one's culture's notions of human excellence. And winning esteem can foster the kind of self-congratulation that obscures an awareness of faults that is the condition for moving away from them. So the appeal to virtue in a social context defined by the pursuit of glory can block an honest assessment of virtue in as much as it implies an appeal to conventionally respectable standards of success. If so, then fostering virtue in such a context merely preserves the moral hegemony of the dominant culture, rendering personal, social, or political reform more difficult.

Moreover, for Augustine, the love of glory is bound up with the fear of death. Rome loved glory because of its desire to pursue a quasi-divine immortality in a tangible form. Thus the Roman desire to build something glorious that will last stems at once from a longing for a shining divine life and a horror at death. The heightened fear of death expands the need for self-assertion and self-aggrandizement. Horror at the apparent oblivion of death leads us to want others to assure us of our own worth. That is, fear of death bears fruit in excessive love of praise and thus of glory.[29] For Augustine, when confronted by our vulnerability, we often both seek the praise of others and tend to exaggerate our estimate of our moral capacities. Thus the fear of death accounts for both the smugness inherent in Rome's virile honor-loving culture, as well as its self-assertive tendency to glory. The pursuit of our own glory and truthfulness about our qualities and limits preclude each other.

This love of glory tends to domination for Augustine. Love of glory is not the same as the desire for power, but it leads to domination by a "slippery slope." The desire for glory is fueled in part by a flight from vulnerability; an assertion of our value and dignity in the face of oblivion. Glory is a zero-sum good, for public recognition is worthless if everyone receives it. Thus cultures devoted to public praise are competitive and evaluative, pursuing a communal life rife with self-assertion and jockeying for position. Commenting on this phenomenon in ancient Greek culture, Robert Vacca points out,

> precisely because nothingness is an abyss ever open before man, his claim on existence acquires a narcissistic intensity, demanding constant reinforcement and reassurance by acknowledgement from others. If this is withheld, the hero's *bié* [elemental masculine force] drives him to destroy the other in ontological self-assertion. Therefore this ideological justification of the hero through honor is at the same time the elevation of force and violence to the highest moral dignity, since *bié* is the essence of the warrior's being and action.[30]

The pursuit of glory thus has deeply paradoxical results. Love of glory can be a spur to virtue, insofar as the desire for public acclaim restrains one's baser impulses. Yet the comparative, evaluative character of glory leads to self-assertion, conflict, insecurity, and thus a drive for mastery.[31] The problematic character of this self-assertive drive for public acclaim takes on an even graver tone when we reflect that it is motivated by the desire to overcome the horror of death. Threats to security—both personal and existential—provoke the struggle for power. Power appears to offer the control that seems necessary in order to manage one's social and existential vulnerability and thus alleviate the anxiety that attends them.[32]

The psychic motives that urge us to grasp at glory also urge us to clutch it tightly once it is acquired. On the level of politics, Augustine understands this psychic motivation as the key to Rome's desire for empire. Rome's lust for domination (*libido dominandi*) of other societies was motivated by its fear of threats to its security. These threats, however, were created by the desire to enhance Roman glory, which is fueled in part by insecurity. Paradoxically, an empire's ambition for greatness both arises out of and fosters a profound sense of vulnerability.

This theme is recapitulated in the later books, wherein Augustine traces the origin and course of the City of Man through history. For him, the two cities arise out of the different choices of Cain and Abel. Cain, the founder of the City of Man, resorted to violence out of envy, jealousy, and a desire to triumph. Paradoxically, however, after settling down to found the first city he remained restless. In a similar way, Augustine believes that empires arise out of a frustration at the inability to be peacefully satisfied, mutual suspicion, envy, and finally, domination (18.2). Fueled as they are by insecurity and anxiety, the more powerful these empires become for Augustine, the more insecure they become.[33] In Augustine's view, as Rome expands to achieve security, she overreaches and overextends, ironically making herself less secure.

For Augustine, the Roman love of glory implies a limited notion of human destiny. In the absence of an afterlife, what else can one do with apparently unlimited human desires except engage in a glorious conquest of the known world that will overcome the hero's annihilation in death through the public recollection of his deeds?

> Those Roman heroes belonged to an earthly city, and the aim set before them, in all their acts of duty for her, was the safety of their country, and a kingdom not in heaven, but on earth; not in life eternal, but in the process where the dying pass away and are succeeded by those who will die in their turn. What else was there for them to love save glory? For, through glory, they desired to have a kind of life after death on the lips of those who praised them. (5.14)

Still, this limited horizon is tragic for two reasons. First, in their attempt to flee from the reality of death, Romans think of Rome as an eternal city. Yet Rome changes and decays.[34] Roman culture aims at a lasting, shining community through the pursuit of glory. Yet the self-assertive pursuit of glory leads to envy, mutual suspicion, frustration, and domination.[35] Thus the love of glory that seeks the empire's eternity is also the cause of its fragmentation and eventual disintegration. Second, the vast majority of Romans pass away into oblivion, forgotten despite their sacrifices for Rome. These sacrifices in pursuit of glory make sense only if the glory of Rome is in the interest of the individuals who have sacrificed. Yet individual sacrifices often require death, and death destroys the possibility of enjoying what one seeks to possess. If the goal of one's personal life is the glory of Rome, what benefit accrues to the individual who dies and cannot enjoy the glory of Rome? Rome forgets most of its heroes. Yet even if it remembers them after they are dead, they cannot enjoy the glory that the living give them. The history of Rome is littered with Romans who seek a shining public recognition yet who pass away into obscurity; as

Augustine says, "smoke has no weight."[36] Thus Romans flee from their temporality and mortality through a self-deceptive obfuscation of human limits.[37]
From Augustine's perspective, even the shining life of heroic sacrifice is not
adequate compensation for death, because death ends the possibility of enjoying human glory. Thus the Roman love of glory for Augustine is an incomplete, and finally, self-deluding yearning for a kind of personal and communal immortality that glory cannot provide.

The ambiguous results of love of glory inform Augustine's political philosophy and philosophy of history. Love of glory is responsible for both Rome's
expansion and decline. Love of glory tends to inflate ambition and thus desire
for greatness. Love of ambition also tends toward irrational domination. Desire for greatness urges Romans on to sacrifice for the public good in a way
that resembles genuine virtue. However, love of glory also exposes in some in-
choate way the fear of vulnerability that drives Roman successes on. Conquest
and domination for security will be the logical result of all this nagging anxiety. The more glory is attained, the less it will assuage the disquiet that gives it
birth. As the Empire extends, she overextends, sowing the seeds of her own destruction.[38]

For Augustine, individual and social life is characterized by an affective dy-
namism that tends to focus life to a point. His formulations of this are familiar: our love is our weight, and a community is an association of rational beings united together by the object of their love. Thus for Augustine every
culture is a determinate answer to the question, "What makes us happy together?" However, while the desires of the human heart drive culture forward,
human desires tend to be partial or fragmentary. For this reason the strength
of a culture is paradoxically the source of its weakness. The love that animates
a particular community will tend to make it pursue its own unique conception of happiness. However, the partiality of its love and thus its conception of
happiness will tend to make a community decline at the same time and for the
same reasons it progresses. Put another way, the grounds of Augustine's praise
of Rome are also the grounds of his critique.

Augustine's critique of Rome serves his goal of praising the City of God, for
the love of human glory obscures the reality of divine glory. For citizens of the
City of Man, who look for human success defined in terms of power and external goods, the shining attractiveness of noble sacrifice that the Romans
pursued forces the City of God into its shadow. Making the City of God intelligible as a reality to be glorified entails delegitimating the Roman claim to
success. From the perspective of the Roman love of glory and worldly success,
the standards and practices of the City of God look like foolishness. Augustine
must uncover the contradictions at the heart of that Roman notion of success
in order to show the wisdom of belonging to the City of God.

Augustine's critique is not aimed at showing the evil of every social structure, although his exuberant rhetoric can sometimes lead people to interpret
him this way. Rather, the ironic consequences of the partiality and failures of
Rome expose in a new way the height and depth of human desire. If a shining, quasi-divine public glory in the service of conquering the known world is
not enough to quell our restless hearts, what is? If the aggressive pursuit of
human glory is based on anxiety and self-delusion about our capacity to transcend our mortality, what way of life might produce both genuine peace and
immortality? If the love of glory which drives Romans to sacrifice for their
country also paradoxically drives them to a self-assertiveness that destroys
their country, what could provide a motivation and standard for service that
builds a genuine common life? If clutching conventional success leads to fragmentation, dissipation, and lust for power, what alternative notions of human
success might succeed in cultivating felicity? The longings and frustrations
implicit in the ironic contradictions of Roman love of glory provide signposts
to the City of God.[39]

After the criticism of Roman practices in *City of God* Books 1–10, Augustine traces the origin, development, and destinies of the two cities throughout
the rest of the book. Revealing the ironic contradictions at the heart of the
Roman Empire allows him to uncover a different notion of human success
and compare it to that found in the earthly city.

Resident Aliens and (Ab)Use

Augustine's presentation of a new notion of success leads to a different notion
of the way to use the world's goods. One important way Augustine parses the
distinction between the two cities is the different ways they use the world's
goods.[40] In this life, citizens of the City of God engage the same goods as the
citizens of the City of Man: spouses, children, friends, careers, money, material goods, and countries, "yet each [City] has its own very different ends in
making use of them" (19.17). Augustine's point is simple: if our lives are transformed by love of God, all our other loves will be transformed as well. Loving
the goods of this world in and through their Creator will lead us to use them
differently.[41]

Augustine points to two experiences that render it difficult to love the
world's goods properly: human restlessness and what I will call the problem
of evanescence. For Augustine, our hearts are restless until they find their rest
in God.[42] He believes we are always seeking an object of worship capable of
bringing our desires to a rest. We become overly attached to created goods to
the extent that we expect them to bring our restlessness to an end. However,

Augustine thinks that if we come to worship them, focusing our apparently infinite desires on finite goods, we tend to place a burden on them that they cannot bear, ruining both them and our own chances for happiness. This is one source of disordered love or abuse of created goods for Augustine. The other source of the problem is this: How are we supposed to deal with evanescent goods? Do we protect ourselves from the grief of impending loss by refusing to love them? Or do we love them, risking both grief and the anxiety that often attends our awareness of their fragility? Apparently we need family, friends, jobs, or possessions to be happy. Yet loving them can result in suffering.[43] One temptation is to protect oneself by pushing these goods away. Another is to clutch them so tightly in an effort to stay their passing that one chokes the joy out of them.

For Augustine, these are the spiritual roots of the tragic dimensions of the City of Man. All created goods are indeed good, but none fully satisfy the longings of the human heart. Simply put, no created good is good enough because each fails to satisfy our apparently boundless desires. Moreover, the evanescence of these goods may lead to anxiety and grief over their inevitable passing. So we are tempted to grasp finite goods all the more tightly as we experience them slipping through our grasp. The City of Man worships these created goods. Yet the disproportion between the boundlessness of our desires and the capacity of finite goods to satisfy them creates the kind of frustrations, anxieties, mutual suspicion, and overgraspingness that tend to pull the City of Man apart:

> The earthly city . . . has its good in this world and rejoices to participate in it with such gladness as can be derived from things of such a kind. And since this is not the kind of good that causes no frustrations to those enamored of it, the earthly city is generally divided against itself by litigation, by wars, by battles, by the pursuit of victories that bring death with them or at best are doomed to death. . . . However it would be incorrect to say that the goods which this city desires are not goods, since even that city is better, in its own human way, by their possession. (15.4)

We could illustrate what Augustine is getting at with a myriad of examples: the suffocation a person experiences in a romantic or familial relationship in which she is worshiped as the conditions for another's happiness, the blindness of xenophobia and nationalism that result when the nation is worshiped as a purveyor of salvation, the myopia that happens when a career is worshiped to the exclusion of family or friends, the glorification of ambition and its attendant projects that leads us to leave the path of wisdom. Employing Augustine's own example, loving the glory of Rome ruins not only Rome, but Romans as well. By worshiping human glory, they place their ultimate hopes in a finite, passing good that cannot satisfy their infinite longings. Unveiling the glory of the City of God requires making sense of the turn to divine glory by showing the ways in which the human efforts to worship finite goods fail to respect their limits. Revealing the ways our worship of passing goods leads to their abuse and our frustration leads to a reconsideration of what might count as proper use.

Augustine does not think that there exists a neutral, indeterminate way of employing the world's goods, in the way that a utility like electricity, for example, might be put to a multitude of uses. Augustine shares the classical notion that a thing's end is its perfection. One cannot use a thing without referring it to the end for which it is being used.[44] The members of the two cities thus engage the same goods, but refer them to fundamentally different ends that fundamentally alter the way they are employed. Properly speaking, for Augustine, there can be no use of a created good that does not acknowledge its ultimate destiny.[45]

So what is proper use? Genuine use of the world's goods entails referring them to their origin and ultimate destiny in God; proper use entails loving created goods in and through their Creator. In the *City of God*, Augustine argues that the world's goods are better loved (that is to say, used rather than abused) if we treat them as pilgrims and resident aliens (19.17). It is helpful to unpack these images and their implications, although I will limit my reflections to the concept of resident alienship.

Imagine a married couple from the United States who have taken long-term jobs in Austria. A host of questions arise. How are they going to educate their children? To what extent should they cultivate Austrian friends? How much should they participate in Austrian public life and culture? If they become too attached to Austria, will they remain American citizens? Should they seek out an American community through which they can make their absent country present? Or will clinging to America ensure that they are not taking advantages of all the experiences Austria offers?

Three approaches to this situation are assimilation, resident alienship, and withdrawal. In the assimilation model, the family manages the tensions of their situation by becoming Austrian, abandoning their old home. In the withdrawal model, the tensions of the situation are managed by holding Austria at arm's length. By arguing for resident alienship, Augustine rejects both of these alternatives. This model is the only way of enjoying Austrian life yet managing the tensions inherent in the situation in order to return to one's true home. In short, the family must live in Austria without being of it. They must engage Austrian life and culture without being defined by it. Thus they will enjoy all the new experiences in their life without forgetting their true home. And to make sure that their true home is not forgotten, they will seek to make the United States, absent from them in its fullness, present by retaining its language, customs, and celebrations in their home. When they celebrate American holidays with the American community they meet in Austria amid American symbols and cultural trappings, America is present to them in faith, hope, and love. If they wish to remain American citizens during their stay overseas, they must struggle to love a community that is at once absent in its fullness yet present in their expectations, desires, and ritual celebrations.

Resident alienship as an image of the Christian life must be related to the two obstacles to proper use, restlessness and evanescence. Christians are both at home and not at home in Creation. The goods they encounter are both enjoyable yet sometimes frustrating, insofar as they cannot bring their desires to a rest. These goods are also fraught with the anxiety of their anticipated passing. Enjoying these goods as resident aliens would be liberating. Freed from the expectation that they will ultimately satisfy, Christians can engage them and enjoy them for what they are, respecting the limits of what they can achieve. For Augustine, our capacity to enjoy our marriages, careers, children, country, or property will increase when we enjoy them for what they can provide and no more. In this way Augustine thinks Christians living as resident aliens are liberated from the frustrations and anxiety stemming from the kind of false expectations associated with Rome's worship of human glory. This does not mean that they employ the world's goods instrumentally. Rather, living as a resident alien provides enjoyments analogous to the kinds of enjoyment associated with one's true home. For Augustine cleaving to God is the condition for the enjoyment of created goods, because through loving God Christians refer finite, evanescent goods back to what is infinite and stable.

Yet while the image of resident alienship shows how the Christian life liberates, it also shows how Christian life constrains. The image has profoundly counter-cultural implications. Resident aliens live as sojourners in a strange land insofar as they adopt different practices, rituals, and standards for human happiness; citizens of the City of God are like resident aliens insofar as they live alongside a culture that is more or less foreign.[46] While this culture is often undeniably good, its good is partial and fragmentary, and so Christians must resist the pressure the surrounding culture exerts on them to assimilate to what it loves. They must engage that culture without being defined by it if they are to use created goods with a view to their ultimate destiny. The Kingdom of God would become incarnate through the celebrations, symbols, rituals, practices, and friendships of the citizens of the City of God. Thus they would speak a different kind of language, have a different vision of life, employ a different set of rituals and traditions, and understand the purpose of their lives and the goods they employ in a fundamentally different way than the culture around them. Politically, for instance, citizens of the City of God would love Rome and work for its good, but for different reasons and to different ends than Romans who are citizens of the City of Man.[47]

Finally, love of Austria and love of the United States is not a zero-sum game. One could easily imagine enjoying one's time in a beloved foreign land in a way that increased love of one's own country. In a similar way, Augustine believes that the love of God and the love of created goods is not a zero-sum relationship; love of God does not come at the expense of love of the world. In fact, love for the goods of the world increases if they are loved in and through love of God. For instance, for Augustine, one's relationships tend to grow closer as the partners move closer to God, as if the friends were moving down two spokes of a wheel toward its hub. By contrast, Augustine ultimately traces the dissipation and fragmentation of Rome to its false worship. Loving earthly goods in and through God allows one to hope that they will be lifted up again in future glory. Refusing to worship our marriages, children, friendships, nations, and ourselves is a necessary condition for their flourishing.[48]

So in Augustine's vision, the love of God would reorder our love and use of the world's goods. Recall that Roman love of glory leads to an empire rife with struggle for domination, conquest, and self-protection. By contrast, Augustine insists that from the perspective of Christian love, authority must be employed to serve the needs of others. Thus Augustine says the person who heads a family in a just way will give direction not out of a "lust for domination," but rather "from a dutiful concern for the interests of others, not with pride in taking precedence over others, but with compassion in taking care of others" (19.14). A few lines later, he insists that God did not want rational beings to have dominion over one another. Hence, the first people given authority were "set up as shepherds of flocks rather than as kings of men" (19.15).

To take a specific example, Augustine points to Theodosius as exemplifying the virtues of a Christian ruler. He praises Theodosius above all for his penance after his order of a massacre at Salonica (5.26).[49] Perhaps Augustine celebrates Theodosius because his actions can be used to the greatest pedagogical effect. In a regime that valorizes self-assertion, mastery, and confident assertions of power, Theodosius publicly humbles himself to atone for a decision that might have seemed logical from a Roman *Realpolitik* perspective. His public abasement surely caused dismay among many traditional supporters of the *imperium*.[50] Yet his willingness to admit his wrongdoing publicly provides a countertype to the self-glorification and self-deceptive ethos inherent in a pursuit of human glory.[51] Augustine's point is that lovers of human glory precisely need to recognize their fallibility, self-deception, false notions of success, and mistaken idea that happiness can be found through mastery and violence. Theodosius' penance is the kind of needed yet unwelcome counterbalance to Roman "virtue" that a reorientation of loves would instill. He shows his subjects that the way through the misery of Roman love of glory is to embrace the mercy of Christ (*misericordia*, 10.3), who took on the role of servant (*servi*) to be a mediator (9.15). This is right worship and religion for Augustine.[52] Theodosius' Christian witness is a way of using his authority to serve others.[53] Whatever the shortcomings and historical inaccuracies of Augustine's appropriation of Theodosius, his point is that politics requires a Christian wisdom that the world sees as foolishness.[54]

Conclusion

Augustine has no political philosophy, if that means a disinterested, theoretical inquiry into the nature and purpose of politics. His goal is practical: to offer a praise of the City of God with a pedagogical and hortatory dimension. He does have a political philosophy, if that means working toward a conception of the earthly community which would harmonize with transformative fruits of belonging to the City of God. He urges his readers to reorient their love to God. He believes that this will bear fruit in a new way of relating to the world's goods. Asking whether Augustine saves or ruins politics misses his point. From the perspective of politics, Augustine's central questions are, "How does a person whose life has been reoriented by love of God and neighbor transform that love into a life of service that uses political action as a vehicle for self-giving? What are the implications of such a life for the individual and the regime in which she or he lives?" Augustine does not offer any specific recommendations for Christians engaged in the active life, perhaps because their talents are so diverse and the regimes in which they find themselves are so different, that any general rule would have only limited use as a practical guide. Rather, Augustine argues for the glory of a Christian life and then leaves room for the free play of practical intelligence. The practical implication of his pedagogy is simply, "Love rightly and do what you will."

However, extrapolating from these reflections leads us to conclude that the engagement Augustine urges is both needful and unwelcome to political regimes.[55] For Augustine, understanding common life is more than a matter of grasping institutional arrangements or the story of jockeying for power. Every community organizes its life around a set of loves that implicitly bespeaks a determinate notion of human flourishing and destiny. Every culture incarnates some deep account of the nature and purpose of human life. For Augustine, one must not cede the meaning of politics to those who abuse it. Our usual notion of politics comes from a tradition that views human beings as asocial and politics as instrumental. On this view, the political task is to ensure the way of our future desires through the public construction of individual freedom. Politics is an artificial system that provides utilities like security and wealth which can be put to any and all private uses. Interest group politics determines the distribution of these utilities and the burdens of paying their costs. Competition, not conviviality, is the law of the jungle. This Machiavellianism is false because it is reductionist; for Augustine, common life is always an expression of the ultimate longings of the human heart.

Thus Augustine shares more with the classical approach to politics than with that of liberal individualism. In the classical tradition, politics is architectonic because it aims at fostering and protecting a way of life; in Aristotle's terms, it seeks a conception of human flourishing. Thus a regime decisively affects every aspect of human life, including the individual's formation.[56] In architecture, for example, the various subcontractors and craftsmen take their cue from the architect, who decides the shape and function of the building. The architect coordinates the work of the subcontractors responsible for lighting or plumbing in light of the end for which the building will be employed. In a similar way, a regime manages the overall shape and direction of the constituent parts of the community because its participants are always acting on some conception of what is good for human beings to be and do when they pass laws or engage in typically respectable practices. To be sure, Augustine takes issue with the notion of the human good most actual regimes cultivate; he does not think most regimes actually foster the virtue and happiness at which they aim. Yet this does not mean he denies that regimes always aim at some determine notion of human flourishing by loving what they love.

Human life requires division of labor, trust, partnerships, and cooperation. Harmonious cooperation requires the practically wise coordination of the various activities of a society. Zoning boards help determine the shape of a community. Tax laws influence our practices of family, justice, and generosity. Criminal laws reflect the way we conceive of our sexuality, our mortality, our need for moderation and responsibility. Thus every political act implies an answer to the question, "How do we become human together?"[57]

For Augustine, Christian political authority serves rather than is served; it exists to coordinate the practices of a whole community in a way that fosters genuine flourishing of every part rather than the aggrandizement of the ruling part. This requires an extraordinarily difficult spirituality because it requires turning away from the temptation of using one's office as an opportunity to pile up power and glory for oneself and one's cronies. As Rowan Williams points out, this means that the spiritual and political are not separate concerns: the spiritual is the genuinely political. Williams sees that Augustine is engaged in a redefinition of the public, designed to show that it is life outside the Christian community which fails to be truly public, authentically political. The opposition is not between public and private, church and world, but between political virtue and political vice. At the end of the day, it is the secular order that will be shown to be "atomistic" in its foundation.[58]

Genuine politics is also a massive exercise in coordination. Thus it also requires a practically wise sense of the overall shape and proper end of the regime as a whole, the needs and potentials of its constituent parts, and an ability to weave those parts into a harmonious, integrated community. When coordinating the activities within a society, a Christian statesman would consistently ask, "What notion of human flourishing and destiny do our practices and institutions imply?" In other words, the Christian engaging in political action must struggle to develop a realistic assessment of the virtues and vices of his or her regime and a notion of the proper end of that regime.

Every political act implies some specific sense of the nature and destiny of the human person. Yet for Augustine, these notions are more or less incomplete in every regime, and these partial notions of the human good are harmful to personal and social life. Augustine thinks that Rome declines because of the partial or fragmentary character of its love of glory; the tragedy of Rome was its limited horizon of human possibility. By implication, he thinks a regime will be less subject to frustration, disharmony, and fragmentation to the extent to which it loves more of the whole human good, to the extent that it understands and acts upon ultimate human destiny when it tries to coordinate cooperative activities for the sake of human flourishing. If Augustine is right that a regime is more flourishing to the extent that its sense of the nature and destiny of human being is more whole, all regimes require efforts to resist their partiality in the direction of wholeness. If so, all political regimes require a critical, countervailing stance even in order to maintain themselves. They need a fuller and richer wisdom about the purpose and meaning of human life than their own loves provide. The kind of coordinating work that practically wise political actors do can only be done well if it is informed by a realistic assessment of the nature and purpose of the community. Thus, for Augustine, Christian faith does more than supply a counternarrative to modernity. It imparts a wisdom about the wide horizon of human possibility that provides a standard for a countervailing critique of political practices, as well as a motive to push against those defects through loving service.

This means that the political actors need the kind of wisdom Christian faith imparts.[59] Christian faith provides an understanding of the restless longings of the human heart as well as the height and scope of human destiny. From this perspective, all existing regimes are found to be partial, only more or less fulfilling the desire of the human heart. The more complete notion of the nature and purposes of the parts of a regime that Christian faith provides could be employed to create a more flourishing community.[60] Thus Augustine thinks that the politics practiced by a member of the City of God is more genuinely political than that practiced by a member of the City of Man. Faith gives political actors a broader sense of the whole to which the parts must be referred to create a flourishing community. Faith also leads political actors to refuse to worship their political activity or their community in a way that is sure to ruin them both. By contrast, the City of Man pursues incomplete, fragmentary desires, while having more or less inadequate notions of human flourishing, and a self-deceptive assessment of its own vices.

However, the Christian is called to be a witness for a way of life that a regime needs, yet will probably push away. Augustine is careful to take into account the way the love of human glory obscures divine glory. Political regimes might require Christian wisdom, but they do not necessarily want it, or even see the sense in it. Christian service to the community consists partly of exposing the blind spots of the community, so as to push it in the direction of a more complete vision. This means that Christians who shoulder authority for the sake of loving service at some point will be misunderstood, and perhaps even persecuted. They are called to work for the betterment of a regime that, more than their fellow citizens, they know to be partial, more or less unjust, and ultimately evanescent, all the while being aware that this self-giving is not going to be easy or appreciated.

Still, while the glory of this way of life may be obscure to many, Augustine thinks it is more real, because it is more realistic, about the problems and possibilities of political life than either classical republicanism or liberal individualism. Augustine urges his readers to citizenship in the City of God and the reorientation of priorities that flow from it, but he does not promise human glory. Rather, he promises struggle, detachment, and self-abandonment. He asks that we serve whatever context we finds ourselves in without any assurance of honor, power, or conventional success (Mark 8:34–38). For Augustine, a genuinely Christian politics must open its arms to the world and also to the cross.

Notes

1. For an account of Political Augustinianism, see Robert Barr, "The Two Cities in Saint Augustine," *Laval theologique et philosophique* 18 (1982) 211–29. For a survey of the literature and an attempt to clear Augustine himself of these charges, see the chapter, "Political Augustinianism?" in Henri deLubac, *Theological Fragments* (trans. Rebecca Howell Balinski; San Francisco: Ignatius Press, 1989) 234–85. Many political theorists argue that the impetus to liberal neutrality, secularism, and tolerance arose from the discord sown by the kind of politically charged religiosity associated with Political

Augustinianism. See, for example, John Rawls, "Justice as Fairness: Political not Meta-physical," *Philosophy and Public Affairs* (Summer 1985) 225; Judith Shklar, *Ordinary Vices* (Cambridge, MA: Harvard University Press, 1984) 5; Jeffrey Stout, *The Flight from Authority: Religion, Morality, and the Quest for Autonomy* (Notre Dame, IN: University of Notre Dame Press, 1981) 13, 235–42.

2. See for example, Hannah Arendt, *The Human Condition* (Chicago: University of Chicago Press, 1958) 14, 50–58. For responses see Peter J. Burnell, "Is the Augustin-ian Heaven Inhuman? The Arguments of Martin Heidegger and Hannah Arendt," in *History, Apocalypse, and the Secular Imagination: New Essays on Augustine's City of God* (eds. Mark Vessey, Karla Pollmann, and Allan D. Fitzgerald; Bowling Green, OH: Phi-losophy Documentation Center, 1999) 283–92; and Rowan Williams, "Politics and the Soul: A Reading of the City of God" *Milltown Studies* 19:20 (1987) 55–72.

3. Reinhold Niebuhr, "Augustine's Political Realism," in *The City of God: A Collec-tion of Critical Essays* (ed. Dorothy Donnelly; New York: Peter Land, 1995) 120.

4. For examples of this general approach see Jean Bethke-Elshtain, *Augustine and the Limits of Politics* (Notre Dame: University of Notre Dame Press, 1998); Her-bert Deane, *The Political and Social Ideas of St. Augustine* (New York: Columbia University Press, 1963); John Figgis, *The Political Aspects of St. Augustine's* City of God (London: Longman's, 1921). Similarly, some argue that Augustine's philoso-phy of history can resist the kind of progressive notions of history and politics as-sociated with the Enlightenment and especially totalitarian ideologies. So, for in-stance, Karl Lowith, *Meaning in History* (Chicago: University of Chicago Press, 1949) 160–73; Eric Voegelin, *The New Science of Politics* (Chicago: University of Chicago Press, 1952).

5. Robert Markus, *Saeculum: History and Society in the Thought of St. Augustine* (Cambridge: Cambridge University Press, 1970) 56, 71.

6. Oliver O'Donovan, "Augustine's *City of God* XIX and Western Political Thought," *Dionysius* 11 (1987) 89–110, esp. 102.

7. Deane, *The Political and Social Ideas of Saint Augustine*, 78. See also R. W. Dyson, *The Pilgrim City: Social and Political Ideas in the Writings of St. Augustine of Hippo* (Suffolk, UK: Boydell Press, 2001) 46–61.

8. P. J. Burnell, "The Status of Politics in Augustine's *City of God*," *History of Polit-ical Thought* 13 (1992) 13–29.

9. See, for example, Paul J. Weithman, "Toward an Augustinian Liberalism," *Faith and Philosophy* 8:4 (1991) 461–80. Of course, other scholars argue that Augustine's po-litical theology diverges from liberalism. See John Millbank, *Theology and Social The-ory* (Cambridge: Blackwell, 1991); Michael J. White, "Pluralism and Secularism in the Political Order: St. Augustine and Theoretical Liberalism," *University of Dayton Review* 22:3 (Summer 1994) 137–53.

10. Unless otherwise noted, all internal citations are to the *City of God*. With some slight modifications, translations are from Augustine, *City of God* (trans. Henry Bet-tenson; New York: Penguin Books, 1984). The Latin text I consulted was *Corpus Chris-tianorum Series Latina*, volumes 47–48 (Belgium: Turnholti, 1954).

11. See Peter Brown, *Augustine of Hippo* (Berkeley: University of California Press, 1967) 311: "The *City of God* is a book about glory."

12. Mark Vessey, "Introduction" in *History, Apocalypse, and the Secular Imagination: New Essays on Augustine's* City of God (eds. Mark Vessey, Karla Pollmann, and Allan D. Fitzgerald, O.S.A.; Bowling Green, OH: Philosophy Documentation Center, 1999), 14. The opening sentence reads, "*Gloriosissimam civitatem dei sive in hoc temporum cursu cum inter impios peregrinatur ex fide vivens, sive in illa stabilitate sedis aeternae, quam nunc expectat per patientiam, quoadusque iustitia convertatur in iudicium, deinceps adeptura per excellentiam victoria ultima et pace perfecta, hoc opera instituto et mea ad te promissione debito defendere adversus eos, qui conditori eius deos suos praeferunt, fili carissime Marcelline, suscepi, magnum opus et arduum, sed Deus adiutor noster est*" (I, preface).

13. Augustine, *Answer to Maximinus the Arian* 2.13.2–9, in *Arianism and Other Heresies* (trans. Roland Teske; Hyde Park, NY: New City Press, 1995).

14. For ancient texts as spiritual exercises see Pierre Hadot, *Philosophy as a Way of Life* (Oxford: Blackwell, 1995).

15. As Rowan Williams points out, "Preoccupation with achievement brings in its wake a preoccupation with power and pre-eminence: the whole point of the quest for glory lies in the urge to gain advantage over another. In contrast, the love and longing for goodness which marks the city of God is of its essence a desire which seeks to share its object" ("Politics and the Soul," 62).

16. "Thus we find in the earthly city a double significance: in one respect it displays its own presence, and in the other it serves by its presence to signify the Heavenly City" (XV.2).

17. "The City of God developed not in the light, but in the shadow" (XVIII.1). Machiavelli provides an obvious example of someone whose worship of conventional success and security leads him to hold the City of God in contempt. Scorn for the "impractical" goods the City of God seeks is a hallmark of Machiavelli's critique of Christianity. He urges a "useful" and "effectual" truth rather than the "imagination" thereof. See Machiavelli, *The Prince* (trans. Leo Paul S. de Alvarez; Prospect Heights, IL: Waveland Press, 1980) 93 (Chapter 15): "And many have imagined republics and principates that have never been seen or known to be in truth; because there is such a distance between how one lives and how one should live that he who lets go that which is done for that which ought to be done learns his ruin rather than his preservation—for a man who wishes to profess the good in everything needs must fall among so many who are nor good."

18. Augustine illustrates this point with brilliant subtlety in the opening chapters of *City of God*, Book 18, wherein he traces the development of the two cities alongside each other. In this sketch, central figures in salvation history like Abraham and Moses are nothing but blips on the radar screens of powerful nations and empires. The people who from one perspective are the pivots on whom the history of human salvation turns are those who from another deserve no recognition.

19. See 3.17 for Augustine's reflections on the ways he reuses material from Roman historians.

20. "Why must an empire be deprived of peace, in order that it may be great?" (3.10).

21. In this vein, Augustine asks his readers to imagine two men. One has limited resources, but is content with them. He is moderate, loyal, compassionate, peaceful, and kind. The other man is rich, but "tortured by fear, worn out with sadness, burnt up

with ambition, never knowing the serenity of repose, always panting and sweating in his struggles with his opponents" (4.4).

22. "What a splendid religion for the weak to flee to for liberation! He asks for the truth that will set him free; and it is believed that it is expedient for him to be deceived" (4.27).

23. Thus Augustine repeatedly tells his audience that the only god really worth worshiping is the god of happiness (e.g., 4.23). It has been argued that by Augustine's time paganism was no longer a living force: James O'Donnell, "The Demise of Paganism," *Traditio* 35 (1979) 45–88. Yet Augustine's concern is not merely pagan religion, but the psychic motivation underlying it—the drive to assure oneself of the external goods that constitute a certain understanding of success. For Augustine, this psychic attitude is the motivation for pagan religion. But in another sense, it is the motivation for empire, conceived as a communal project devoted to assuring such success.

24. "The only man who would not be satisfied with this God is the man who is not satisfied with his gift. I repeat, the only man who would not be satisfied with God, the giver of happiness, as worthy of his worship, is the man who is not satisfied with happiness itself as worthy of his acceptance" (4.25).

25. "The kingdoms of the East had enjoyed renown for a long time, when God decided that a Western empire should arise, later in time, but more renowned for the extent and grandeur of its dominion. And, to suppress the grievous evils of many nations, he entrusted this dominion to those men, in preference to all others, who served their country for the sake of honor, praise, and glory, who looked to find that glory in their country's safety above their own and who suppressed greed for money and many other faults in favor of that one fault of theirs, the love of praise" (5.14).

26. See Rowan Williams, "Politics and the Soul," 61: "The remarkable success of the early Roman republic is not due to the favor of the Roman gods (we have already seen in Books II and III that they show little sign of being concerned for the welfare of their worshipers), nor simply to immanent causes like the extraordinary power of disinterested virtue. Augustine's explanation is at once cynical and theological: the lust for glory restrains the more obvious factors making for disintegration in the state; and God elects to raise up a new empire over against the ancient tyrannies of the east, one which at least represents some kind of judgment upon the unbridled *libido dominandi* of those older systems."

27. Among many examples of his praise of Roman virtue is Augustine's account of Curtius, who "spurred on his horse and hurled himself, fully armed, into a gaping chasm in obedience to the oracles of his gods. They had ordered that the best possession of the Romans should be consigned to that abyss, and the Romans could only interpret this as referring to their excellence in warriors and in arms; hence it appeared that at the gods' command a fully-armed warrior must hurl himself to that death" (5.18).

28. "The Roman Empire was not extended and did not attain glory in men's eyes simply for this, that men of this stamp should be accorded that kind of reward. It has this further purpose, that the citizens of that Eternal City, in the days of their pilgrimage, should fix their eyes steadily and soberly on those examples and observe what love they should have towards the City on high, in view of life eternal, if the earthly city had received such devotion from her citizens, in their hope of glory in the sight of men" (5.14).

29. By contrast, in *City of God* 13.4 Augustine points to the martyrs who overcome their fear of death through belief in a different kind of glory.

30. Robert Vacca, "The Theology of Disorder in the *Iliad*," *Religion and Literature* 23 (1991) 1–22, quotation from p. 17. For an account of the social and political consequences of love of glory in the ancient world, see my *Revaluing Ethics: Aristotle's Dialectical Pedagogy* (Albany: State University of New York Press, 2000) Chapter 2.

31. For example, Augustine says, "The man who covets glory either 'strives by the right way' for it or 'struggles by trickery and deceit,' desiring to seem a good man without being so" (5.19).

32. See Peter Brown, "Political Society," in *Augustine: A Collection of Critical Essays* (ed. Robert Markus; Garden City, NY: Doubleday Anchor Books, 1972) 320–21: "Those who refuse to recognize dependence are those most overtaken by the urgency of domination, or the need to secure the dependence of others."

33. Thomas Hobbes, the great theorist of power, recognizes the link between the drive for power and security, on the one hand, and restless anxiety on the other: "So that every man, especially those that are over provident, are in estate like to that of *Prometheus*. For as *Prometheus*, (which interpreted is, *The prudent man*,) was bound to the hill *Caucasus*, a place of large prospect, where, an Eagle feeding on his liver, devoured in the day, as much as was repayred in the night: So that man, which looks too far before him, in the care of future time, hath his heart all the day long, gnawed on by feare of death, poverty, or other calamity; and has no repose, nor pause from anxiety, but in sleep" (*Leviathan* [NY: Penguin Books, 1968] 169, emphasis in the original).

34. Indeed, the myth of the eternity of Rome may have contributed to its downfall. See Stephen Williams and Gerard Friell, *Theodosius: The Empire At Bay* (New Haven: Yale University Press, 1994) 26: "The constant invocation of a changeless, eternal Rome by the orators and historians, their effortless comparisons with the fabulous Catos and Scipios of the distant past, was more than just a natural reverence for tradition and continuity. It verged on the classical hypnotic fixation, which continued even up to the Enlightenment when Gibbon was writing. It presented Rome as a kind of inviolate essence, transcending all upheaval and change, and in doing so soothed and blunted the critical faculties of many contemporaries who had to grapple with a radically different world."

35. These are the vices Augustine identifies with the origin of empires as well. See 18.2.

36. "As far as I can see, the distinction between victors and vanquished has not the slightest importance for security, for moral standards, or even for human dignity. It is merely a matter of the arrogance of human glory, the coin in which these men 'received their reward,' who were on fire with unlimited lust for glory, and waged wars of burning fury. Is it the case that the conqueror's lands are exempt from taxes? Have the victors access to knowledge forbidden to the others? Are there not many senators in other lands, who do not know Rome even by sight? Take away national complacency, and what are all men but simply men? If the perverse standards of the world would allow men to receive honors proportional to their deserts, even so the honor of men should not be accounted an important matter; smoke has no weight" (5.18).

37. Cf. Robert Dodaro, "Eloquent Lies, Just Wars and the Politics of Persuasion: Reading Augustine's *City of God* in a 'Post-Modern' World," *Augustinian Studies* 25

(1994) 77–137, esp. 89–90, "The central thesis of the mature Augustine that original sin produces an abiding fear of death, also establishes this fear as the cornerstone of all political ideology and of the defensive social and political behaviors which they sustain. . . . For the Augustine of the *City of God*, empire maintenance, with the attendant subjugation of peoples and the religious, intellectual, and cultural props which legitimate it is the most grotesque social manifestation of this fear of death. However, just as the objective evil which empires sustain has to be veiled from the view of its practitioners, so too must the fear of death which motivates empire maintenance be veiled from the view of all concerned. Hence every act of political deception occurs on two levels: there is the lie or distortion itself which political authorities and their rhetors create and pass on to the public, and there is the self-deception which veils the lie from the officials who tell it."

38. As Rowan Williams says, "In short, while it [Rome] may be empirically an intelligible body, it is constantly undermining its own communal values which answer to the truest human needs" ("Politics and the Soul," 60).

39. "One part of the earthly city has been made into an image of the Heavenly City, by signifying (*significando*) something other than itself, namely, that other City; and for that reason it is a servant. For it was established not for its own sake but in order to signify another City; and since it was signified by an antecedent sign, the foreshadowing sign was itself foreshadowed" (15.2).

40. "We see, then, that all man's use of temporal things is related to the enjoyment of earthly peace; whereas in the Heavenly City it is related to the enjoyment of eternal peace" (19.14).

41. Clearly, this brings up Augustine's famous distinction between *uti* and *frui*, by which he divides the objects of love into those which ought to be used and those which ought to be enjoyed. For a good sketch of the distinction, its importance and development in Augustine's thought, as well as the scholarly controversies surrounding it, see William Riordan O'Connor, "The *Uti/Frui* Distinction in Augustine's Ethics," *Augustinian Studies* 14 (1983) 45–62. Since Augustine does not bring this distinction up explicitly in *City of God*, I shall bracket the issue, focusing instead on the way Augustine reconceptualizes the notion of "use" in the *City of God*.

42. *Confessions* 1.1.1.

43. See 19.3–9 for an extended treatment of the problem. This theme is present in many spiritual traditions. The Buddha, for instance, says life is like honey on a knife; we get cut even as we lick its sweetness. See Walpola Rahula, *What the Buddha Taught* (New York: Grove Press, 1974) 17–29.

44. O'Donovan, "Augustine's *City of God* XIX and Western Political Thought," 91, 97.

45. See O'Donovan, "Augustine's *City of God* XIX and Western Political Thought," 97: "He more than once maintained that there was no 'use' of things to wrong ends, but that the proper term was 'abuse' and his preferred habit was to describe the wicked as 'wishing to make use' of things that they ought to enjoy rather than as actually doing so."

46. "So the earthly city, whose life is not based on faith, aims at an earthly peace, and it limits the harmonious agreement of citizens concerning the giving and obeying of orders to the establishment of a kind of compromise between human wills about the things relevant to mortal life. In contrast, the Heavenly City—or rather the part of

it which is on pilgrimage in this condition of mortality—must needs make use of this peace also, until this mortal state . . . passes away. And therefore, it leads what we may call a life of captivity in this earthly city as in a foreign land, although it has already received the promise of redemption. . . . And yet it does not hesitate to obey the laws of the earthly city by which those things are regulated; and the purpose of this obedience is that, since this mortal condition is shared by both cities, a harmony may be preserved between them in things that are relevant to this condition" (19.17).

47. O'Donovan points out that it is a mistake to think "that the City of God and the earthly city get on together by having a common use and different ends. From this misreading we would conclude that the earthly city is a neutral institution of shared means to private ends. . . . [But] Augustine does not think that the earthly city is constituted in the same way as the relation between the earthly city and the heavenly city is constituted. He would not say that there was a common use but differing ends among the members of the earthly city. There is in fact a common end, eternal punishment, and no use in the proper sense at all, because there is no utility, no real final good which gives value to the pursuit of intermediate goods" ("Augustine's *City of God* XIX and Western Political Thought," 98).

48. "God, then, created all things in supreme wisdom and ordered them in perfect justice; and in establishing the mortal race of mankind as the greatest ornament of earthly things, he has given to mankind certain goods in this life. These are: temporal peace, in proportion to the short span of mortal life—the peace that consists in bodily health and soundness, and in fellowship with one's kind; and everything necessary to safeguard or recover this peace—those things which are appropriate and accessible to our senses, light, speech, air to breathe, water to drink. . . . And all this is granted under the most equitable of condition: that every mortal who uses aright such goods, goods designed to serve the peace of mortal men, shall receive goods greater in degree and superior in kind, namely, the peace of immortality, and the glory and honor appropriate to it in a life which is eternal for the enjoyment of God and one's neighbor in God, whereas he who wrongly uses those mortal goods shall lose them, and not receive the blessings of eternal life" (19.13).

49. Butheric, the commander of Salonica, refused to allow a star charioteer accused of rape to compete in the hippodrome. A riot ensued, and in the chaos Butheric and several officers were murdered and their corpses mutilated and dragged through the streets. Theodosius, by now Emperor of both East and West, was furious: "Accordingly on a certain day when the people once again thronged excitedly into the hippodrome for the races, at a signal the gates were barred. Without pity, deaf to the screams and entreaties of the people (or even enflamed by them) the troops proceeded over several hours to butcher the spectators indiscriminately. According to Theoderet, 7,000 people of both sexes and all ages were slaughtered" (Williams and Friell, *Theodosius*, 68). Theodosius, however, came to regret his decision and, putting aside his imperial trappings, did public penance for several months in the cathedral of Milan.

50. Williams and Friell, *Theodosius*, 70.

51. See Dodaro, "Eloquent Lies," 94: "Hence, Augustine contrasts self-glory as a value in Roman political life with confession, a rhetoric of a different sort, one which 'decenters the subject' by rendering the politician more conscious of his or her own infallibility, and hence more likely to render just judgments."

52. "We are commanded to love this one Good with all our heart, with all our soul, with all our strength; and to this Good we must be led by those who love us; and to it we must lead those whom we love. . . . For if a man loves himself, his one wish is to achieve blessedness. Now this end is 'to cling to God'. Thus, if a man knows how to love himself, the commandment to love his neighbor bids him to do all he can to bring his neighbor to God. This is the worship of God (*Dei cultus*), this is true religion (*vera religio*); this is right devotion (*recta pietas*); this is the service we owe to God (*Deo debita servitus*)" (10.3).

53. It may seem strange to hold out Theodosius' Christian witness as a form of loving service. However, as Oliver O'Donovan points out, when talking about love of neighbor, Augustine does not give much thought to the needs of the body. He means "evangelism." One's neighbor "is a man, and men find their blessedness in God. The only service of lasting significance that we can render him is to lead him to that blessedness" (*The Problem of Self-Love in St. Augustine* [New Haven: Yale University Press, 1980] 112).

54. "Consequently, in the earthly city its wise men who live by men's standards have pursued the goods of the body or of their own mind or both. Or those of them who were able to know God 'did not honor him as God, nor did they give thanks to him, but they dwindled into futility in their thoughts, and their senseless heart was darkened in asserting their wisdom'—that is, exalting themselves in their wisdom, under the dominion of pride—'they became foolish, and changed the glory of an imperishable God into an image representing a perishable man.' In the Heavenly City, on the other hand, man's only wisdom is the devotion which rightly worships the true God and looks for its reward in the fellowship of the saints . . . 'so that God may be all in all'" (14.28).

55. I am using "regime" in Leo Strauss' sense: "We shall translate *politeia* by 'regime', taking regime in the broad sense in which we sometimes take it when speaking, e.g., of the Ancien Regime of France. The thought connecting 'way of life of a society' and 'form of government' can provisionally be stated as follows: The character, or tone, of a society depends on what the society regards as most respectable or most worthy of admiration. But by regarding certain habits or attitudes as most respectable, a society admits the superiority, the superior dignity, of those human beings who most perfectly embody the habits or attitudes in question. That is to say, every society regards a specific human type (or a specific mixture of human types) as authoritative. . . . In order to be truly authoritative, the human beings who embody the admired habits or attitudes must have the decisive say within the community in broad daylight: they must form the regime. When the classics were chiefly concerned with the different regimes, and especially with the best regime, they implied that the paramount social phenomenon, or that social phenomenon then which only the natural phenomena are more fundamental, is the regime" (Leo Strauss, *Natural Right and History* [Chicago: University of Chicago Press, 1953] 136–37).

56. Aristotle, *Nicomachean Ethics* 1141b21; 1141b24–28; *Politics* 1252a1–8; 1260a17–19.

57. *Nicomachean Ethics* 1093a27–1094b10.

58. Williams, "Politics and the Soul," 58.

59. Of course, other religious and philosophical traditions could supply an analogous kind of wisdom born from an analogous sense of the human person. But doing the comparative philosophy and theology required to flesh this point out fully is obviously beyond the scope of this chapter.

60. I could illustrate this point with the following: "Some time ago in a conversation with Wes Jackson in which we were laboring to define the causes of the modern ruination of the farmland, we finally got around to the money economy. I said that an economy based on energy would be more benign because it would be more comprehensive. Wes would not agree. 'An energy economy still wouldn't be comprehensive enough.' 'Well,' I said, 'then what kind of economy *would* be comprehensive enough?' He hesitated for a moment, and then, grinning, said, 'The Kingdom of God'" (Wendell Berry, *Home Economics* [NY: Farrar, Strauss, and Giroux, 1987] 54).

61. *City of God*, 19.7, where Augustine says that Christians must be willing to engage their civic duties despite the injustice and partiality of existing political orders. Also there is this passage: "While this Heavenly City, therefore, is on pilgrimage in this world, she calls out citizens from all nations and so collects a society of aliens, speaking all languages. She takes no account of any difference in customs, laws, and institutions, by which earthly peace is achieved and preserved—not that she annuls or abolishes any of those, rather, she maintains them and follows them" (19.17).

Part III

AUGUSTINIAN INFLUENCE
AND PERSPECTIVES

10

Toward a Contemporary Augustinian Understanding of Politics

Todd Breyfogle[1]

<hr style="height:5px;background:black;border:none;" />

THE INTEREST IN AUGUSTINE IN contemporary political theory is in some ways perplexing. There can be no doubt, as several scholars have noted, that Augustine's examination of the self is of interest to our own self-obsessed age.[2] He has been appealed to, especially, by those authors in political theory who have engaged in reflecting on the "crisis" of modernity.[3] Just as the defenders of Augustine have indeed been varied and devoted to different aspects of his thought, so too modern criticism of Augustine has been harsh and varied. In short, modern uses of Augustine have landed the African bishop simultaneously in opposing camps.

Thus, Augustine has been seen both as the hope of post-war Europe and as the decisive contributor to "creating the present condition of the earth, a planet in ecological and nuclear crisis."[4] His work has been seen both as the origin of ideology and as a powerful critique of ideology.[5] His political realism has been lauded on the one hand and criticized as overly pessimistic on the other.[6] Similarly, "political Augustinianism" has been viewed as risking complacency in the face of despotic rule, yet at the same time Augustine's thought has been identified with the German liberation theology of Jurgen Moltmann.[7] Augustine's hermeneutics of suspicion have been likened to that of Noam Chomsky, while his hermeneutics of tradition has found its contemporary expression in the person of Russell Kirk.[8] Scholars have identified Augustine as holding that political rule is, variously, good and natural to human beings, neutral, and an artificial and necessary evil.[9] Political philosophers have seen Augustine as evocative of the ancient polis, and as the *locus classicus* of medieval spiritual representation.[10] Others have seen in Augustine the roots of varieties of modern liberal politics, with resonances in Hobbes, Tocqueville, and in contemporary attempts to advocate a revised Augustinian-Thomistic narrative.[11] Against authoritarian interpretations, Augustine has been advanced as offering a politics of limits, as an advocate of modern skepticism and the desacralization of politics, as well as the source of a postmodern, or perhaps post-postmodern, skepticism and resacralization of politics.[12]

How would one make one's way through such a bewildering array of contradictory contemporary interpretations? Indeed, how could one add any clarity to this mass of assessments, particularly given Isidore of Seville's famous caveat that anyone who claims to have read all of Augustine is a liar? This multiplicity should caution us against the notion that Augustine had "a theory" of politics and should make us think twice before identifying Augustine with any particular strain of political thought—ancient or modern.

We are not alone: even a superficial survey of medieval political debates shows Augustine quoted on opposing sides of the argument at hand, the supporter of conciliarists, monarchists, and papalists alike. Such are the perils of writing so much, with such sophistication and attention to specific circumstances as well as perennial human predicaments.[13] Any rich and prominent author is bound to be invoked by contradictory partisans. The very multiplicity of opinion suggests two things: that interpreters are (perhaps necessarily) prone to cast Augustine according to their own likes and dislikes; and that the very variety suggests that Augustine, like any great thinker, possesses a richness which is both suggestive and not easily pinned down. But the ambiguities in Augustine's reflections on politics derive from two more fundamental aspects—one general, one specific—of his thought.

The first, general ambiguity of Augustine's thought concerns his political terminology. Augustine is intentionally ambiguous and inconsistent in his use of terminology for considered philosophical and rhetorical reasons. Signs (words, concepts) never exhaustively or accurately describe things, and reliance on a single word or concepts runs the risk of reifying and so falsifying the thing itself.[14] Moreover, language evokes sufficiently diverse understandings that Augustine uses diverse terms in the hopes that at least one term or expression will adequately communicate with diverse readers.

While Augustine is notoriously inconsistent with his terminology, it is nonetheless perhaps in the realm of political vocabulary that Augustine has the most to offer to a contemporary understanding of politics. Augustine does not, of course, speak of "politics" and has no theory of the "state." The insistence on the use of modern political terminology with respect to Augustine, even with caveats, has done much to obscure the contours of Augustine's thought.[15] Moreover, Augustine wrote no systematic treatise on politics as such, nor did he discuss (i.e., qua political science in the style of Plato, Aristotle, or later Aquinas) the best regime. The variety intrinsic to Augustine's own expression is compounded by the ambiguities created by the similarities and difference between our political symbolization and his. We are heirs, conceptually and linguistically, to a Roman-Christian jurisprudence, but Augustine's vocabulary affords no simple correspondence between his era and ours, and it is difficult for us to be fully conscious of (or fully to set aside) the presuppositions, prejudices, and preconceptions of our age.

Second, and more specific to the present topic, I would like to suggest that the considerable interpretive divergences surrounding Augustine's work are intrinsic to his formulation of the "two cities" itself. I wish, first, to recast this formulation in terms of prudential attachment to and detachment from each of the cities, and then articulate three often overlooked implications of Augustine's political anthropology. My aim in what follows is to be suggestive rather than conclusive.[16] Many of my debts will be clear, but I trust that my greatest debt will be to Augustine himself. The very spirit of such an undertaking is faithful to Augustine, for Augustine recognized that reflection on political things is always the prudential consideration of contingent circumstances largely dependent upon a people's self-understanding of their age.

*

Augustine, it is well known, held that human beings live in tension between the heavenly and the earthly and are characterized by a divided soul, caught between the fear of death and the desire for a peaceful soul at rest in God. "Our hearts are restless," Augustine writes at the beginning of the *Confessions*, "until they find rest in Thee."[17] In this context, Augustine's formulation of the two cities both incorporates and redefines the classical understanding of the *polis*. First, it universalizes human attachments to one another irrespective of political boundaries. Second, the good life for human beings no longer finds its highest expression in participation in the life of the *polis*, but takes its bearings from a transcendent, transpolitical end—the contemplation of God in faith and virtue. Third, Augustine denies any human institution a claim to divine sanction or perfect justice; there is no historical progress after Christ, but only providential justice.[18]

At the same time, however, the city continues to have a role to play in the formation of excellent souls.[19] Political rule is held to be a good, subordinate only to the body, freedom, family, and friends, and above honor (or favor) and possessions (*pecunia*). Indeed, the *civitas* has proximity to the family insofar as it is "usually held to have the place of a parent." In regulating "these things which may be called ours for a time," temporal law "maintains order through fear" of the loss of possessions and properly serves as exemplary of natural law in the identification and promotion of virtue.[20] Augustine's assertion that the *civitas terrena* is a qualified good should not detract from the fact that he does see the city as good.

The framework of the two cities, caused as they are by two loves—love of self to the exclusion of God and love of God to the exclusion of self—serves notice that spiritual and civil peace derives from the right ordering of human loves.[21] The city is good insofar as the loves which animate it are rightly ordered and referred to God. This does not render the *civitas terrena* a pale imitation of the *civitas Dei*, but rather the imperfect expression of human loves which can be perfected only eschatalogically.[22] The multiplicity of interpretations of Augustine come down to this: human beings must be simultaneously attached to and detached from both the earthly city and the heavenly city. How to manage such a disposition is the subject of Augustine's political anthropology generally. The love of neighbor and love of God inform one another, but the practical management of these loves in daily life is a difficult task.

The *libido dominandi* and *amor sui* prompt, for Augustine, diseased attachment to the world. Yet, the command to love one's neighbor requires some attachment to this life. How are detachment and attachment to be reconciled? In political terms, how does one keep allegiance to the *civitas Dei* while not neglecting the demand to manifest *caritas* in this earthly life? Let me phrase the matter somewhat differently. How do we pursue justice knowing that justice will never in this life be attained? How does one cultivate and sustain a love of justice while recognizing that no human arrangement will do anything but approximate the shadow of justice?

The *City of God* is of course the *locus classicus* for Augustine's political reflections and the sensitive reader will detect Augustine's running conversation with at least the ideas of Plato's *Republic*, Aristotle's political and ethical works, and certainly Cicero's *Republic*, from which he quotes explicitly. Nonetheless, his account of classical regime theory lasts barely half a dozen lines—what matters is not the form of the rule but who exercises it; the character of a democracy or aristocracy or monarchy depends on the character and loves of the people.[23]

Augustine shuns modern tendencies toward abstract notions of a just regime or social structures, for such abstractions subordinate the varieties of actual virtue in concrete terms. Additionally, such abstractions seek to legislate a uniformity of virtue, which by definition eliminates virtue's prudential component and precludes the exercise of true *caritas* as a specific response to a specific circumstance. In contrast to "the state," "class struggle," or "social forces," Augustine speaks concretely of *res publica, populi, civitates, utilitas, ius, lex, caritas, amor, mores, societas, amicitia,* and *veritas*. This is not the occasion to explore each of these terms of Augustine's political anthropology (but we shall shortly return to the last three—*societas, amicitia,* and *veritas*).

Nonetheless, these orienting terms of Augustine's political anthropology prompt us to recast our own thinking about Augustine's fundamental political question—What binds a people together?—in more concrete terms.

But even the inattentive reader who encounters the *City of God* as a whole, rather than anthologized, discovers that Augustine's account of political things is intertwined with discussions of demons, pagan worship, scriptures' record of the Fall, eternal beatitude, and so forth. This is to say that, for Augustine, politics is a part of the human condition, but only a part. In Augustine's mind, in contrast to the dominant thinking of our age, the destiny of man presents itself in other than purely political terms.

One might properly speak of Augustine's political anthropology, where politics becomes adjectival rather than substantive. Civil theology treats man as a citizen. Natural theology treats man as an animal. Only Christian theology, for Augustine, treats man as a person made in the image of God.[24] He does, of course, speak of the individual, and while the self is in some sense isolated before and in the love of God, the self is always directed outward by the command to love one's neighbor. Augustine does not define the *civitas* in terms of justice, or in terms of peace, or sovereignty, but of love. That is to say that the character of a city is defined by the character of its people and their loves.[25]

Attachment and detachment are inherent in *caritas* itself; worship and action, contemplation and necessity will always be in tension: "The love of truth longs for a condition of holy leisure; the necessity of love requires that we engage in the just work required of us."[26] Part of understanding this tension is to recognize that *caritas*, for Augustine, is not mere overflowing sentiment in modern terms.[27] On the contrary, love (wanting what is best for one's neighbor) and justice (giving to each what is due him) both require prudential judgment. It is precisely exercising this judgment which is the stuff of virtue in general for Augustine.

The prudential judgment which informs *caritas* is itself governed by two limitations, one epistemological and one personal. Quite simply, it is difficult for us to discern what is best for ourselves, much less for another, and even if we could, we are limited beings who do not have the physical or spiritual capacity for perfect divine love. In judging what is appropriate for one's neighbor, *caritas* comes to make use of individual habit, collective custom, and established conventions as to standards of virtue and justice. This, of course, is anything but blind acquiescence to the status quo. The *civitas Dei*, and Christ its builder and maker, always offer a standard by which the imperfections of the earthly city are made clear. But Augustine recognizes that earthly peace is sufficiently fragile,[28] and the terrors of an unleashed *libido dominandi* so evil, that anything other than minor and halting reform is to fall into the error of Pelagianism, of pursuing "perfection as the crow flies."[29] There will always be imperfections in the world, regardless of the structure of institutions, because of the limitations and imperfections of men. Augustine would view the modern individual and collective quest for perfection—with the force of the modern bureaucratic state behind it—as a form of Pelagian hubris which, at best, discloses a lack of self-understanding and, at worst, exhibits self-deception of a most pernicious sort.

⋆ ⋆

It is the genius of modern political thinkers to have devised political and legal institutions which moderate our worst tendencies. But those thinkers recognized that nonpolitical associations also restrained our nonangelic propensities and fostered the formation of character in the democratic citizenry.[30] The continued interest, among political theorists and others, in communitarianism and civil society underscores the contemporary importance of informal, nonstate associations in forming the social and political habits appropriate to a democratic regime. It is Augustine's specifically noninstitutional understanding of political things, then, which may be of most salutary interest to contemporary political thought.[31]

What sort of political relationships, then, does Augustine envisage? To begin with, for Augustine, political relationships are always specific relationships between persons, that is, between father and son, between neighbors, between official and subordinate, and between trading partners. The relationship between the citizen and "the state" or the ruling power is an abstraction of what is properly understood as the concrete relation between a particular citizen and a particular official in the political bureaucracy.[32] The official may represent the ruling power, but any formal bureaucratic relationship is always informed by personhood and accompanied by individual responsibility. If the persons are Christian, their dealings should exhibit the charity appropriate to Christianity as well as the duty or fidelity appropriate to the position. There is no abstract notion of Christian government apart from the individual Christian actions of those in government, as Augustine's discussion of pagan and Christian emperors makes clear.[33] This analysis does not dismiss the inescapable tension between Christian charity and public duty, though Augustine was more willing than many in our own day to see fidelity to public duty as itself an exercise of Christian charity on behalf of the common good.[34]

Beyond the specificity of relationships, there are three primary terms—*societas, amicitia,* and *veritas*—which orient the practical side of Augustine's analysis of the two cities, terms which are often neglected in contemporary appropriations and which are important for articulating a contemporary Augustinian understanding of politics.

By *societas*, Augustine means something much different from our contemporary usage. Far from being the abstract collective entity which provides for common goods or to which identity references are made, Augustine means "association."[35] Thus, *societas* is the sum total of those innumerable single and repeated engagements between people, engagements as diverse as trade, neighborliness, familial relations, and civic friendship. In classical Latin, and especially in Cicero, *societas* encompasses "fellowship" and collective unions for common purposes as well as "partnership," especially in trading relationships.[36] These relationships are not "political" strictly speaking, except insofar as they take place in the *civitas* or are governed, for example, by rules of international commerce. The web of associations which constitute *societas* are, then, essentially individual encounters which, nonetheless, have a public and often political significance.[37] That is, these associations are primarily individual engagements of mutual benefit which have derivative secondary (if often unintended) effects for the city as a whole. In distinguishing between the primary individual and secondary public effects of these individual associations, we must be careful not to confuse Augustine's position with the formal contemporary distinction between "public" and "private." For Augustine, the description of a "private" good is almost always pejorative, but his judgment pertains not to the sphere of action but to the way in which the action was pursued. For Augustine, a private good is frequently a good referred only to oneself and is one which cannot be enjoyed by others, only by me. Mutual exchanges of commerce or goodwill are not, therefore, properly termed "private" for Augustine in the way in which we use the term today.[38]

Just as the ordering of one's soul yields ordered and harmonious relationships with others, so too harmonious individual associations produce an ordered and harmonious city. But this public harmony, is, at it were, a byproduct of these individual relationships. If there is not justice in an individual, Augustine contends, how can there be any justice in a city composed of such individuals.[39] Thus, earthly peace and just rule are common goods, but goods which are ancillary to people pursuing essentially individual relationships. The household is "the beginning, or rather a small component part of the city, and every beginning is directed to some end of its own kind, and every component part contributes to the completeness of the whole of which it forms a part. The implication is quite apparent, that domestic peace contributes to the peace of the city—that is, the ordered harmony of those who live together in a house . . . contributes to the ordered harmony concerning authority and obedience obtaining among the citizens."[40] It is a mistake to read this passage, and others like it, as suggesting the city is the household writ large; Augustine does not contend that political authority is essentially the extension of paternal authority. The well-ordered household contributes to the good of the city precisely because it pursues an end "of its own kind," its proper, private end. That said, it is worth noting that the character of the civic order reflects the character of the souls and relationships which make up that order. This is what Augustine means when he says that the "two cities are formed by two loves," and that in the absence of justice there is no difference between Alexander's empire and a band (*societas*) of thieves.[41]

This harmony of the well-ordered *civitas* depends upon law as both a rational and customary mechanism for regulating the inevitable conflict of human wills. Civil government is the mediation of conflicting wills and passions by a minimal standard of rationality. Indeed, when Augustine offers (in *City of God* book 19) his reformulation of Cicero-Scipio's definition of a republic (originally advanced in *City of God* book 2) Augustine expressly adds the word "reasonable": the *civitas* is "an assemblage of reasonable beings bound together by a common agreement as to the objects of love."[42] Political authority exists to secure "a compromise between human wills in respect of the provisions relevant to the moral nature of man."[43] But the invocation of political authority is the exception to that network of rational, self-regulating associations which constitute *societas*.

The bare minimum of a definition of a people—Cicero-Scipio's definition, which Augustine refines but does not abandon—presupposes a common understanding of *ius*, what is mine and thine, and the derived *leges* which regulates disputes about *ius*.[44] So too it depends upon the customary relationships of any established society, together with the individual habits and collective traditions which regulate daily life. The legal and customary rules of political society improve the souls of men by directing human action, placing limits upon or restricting those actions, and punishing those whose actions transgress those rules. Augustine's notion of a "common good" is robust precisely because of its concrete particularity—*societas* cannot be modified apart from changes in the individual souls which compose it. In reflecting on political things, Augustine always has in view the improvement of the individual soul, whose improvement will naturally though perhaps imperceptibly contribute to the common good.[45] Right living and a rightly ordered soul will produce a more noble civic order. That said, political rule, for Augustine, is a qualified good—a good because it keeps the peace and improves the soul, qualified because, in ameliorating the effects of sin, it is itself required by sin.

Amicitia, the second important term I wish to highlight here, has some overlap with *societas*, for Augustine's understanding of *societas* includes what I shall call the weak understanding of friendship. The term friends, Augustine writes, "may mean those in the same house, such as a man's wife or children, or any other members of the household; or it can mean all those in the place where a man has his home, a city, for example, and a man's friends are thus his fellow-citizens; or it can extend to the whole world, and include the nations with whom a man is joined by membership of the human society; or even to the whole universe, 'heaven and earth' as we term it, and to those whom the philosophers call gods, whom they hold to be a wise man's friends. . . ."[46] Friendship in this weak sense is both included in the relationships of the city and extends well beyond the relations of citizens to take the whole universe as its field. Friendship in this weak sense transcends the bonds of mere citizenship, and indeed even the formal concrete associations of *societas*, for the weak sense of friendship presupposes a predisposition toward association among all human beings even before those associations are formed. This universalizing propensity confirms that the fundamental human bond is not that of shared political citizenship.

But if friendship in its weak sense opens more widely, there is also a strong sense of *amicitia* as Augustine conceives it, and it is this strong *amicitia* that plays an important role in Augustine's understanding of human attachments.[47] For the engagements of *societas*, being the products of utility and general good will, are supplemented by stronger ties which bind a people together. The superficial order of *societas* is largely an engagement of performance of contract or simple noninterference whose public good is ancillary rather than primary. Friendship in the strong sense, on the other hand, is a good in itself (referred always, of course, to God) to be enjoyed for its own sake, apart from a sense of obligation or necessity. Indeed, Augustine speaks of the highest spiritual good in terms of friendship with God.[48] Relationships of *amicitia* in the strong sense are also the freest of human associations because they are most distant from utility and obligation. While these strong friendships support the *civitas*, they may also subvert tyrannical rule by cementing humane allegiances which transcend political injustice.[49] The political implications of strong friendship are portrayed acutely in *1984* by George Orwell, in whose dystopia the love of another becomes perhaps the most traitorous and subversive crime.

The relative detachment of the engagements of *societas* is supplemented (and counteracted) by the attachment of relationships of *amicitia*. Friendship is both the source of knowledge of others and the strengthening of our souls, for friendship nourishes the soul, the way food nourishes the body.[50] Friendship, like food, both changes and is changed by the soul.

In a fascinating passage from the early treatise *83 Diverse Questions*, Augustine describes in some detail the strong attachments of friendship. "We should bear one another's burdens in love, and also in friendship," Augustine writes, "just like the deer crossing a channel line up and place their heads upon one another to ease the burden, taking turns in front."[51] Augustine continues, quoting Solomon (Proverbs 5.19): "'Let the deer of friendship and the foal of your

affections converse with you.' For nothing so proves friendship as the bearing
of a friend's burden." To bear a friend's burden is not only to support him, but
to endure his ills (e.g., obstinacy or talkativeness) until he reaches a cure. Some
degree of empathy is also required, though only for the purpose of helping and
not for imitating the malady which afflicts another. When bearing one another's burdens, we should think of Christ's *kenosis* (Augustine cites Philippi-
ans 2.4–8) and look not to our own interests but to those of the other. So too
we should consider what we would want offered if we endured the same weakness, just as Paul said that he has become all things to all men (I Cor. 9.22).[52]

Friendship, for Augustine, transcends social rank. Indeed, Augustine un-
dercuts the Aristotelian requirement that friendship be among political and
social equals—we are all equal in the sight of God—without doing away with
the prudential aspect of friendship and the reality that true friendship will be
very rare. The humility of friendship requires that we should esteem others as
superior—such an attitude will "crush pride and kindle charity"—keeping in
mind that another might have some great hidden quality of which we are unaware.[53] Friendship both gives the other the benefit of the doubt as well as giving him what is due:

> Moreover, in the case of some man whom one does not know, one must not pass
> any judgment at all; and no one is known except through friendship. And for this
> reason do we bear more steadfastly the bad points of our friends, because their
> good points delight and captivate us. Accordingly one must not reject the friend-
> ship of anyone who offers himself for the association of friendship. [It is] not
> that he should be received immediately, but he should be desired as one worthy
> of being received, and he should be so treated that he can be received. For we can
> say that a person has been received into friendship to whom we dare pour out all
> our plans. And if there is someone who lacks the courage to offer himself [to us]
> in the making of friendship, because restrained by some temporal honor or rank
> of ours, we must come down to him and must offer to him with a certain gen-
> tleness and humility of soul what he himself does not of himself dare ask. Al-
> though somewhat rarely, of course, nonetheless it does happen from time to
> time in regard to someone whom we want to receive into friendship that we
> learn of his bad qualities before we learn of his good, and offended and, as it
> were, driven back by them, we give up on him and do not pursue an investiga-
> tion of his good qualities, which are perhaps somewhat hidden.[54]

Bearing friends' burdens and enduring their weaknesses is in keeping with the
example of Christ, who endured our ill habits in anticipation of our being
made whole: "by loving Christ we easily bear the weakness of another, even
him whom we do not yet love for the sake of his own good qualities, for we
realize that the one whom we love is someone for whom the Lord has died."[55]

Friendship requires not only discernment in the selection of friends but also judgment in their correction. Indeed, one must resist the fear of giving offense or of losing a good friendship which often keeps us from reprimanding others for their misdeeds, Augustine notes.[56] Augustine also cautions against the spiritual perils of those friendships which are referred to self and not to God.[57]

Societas, then, describes the relations in which we pursue the necessities of life and delight in associations of good will which, because the human capacity for deep love is limited, fall short of the intense intimacy of friendship. *Amicitia*, in turn, describes those rare strong friendships which fulfill and restore the soul and so sustain in us the openness and good will that weaker friendships and associations of *societas* require. Together, *societas* and *amicitia* orient, for Augustine, our detachment from and attachment to the life of the *civitas*. Augustine's prudential rule—"first, to do no harm to anyone, and, secondly, to help everyone whenever possible"[58]—would seem to be informed by these principles. Namely, in the realm of *societas*, one should take care not to do harm. In the realm of *amicitia*, one should seek to improve the soul of our neighbors.

Both *societas* and *amicitia* presuppose and are thus qualified by a third term, *veritas*. For *societas* and *amicitia*, like all things for Augustine, are informed by a love which is referred either to God or to self, and so both require the standard of truth, insofar as it can be apprehended. What is it in human relations, Augustine asks, that the soul receives? "Another soul which it assimilates to itself by receiving it into its friendship. And what is it that the soul gets through itself and does not change? The truth." [59] *Veritas* is essential for the weak relations of *societas* (performance of contract, avoidance of calumny, etc.) and for the strong associations of *amicitia*, in which truth itself binds the friends together. In both cases, furthermore, truth is inherent to justice—rendering unto each what is due. And so, when Augustine contends that Rome was never truly a republic because it lacked justice, he indicts Rome's lack of commitment to truth, both with respect to its public narrative of itself (one of misrepresentation and self-deception in pursuit not of justice but the *libido dominandi*) and with respect to its ignorance of Christ, the Truth.[60] In one sense, the contemporary slogan "no peace, no justice" has an Augustinian ring. But Augustine also notes that justice is dependent on truth, and so the Augustinian corollary to this slogan would be: "no truth, no justice." Thus, the critical Augustinian question of any society is not only the question does it possess justice, but does it "live in truth"?[61] Does a political regime tell things as they are? Do people possess some sense of what is and is not true, what are the limits of human action and the responsibilities enjoined upon human beings?

Pilate asked the question, What is truth? This is the question that any body—political or individual—tempts itself to ask as a rhetorical question. It is the sceptical question which presupposes no answer and so has the potential for either benign relativism or malignant nihilism. Asked rhetorically, it is a political question which is most pernicious to ask, for it gives license to the despot and relieves the democratic leader of the responsibilities of moderating the desires of the people. At its root, it renders individual and political acts solely the provenance of power, and hence of will. In the realm that does not adhere to justice, truth, and so justice, becomes the will of the stronger.

Yet, for Augustine, the question "What is truth?" yields a healthy scepticism, one which is consistent from his initial elaboration of scepticism in the early dialogue *Contra Academicos* to its mature expression in the *City of God.* Augustine is sceptical of the unexamined life and of all political ideologies, for he recognizes that no republic possesses justice, and that therefore no regime or political cause can claim the soul's primary allegiance. Neither one's will nor one's reason can be subordinated to a regime or cause. *Veritas*, like *societas* and *amicitia*, informs the city but extends well beyond it and, in so doing, anchors it to justice.

Augustine is able to resist both the will to power and the apathy of radical deconstruction because he recognizes that Pilate's question—the answerless question which obliterates moral and political freedom—is wrongly formulated. The question, for Augustine, is not "What is truth?" but rather, "Who is Truth?" Metaphysical and epistemological abstraction is transposed into the realm of concrete personal encounter. And for Augustine, Christian scepticism is always rooted in the person of Christ the Truth.

Christ the Truth, for Augustine, is also Christ the Judge who judges things according to how they are, not how he would like them to be. So too Augustine, in evaluating political things, takes as his starting point human affairs as they really are, not as they might be, for truth demands that we be accurate in our consideration of the frailty and violence of human sin. In this respect, Machiavelli and Hobbes share with Augustine the impulse to follow the ugly truth about human beings, to follow the truth of the matter, as Machiavelli put it, rather than the imagination of it.[62] But at the same time, Augustine appeals to the best in human beings in his recognition of the cooperative good will of *societas* and the noble unity of *amicitia*. Truth requires Augustine to attend simultaneously to both our basest and highest longings. Augustine expects neither too little nor too much from political associations.

And while Augustine may be the first proponent of a strong doctrine of negative liberty vis-à-vis civic life, he combines this with a strong conception, retained from classical antiquity and from scripture, of positive liberty.[63] *Societas, amicitia,* and *veritas* combine to place *freedom from* and *freedom for* in balance. In his pastoral letter on St. Augustine, John Paul II articulates the balance this way:

All other freedoms which Augustine illustrates and proclaims find their place among these two, which mark the beginning and the end of salvation: the freedom from the dominion of the disordered passions, . . . and the freedom from time that we devour and that devours us, in that love permits us to live anchored to eternity. But love, as he also observes, works "with liberal sweetness," so that "the one who observes the precept with love, observes it in freedom." "The law of freedom is the law of love."[64]

* * *

Societas, amicitia, and *veritas* are three Augustinian touchstones by which we might begin to take our bearings in reflecting on our contemporary political arrangements. For Augustine's thought may be instructive as an attempt to re-formulate the traditional link between virtue and the city in new terms, terms which take account, on the one hand, of the moral order which makes social existence possible and, on the other hand, of the fundamentally flawed char-acter of men in civil society.[65] Augustine suggests that people get the sort of ruler they deserve. This is a principle of divine providence and justice, and correspondingly Augustine intends this judgment as both a sobering and a comforting one.[66] What it suggests about our own time is something each of us must continue to evaluate for ourselves.

It is Augustine's genius to have charted a path for us between the brambles of triumphalist attachment to politics on the one hand and ascetic detach-ment on the other, and, between them, pure indifference.[67] Maintaining pro-portional attachment and detachment simultaneously without slipping into indifference is the Augustinian challenge. Augustine—in that "*opus magnum et arduum*" which is the *City of God*—rendered the truth of the person of Christ coherent with the best of ancient political philosophy and practice. Nonetheless, crucial questions remain. Can a contemporary Augustinian un-derstanding of politics be sustained without reference to the Incarnation? Similarly, can the hierarchical, neoplatonic metaphysics of participation on which Augustine's ethical vision is based be persuasive to the modern mind? How can the impatience of the modern spirit reconcile itself to Augustine's account of God's inscrutable providential order? Can Augustine's insights into political things be separated from his theological positions? What theological (and antitheological) suppositions in modern thought does a consideration of Augustine help lay bare? How are we to form an inclusive, diverse, non-coercive polity with a substantive collective vision of human flourishing while remaining simultaneously skeptical about the epistemological foundations of that substantive collective vision?

It would seem hardly likely that any attempt at a purely Augustinian syn-thesis would be possible, or indeed desirable, in the political world we cur-rently inhabit. But Augustine challenges us not to lose sight of Truth in our daily activities so that our human associations, whether weak or strong, are increasingly infused by an expansion of love and the restriction of the *libido dominandi.* A contemporary Augustinian understanding of politics thus invests the contemporary order of meaning with a new direction. Augustine does not present the destiny of man in political terms; rather, he presents politics in terms of the twin destiny of man. In assessing a synthesis adequate to our own political circumstances, perhaps we are neither waiting for Godot, nor for a new St. Benedict, but for a new and different St. Augustine.

Notes

1. This chapter is a revised version of a paper presented on a panel at the American Political Science Association meeting in Washington, D.C., in August 1997. I am grateful to panel organizer Charles Mathewes for his invitation, and to fellow panelists Jean Bethke Elshtain, Joshua Mitchell, Timothy Fuller, and Charles Mathewes for their comments on that occasion.

2. Jean Bethke Elshtain, *Augustine and the Limits of Politics* (Notre Dame: University of Notre Dame Press, 1995) and Joshua Mitchell, *The Fragility of Freedom: Tocqueville on Religion, Democracy, and the American Future* (Chicago: University of Chicago Press, 1995).

3. For example, in addition to Elshtain and Mitchell, see also Eric Voegelin, *The New Science of Politics* (Chicago: University of Chicago Press, 1952), Hannah Arendt, *Between Past and Future: Eight Exercises in Political Thought* (New York: Viking, 1954), and, *Love and St. Augustine,* ed. J. V. Scott and J. C. Stark (Chicago: University of Chicago Press, 1996). The spirit of Augustine is implicit in much of Michael Oakeshott's reflections on modern political life: see Glenn Worthington, "Michael Oakeshott and the *City of God,"* *Political Theory* 28:3 (June 2000), 377–98.

4. In a speech shortly after the Second World War, Albert Camus asserted that only Christianity could sustain the moral and physical requirements of rebuilding Europe. For Camus' persistent Augustinianism, see Herbert R. Lottman, *Albert Camus: A Biography* (Corte Madera, CA: Gingko Press, 1997), 726–27, n.5. The quotation is from Margaret Miles, *Desire and Delight: A New Reading of Augustine's* Confessions (New York: Crossroad, 1992), 98.

5. Karl Jaspers, *Plato and Augustine* (New York: Harvest, 1962), 119: Augustine "discloses unmistakably a will to power, having as its corollary a will to submission, which in the main point has relinquished all striving to think independently." Augustine's critique of ideology is well articulated by Ernest Fortin, *Political Idealism and Christianity in the Thought of St. Augustine* (Villanova: Villanova University Press, 1972).

6. Reinhold Neibuhr, "Augustine's Political Realism," in *Christian Realism and Political Problems* (New York: Scribner's, 1953), 119–46.

7. H.-X. Arquilliere, *L'Augustinisme Politique* (Paris: J. Vrin, 1955). The affinities with Moltmann are asserted by R. A. Markus, *Saeculum: History and Society in the Theology of St. Augustine* (Cambridge: Cambridge University Press, 1970). See also Peter

J. Burnell, "The Problem of Service to Unjust Regimes in Augustine's *City of God*," *Journal of the History of Ideas* 54:2 (1993), 177–88.

8. R. Dodaro, "Eloquent Lies, Just Wars and the Politics of Persuasion: Reading Augustine's *City of God* in a 'Postmodern' World," *Augustinian Studies*, 25 (1994), 77–138, makes the identification with Noam Chomsky. For Kirk's debt to Augustine, see Jeffrey O. Nelson, "An Augustine for Our Age," *The University Bookman* 34:2, (1994). See also, R. Dodaro, *Language and Justice: Political Anthropology in Augustine's De Ciuitate Dei* (unpublished D.Phil. thesis, Oxford).

9. Natural: Peter J. Burnell, "The Status of Politics in St. Augustine's *City of God*," *History of Political Thought*, 13:1, (Spring 1992), 13–29; J. N. Figgis, *The Political Aspects of St. Augustine's 'City of God'* (Gloucester, MA: Peter Smith, 1963). Neutral: R. Markus, *Saeculum*. Artificial: Neibuhr, *Christian Realism*. See further: H. A. Deane, *The Political and Social Ideas of St. Augustine* (New York, 1963); O. M. T. O'Donovan, "Augustine's *City of God* XIX and Western Political Thought," *Dionysius* 11 (December 1987), 89–110; and Paul J. Weithman, "Augustine and Aquinas on Original Sin and the Function of Political Authority," *Journal of the History of Philosophy* 30:3 (July 1992) 353–76 and "Toward an Augustinian Liberalism," *Faith and Philosophy* 8:4 (October 1991) 461–80. In his various works, Peter Brown's assessment of Augustine is not clear on this topic. See P. Brown, "Political Society," in *Augustine: A Collection of Essays*, ed. R. A. Markus (New York: Anchor Books, 1972) 331–35, and "St. Augustine's Attitude to Religious Coercion" in *Religion and Society in the Age of St. Augustine* (New York: Harper and Row, 1972) 262–78.

10. See Arendt, *Between Past and Future* and *Love and St. Augustine*; Eric Voegelin, *The New Science of Politics*; and James V. Schall, "On the Place of Augustine in Political Philosophy," *The Political Science Reviewer*, vol. 23, 1994, 128–65.

11. Hobbes: Michael Oakeshott, "Introduction to *Leviathan*" and "The Moral Life in the Writings of Thomas Hobbes" in *Rationalism in Politics and Other Essays* (Indianapolis: LibertyPress, 1991) 221–94, 295–350; Tocqueville: Joshua Mitchell, *The Fragility of Freedom*. Thomas Aquinas: see Alasdair MacIntyre, *Three Rival Versions of Moral Enquiry* (Notre Dame: University of Notre Dame Press, 1990), with Christopher J. Thompson, "Benedict, Thomas, or Augustine? The Character of MacIntyre's Narrative," *The Thomist*, 59:3, (July 1995), 379–407.

12. See, respectively: Jean Bethke Elshtain, *supra*; Michael Oakeshott, *The Politics of Faith and the Politics of Scepticism*, ed. T. Fuller (New Haven: Yale University Press, 1996); John Milbank, *Theology and Social Theory: Beyond Secular Reason* (Oxford: Basil Blackwell, 1990).

13. Secondary literature is rife with considerations of the polemical occasions that gave rise to Augustinian doctrinal and theoretical formulations. Augustine was painfully aware of his works being misread or misinterpreted in his own lifetime. Mark Vessey has shown how Augustine took pains, late in life, to shape the way in which he would be read on doctrinal matters after his death: see "*Opus Imperfectum*: Augustine and His Readers, 426–35 A.D." *Vigilae Christianae* 52 (1998) 264–85. A similar consideration of the steps Augustine may have taken to offer a lens on how he wanted to be interpreted on *political* matters would be a most useful study.

14. See, e.g., Augustine's discussions of language and thought in *De magistro* and *De doctrina christiana* and R. A. Markus, "St. Augustine on Signs" in *Augustine*, ed. Markus.

15. See *O'Donovan*, "Augustine's *City of God* XIX" (p. 99): "Augustine simply had no conception of the state. Only the 'earthly peace', 'the temporal peace of the meantime, common alike to the good and to the wicked' ([*De civ. Dei* 19.]26)—not an institution, but simply a condition of order—is common to both communities." For example, both Markus, *Saeculum*, and Milbank, *Theology and Social Theory*, note the anachronism of such terms and proceed to use them, their caveats notwithstanding.

16. I make no attempt here to engage directly the considerable, and growing, literature on Augustine's political thought. Correspondingly, the notes are intended, in most instances, simply to direct the reader to further study. The major studies and well-known, useful bibliographies are compiled in two very thoughtful articles: E. TeSelle, "Toward and Augustinian Politics," *Journal of Religious Ethics* 16 (1988) 87–108 and J. V. Scott, "Political Thought, Contemporary Influence of Augustine" in *Augustine Through the Ages: An Encyclopedia*, ed. A. Fitzgerald (Grand Rapids: Eerdmans, 1999) 658–61. Two titles which have appeared since Scott's article and which are worth noting here are: Donald X. Burt, *Friendship and Society: An Introduction to Augustine's Practical Philosophy* (Grand Rapids: Eerdmans, 1999); and Augustine, *Political Writings*, E. M. Atkins and R. J. Dodaro, eds., (Cambridge: Cambridge University Press, 2001). I have not seen M. Hanby, *Augustine and Modernity* (London: Routledge, 2003).

17. *Conf.* 1.1.

18. It is important to note that desacralization does not necessarily mean liberal neutrality. See John Bowlin, "Augustine on Justifying Coercion," *Annual Society of Christian Ethics* 17 (1997) 49–70.

19. The most recent attempt to argue this point is John von Heyking, *Augustine and Politics as Longing in the World* (Columbia: University of Missouri Press, 2001).

20. *De Libero Arbitrio*, I.109ff. Cf. *De civ. Dei* 19.13, where A's account of the good things includes peace but not civil government.

21. "Accordingly, two cities have been formed by two loves: the earthly by the love of self, even to the contempt of God; the heavenly by the love of God, even to the contempt of self" (*De civ. Dei* 14.28 [trans. Dods, New York: Modern Library, 1950, p. 477]).

22. See F. E. Cranz, "De Civitate Dei, XV, 2, and Augustine's Idea of the Christian Society," in *Augustine*, ed. R. A. Markus, 404–21. Also, O'Donovan, "Augustine's *City of God* XIX."

23. *De civ. Dei* 2. 21.

24. Augustine's critique of civil and natural theology is centered in *City of God* book 6; his elaboration of understanding the person is centered in books 11-14 of *City of God*.

25. In revising Cicero-Scipio's definition quoted in *City of God* 2.21, Augustine writes: "a people is an assemblage of reasonable beings bound together by a common agreement as to the objects of their love," and "in order to discover the character of any people, we have only to observe what they love" (19.24, trans. Dods, p. 706). O. M. T. O'Donovan, *Common Objects of Love: Moral Reflection and the Shaping of Community* (Grand Rapids: Eerdmans, 2002) offers a characteristically perceptive series of Augustinian reflections on this subject, shaped, in part, by the events of September 11, 2001.

26. *quam ob rem otium sanctum quaerit caritas veritatis; negotium iustum suscipit necessitas caritatis* (*De civ. Dei* 19.19).

27. It is one of the singular faults of A. Nygren's great study of *agape* and *eros* to have divorced Christian *caritas* from its classical ethical and metaphysical roots. A. Nygren, *Agape and Eros*, (2 parts), rev. ed., trans. P. S. Watson (London, 1953). Compare E. Gilson, *The Christian Philosophy of St. Augustine* (New York: Vintage, 1967), 137: "Loving another with one's whole soul does not mean disowning or sacrificing oneself; it means loving another as oneself, on a basis of perfect equality." And again: "We should note how this conception of Christian charity embraces the notion of justice, to which we often feel inclined to oppose it. The view commonly expressed today, to the effect that the Christian idea of charity is an antiquated notion for which modern times have substituted the ideal of justice, rests on a complete ignorance of Christian doctrine as St. Augustine interpreted it. From this text of Augustine it is clear that there is not more justice in the so-called modern ideal of justice, but less charity." (Gilson, p. 312 n. 45). See also *In Epist. Joan. ad Parthos* 8.4-5; J. Burnaby, *Amor Dei: A Study in the Religion of St. Augustine* (London, 1938) and O. M. T. O'Donovan, *The Problem of Self-Love in St. Augustine* (New Haven: Yale University Press, 1980).

28. "If, then, safety is not to be found in the home, the common refuge from the evils that befall mankind, what shall we say of the city? The larger the city, the more is its forum filled with civil lawsuits and criminal trials, even if that city be at peace, free from alarms or—what is more frequent—the bloodshed of sedition and civil war. It is true that cities are at times exempt from those occurrences; they are never free from the danger of them." *De civ. Dei* 19.6.

29. The phrase in Michael Oakeshott's, "The Tower of Babel" in *Rationalism in Politics*, 466. In political rather than theological terms, one might identify the Pelagian impulse with Voegelin's 'gnosticism', Ellul's 'technique', and Oakeshott's 'rationalism.' See Voegelin, *supra*, Jacques Ellul, *The Technological Society* (New York: Vintage, 1964); Michael Oakeshott, "Rationalism in Politics," in *Rationalism in Politics*, 5–42.

30. Madison, *Federalist* No. 10. Character formation as requisite in regimes based on principles of negative liberty is a persistent theme in classical liberal thought. See, for example, the conclusion of Constant's famous essay "The Liberty of the Ancients Compared with that of the Moderns," in Benjamin Constant, *Political Writings*, ed. B. Fontana (Cambridge: Cambridge University Press, 1988), 309–28.

31. Augustine's emphasis on the non-institutional character of political life parallels Oakeshott's treatment of the "superficial order." See Oakeshott, *Politics of Faith*.

32. Augustine's letters bear this out. Roman bureaucratic structures and traditions of patronage assured the inescapability of personal relations in the practice of politics. For a brilliant study of personal politics in action in Augustine's day, see N. B. McLynn, *Ambrose of Milan* (Berkeley: University of California Press, 1994).

33. *De civ. Dei* 5.24-25.

34. The just man is always enjoined to love and serve his neighbor, and is always bound to "the claims of truth and duty" (*De civ. Dei* 19.19). One may indeed lead a contemplative life, but the Christian is required to accept the burden of service if it is imposed upon him. On the common good more generally, see R. A. Markus, "*De Civitate Dei*: Pride and the Common Good," *Augustiniana* (1990), 245–59; N. J. Torchia,

"The Commune/Proprium Distinction in St. Augustine's Early Moral Theology," in *Studia Patristica* 22, ed. E. A. Livingstone, (1989), 356–63; J. V. Scott, "Augustine's Razor: Public vs. Private Interests in *The City of God*" in *"The City of God": A Collection of Critical Essays*, ed. D. F. Donnelly (New York: Peter Lang, 1995).

35. See Fortin, *Political Idealism*, as well as Oakeshott's discussion of association in "Talking Politics" in *Rationalism in Politics*, 438–61.

36. E.g., Cicero *De Leg.* 1.10.28, *De Off.* 3.6.32, and *Quint.* 3.11.

37. In the *Apology*, Plato's Socrates says that he has lived a private life, but it is clear that this private life has profound political consequences.

38. See e.g., *De. div. quaest. 83*, 79; in this, Augustine adds a moral color to the Latin "*privatus*" which, for classical authors, simply distinguished one's domestic matters from one's concerns qua citizen. See also Torchia, "The Commune/Proprium Distinction" and Scott, "Augustine's Razor." See also the discussion in n. 45, below.

39. *De civ. Dei* 19.21.

40. *De civ. Dei* 19.16. For a different interpretation of this passage and a fuller discussion of the household in Augustine, see the article by Kevin Hughes in this volume. The contrasting interpretations are best articulated in O'Donovan, "Augustine's *City of God* XIX" p. 104 and Rowan Williams, "Politics and the Soul: A Reading of the *City of God*," *Milltown Studies*, 19/20 (1987) p. 64.

41. *De civ. Dei* 4.4.

42. *rationalis multitudinis coetus, rerum quas diligit concordi communione sociatus* (*De civ. Dei* 19.24); cf. *De civ. Dei* 2.21. Also *De civ. Dei* 1.15, where the *civitas* is solely a "harmonious collection of individuals (*concors hominum multitudo*)."

43. *De civ. Dei* 19.17.

44. See O'Donovan, "Augustine's *City of God* XIX." Also, *De libero arbitrio*, 1.7: "For a nation consists of men, united under one law which, as I have said, is temporal (*Nam ex hominibus una lege sociatis populus constat, que lex, ut dictum est, temporalis est*)." An important part of Augustine's treatment of the matter is his identification of *ius* with the private and *lex* with the public. See, for example, *De div. Quaes*: "Every soul, to some degree, exercises an authority belonging to it in virtue of a certain private law (*ius priuatum*), and, to some degree, is constrained and ruled by universal laws analogous to public laws (*leges publicae*)." *Ius priuatum* is that which I rightly have control over (mine not thine, including body, soul, family, property, etc.). These are givens for Augustine, which is to say that they are inherent from nature (body, soul) or rightful inheritance (family, property, citizenship) or ability (offices, honors). Without *ius*, there is nothing for *lex* to do. Reference to universal law or *lex natura* would seem necessarily to entail a common moral authority—things possessed or acknowledged by all—in contrast to things held individually. This cuts both ways, as is the case so often in Augustine. What is private is good clearly, for these are things granted by God and by tradition. But universal and public law "constrain and rule" the inherent tendency of human beings to look inward rather than outward.

45. Not unlike, perhaps surprisingly, Adam Smith's discussion of the 'invisible hand.' See also Weithman, "Augustine and Aquinas on Original Sin" for an interesting comparison of Augustine and Aquinas.

46. *De civ. Dei* 19.3.

47. *De civ. Dei* 10.1: " 'religion' is something which is displayed in human relationships, in the family . . . and between friends." The Latin *religio* means not only "religion" but that which binds. Thus, there is a particular, rather than general, piety associated with strong friendship

48. *De Gen. C. Manich.* 1.4; *In Jo. Ev. Tr.* 110.6; *Trin.* 1.21.

49. On Augustine and service to unjust regimes, see Burnell, "The Problem of Service."

50. See *De div. Quaes.*, 39.

51. *De div. Quaes.*, 71.1. See Pliny, *Nat. Hist.* Bk 8 p. 83 (Rackham, trans.).

52. *De div. Quaes.*, 71.1-4.

53. *De div. Quaes.*, 71.5.

54. *De div. Quaes.*, 71.5-6.

55. *De div. Quaes.*, 71.7.

56. *De civ. Dei* 1.9.

57. See, e.g., *De civ. Dei* 19.8 and *Conf.* 4.

58. *De civ. Dei* 19.14.

59. *De div. Quaes.* 39.

60. *De civ. Dei* 19.21; Augustine's conclusion serves as a summary of the evidence mustered against Rome in the first five books of *City of God*.

61. I borrow the phrase and its implications from Vaclav Havel, *Living in Truth*, ed. Jan Vladislav (London: Faber, 1987). Havel's work is permeated by a profound sense of the metaphysical and ethical degradation that accompanies a political regime which suppresses the public and private recollection and expression of truth.

62. See also P. D. Bathory, *Political Theory as Public Confession* (New Brunswick: Transaction, 1981) p.13 n.18: "Though sometimes compared to Machiavelli because of his political realism, Augustine in fact offers a powerful alternative to Machiavellian civic education."

63. The distinction between positive and negative liberty finds its classic modern expression in Isaiah Berlin, "Two Concepts of Liberty," in *Four Essays on Liberty* (Oxford: Oxford University Press, 1969) 118–72.

64. John Paul II, "Pastoral Letter on St. Augustine" (Boston: St. Paul Editions, 1986), 25.

65. See O'Donovan, "Augustine's *City of God* XIX," 102, and Fortin, *Political Idealism*.

66. *De civ. Dei* 5.19.

67. See T. S. Eliot, *Little Gidding*, III.

11

Sexual Purity, "The Faithful," and Religious Reform in Eleventh-Century Italy: Donatism Revisited

Louis I. Hamilton

S OMETIME IN THE LATER PART of 1059, Peter Damian sat before an angry and dangerous crowd of Milanese laity and clergy. "Everything, I might say seemed to point to my death, as my friends frequently advised me, some of these people were thirsting for my blood."[1] Damian had arrived in the city three days earlier, accompanied by Anselm da Baggio (the future Alexander II), to help calm civil unrest over the behavior of the Archbishop Guido, and now found his own life in danger.

The course of events that brought Damian to Milan and placed him in mortal danger can be traced back at least a decade to early debates concerning the reform of the clergy. Increasing anxiety about the sexual purity of the clergy ranging from marriage or concubinage (nicolaitism), masturbation, to practices we now call homosexuality, and paedophelia (the last three all called sodomy), were linked to the practice of paying fees for ecclesiastical office (simony) that had come to dominate the discussion of church reform.[2] It was increasingly the position of reformers, lay and clerical, that greater monastic discipline among clergy would help promote a more eschatologically pure church, a church more properly primitive and apostolic.[3] In order to encourage these reforms, a Roman synod in April of 1059 had endorsed the growing lay practice of boycotting the liturgies of clerics who were known to have wives or live with women. (These were the so-called liturgical strikes, *sciopero liturgico*, as Italian historians have named them after contemporary labor actions.)[4] This Roman endorsement intensified an already violent situation in Milan.[5]

R. I. Moore has suggested that the ultimate reform position on such boycotts implied a kind of Donatist theology of the priesthood.[6] It implied an anxiety over the legitimacy of the sacraments performed by simoniacs and nicolitains. More traditionally, historians have seen the reformers debate the question of "Donatism" without embracing it, because of the work of Peter Damian against the influence of Humbert of Silva Candida.[7] Historians have long recognized the political nature of the so-called investiture contest of the late eleventh and twelfth centuries.[8] The at times bloody struggle between German emperors and the Roman popes to define their proper roles within Christendom has been described by Norman Cantor as "the first of the great world revolutions of western history" that completely altered European society by attempting to distinguish between the spheres of church and state.[9] But that distinction was a long way off; in the eleventh century bishops were lords, and kings were quasi-sacral figures.[10] This means that theological treatises could properly have both overt and covert political implications.[11] It has been argued by Moore that the debate over "Donatism" in the eleventh century was part of a process that encouraged civic uprisings against episcopal and lay authorities (such as that confronted by Peter Damian in Milan) that ultimately offered a forum for broad political and religious dissent within Europe, especially urban Europe.[12] In short, in the eleventh and twelfth centuries, the possibility existed to throw into doubt the sacramental worthiness of your bishop, and thereby overthrow your episcopal lord.

Historians have generally agreed, and even Moore has conceded, that Peter Damian was central to preventing the reformers from embracing the "Donatist" position outright.[13] It is my contention that, while it is correct that Damian was the strongest voice for the Augustinian position in the middle of the eleventh century, he himself helped foment the anxiety that loaned credence to the "Donatist" argument. In fact, many of his own arguments concerning clerical sodomy were later used against him by Humbert of Silvia Candida, his most significant opponent and the strongest voice for the "Donatist" approach. It was, at mid-century, an anxiety about the purity of the sacraments expressed consistently in sexual terms. The persistence of the question was closely connected to this ambivalence in Damian's thought and preserved in Humbert's writings.

The Donatist schism originated after the Diocletian persecution of 303 to 305 in Roman Africa.[14] During the persecution, fissures had emerged within the Christian community over how best to endure. Some felt that the example of the great African martyrs was the only proper model for Christians in a time of persecution. Others pursued compromise with authorities in order to preserve their own lives and the lives of members of their Christian community. Those who handed over (*traditio*) copies of the Scriptures to Roman authorities were considered apostates, while those who had failed to more actively resist the Romans were viewed by some, but not all, with greater sympathy. After the persecution, the election of a bishop in Carthage (Caecilian), believed to have endorsed a more moderate resistance, led to schism. A rigorist party of clergy and laity emerged to depose Caecilian and elect a priest whose successor was Donatus (d. 347) from whose name came the dismissive term Donatism used by the opposing, self-titled, Catholic, party of clerics and laity. The Emperor Constantine's initial attempts at a peaceful solution failed and he resorted to more coercive tactics, setting an important precedent that would be remembered in the Middle Ages. Augustine entered the fray, as priest of Hippo in 393, with his *Psalmus contra partem Donati*, followed by a large number of works, the most important of which were perhaps his *De baptismo* (c. 400–01) and *De unico baptismo* (410). After the situation grew increasingly violent, Augustine endorsed a hardened imperial policy that resulted in the "Edict of Unity" in 405, penalizing the Donatists as heretics. All of this confirmed the Donatists' self-understanding as the true church of the martyrs and did little to diminish their cause. Only the Vandal and later Muslim invaders ended the controversy.

Theologically the controversy had a longer-lived legacy. It drew Augustine into some of his most profound thinking on the priesthood, ecclesiology, and the sacraments. Central to the Donatist position was that, as the true church, they possessed the true sacraments, that their rites were the sanctifying rites. Peter Brown's summation is most helpful,

> The anxiety, that genuinely haunted Donatist bishops, was that, by tolerating any breach in a narrow and clearly defined order of ritual behavior, they might alienate God from His Church. . . . Anyone who reads a Donatist pamphlet . . . will be struck by the power of the idea of ritual purity that stemmed straight from the Old Testament: the fear of a sudden loss of spiritual potency through contact with an "unclean thing," and the elementary imagery of "good" and "bad" water. . . . The Donatist enthusiast would carry clubs they called "Israels"; they would "purify" Catholic basilicas with coats of whitewash; they would destroy the altars of others.[15]

Thus, the Donatist party insisted upon both the rebaptism of Catholic converts and the impurity of Catholic sacred space as consecrated by impure Catholic bishops.[16] For the Donatists, compromised priests administered impure sacraments, that "made one dirtier" rather than cleansing.[17] The Donatist Bishop Petilian stated their position thusly, "what we look for is the conscience of the giver, giving in holiness, to cleanse that of the recipient."[18]

Augustine resisted this logic consistently throughout his episcopal career. The Augustinian position was that the priest was the conduit of sacramental grace and that, therefore, the purity of the priest was irrelevant to the efficacy of the sacrament. The Donatists, according to Augustine's logic, had valid baptism and need not be rebaptized before becoming Catholics. As violators of the unity of the church, however, the Donatists had cut themselves off from the fruits of baptism, the forgiveness of sins and eternal life.

Thus, by calling for a liturgical strike against simoniac clerics in April of 1059, the Roman synod was running the risk of endorsing something akin to a de facto "Donatism." In point of fact, the question, whether or not to endorse a "Donatist" position, *de iure*, was an open one in the middle of the eleventh century. The supremacy of the Augustinian position was not presumed and its ultimate triumph ought not to be taken for granted.

Ten years earlier, at the Lateran Palace, Leo IX had attempted to depose all bishops who were unable to demonstrate that they had obtained their office without simony. More to the point, Leo wanted to declare all consecrations by simonists invalid. Given that "simony" here included practices ranging from outright bribery of parties involved in the nomination and election of the bishop (from nobles, to common clerics, and the laity) to the very common practice of paying a prescribed fee upon taking office, Leo's zeal created a crisis.[19] It was loudly observed that, were Leo's plans to be carried out, the divine services would essentially cease to take place.[20] Ultimately Leo was forced to back down and required instead a forty day penance by all who had knowingly accepted consecration from or been ordained by a bishop guilty of simony. Similar canons were promulgated in a synod in Mainz that same year.[21] Further, Peter Damian records that Leo reconsecrated bishops who had been ordained by simonists, an essentially "Donatist" position, as historians have noted.[22] It is important to note that at this stage the argument against the invalidity of rites performed by simoniacs, that is, the argument for a less rigorist position against simoniacs, was a practical one. The debate was not about sacramental theology, but about whether or not the church could practically sustain such rigor. Further, Damian and Bonizo of Sutri record that all wives and concubines of Roman area clergy were to be declared unfree and the property of the church; this suggests that nicolaitanism was discussed alongside of, and linked to, the question of valid consecration.[23]

Up to this point I have been narrating a complex but standard view of these periods and their debates. What I will proceed to argue will be less conventional. I will suggest that the ensuing debates over the validity of the sacraments performed by nicolaitans and simonists did not mark a triumph for the Augustinian viewpoint, but rather, a practical triumph, in part, for the "Donatist" position. This practical triumph occurred because, from the outset, one of the most sophisticated readers of Augustine of his day, Peter Damian, confused the issue. Damian, depending on the circumstance, variously attempted to link or distance the validity of the sacraments from the purity of the priest. In short, what we discover is that Damian's initial enthusiasm for such a linkage in 1049 is reversed during the debate with Humbert of Silva

Candida in the 1050s and ultimately in the Patarine affair. Then, his moderate, Augustinian stance held sway. However, after Damian's death, under more hostile conditions, a clearly "Donatist" position regarding the dedication of churches, in particular, emerged among reformers attempting to draw upon a basis of popular support.

In the latter half of 1049, Peter Damian sent a small book in the form of a letter to Leo IX. This has come down to us as his *Liber Gomorrhianus*.[24] In the letter he outlined for Leo what he saw as a growing problem among the local clergy accompanied by a stern warning.

> In our region a certain abominable and most shameful vice has developed. . . .
> The befouling cancer of sodomy is, in fact, spreading so through the clergy or
> rather . . . is raging with such shameless abandon through the flock of Christ, that
> . . . [i]t would be better for them to perish alone as laymen than, after having
> changed their attire but not their disposition, to drag others with them to de-
> struction, as Truth itself testifies. . . . "But if anyone is a cause of stumbling to one
> of these little ones, it would be better for him to be drowned in the depths of the
> sea with a great millstone around his neck." (Mt. 18.6). Unless immediate effort
> be exerted by the Apostolic See, there is little doubt that, even if one wished to
> curb this unbridled evil he could not check the momentum of its progress.[25]

Damian described the growing sexual scandal as including masturbation, mutual masturbation, interfemoral coitus, and anal intercourse, but these practices encompassed a wide variety of possible variations.[26] By extension the scandal included what we would call pedophelia and even concubinage.

Damian dealt with the former in a section entitled, "Of Clerics or Monks Who Are Seducers of Men."[27] Here he quoted at length from Basil the Great, as he read him in Burchard's *Decretum*:

> Any cleric or monk who seduces young men or boys, or who is apprehended in
> kissing or in any shameful situation, shall be publicly flogged and lose his cleri-
> cal tonsure. Thus shorn, he shall be disgraced by spitting into his face, bound in
> iron chains, wasted by six months of close confinement. . . . Following this pe-
> riod he shall spend a further six months living in a small segregated courtyard . . .
> [and] never again allowed to associate with young men for the purposes of im-
> proper conversation or advice.[28]

Damian observed that if such were the punishment appropriate to kissing, the punishment for more significant forms of sexual contact ought to be even more severe. Indeed, such people should not be allowed to handle the sacraments even after they have confessed and done penance.[29]

The sexual crisis clearly had implications extending beyond homosexual relations for Damian, implications that could affect the discussion over clerical celibacy. For Damian, sexual relations between a cleric of superior with one of inferior rank was a form of spiritual incest. In a section entitled, "Of Bishops Who Practice Impure Acts with Their Spiritual Sons," Damian argued that bishops who ordained priests were spiritual fathers to those whom they ordained, since it was a form of second baptism.[30] According to contemporary canons this spiritual relationship prohibited a sexual relationship.

> If a man violates a woman for whom he has stood as godfather, will anyone hesitate in deciding that he be deprived of Holy Communion, or in ordering that he undergo the ordeal of public penance according to the norms of the sacred canons? For it is written that "spiritual begetting is greater than physical." . . . It follows therefore that the same sentence is rightly inflicted on him who . . . by sacrilegious intercourse abuses his spiritual daughter, and on him who in his foul lust defiles a cleric whom he has ordained.[31]

In fact, Damian concluded, the homosexual spiritual incest is worse because it is also a violation of the law of nature. Bestiality would be preferable since only one soul is lost.[32] Be that as it may, this implies a logic whereby the bishop must remain chaste as the spiritual father of his congregation. Therefore, "both he who seduces his own daughter or his daughter by baptism, and he who sins shamefully with his son begotten in sacramental penance, are guilty of the same crime."[33] Thus, Damian's anxieties about sexual purity had implications for Nicolaitans as well; they too were a threat.[34]

More to our point these sins threatened the validity of the sacraments. Damian does much to undermine the sacramental legitimacy of priests who committed these acts in three sections entitled, "That the Services of an Unworthy Priest Will Spell Ruin for the People"; "That God Is Unwilling to Accept Sacrifices from Unclean Hands"; and "That No Holy Oblation, Soiled by Impurity, Is Acceptable to God." These chapter headings alone suggest a link between the worthiness of the priest and the validity of the sacrament, but it is notoriously difficult to know the origin of such headings in medieval treatises. His argument here turns on two points, one logical, the other exegetical. The logic of his argument depends on the medieval understanding of the priest as mediator. One cannot act as a mediator in a dispute with a powerful person, unless one knows the powerful person. Likewise, "how can one dare to act as an intercessor for the people before God if, in view of his life, he knows that he is not on friendly terms with the grace of God? Again, how can one ask him to pardon others if he does not know if God is well disposed towards him?" The matter is all the worse if the intercessor is someone with whom God is angry with.[35] Thus the sacral authority of the priest, the capacity of the priest to act as mediator, was severely compromised by these sexual sins. Damian has here pushed the orthodox position on the validity of its sacraments to its furthest limit by suggesting, but not insisting on, a link between sacerdotal behavior and the efficacy of the sacrament.

For scriptural support against "those of you who sneer at heeding my writing," Damian turned to Proverbs and Isaiah. Both passages depend on the question of purity. The former is clear, "The sacrifices of the unclean is abhorrent to the Lord" (Prov. 15.8). The passage from Isaiah depends on the ancient understanding of semen as blood which Damian would have known through Isidore of Seville.[36]

> Bring me your worthless offerings no more, the smoke of them fills me with disgust.... They lie heavy on me, and I am tired of bearing them. When you stretch out your hands I will turn my eyes away from you; when you multiply your prayers, I shall not listen. Your hands are covered with blood. (Is. 1.10–15)

Damian noted that the agitation of the blood in arousal converted it into semen, and, therefore, the condemnation of Sodom and Gomorrah was not for physical violence but for sexual sin.[37] This sexual sin caused God to reject their sacrifices.

This intense link between sexual purity and sacramental validity would only seem possible by carefully ignoring the Augustinian position. Indeed, Damian makes no direct use of Augustine's writings in the *Book of Gomorrah*. He does, however, refer to Augustine's reputation as a "prosecutor of Manichaeans and Donatists." It is this reputation that was formative, not Augustine's actual writings—a reputation Augustine earned through Possidius' *Vita Augustini* as much as through his own writings.[38]

Damian ended his book by requesting that Leo instruct him as to how best to deal with the matter, and whether indeed all such offenders should be expelled from holy orders. His appeal urges the pope to act forcefully, "that a prostrate Church may everywhere rise to vigorous stature."[39] If this is not a deliberate sexual pun, it suggests a real anxiety on Damian's part for the uncompromised masculinity of the church. While it is impossible to know the actual extent of these practices in the period, it is clear that Damian here presents a growing anxiety about the sexual purity of the clergy. Leo's response is likewise concerned with the relationship between sexual purity and the purity of the church. Leo praises Damian, saying that he had, "arrived at the resplendent bed of sparkling purity."[40] The relationship between clerical and ecclesiastical purity is endorsed even as the pope tempers Damian's harsh demands.

> If [these priests] had lived purely, they would be called, not only the holy temple of the Lord, but also his very sanctuary, in which with snow white splendor the illustrious Lamb of God is offered, by whom the foul corruption of all the world is washed away.[41]

But Leo offered penance to those who masturbate alone, mutually, or inter-femoraly as long as they have not done these things "for a long time." Those who have done so continuously or who have had anal intercourse were to be removed from orders.[42]

While the exact date of the *Book of Gomorrah* is unknown, its composition roughly coincided with the Lateran synod of April 1049. There, Leo IX pushed, unsuccessfully, to declare all ordinations by simoniacs invalid. Leo may have himself reconsecrated those who received orders from simoniacs.[43] The cardinal and bishop, Humbert of Silva Candida, would argue this position vigorously. Leo pressed the bishops to debate the matter of the validity of ordinations by simoniacs, and this prompted a very different response from Damian.

In the summer of 1052, Damian sent to Leo a book he described as his *Most Gratuitous Book* (*Liber Gratissimus*) as it discussed the ordinations of those freely ordained by simoniac bishops. Perhaps because he was confronted with the question more directly, or perhaps because the question was no longer a narrowly sexual one, he reversed his earlier thinking and took the Augustinian stand against connecting the validity of the sacrament to the purity of the priest. Damian's argument is thoroughly dependent on Augustine, "[Christ] distributed his spiritual gifts through ministers of his word, and still as their source retained within himself the fullness of all graces."[44] Here he extends Augustine's argument against the Donatists to the question of reordaining priests. Damian concludes that Christ is the minister of the sacraments, while the bishop only acts as the external minister. As there is only one who baptizes, Christ, so there is only one who ordains.[45] Gone is Damian's previous concern for the effective mediation of the particular priest.

Without directly naming his *Book of Gomorrah*, Damian completely abandoned his previous stance. In a section entitled, "That the Gift of God is not Defiled by Unclean Ministers," he insisted that the sins of the ministers do not sully the purity of the sacrament.

> [I]s there any wonder that the most high and infinite Spirit should touch ever so lightly with his splendor the dark and squalid hearts of certain men, only to remain clean and unsullied in his own purity? Anyone who ordains, therefore, and is guilty of any crime—whether he is proud, *or lustful*, whether he is a murderer, or even a simonist—he is indeed tainted and undoubtedly steeped in deadly leprosy, but the gift of God that is passed on through him is defiled by no one's corruption, nor infected by anyone's disease. That which flows through the minister is pure, and passes to a fertile soil, clean and limpid.[46]

Now, only three years after *The Book of Gomorrah*, Damian stated clearly that sexual sin did not sully the purity of the sacrament. In 1049 he stated, "Almighty God himself refuses to accept sacrifice from your hands."[47] The anxiety over sacramental purity had somehow dissipated for Damian in the intervening years.

Damian may have read more of Augustine's own sacramental theology, but it is interesting to note that his *Liber Gratissimus* is almost entirely dependent on Augustine's *Commentary on John* and not his anti-Donatist materials. Damian makes only one possible reference to the *De baptismo* but that might also reflect only a reading of the *Commentary on John*.[48] In any case, Damian had, by 1052, familiarized himself with the history of the Donatist controversy, that rebaptism was their heretical teaching, and that this was condemned by the Council of Carthage in 401. He even provided an account of the controversy in the *Liber Gratissimus*.[49] Therefore it appears probable that Damian's distancing himself from his earlier position was the result first of his ongoing exploration of the canons, and then a rereading of Augustinian materials, although not the most germane texts.[50]

In this way, Damian may have familiarized himself with the Donatist position well enough to realize that their stance on rebaptism included an argument for the rededication of churches. This logical extension would have made sense to Damian whose contemporaries viewed the dedication as a kind of baptism.[51] In either case he saw that questioning the ordinations of simoniac bishops would have dire implications for the basilicas of Europe.

> To this we may add that, if it is once admitted that a sacrament administered by such men be judged invalid, all basilicas dedicated up till now would have to be destroyed along with their altars.[52]

Damian recognized that this neo-Donatist position that questioned the consecration of priests by simoniac bishops would extend naturally to the consecration of sacred space and that all sacred spaces would be thrown into doubt. This was a warning that would prove most prophetic.

Despite Damian's extensive reliance on the authority of Augustine and the canons, the question was far from resolved in 1052. In 1057 and 1058 Humbert would compose the first two books of his *Three Books Against the Simoniacs*. Humbert argued against Damian's position, if not Damian himself, that the ordinations of simonists were invalid.[53] As part of this effort, Humbert marshaled arguments from Augustine as well as an extensive scriptural exegesis. Humbert first needed to distance his position from the Donatist position that Damian had clearly laid out in his *Liber Gratissimus*. Humbert did so by first recognizing, begrudgingly, that rebaptism was not licit, as long as the baptism had been performed in a proper manner.[54] "God has permitted," Humbert concluded, "that which he did not want." But Humbert went on to observe that even though such baptism is accepted, those rejoining the church are confirmed by the laying on of the hands of the bishop.[55] In this manner Humbert attempted to weaken the connection between reordination of priests ordained by simoniac bishops—since the practice of admitting those baptized by heretics also involved the laying on of hands.

Additionally, and most importantly, Humbert argued that these were not *re*ordinations at all, rather that was a title falsely assigned by his detractors.[56] The only proper ordination was by a known Catholic bishop. Just as lay heretics were not allowed to receive communion, nor were clergy to be taken up into the clergy without the imposition of hands by a Catholic bishop.[57] Heretics, such as simoniacs, never received the sacrament and thus could not impose it on others. Therefore, there was no reordination only genuine ordination or no ordination.[58]

In the central chapters of his second book he appears to address Damian's arguments most directly. In fact, Humbert takes up the exegesis that Damian had presented in his *Book of Gomorrah*, arguing, as had Damian, from Isaiah 1.15, "When you extend your hands, I avert my eyes from you. When you multiply your prayers, I do not hear them. Your hands are full of blood." The hands of simoniacs are bloody, because "of the many contaminations they accept." They have made their souls into whores.[59] Humbert sees the same connection between the purity of the priest and the validity of the sacrament that Damian had argued in favor of in the *Book of Gomorrah* and against in the *Liber Gratissimus*. Damian's own inconsistencies were being used against him. Simoniacs were foxes who, as they had destroyed the vine of Sodom, might damage the flowering vine of Christ.[60]

Humbert attempted to circumvent the Donatist argument by confusing the Augustinian position. In the chapter entitled, "On the sentences of Augustine, in which every heretic is convicted of denying Jesus Christ's Incarnation," Humbert attempted to co-opt Augstine to his position. Referencing Augustine's Treatise on the *First Epistle of John* directly, "Certainly every [heretic] who goes out from the Church, and they are cut off from the unity of the Church, are antichrists; let no one doubt this."[61] Humbert urged a surprising reading of Augustine, "Let your charity consider the great sacrament. Examine what the Lord God will have inspired and what is being insinuated to you under a veil. Behold they go out from us and are made Donatists."[62] Humbert, in what one can only presume was a deliberate rhetorical strategy, conflated the Augustinian position on heretics with his anti-Donatist polemic—with Augustine's own text—in order to deflect the charge of "Donatism" away from Humbert himself.

Similarly, Humbert pushed the limits of the Augustinian stance on the sacraments of heretics. Following Augustine, Humbert argued that while heretics had the outward sign of the sacrament they had cut themselves off from its inner grace. "Whence, only the visible bread of the sacrament appears to them, but the invisible bread of the Spirit is absent." Not one to leave well enough alone, Humbert extended this argument to all of the sacraments and saw in them more than simply the absence of grace.

> Whence, only the visible bread of the sacrament is present to him, but the invisible bread of the Spirit is absent. Which is, just the same, believed of the water of baptism, of the oil of sanctification, and of the other ecclesiastical sacraments. And o' if only the very visible sacraments might remain pure for them, just as they appear, and simple, and only in their natural character, and not some pollution existing in them; what is worse, it is the bread of pollution and a lie, as is whatever is theirs, just as the Holy Spirit attested, through the prophet Hosea. . . . "Ephraim has returned to Egypt, and in Assyria ate polluted food. They did not pour out wine as libation to the Lord and their sacrifices were not pleasing to him, as bread of mourning. Everyone who ate it was contaminated. . . . In the house of God they are sinning profoundly just as in the days of Gibeah."[63]

For Humbert, the words of the prophet were a warning that the sacraments performed by sinners were polluted and tainted with the sin of the priests. They were a warning to the eleventh-century church that the sacrifices of sinning clerics would bring condemnation from God.

Humbert also discovered in the warning of the prophet an anxiety over the polluting nature of sexual sin in particular. Again, he found himself championing the position Damian took in the *Book of Gomorrah*. For the sin of Gibeah was, as at Sodom and Gomorrah, the threatened male sexual assault of another male.[64] The citizens of Gibeah were, "effeminates and other sodomites, others however were the defenders of them."[65] These were to be understood as the heretics within the church, "Surely such are the little gatherings of heretics, which make the house of God a cave of mercenaries and a brothel."[66] In one push, Humbert connected anxiety about sexual purity, in particular male homosexuality, to both simony and nicolaitism. In short, he has recapitulated and extended Damian's own argument from the *Liber Gomorrah*.[67]

In 1058, Humbert wrote the last of his *Three Books*. Here his argument linked the evils of simony to the influence of lay rulers within the church. Lay influence on the ecclesiastical elections, Humbert argued, had led to the moral decline of the church. He focused particularly, but far from exclusively, on the problem of lay rulers investing bishops with the symbols of their office—the ring and crosier—as the point of the wedge dividing the church from its sacred mission.[68] For our purposes it is important to note that here Humbert took up the "Donatist" position in favor of the need to purify altars and churches dedicated by heretics. While he did not use the term *rededicare*, this is because he did not believe they were ever properly consecrated, the natural extension of his previous arguments. Rather these altars needed to be reconciled.[69]

In April of 1059, as was noted above, the laity was called upon to strike against simoniac and nicolitain clergy: "Let no one hear the mass of a priest who is known without a doubt to have a concubine or taken a wife."[70] Indeed, despite his effort in the *Liber Gratissimus*, Peter Damian himself continued to cloud the issue. In the first half of the year he sent a letter to Pope Nicholas II, where he interrogated an imagined nicolitain.

> Clearly, if a father incestuously seduces his daughter, he will be promptly excommunicated, forbidden communion, and either sent to prison or exiled. How much worse, therefore, should be your degradation, since you had no fear of perishing with your daughter, not indeed in the flesh, which would be bad enough, but rather with your spiritual daughter? All the children of the Church are undoubtedly your children. . . . Moreover, since you are the husband, the spouse of your church, symbolized by the ring of your betrothal and the staff of your mandate, all who are reborn in her by the sacrament of baptism must be ascribed to you as your children. Therefore, if you commit incest with your spiritual daughter, how in good conscience do you dare perform the mystery of the Lord's body?[71]

The nicolitain committed a spiritual incest that left him polluted and, therefore, ought not dare perform the sacraments lest he introduce contagion into the church, "And thus you contaminate by your actions the doorkeeper, the lector, the exorcist, and in turn all the sacred orders, for all of which you must give an account before the severe judgment seat of God." And he begged the pope to take a rigorous stand against the impurity of the nicolitains: "do not by conniving and dissimulation loosen the reigns on this raging impurity. This disease is spreading like a cancer, and its poisonous breed will reach out endlessly unless its evil growth is cut off by the scythe of the gospel."[72]

Significant portions of the Italian clergy and laity took this seriously indeed. This call to liturgical strike played upon the anxiety concerning the relationship between the purity of the sacrament and the minister's own spiritual worthiness. As has been noted by R. I. Moore, and as we have seen, this anxiety resonated deeply within European society.[73] In Milan it helped to foment the increasingly violent tensions within the city that would bring Peter Damian there later in the same year.

In 1056, the cleric Ariald of Cariate began preaching against simony and nicolaitism in the countryside around Milan. He soon brought his message to the city itself and his message began to attract significant support within the city. There is much debate as to the origins of this support but it seems to have been divided vertically rather than horizontally within the city, entire households supporting or opposing the reforms and even the divisions within the households were between peers.[74] His supporters became known as the patarines, although the origin of the word is unclear. They referred to themselves, among other things, simply as "the faithful."[75] In May of the next year the group grew violent, compelling priests to renounce their concubines. Violent strife continued in the city, and "the faithful" took the occasion of the absence of the Archbishop Guido, a known simoniac, from the city, as an opportunity to force his ouster.

This was the occasion for Peter Damian's mission to Milan late in 1059. He later reported the matter to the deacon Hildebrand (the future Gregory VII). Damian was clearly impressed by his own success and the success of "the faithful," that is, the patarines. The Roman Church, he observed, was like a general armed with the canons and "supported by the forces of the faithful."[76] The success of the battle was not clear at the outset. A few days after his arrival in the city the rumor spread that Damian's legation would mean the end of the independence of the Milanese Church. Bells rang out in the city, a horn was sounded, and an angry mob of clerics and laity, now as eager to defend the liberty of their church as they had been for its reform, gathered in the cathedral.[77] Damian feared for his life, but chose to seat himself before the crowd. Here the Archbishop Guido, perhaps tired of the ever-threatening mob, perhaps hoping for leniency from Damian, chastised the crowd and offered to seat himself at the cardinal's feet. Thus, with some effort, Damian was able to address the people gathered. He asked them to check their own ecclesiastical records and see whether or not, since the time of Ambrose, the Milanese Church had not in fact accepted the primacy of Rome. Having thus convinced the crowd, he turned to the question of reforming the local clergy.[78]

Much to Damian's horror, a quick survey of the gathered clerics revealed that, "hardly anyone in the whole assembly was found to have been promoted to orders without payment."[79] That is, that nearly all were guilty of simony, and a strict system of payment existed for rising through the Milanese clerical ranks.[80]

> It seemed to be the total overthrow of the Christian religion to see how these men had desecrated the sacred mysteries in all the churches of this wide-spread diocese and of this noble city. But for me to exempt a few would have caused a dispute, since almost all of them were guilty; nor did it seem permissible to impose varying sentences on them, since the inducement was the same for all. This also added to my worry that, unless this case were concluded with some measured decision, the furious mob would not be quieted without a great number of men being massacred.[81]

It is clear from his own response that Damian saw the practice of simony as a desecration of the sacraments, and that this simoniac church was the "overthrow of the Christian religion." It is implied that Damian had considered some punishment more harsh than simply penance (his ultimate decision) since he was initially uncertain as to how to handle the matter. Damian thought first of Pope Innocent I, "where many have sinned, the crime cannot be punished." Then he recalled the treatment of other heretics,

> I was also reminded of the discretion used by the holy pontiffs and the original authors of the canons in dealing with Donatists, Novatians, and others who were ordained in various heresies.[82]

Damian's assessment of the situation was as, first, a desecration of the sacraments; second, a practical concern—how to reform a church where nearly the entire clergy has engaged in the matter; and, third, that while the precedent of leniency was taken from the Donatist, it was not primarily as a theological matter (this relates to the second point). Damian offered the simonists and the nicolaitans the opportunity to publicly renounce their sins and do penance. The oath of Archbishop Guido is a telling reaffirmation of the sacramentally corrupting influence of simony,

> Your holy devotedness [Guido] . . . is not unaware of the detestable custom that grew up from old in this holy church . . . of how hateful to God it is, how shameful and perverse and condemned by the authority of all the holy canons, and of how it is spread to the souls of innocent people by contaminating them with its deadly and pestilential leprosy. . . . I also denounce the heresy of the Nicolaitans and promise, insofar as it will be possible for me, that not only priests, but also deacons and subdeacons, shall be bound by the same attestation mentioned above: to abandon their abominable union with wives or concubines.[83]

While Damian's moderate handling of the Milanese clergy has been presented as a triumph of the Augustinian, anti-Donatist position, it still called into doubt the legitimacy of sacraments performed by sinning clerics by stating that innocent people could be contaminated by the sacraments of simoniacs.[84] Moreover, Damian seems to have been more concerned with the practical matter of reforming the Milanese Church, than with Augustinian theology.

But Damian had not entirely forgotten his *Liber Gratissimus*. In 1061, he added an addendum to the work, noting that Nicholas II had ruled in council on the matter or reordination. Damian's addendum makes it clear that the debate in council had been both heated and confused. Again, the decision was a practical one,

> That those who were hitherto ordained freely by simonists should remain . . . but that those not yet promoted by them would not in the future be permitted advancement; but with this proviso, that as a result of the severity of the sentence neither the entire ecclesiastical order should be destroyed, nor that in view of its leniency the plague of simony should [continue] all with a view that what in past ordinations had been valid should for future ones be totally forbidden.[85]

A moderate stance was taken in 1061, but this was hardly a clear triumph for the Augustinian position on the relationship between sacrament and priest.

Once we understand that Damian himself, the supposed defender of the Augustinian position, was hardly clear on the matter and was often driven by immediate practical concerns in his own dealings with these questions, it is more clear why "Donatist" positions persisted within the reform movement. The reasoning of Humbert, alongside the reasoning of Damian's *Book of Gomorrah* and *Letter 61*, continued to exert its influence over the reformers. Thus, the reformers did call into question the legitimacy of sacraments performed by simoniacs and did perform them over. In 1052, Damian had warned that, were the reformers to follow the logic of the Donatist positions, they too would have to question the validity of churches and altars dedicated by sinful bishops. In fact, reforming popes would do precisely that.

The question was far from resolved in 1061. In the reign of Alexander II and Gregory VII, the laity continued to be encouraged to boycott the liturgies of clerics suspected of being unchaste or simoniacs. These Milanese clerics were called the ministers of Satan by Gregory VII.[86] And clergy and people continued to refuse the sacraments from priests they considered unworthy.[87] Even Damian himself would be accused of simony when he attempted to come to a similar Augustinian conclusion in Florence in 1067 as he had in Milan in 1059. Thus, as R. I. Moore puts it, the reformers were willing to come "perilously close to the Donatist position" in form if not in theology because it allowed them to exert a disciplinary force in the church.[88] Evidence of confusion might also be found in Urban II both reordaining clerics ordained by the antipope Guibert of Ravenna and confirming the illegitimacy of reordinations.[89] That this was a matter of ecclesiastical discipline (and, so, authority) rather than a theology of reordination only emphasizes the need the reformers seem to have felt to soften the strictly Augustinian position.

Perhaps the most persistent manner in which the reformers would adhere to a de facto "Donatist" position was in the matter of consecrating churches. While the reformers of the eleventh century do not appear to have openly *re*-consecrated churches, they did often take opportunities to perform another consecration of a church. The canon law collection compiled by the pro-gregorian Anselm II of Lucca (the nephew of Alexander II) prior to 1085 allowed for a new consecration if an altar was moved, and thus even a relatively minor change within the church structure could be an occasion for a licit, additional consecration.[90] Anselm's collection also offered the precedent of Gregory I (re)dedicating Arian churches when they became Catholic.[91] Anslem's collected canons also noted that if the dedication was in doubt it could be performed again.[92] Most impressively the canons suggested that no Mass was to be said in a church whose dedication was not consented to by the papacy, nor were oratories to be consecrated without papal permission.[93] These canons could throw into doubt the consecration of countless churches, altars, and oratories throughout Christendom. Moreover, they could provide the opportunity for these to be dedicated by reforming loyalists. As we have seen, this is very close to the Donatist position of rededicating churches even though Anselm denied the validity of reordaining clerics. The matter would have been further confused for contemporaries because ordination and dedications might both be referred to simply as consecrations.[94]

In fact, Paschal II's dedication of S. Maria in Parma in 1106 after deposing its Bishop Cadalus, the antipope Honorius II, suggests such a (re)dedication.[95] Dedicating the cathedral well after reconstruction of the middle of the eleventh century at the end of the council that reconciled the city of Parma (that had supported its bishop, Cadalus), and appointed a replacement, was an opportunity for Paschal to assert his own authority in the rebellious city.[96] The chronicle's reference to Paschal proceeding to make many places "fruitful" throughout Italy and France, might contain an echo of rededication.[97] Such a dedication helps explain the ongoing confusion over the matter of the legitimacy of sacraments as Paschal had confirmed the ordinations of schismatics and heretics at Guastella in 1106, referencing the Donatist controversy among other previous heresies.[98] Both the need to reconfirm the official position on reordination and the likely rededication at Parma suggest an ongoing confusion on the matter. Likewise the multiplicity of twelfth-century dedications at S. Lorenzo in Lucina (possibly four) are also suggestive of the need to reassert control over the church during the Anacletan schism by means of the rededication.[99]

The confusion over the matter persisted into the twelfth century while Innocent II stuggled with Anacletus for authority over the Roman church. Gerhoh of Reichersberg would offer a logic to justify the "Donatist" position regarding the rededication of altars based upon his own reading of Augustine in 1130. Gerhoh would transform the Augustinian argument by asserting a distinction between the reconsecration of people (rebaptism or reordination) on the one hand and reconsecration of things (altars, churches) on the other. Since the fruitfulness of the sacrament performed by a heretic depended on the good will (and ignorance) of the recipient, and since objects such as altars and walls had no reason, their consecration by heretics could have no effect.[100]

The height of this "Donatist" position toward the dedication came at the Lateran Council of 1139 when Innocent II ordered the destruction of altars consecrated by certain episcopal supporters of Anacletus.[101]

> Geoffrey bishop of Chartres, as noted above, legate of all of Aquitane having taken up the command of the Lord Pope, eagerly traveled to every region of Gaul

himself, and also of Aquitaine, he destroyed all altars of the holy churches by his own hands, which either Girard, that author and protector of sedition, or Giles, bishop of Brescia, or their accomplices, consecrated anointing with the chrism of benediction in that hateful schismatic time, not leaving a stone upon a stone which he might tear down, he leveled [them] entirely to the ground; and as reason dictated, he took care to restore others in their place.[102]

With this, Peter Damian's worst fears had become, for a moment at least, a reality. Using the canons of the day, Innocent was able to carry out a Donatist-style purge of impure churches and rededicate their altars under the guise of restoration.[103] Innocent used the confusion over the validity of dedications performed by heretics as an occasion to mark his own triumph over the Anacletan party.

In part, the reformers needed to blur the Augustinian position because much of their own authority depended upon an increasingly popular perception of their leaders as the more monastic, more pure and worthy, as R. I. Moore and others have suggested.[104] Indeed, the Cathars would push the question of purity even further.[105] However, what has not been appreciated heretofore is that while Peter Damian did take up the Augustinian position in his *Liber Gratissimus*, and while this became the official position of the Roman Church, Damian himself must also bear some responsibility for undermining the argument. Humbert's arguments in his *Three Books against Simoniacs* echo Damian's earlier *Book of Gomorrah* in important ways, and he can no longer be seen as a lone voice in the eleventh century.[106] Damian's own position on reconsecration would have been clearer, more consistent, without the *Book of Gomorrah*. Throughout the eleventh, into the twelfth century, and beyond, an anxiety about the purity of the clergy and the sacramental functions they performed would persist and shape the claims to legitimacy of reformers and innovators within the church.[107]

Notes

1. Peter Damian, *Letters*, 4 vols., tr. by Owen J. Blum, O.F.M. (Washington, DC, 1989), vol. 3, *Letter 65*, p. 26. The correspondence was in December, but the precise date of the events is unclear.

2. For the overall idea of sexual impurity as articulating transgressions and boundaries within community, see Mary Douglas, *Purity and Danger: An Analysis of Concepts of Pollution and Taboo* (London 1978, 1966), pp. 3–4. Most recently she has connected this to the sacred space of the Temple in Leviticus, in Douglas, *Leviticus as Literature*, p. 90 and again 235–37. On these sexual practices see, John Boswell, *Christianity, Social Tolerance, and Homosexuality: Gay People in Western Europe from the Beginning of*

the Christian Era to the Fourteenth Century (Chicago, 1980); James A. Brundage, "Concubinage and Marriage in Medieval Canon Law," in *Sexual Practices and the Medieval Church*, ed. by Vern L. Bullough and James A. Brundage (Buffalo, 1982), pp. 118–28; and Mark D. Jordan, *The Invention of Sodomy in Christian Theology* (Chicago, 1997), esp. pp. 45–66, concerning Damian. Jordan considers Damian the inventor of the term "sodomy" (*sodomita*), *Invention of Sodomy*, p. 29, but overlooks the "Donatist" implications of Damian's arguments. An excellent overview of the reform is Uta-Renate Blumenthal, *The Investiture Controversy, Church and Monarchy from the Ninth to the Twelfth Century* (Philadelphia, 1988).

3. The rhetoric of Christian religious reform is almost by definition an appeal to a primitive ideal, Gerhart Ladner, *The Idea of Reform: Its Impact on Christian Thought and Action in the Age of the Fathers* (Cambridge, 1959); Beryl Smalley, "Ecclesiastical Attitudes toward Novelty: c. 1100–c. 1250," in *Church, Society and Politics: Papers Read at the Thirteenth Summer Meeting and Fourteenth Winter Meeting of the Ecclesiastical History Society*, ed. by Derek Baker (Oxford, 1975), pp. 113–31; for an overview of the monastic ideal see Blumenthal, *Investiture Controversy*, pp. 7–22.

4. Giuseppe Fornasari, *Medieoevo riformato del secolo XI: Pier Damiani e Gregorio VII* (Naples, 1996), pp. 31–49; Fornasari, "S. Pier Damiani e lo 'sciopero liturgico,'" *Studie Medievali*, ser. 3 an. 17, f. 2 (1976), pp. 815–32; Ernst Werner, "Pietro Damiani ed il movimento popolare del suo tempo," *Studi Gregoriano* (1975), pp. 289–314; Constanzo Somigli, "San Pier Damiano e la Pataria," *San Pier Damiano nel IX centenario della morte (1072–1972)*, 4 vols., Centro studi ricerche sulla antica provincial ecclesiastica ravennate (Cesena, 1972), vol. 3, pp. 193–206; Cinzio Violante, *La Pataria e la riforma ecclesiastica* (Rome, 1955).

5. Blumenthal, *Investiture Controversy*, p. 95.

6. Prof. Richard Landes encouraged me to consider this possibility more seriously. R. I. Moore, *The Origins of European Dissent* (Toronto, 1994).

7. For the extensive historiography on the question, see John Gilchrist, "'Simonica Haerisis' and the Problem of Orders from Leo IX to Gratian," *Proceedings of the Second International Congress of Medieval Canon Law, Boston College*, ed. S. Kuttner and J. Joseph Ryan, Monumenta iuris canonici, Series C: Subsidia, vol. 1 (Vatican City, 1965), pp. 209–35. Reproduced in *Canon Law in the Age of reform 11th-12th Centuries* (Aldershot, 1993). The traditional view of the matter was first articulated by Louis Saltet, *Les Réordinations* (Paris, 1907).

8. The literature on the struggle between the German emperors and the Roman papacy is almost limitless. The most important of these older studies are Gerhart B. Ladner, *Theologie und Politik vor dem Investiturstreit* (Baden, 1936); Gerd Tellenbach, *Church, State, and Christian Society at the Time of the Investiture Contest*, tr. by R.F. Bennett (Oxford, 1970); Walter Ullmann, *The Growth of Papal Government in the Middle Ages: A Study in the Relation of Clerical to Lay Power* (3rd ed., London, 1970). For an excellent overview of the period and a more complete outline of the historiography (though far from exhaustive), see Blumenthal, *Investiture Controversy*. Recent biographies of the central figures by two of the most important historians of the period are also essential reading: H. E. J. Cowdrey, *Gregory VII, 1073–1085* (Oxford, 1998) and I. S. Robinson, *Henry IV of Germany, 1056–1106* (Cambridge, 1999).

9. Norman Cantor. *Church, Kingship, and Lay Investiture in England* (Princeton, N.J., 1958), p. 7.

10. The classic studies are Marc Bloch, *Les rois thaumaturges: etude sur le caractère surnaturel atribué a la puissance royale particulièrement en France et Angleterr* (Paris, 1961); and Ernst Kantorowicz, *The King's Two Bodies; a Study in Medieval Political Theology* (Princeton, 1957, 1985).

11. I. S. Robinson suggests that Peter Damian was highly influential in this regard, "'Political Allegory' in the Biblical Exegesis of Bruno of Segni," *Recherches de Théologie Ancienne et Médiévale* 50 (1983), pp. 69–98.

12. Moore, *European Dissent*, pp. 1–20, esp. pp. 3–4, 12, and 20.

13. Blumenthal, *Investiture Controversy*, p. 76; Moore, *European Dissent*, p. 61.

14. What I offer here is a brief outline of the controversy and its theology; for a more detailed scholarly treatment see: T. D. Barnes, "The Beginnings of Donatism," *Journal of Theological Studies* n.s. 26 (1975), pp. 13–22; François Decret and Mhamed Fantar, *L'Arfique du Nord dans l'Antiquité: Histoire et civilization des origins au ve siècle* (Paris, 1998), pp. 135–89; W. H. C. Frend, *The Donatist Church* (Oxford, 1952, 1985); Jean-Louis Maier, ed., *Le Dossier du Donatisme*, 2 vols. (Berlin, 1987, 1989); R. A. Markus, "Christianity and Dissent in Roman Africa: Changing Perspectives in Recent Work," *Studies in Church History* 9 (1972), pp. 21–36, reprinted in *From Augustine to Gregory the Great: History and Christianity in Late Antiquity* (London, 1983); Markus, "The Problem of 'Donatism' in the Sixth Century," in *Gregorio Magno e il suo tempo*, I, Studi Storici 33 (Rome, 1991), pp. 159–66, reprinted in *Sacred and Secular* (London, 1994); Peter Brown, *Augustine of Hippo: A Biography* (Berkeley, 2000); Brown, "Religious Dissent in the Later Roman Empire: The Case of North Africa," *History* 46 (1961), pp. 83–101, reprinted in his *Religion and Society* (London, 1977); and G. G. Willis, *Saint Augustine and the Donatist Controversy* (London, 1950). Also helpful to me in creating this summary were R. A. Markus, "Donatus, Donatism," in *Augustine through the Ages, An Encyclopedia*, ed. Alan D. Fitzgerald, O.S.A. (Grand Rapids, Mich., 1999), pp. 284–87; Maureen A. Tilley, "Anti-Donatist Works," ibid., pp. 34–39; Pamela Bright, "Donatist Bishops," ibid., pp. 281–84; and William Harmless, S. J., "Baptism," ibid, pp. 84–91.

15. Brown, *Augustine*, pp. 218–19. Optatus of Milevis, *De schismate Donatistarum* in *Optat de Milève Traité Contre les Donatistes*, Source Chrétiennes, nos. 412–13 (Paris, 1995) Vi, 1–3; Augustine, Epistulae, 29, 12, Corpus Scriptorum Ecclesiasticorum Latinorum (Vienna, 1865–), 34.1.114–22 and 34.1.29, respectively.

16. Bright, "Donatist Bishops," p. 282.

17. Augustine quoting Petilian in *Contra litteras Petiliani*, CSEL 52, 2.2.4.

18. Ibid., 2.3.6 and 3.8.9.

19. Damian will encounter this last problem and appears to worry about Leo's solution in Milan, *Letter 65*, pp. 29–30.

20. Blumenthal, *Investiture Controversy*, p. 74.

21. Ibid., p. 74.

22. Ibid., p. 75.

23. Ibid., p. 74.

24. I am using Blum's translation: Damian, vol. 1 *Letter 31* (*L Gom*). See *San Pier Damiani, Liber Gomorrhianus: Omossesualità ecclesiastica e riforma della Chiesa*, ed. by

Eduardo D'Angelo (Torino, 2001); Peter S. Payer, *Peter Damian: Book of Gommorah. An Eleventh-Century Treatise against Clerical Homosexual Practices* (Waterloo, Ont., 1982); Vern L. Bullogh, "The Sin against Nature and Homosexuality," in *Sexual Practices and the Medieval Church*, pp. 14–21; and Boswell, *Christianity, Social Tolerance, and Homosexuality*, emphasizes the coolness of Leo's response to Peter Damian, p. 212.

25. Damian, *Letter 31*, p. 6.

26. *LGom.*, p. 7. On the antecedents for these classifications see Jordan, *Invention of Sodomy*, pp. 52–53.

27. As is often the case in such texts, it is not clear whether the titles of the individual chapters are original to Damian or not. If not they reveal, at least, something of the initial reception of the text, as they are associated with its earliest manuscripts. Thus they either represent what Damian intended or what his earliest readers thought he intended.

28. *LGom.*, p. 28; Burchard, *Decretum*, 17.35, PL CXL (1853); see Kurt Reindel (ed.), *Die Briefe des Petrus Damiani*, vol. 1, MGH, *Die Briefe der deutschen Kaiserzeit*, 4 vols. (Munich 1983), vol. 1, p. 308, n. 36.

29. Damian, quoting Pope Siricius, "Although now cleansed of the stain of every sin, those who were once vessels of vice must not take in hand the instrument for administering the sacraments." *LGom.*, p. 30. Jordan is partly correct, but Damian is *posing the question* whether sodomy is a sin that cannot be repented; Leo answers otherwise. Jordan, *Invention of Sodomy*, p. 67.

30. *LGom.*, p. 16.

31. *LGom.*, pp. 15–16.

32. *LGom.*, p. 16.

33. *LGom.*, p. 19.

34. Damian will pick up this logic in *Letter 61*, written in 1059.

35. *LGom.*, p. 38.

36. Isidore of Seville, *Etymologies*, 9.6.4 ed. by Marc Reydellet (Paris, 1981–).

37. *LGom.*, pp. 39–40.

38. Possidius, *Vita Augustini*, Herbert T. Weiskotten, ed. and tr., *Sancti Augustini Vita scripta a Possidio episcopo*, (London, 1919) (chpts. 14–16). Damian's reputation as an Augustinian voice in the eleventh century depends only partly on the *Liber Gratissimus*; see Michel Grandjean, "Pierre Damien lecteur d'Augustin. A propos del l'interprétation du marriage de Jacob," *Revue des Études Augustiniennes* 36 (1990), pp. 147–54.

39. *LGom.*, p. 53, "et jacentis Ecclesiae status undique ad sui vigoris jura resurgat."

40. Ibid., p. 3.

41. Ibid., p. 4.

42. Ibid., p. 5.

43. Blumenthal, p. 74.

44. Blum, Damian, *Letter 40* (*LGrat.*), p. 114. Augustine, *In Iohannis evangelium tractatus CXXIV*, ed.by R. Willems O.S.B., Corpus Christianorm 36 (Turnholt, 1954), 5.9, 45.

45. *LGrat.*, pp. 117–20 see N. M. Haring, "The Augustinian Axiom 'Nulli Sacrameto injuria facienda est'," *Mediaeval Studies* 16 (1954), pp. 87–117.

46. *LGrat.*, p. 139, emphasis mine.

47. *LGom.*, p. 39.

48. *LGrat*, p. 167.

49. *LGrat*, pp. 171–73.

50. For Peter Damian as canonist, see Fornasari, *Medieoevo riformato*, pp. 353–410; John Joseph Ryan, *Saint Peter Damiani and His Canonical Sources; A Preliminary Study in the Antecedents of the Gregorian Reform* (Toronto, 1956).

51. Brian Vincent Repsher, 'Locus est Terribilis': *The Rite of Church Dedication in Medieval Christendom* (Ph.D. Dissertation, The University of North Carolina at Chapel Hill, 1994).

52. *LGrat.*, p. 184.

53. See n. 1 of Blum, Damain, *Letter 40*, p. 111.

54. Humbert, *Libri tres adversus simoniacos*, ed. by F. Thaner, Monumenta Germaniae Historica, Libelli de Lite (Ldl) (Hannover, 1891), t. 1, p. 115.

55. Humbert, *L Tres*, p. 116.

56. Ibid., p. 113.

57. Ibid.

58. Ibid., pp. 112–13.

59. Ibid., pp. 170–72 at p. 171: *A quorum sanguinulentis manibus non solum nil sanctifications, sed etiam plurimum contaminationis acceperunt, in tantum ut facta sit meretrix anima eorum quondam fidelis plenaque iudicii.*

60. Ibid., p. 167.

61. Ibid. p. 172, Augustine, *Tractate 3 On the First Epistle of John*, n. 7 (1), tr. by John W. Retting (Washington D.C., 1995), p. 165.

62. Humbert, *L Tres*, p. 167.

63. *Unde panis visibilis sacramenti tantummodo eis adest, sed invisibilis panis Spiritus abest. Quod nichilominus de aqua baptismatis, de unctione sanctificationis et ceteris ecclesiasticis sacramentis credendum est. Et o utinam ipsa visibilia sacramenta remansissent eis pura, sicut videntur, et simplicia et in sua tantum natura, et non inesset eis pollution aliqua, sed quod peius, panis pollutionis et mendacii est, et quicquid eorum est, sicut Spiritus sanctus per prophetam Osee . . . , Reversus est Effraim in Aegyptum, et in pollutum comedit. Non libabunt vinum Domino, et non placebunt ei sacrificial eorum quasi panis lugentium. Omnes, qui cemedunt eum, contaminabuntur. . . . In domo Dei eius profunde peccaverunt sicut in diebus Gabaa.* Ibid., p. 174.

64. Judges, 19. 22–30.

65. Humbertus, *L Tres*, p. 174: *qui habitores Gabaa effeminatos, et Sodomitas alios, alios autem defensores eorum narrat.* Jordan overlooks Humbertus and only addresses Gibeah briefly, *Invention of Sodomy*, pp. 30–31.

66. Ibid.: *Nimirum talia sunt haereticorum conventicula, quae domum Dei faciunt speluncam latronum, et lupanar.*

67. Blumenthal says that the *Libri tres* "found barely an echo among his contemporaries," *Investiture Controversy*, p. 76; Gilchrist, "Simoniaca Haresis", p. 226.

68. Blumenthal, *Investiture Controversy*, pp. 89–91.

69. Humbert, *L Tres*, p. 223.

70. P. Jaffe, *Regesta pontificum romanum ab condita ecclesia ad annum post Christum natum MCXCVIII* (1885–88), 4399. As quoted from Giuseppe Fornasari, "S. Pier Damiani e lo 'sciopero litugico'," *Studi Medievali*, ser. 3, an. 17, f. 2 (1976), pp. 815–32, at 819. *Ut nullus missam audiat presbyteri, quem scit concubinam indubitanter habere aut subintroductam mulierem.*

71. Damian, *Letter 61* pp. 10–11.

72. Ibid., pp. 11–12.

73. Moore, *European Dissent*, pp. 60–63. In addition to the material in note 14 above, for the Pataria, see G. Cracco, "Pataria, *opus* e *nomen*," *Rivista di storia della chiesa in Italia* 28 (1974), pp. 357–87; H.E.J. Cowdrey, "The Papacy, the Patarenes and the Church of Milan," *Transactions of the Royal Historical Society* ser. 5, n. 18 (1968), pp. 25–48; and Cowdrey, "Archbishop Aribert II of Milan," *History* 51 (1966), pp. 1–15.

74. Moore, p. 57.

75. Cracco, "Pataria: *opus* e *nomen*," 369–75.

76. Damian, *Letter 65*, p. 25.

77. Ibid., p. 26.

78. Ibid., pp. 26–29.

79. Ibid., p. 29.

80. Ibid., p. 34.

81. Ibid., pp. 29–30.

82. Ibid.

83. Ibid., pp. 33–35.

84. Here I am offering a reassesment of R. I. Moore on the matter. Moore sees this moment as the death blow, ultimately, to such future dissent, *European Dissent*, p. 61. I am suggesting that Damian was hardly clear on the Augustinian question and left a wide berth for such future dissent. Therefore, the subsequent similarities in the policy of Alexander II and Gregory VII to those of Humbert that Moore observes, are as much the result of Damian's own efforts. Indeed, we have already seen that Humbert's work closely paralleled the arguments found in Damian's *Book of Gommorah*.

85. *LGrat*, p. 214.

86. *Epistolae vagantes*, ed. H. E. J. Cowdrey (Oxford, 1972), pp. 22–24.

87. Moore, *European Dissent*, p. 62.

88. Moore, *European Dissent*, p. 61.

89. For the former see *Le Liber Pontificalis: texte, introduction et commentaire*, ed. by Louis Duchesne (Paris, 1955–57), v. II, p. XXIV. The latter at the Council of Piacenza in 1095; see Moore, *European Dissent*, p.188.

90. Anselm II, Bishop of Lucca, *Anselmi episcopi lucensis Collectio canonum: una cum collectione minore iussu Instituti Savigniani*, ed. by F. Thaner (Oeniponte, 1906–15), Bk. V, c. 13. For an overview of the collection and the life of Anselm II, see, Kathleen Cushing, *Papacy and Law in the Gregorian Revolution.* (Oxford, 1998).

91. *Anslemi* Bk. V, c. 22, as well as c. 21, based on a false epistle of Pope John I.

92. *Anselmi*, Bk. V, c. 23.

93. *Anselmi*, Bk. V, c. 6 and c. 26 respectively.

94. As noted by Gilchrist, "Simoniaca Haeresis", p. 222; and Haring, "Augustinian Axiom," p. 102. Haring observes that Anselm did not take a rigorous Augustinian

stand on other sacraments performed by heretics, but rather a somewhat tempered position emphasizing the possibility of reimposition of hands and ignoring Augustine on reordination, ibid., pp. 99–100.

95. Donizo of Canossa, *Vita Mathildis, celeberrimae principis Italiae: carmine scripta a Donizone presbytero*, ed. by Luigi Simeoni, Rerum Italicarum Scriptores, t. 5, pt. 2 (Bologna, 1940), 1114–20.

96. Uta-Renate Blumenthal, *Early Councils of Pope Paschal II, 1100–1110* (Toronto, 1978), p. 52.

97. Donizo, *Vita Mathildis*, 1122. It was the contemporary theological position that the sacraments of heretics failed to flourish: Gilchrist, "Simoniaca Haeresis", p. 224.

98. Blumenthal, *Early Councils of Pope Paschal*, pp. 53, 55–56.

99. Louis I. Hamilton, *Power of Liturgy and the Liturgy of Power in Elventh- and Twelfth-Century Italy*, Appendix B.

100. Gerhoh of Reichersberg, *Liber de Simoniacis*, Ldl, vol. 2, pp. 267–68.

101. Mary Stroll, *The Jewish Pope, Ideology and Politics in the Papal Schism of 1130* (Leiden, 1987), pp. 134–35.

102. J. D. Mansi, *Sacrorum conciliorum nova, et amplissima collectio* (Venice, 1776, repr. Paris, 1903), v. 21, 535–36: *Gaufridus etiam Carnotensis episcopus, ut supra dictum est, totius Aquitaniae legatus accepta domni papae praeceptione, omnem Galliae regionem, ipsius quoque Aquitaniae, studiose circumiens, omnia sanctarum ecclesiarum altaria, quae vel Girardus ille seditionis autor & obtentor, vel Gilo Tusculanensis episcopus, aut eorum complices, chrismalis unctionis benedictione in illius odiosi schismatic tempore consecraverant, propriis manibus dissipavit, nec reliquens lapidem super lapidem, quem non destrueret, solo funditus adaequavit: & ratione dictante, alia eorum loco restaurare curavit.*

103. Compare with Optatus, *De schismate Donatistarum*, Vi, 1.

104. E. Pásztor, "Una fonte per la storia dell' età gregoriana: la Vita Anselmi episcopi Lucensis," *Bollettino dell'istituto storico italiano per il medio evo e archivio Muratoriano* 72 (1960), 1–33. Moore, *European Dissent*, pp. 47–49.

105. Moore, *European Dissent*, pp. 168–240.

106. As suggested by Blumenthal, *Investiture Controversy*, p. 76; and Gilchrist, "Simoniaca Haeresis", p. 234.

107. For the ongoing twelfth-century debate, see Haring, "Augustinian Axiom," pp. 109–117.

12

The Enchanted City of Man: The State and the Market in Augustinian Perspective

Eugene McCarraher

ONE OF THE OLDEST TALES TOLD about modernity is entitled "The Disen-chantment of the World." Written by Max Weber, it relates the story of a once-enchanted place, full of "mysterious incalculable forces" that inhabited or controlled our world. Beholden to the whimsy or providential design of a pantheon of spirits and deities, the world of enchantment could be magically or prayerfully entreated. Rocks, trees, rivers, and rain pulsed with invisible but potent beings, as did the affairs of human communities. Families, tribes, and empires bore a sacral character enlivened by "pneuma, which swept through the great communities like a firebrand, welding them together." But with Protestantism, science, bureaucracy, and capitalism, the company of enchant-ment was evicted from the earth, and its dispossession defines modernity. The sciences dispelled the ontology of mystery, while the new political and eco-nomic knowledges gave starkly terrestrial accounts of power. The prose of rea-son hushed the poetry of enchantment in the state and the capitalist market. Moderns inhabit an "iron cage," Weber wrote, prisoners of their quest for free-dom from the lies and terrors of enchantment.[1]

In this chapter, I will draw upon St. Augustine to suggest that this tale of disenchantment conveys a misleading account of modernity. Relying heavily on the *City of God*, and enlisting the insights of "radical orthodoxy" in con-temporary theology, I propose that the modern city of man remains an en-chanted abode. Far from being "secular" modes of political and economic ra-tionality, the nation-state and the capitalist market are unmistakable forms of fetishism, sacral orders which captivate and mobilize our perverted celestial desires. While the assertion that secular polities and markets have their own "gods" is certainly not a new one, it has rarely if ever gone beyond moralism, in large measure, I would contend, because of what John Milbank has baldly condemned as the "false humility" of modern Christian theologians, their reluctance to put their conceptual and imaginative resources at the center of Christian intellectual life.[2] By turning (or rather *returning*) to theology, I will demonstrate how a variety of twentieth-century intellectuals, many of them professedly "secular," have discerned the sacral quality of modern political and economic life. From the "beloved community" or "common faith" imagined by American Progressives, to the "money complex" and "commodity fetishism" described by Freudian and Marxist critics, an array of writers has dimly perceived the reality behind "secularity"—modernity's concealed enchantment, its repression, displacement, and renaming of the sacred.

This essay, then, is an attempt to foster an Augustinian reformulation of political and cultural criticism. Over the last decade, Christian intellectuals have been enjoined to entertain "the outrageous idea of Christian scholarship" and to clothe the "naked public square" in a decent theological drapery. I write from a conviction that the preponderance of Christian scholarship in this vein has been anything but "outrageous," and that its fire-breathing modesty reflects a threadbare and mediocre theology. At the same time, calls for a more robust religious presence in the public world assume the "secularity" of modern politics, identify that secularism solely with the political left, and bestow a benediction on the liberal capitalist order.[3] In my Augustinian reading I aim to avoid both these forms of obfuscation. Christian intellectuals should use theology, not as some invertebrate "spirit" which "informs" their writing, but as the conceptual architecture in which they formulate problems and incorporate other traditions. When they do, they'll discover that the "naked public square" has always worn the raiment of the sacred, and that the battles between "secular" and "religious" citizens—as well as the conflicts between "liberal" and "conservative" believers—have always been conducted on the ideological terrain of the state and capitalist market. If we both forsake the banality of moralism and allow Augustine to be, like the gospel he loved, "ever ancient, ever new," we might see the perversity of our age in all its folly, sadness, and redeemable grandeur.

Tales of Two Cities:
The Bishop of Hippo as Melancholy
Conservative, Liberal Reformer, and Christian Socialist

Anyone who claims an Augustinian mantle must recognize that there are several fabrics and styles. While this is not the place for a meticulous assessment of the literature on Augustine's historical, social, and political ideas, I will sketch what I see as the main lines of interpretation and justify my own selection from among the various Augustines. There are three Augustines who emerge from this literature, and their differences arise over two related themes in the bishop's work: the relationship of the "earthly city" and the "heavenly city," and the meaning of the Church, especially its ecclesiology (its account of its nature and organization) and its soteriology (its account of salvation). Like many apparently pedantic disputes, these differences harbor subtle but enormously dissimilar political implications. I will also contend that Augustine advances a "sacramental" view of creation which allows us both to offer a Christian version of "enchantment" and to ground political theology in a sacramental, "enchanted" metaphysics.

It's fair to say that the most hallowed and influential Augustine is the figure I'll dub the Melancholy Conservative, the gloomy Christian gus of Roman antiquity. This bishop of Hippo presides over the "Constantinian" concordat between the church and imperial might; provides, in the *City of God*, the *ur*-text of the "just war" tradition; and sanctions, in the (uncomplimentary) words of the theologian Andrew Shanks, "a fully comprehensive scheme of cultural hegemony." But this ecclesial pillar of imperial stability is an odd brand of conservative, one who likens the state to a gang of thieves and relishes its humbling by barbarians. Though insistent, like any conservative, on the primacy of social order, this Augustine has no illusions about the earthly city's pretensions to virtue. Every social and political order bears the mark of *libido dominandi*, the lust for power and mastery that enslaves every sinful creature. The conflicts within and without the empire, and the violence required to quell them, belie Rome's claim to be an exemplary commonwealth—its avowal, as Augustine cites Cicero's *De Republica*, to constitute "an association united by a common sense of right and a community of interest." "That commonwealth never existed," Augustine comments tersely; Cicero's description is "a fancy picture" because "there was never real justice in the community." Still, despite Rome's self-delusion, the sinful condition of humanity mandates restraint and subordination, and so earthly order—itself corrupted by sin—must be paramount in political life. In this scheme of politics, the Church is an eminently serviceable institution. Since the visible Church and the heavenly city are related but not identical, the love and peace of celestial community can have no purchase on terrestrial affairs. While the Church saves souls, it cannot overturn injustice, and it brings the gospel to bear on social and political life only in the most temperate and truncated manner. Thus, what Herbert Deane succinctly calls Augustine's "political and social quietism" derives, not only from his rueful vision of human corruption, but from an ecclesiology that defines the Church's political relevance in terms of regulation, not transformation.[4]

While the Melancholy Conservative held sway from antiquity through much of the twentieth century—a tribute, as it were, to the durability of the Constantinian bargain—Augustine the Liberal Reformer has emerged in the years since World War II. This incarnation takes two forms, one which resembles the Melancholy Conservative, and another which anoints him a harbinger of social and political modernity. The first Reformer stalks the pages of Reinhold Niebuhr and Jean Bethke Elshtain. In Niebuhr's view—articulated in the early 1950s as American Protestant intellectuals sought moral and political high ground in the early days of the Cold War—Augustine is "the first great 'realist' in Western history." Not quite a cynic, Niebuhr's Augustine agrees with the Melancholy Conservative that, in the earthly city, power is checked and channeled only by another power, and that earthly order requires hierarchy and deference. "Without some form of subordination," Niebuhr wrote with masterly *gravitas*, "the institutions of civilization could not exist." But Niebuhr considered Augustine's realism "excessive" and "indiscriminate," and complained that the bishop could not distinguish between legitimate and illegitimate forms of subordination. This careful appropriation allowed Niebuhr to induct Augustine into the ranks of "Christian realists," Protestant intellectuals who sought theological sanction for the reformist and imperialist ambitions of Cold War liberals. Augustine's alleged appreciation of the truth in *realpolitik* made him indispensable to Protestants eager to purge the liberal tradition of illusions about the plasticity of human nature and the inevitability of historical progress. It also hallowed him in the eyes of secular "vital centrists" such as Arthur Schlesigner, Jr., who comprised a "tough-minded" liberal cohort of the postwar policy and academic elite. At the same time, Augustine's alleged refusal to acknowledge "the sense of justice in the imperial constitution" lent credibility to Niebuhr's affirmation of "the creative and ambiguous character of American hegemony" in the non-Communist world.[5]

Niebuhr's construction of an Augustinian "realism" depended on his simultaneous erasure of Augustinian ecclesiology. Niebuhr downplayed the social and cultural character of the antagonism between Augustine's two cities. Correcting Augustine's trope of the "two cities" which inhabit the same geographical and political space, Niebuhr maintained that the problem of the cities' intermingling was not that "two types of people dwell together" but that "the conflict between love and self-love [rages] in every soul." Thus, Niebuhr's reading of the *City of God* as a primer in political realism continued in his vein of the 1930s, when, even as a socialist, he had cast the problem of political morality in the liberal individualist terms of "moral man" and "immoral society," not in terms of Christian and non-Christian communities of political identity. Indeed, Niebuhr the Protestant socialist could become the *pontifex maximus* of Cold War liberalism because, as he argued in *Moral Man and Im-*

moral Society (1932), "pure religious idealism does not concern itself with the social problem." This understanding of the earthly-heavenly divide as a primarily internal conflict enabled Niebuhr to "realistically" cede the terrain of politics to secular expertise. Despite Niebuhr's reputation for political engagement, his reading of Augustine described a church even more politically lifeless than the *ecclesia* of the Melancholy Conservative.[6]

Writing a generation later, Elshtain brought Augustine into the ranks of a reform tradition much more battered and bewildered than Niebuhr's. More pointedly than Niebuhr, Elshtain contended that Augustine underwrites a "politics of limits" and a "chastened form of civic virtue" that recognizes the illusory and dangerous nature of utopianism. Augustine, she maintained, offers only a "*via negativa*," a "negative of ideology" which leavens a politics committed only to "prevent[ing] the worst from happening." This eminently reasonable and uninspiring stance lames a thesis more muscular and tantalizing than anything in "Christian realism": "the Augustinian is always a radical *in situ*" who must courageously repudiate any illegitimate allegiances demanded by earthly power. Because Elshtain does not flesh out this "radicalism" in terms of ecclesiology, her ideal of the Augustinian maverick who lives "the ethic of the pilgrim" has no concrete collective existence.[7] Like Niebuhr's concentration on the individual soul, Elshtain's account of Augustine rendered the church politically irrelevant, even invisible.

Where Niebuhr and Elshtain emphasized the "chastened" quality of Augustinian liberalism, R. A. Markus affirmed what he considered "the neutral, pluralist society of the Augustinian tradition." Conceding Augustine's melancholy conservatism—civil community is a device for "keeping chaos and disintegration in check"—Markus discerned a more positive ecclesiology by whose terms the Church must "support, and sometimes inspire" ideas and movements for social reconstruction. In Markus's hands, Augustine became a precursor of the "secular city" theology that marked the 1960s. Clearly indebted to Harvey Cox, Jurgen Moltmann, and other "theologians of hope," Markus found in Augustine support for selective but vigorous political engagement. Although Markus's Augustine rejects all attempts to compromise the transcendence of the heavenly city, he nonetheless calls on Christians to subject all earthly orders to "a critical scrutiny in the perspective opened by the hope of the Kingdom." In the Markusian brand of Augustinian politics, Christian hope became "a searchlight" which illuminates "opportunities for protest." But this activist Augustinianism stopped well short of the radical and often Marxist politics that enlivened "liberation theology." Markus explicitly avowed that "liberal reformism" was his preferred métier, and admonished Augustinian liberals to respect "the fragmentary, piecemeal, *ad hoc* character of political enterprise." Christians must seek, not a revolutionary transformation of society, but "provisional goals" that address specific problems.[8]

With its wariness of radical, "totalizing" solutions to earthly injustice, Markus's "provisional" Christian politics reflected the post-1945 turn in liberalism, social democracy, and "Christian democracy" toward a technocratic composure of social and political conflict. Terrified by fascism, disillusioned by Stalinism, and unsatisfied by laissez-faire, reformers in the North Atlantic world drew upon the burgeoning culture of professionalism to fashion the keywords of postwar political discourse: "chastened," "provisional," "sober," and "mature," all the nestorian refrains of gray-flanneled power. Epitomized in Daniel Bell's (premature) announcement of the "end of ideology"—a dictum recently airbrushed and reissued by Francis Fukuyama as "the end of history"—this new parlance betokened the multi-credentialed sagacity of technical specialists, bureaucratic managers, and policy analysts.[9] Thus, even theologians who saw more ground for political hope than Niebuhr (or later Elshtain) could not shake the conviction that theology held little distinctive political promise.

Yet the Christian political ferment of the 1960s was not restricted to advocates of a "secular" or "provisional" politics. While considerable attention has been paid to "liberation theology," the most intellectually vibrant development in the Christian social thought of the period was among Catholics linked to the British New Left. Combining Marxist philosophy and Catholic theology with greater sophistication than liberation theologians, the "Slant" group, as they were called, rejected what Terry Eagleton considered the "tepid liberalism" of Vatican II Catholicism and its "embracement of social engineering and managerialism"—the politics, that is, of Augustine cast as Liberal Reformer. For the most part bereft of references to Augustine, *Slant* addressed one of the classic Augustinian concerns: the nature of the heavenly city. The Church, Eagleton wrote, was the earthen vessel of all genuinely revolutionary social thought. Just as, in Marxist-Leninist theory, the party was the enlightened vehicle of class struggle at the political level, so Christians as the body of Christ constituted "a revolutionary vanguard . . . working to dissipate the layers of false consciousness." But in order to dispel the illusions of unbelief, Christians needed a precise vocabulary of revolution, one which *Slant* could not discern in the stampede to join "the world come of age," to use the Bonhoefferesque phrase then in vogue among "secular" Christians. Impatient with invocations of "religion" in the tiresome and undisciplined enthusiasm of "secular city" Christians, Eagleton noted that "religious sentiment, shorn of its factual context of theological truth, could be conveniently blended into any version of life which needed some emotive underpinning." Theology, he suggested, was the revolutionary lexicon of Christianity, the discursive and ritual language through which Christians saw in the risen Christ "the ground of the historical movement . . . for communal liberation" and in the Eucharist "the symbolic transcendence of all historical alienation." Pointing to the Oxford Movement and its political incarnation in the "Christian socialist" movements of the late nineteenth and early twentieth centuries, Eagleton praised their insistence on "the concrete cooperative community of the church as an image of ideal human society." Because of this twofold emphasis on discursive particularity and "high" ecclesiology, Christian social thought could proceed, Eagleton observed shrewdly, "in theological rather than merely religious terms."[10]

Although *Slant* broke apart in the 1970s, their concerns with the intellectual and institutional integrity of Christian political identity have taken a new and distinctly Augustinian form in "radical orthodoxy," an Anglo-American, Anglican-Roman Catholic movement in theology. Beginning ostensibly as a critique of modern theology, radical orthodoxy associates this intervention with a line of social and political criticism inaugurated in the mid-nineteenth century among the socialist heirs of the Oxford Movement—precisely those Christian radicals celebrated by Eagleton.[11] Because ecclesiology was central both to the Oxford Movement and to the varieties of British Christian socialism, the work of Augustine figures centrally in their work. It is here that we discover Augustine as Christian socialist, and it is this Augustine who provides contemporary Christians with the fundamentals of a distinctive political and cultural criticism.

The Christian socialist Augustine arguably made his first appearance in John Neville Figgis's brief but brilliant *The Political Aspects of St. Augustine's 'City of God'* (1921), a milestone in Christian political thought. An Anglican priest and a leader of the Church Socialist League, one of the more radical elements of the Christian socialist movement before World War I, Figgis wrote, like Augustine, in the smoky twilight of a civilization racked by war and despair. Although, in Figgis's view, Augustine's political remarks "never amount to a theory" either of politics or of history, they do convey a political sensibility informed by theology. While Figgis refused to squarely pit the visible Church squarely against organized earthly power—"the primary distinction" for Augustine is always between "the body of the reprobate and the *communio sanctorum*"—he highlighted the decisive difference between the incarnate celestial city and the unregenerate earthly metropolis. "The Civitas Dei," Figgis contended, "can mean nothing less than the social life of the children of God." As such, it is irreducibly "a social life" in opposition to "another form of social life." Thus Figgis discovered in Augustine an ecclesiology that countered both liberal individualism (which finds both apotheosis and indictment, he noted, in Nietzsche's "will to power") and conservative pietism (which falsely promises "earthly security under the aegis of the Church").[12]

Meanwhile, to a degree unmatched (and even unimagined) by Augustine's conservative and liberal interpreters, Figgis recognized the enchanted, sacral character of the earthly city's affairs. The structuring conflict of the *City of God*, he recalled, is not that of "sacred and secular" but of "Christianity and Paganism"—"two religions," he emphasized, which express two opposing passions, "the passion for God and the passion for self." The religious nature of *libido dominandi* was evident to Figgis in the noble ideals of the earthly city. Humanist concerns with truth, beauty, and justice, even when bereft of religious or theological formulation, require some "infusion of the other-worldly principle." Moreover, Figgis noted the centrality of sacrifice among the virtues intoned by both patriots and merchants. Whether in dying for country or in saving for investment, something or someone "must die to live," in Christian parlance.[13]

Yet Figgis retreated from some of the political implications of his own insights. Referring to the conclusion of Blake's "Milton" which served as the anthem of the Labour Party, Figgis mused that the bishop never thought to "build Jerusalem in Africa's bright and sunny land" and dismissed the idea that Augustine had proposed a "programme on socialistic lines." But this pedantic concession to historical exactitude also robbed Figgis of an opportunity to envision, through an Augustinian prism, a socialist, Christian modernity. Could not "the social life of the children of God" have provided the partisan of the Church Socialist League with a warrant to translate ecclesiology into a vital Christian socialism? Perhaps the wartime demise of British Christian socialism had lamed Figgis's political will and stymied his theological imagination. A similar failure of nerve prevented Figgis from expanding on his discernment of the errant sacrality of the earthly city. Declaring that Augustine "discarded the principles of religion in the idea of a commonwealth"—an assertion that both flew in the face of the text and contradicted his insight into the enchanted nature of "paganism"—Figgis ended up confirming one of the central platitudes of modernity. "The sharp distinction between secular and sacred, holy and profane," he asserted, "was enormously strengthened by St. Augustine."[14]

Figgis's successors in "radical orthodoxy" acknowledge a liberal moment in Augustinian theology—Augustine *does* "contribute to the invention of liberalism," Milbank concedes, because he can not envision a politics of complete justice—but they locate it in their larger repudiation of an "ontology of violence" which undergirds political thought from antiquity to our post-modern era. In this view, the Melancholy Conservative and the Liberal Reformer are present but not decisive. While Augustine saw that the curbing of sin is itself afflicted by sin—indeed, by a sin potentially more self-deluded about its virtue than the wrong it curtails—his "pastoral" and "pedagogical" legitimation of coercion opens the door much too widely, Milbank thinks, to complicity in the designs of *imperium* and *libido dominandi*. Thomas Aquinas trundled through this door, Milbank believes, with a "spiritualized" account of the Church which, in defining it as "an organization specializing in what goes on inside men's souls," both depoliticized Christianity and turned politics into the management of conflict. (It is on this score that Milbank attacks both Markus and Niebuhr, the Melancholy and the Liberal.) Still, although Milbank cites Augustine's "Christian prince" as a kind of halfway covenant between *ecclesia* and *imperium*, his defense seems more obligatory than compelling. Indeed, Milbank—as well as Rowan Williams and Graham Ward—identifies in Augustine the sources of a political imagination that enables us to repudiate punishment, coercion, manipulation, and war, and to completely "unthink the necessity of violence."[15]

The radical orthodox construction of Augustine—one which leads, especially in Milbank, to a "Christian socialist" political theology—is a remarkably ambitious intellectual project, and it gives us a prism through which we can see the enchantment of the earthly city. Augustine's account of history in the *City of God* secures "a true Christian metanarrative realism," Milbank claims, which provides "the original possibility of critique that marks the western tradition." Liberalism and Marxism, he asserts, are "abridgements" or "parodies" of this historical theology—perversions, in Augustinian parlance, of the Christian critical lineage.[16] (One is tempted to say that the *City of God* is the *Das Kapital* of Christian theology.)

Political theology must rest, Milbank argues, on what he describes as "Augustine's vision of the ontological primacy of perfection"—in other words, on the conviction that creation is peaceful, abundant, and sacramental. Because Christians believe that God is a God of love and power, and that God's creation partakes of these qualities, they trust in God and the real goodness of the world. Thus, the Christian virtue of charity is not an idealistic moralism but the clearest and profoundest realism, a faith that is literally true to life, an authenticity that arises from "the assumption of plenitude, our confidence in God's power."[17] In direct opposition to the skinflint wisdom of modern economics, we could say that we always live beyond our means, because there's really no other way we can live.

Creation is not just abundant, but sacramental as well. On this score, I would contend that Augustine formulates a Christian version of enchantment which explains the divine presence in the material world. When Augustine claimed that "the invisible realities of God are apprehended through the material things of his creation," he rooted his assertion in what Ward has described as a "doctrine of divine participation in creation" whereby "the corporeal and the incorporeal do not comprise a dualism." When read theologically, the visible, material realm "manifests the watermark of its creator." Thus, what we rightly desire through material goods—be they delicious foods, attractive clothing, or beautiful bodies—is the God whose trademark (to change the metaphor) is everywhere. The ritualized sacraments of the Church, especially the Eucharist, are unique bearers of God's presence, efficacious "means of grace" which cultivate our receptive expectation. This is why Augustine contended in the *City of God* that worship is the basis of all other virtues, since, in Milbank's words, it "gives everything back up to God, hangs onto nothing and so disallows any finite accumulation which will always engender conflict."[18]

To worship properly and to see the mark of God, we must enter the Church, the earthly, social manifestation of the "heavenly city" whose fullness awaits us. As an anticipatory community ("proleptic" in theological jargon), the Church affords the sacramental view of creation, performs those liturgies which enable us to "read" things and desire rightly, and practices that charity whose assurance is plenty. As Figgis realized, it is "the social life of the children of God." Salvation—"the restoration of being," in Milbank's words—simply *is* participation in this particular form of social life, and so the Chruch is the "*telos* of the salvific process."[19]

But this means that the Church is not an exclusively "spiritual" community, since such a conception would reproduce socially a dualism alien to Christian ontology. As "the heavenly city on pilgrimage through this world," in Augustine's words, the Church is both a *polis* and an *oikos* whose way of life, if followed seriously, has revolutionary political consequences. Since men and women, created in God's image and likeness, are irreducibly social beings—the anthropological implication of Trinitarian doctrine—then their exchanges of goods and services within "the restoration of being" must reflect a conviviality, a joy in creativity, and a lack of concern for accumulation that rests on the assurance of abundance. As Augustine puts it in the *City of God*, any goodness is "enjoyed more widely by the united affection of partners," and "anyone who refuses to enjoy this possession in partnership will not enjoy it at all." At the same time, in a sacramental fashion, human labor becomes *poesis*, a portal onto divinity, a way to "open up our awareness of the sacred in the presentation of compelling forms." Among radical Augustinians, the political economy of sacrament takes a variety of (often vague and suggestive) forms. For D. Stephen Long, it is "the divine economy"; for William Cavanaugh, it is "eucharistic anarchism"; for Milbank, it is "Christian socialism," an economy of worker-controlled production and consumption that recalls the "guild socialism," not only of the Fabian G. D. H. Cole, but of Figgis's Church Socialist League.[20]

Unfortunately, in our sin—what Augustine famously called our "perversion" or errant love—we invert the real state of things, misread the sacramental marks, do wrong in the faith that we are doing right, and attribute to earthly goods and ultimately to ourselves the power possessed by God alone. We enter what Augustine called the "earthly city," a state of being founded on *libido dominandi*, a lust for power kindled by our errant love, a lack of trust in the peace and abundance of God. For all their claims to maturity and realism, the unredeemed citizens of the earthly city inhabit a dreamworld of scarcity whose all-too-real consequences are anxiety, fear, conflict, and death. But because we still bear the *imago dei*, our art, technology, commerce, and politics—evidence, Augustine wrote, of "the blessings we enjoy" from God—are warped into grotesquerie. As Oliver O'Donovan puts it, "disorder is predatory on some order." We create what Augustine called a *perverse imitatur*, a distorted representation of the heavenly city, the illustrious but crippled product of our longing.[21]

When *perverse imitatur* takes political and economic form, it becomes, to use Augustine's example, *imperium*. "So long as it enjoys material prosperity and the glory of victorious war" (he wrote in the stunning Book II chapter 20 of the *City of God*), the citizens of the earthly *imperium* are happy. "We should get richer all the time, to have enough for extravagant spending every day"— the logical culmination of an ontology of scarcity with no faith in sacramental plenty. This paradise of deficiency fosters a culture of individualism whose first commandment is that "anyone should be free to do as he likes about his own, or with his own, or with others, if they consent." The earthly *imperium* is a boundless marketplace mastered by "providers of material satisfactions" who cultivate not the honor and morality but rather the "docility of their subjects." Just as Christian love depends on worship, imperial docility rests on wrongful worship; Rome, Augustine asserted elsewhere, "has made to herself . . . false gods whom she might serve by sacrifice."[22] Caesar and Mammon, while lenient in their way, are also demanding: incessant work and lethal devotion become the means to restore fulfillment. Where Christians accept the sacrifice already made by a Lamb, the denizens of *imperium* sacrifice themselves as lambs for the sake of their divinities. Accumulation and death—the sacrifices of enjoyment and of life itself—become the order of the day.

We can now summarize the outlines of an Augustinian criticism of the modern state and the capitalist market. Both are perverse imitations of the heavenly city. Both live as parasites on a divine order. Both are fetishes in which desires for beatitude find a false and beleaguered fulfillment. Both beguile with their own soteriology. While the capitalist corporation claims a bogus sacrality, the nation-state shows more clearly the perversion of ecclesia. While the civil religions of modern states have their own liturgical simulacra, the capitalist market in commodities exemplifies more profoundly the perversion of sacrament.

"Extra republicam nulla salus": Enchantment, Redemption, and the Soteriology of State Fetishism

Modern political thought rests on repression of its redemptive hopes. While this assertion defies the conventional wisdom of both its advocates and its detractors, it also rehearses the insight of several "secular" political intellectuals.

On this score, we have arguably only begun to reap the fruit of Christian socialist Augustinianism. Because it defines modern "secularity" as, in part, the creation of a political space of untrammeled human will-to-power, Milbank's account of the invention of modern political science by Machiavelli, Hobbes, Locke, and Spinoza comports with the traditional tale of disenchantment that I am trying to discredit. If we want to embellish Milbank's own best insights, we might turn to William Cavanaugh, who, upholding the claim that Augustine understood the Roman *imperium* as "a dim archetype" of the Church, argues that the modern nation-state is "a simulacrum, a false copy, of the Body of Christ" and that it offers "an alternative soteriology to that of the Church." As Cavanaugh wittily encapsulates the soteriology that is modern political theory, "*extra republicam nulla salus.*"[23]

Though it would be easy to classify and dismiss Cavanaugh's insight as a piece of theological ingenuity, it echoes some of the most provocative work in political anthropology, particularly that of Michael Taussig on "state fetishism." Drawing not only on Marx but on Emile Durkheim, Taussig contends that the modern nation-state is a new form of sacred space, a polis every bit as enchanted as those of "primitive," ancient, or medieval peoples. In Taussig's view, Durkheim's analysis of totemism in *The Elementary Forms of Religious Life* (1912), while problematical in its methodology and evidence, illuminates nonetheless the ready and often violent devotion to "the State" on the part of modern citizens. Durkheim himself noted that the study of totems— objects or symbols that signified and possessed the enchanting spirit of a clan—pointed to the totemic quality of modern social and political order. The totem, Durkheim explained, drew its power from the communal consciousness of a clan, membership in which was essential, not just for survival, but for moral identity and sacral connection—in Augustinian terms, for salvation. If, in Durkheim's words, "society is to its members what a god [or a totem] is to its faithful," and if "society never stops creating new sacred things," then modernity could be characterized in terms of its own totems, its own enchantments, its own social and symbolic order of sacrality. Taussig is especially impressed by the importance of death in modern political culture. The modern state "has a deep investment in death," he remarks, because death "endows the Nation-State with life, a spectral life, to be sure." Consider, he asks, the meaning of the tomb of the unknown soldier. (Christians might recall that their hope begins with an *empty* tomb.) But where, for Durkheim, the social sciences inherit and transmute enchanted or theological accounts of social life into secular scientific knowledge—a conversion, we might observe, which makes social scientists a modern clerisy—Taussig appropriates Durkheim not to sanction but to transcend the modern and specifically liberal nation-state.[24]

Although Taussig puts a Marxist, "secular" twist on the persistence of political enchantment—"Get in touch with the fetish!" he urges, acknowledge its roots in social reality and turn it in revolutionary directions—I would contend that an Augustinian political criticism should recognize and incorporate the wisdom in Taussig's insight.[25] Following Cavanaugh and Milbank, we could argue that the modern state, like Augustine's Roman *imperium*, is a totemic or fetishistic creation. It is an ecclesial caricature to which human beings perversely ascribe redemptive powers, for which they will suffer death so as to give life, and in which their participation becomes the very meaning of salvation. Inescapable but always perverse, citizenship in the nation-state is an image and likeness of discipleship in the heavenly city on earth.

Much of modern political theory could be interpreted as the soteriology of the nation-state. As Joshua Mitchell and William Cavanaugh have perceptively demonstrated, early modern political philosophy was justified, in Mitchell's words, "not by reason alone" but by the transfiguration of traditional religious identity. Because it posed a transnational challenge to the moral authority of the state—a challenge that needed to be eliminated, curbed, or, better yet, transmuted—the Church became, Cavanaugh writes, "the primary thing from which the state is meant to save us." So if the state was, as Thomas Hobbes put it, "a mortal god," then the new deity required an enchanting ensemble of ritual, moral codes, and theology. Perhaps the most elaborate theorization of this state fetishism is Jean-Jacques Rousseau's promotion of a "civil religion" in *The Social Contract* (1762). Rousseau maintained unashamedly that the modern state is a revival of paganism—not only, as in Milbank's Augustinian view, because of its ontology of violence, but also because, as Augustine himself would have seen, it claims sacral status and ultimate devotion. Rousseau's remark that "the founders of nations have resorted to divine authority and attribute their own wisdom to the gods" appears cynical only if we forget his attempt to collapse religion into the state. Indeed, Rousseau emphasized more forcefully than any other modern political thinker the soteriological nature of modern nationalism. "Anyone who dares to say 'there is no salvation outside the Church' must be expelled from the state—unless the Church is the state and its pontiff the ruler." A "religion of the citizen," he continued, has "its gods, its own protectors and guardians . . . its dogmas, its rites, its visible form of worship." Everything outside the boundaries of the state, and therefore of the civil religion, is "faithless, alien, and barbarian." This is why Rousseau vilified Christianity with special vehemence. Because believers practice an allegiance that transcends and even conflicts with their duties to the state, Christianity "detaches them from the state, as from everything else on earth."[26]

While students of American political culture—drawing conventionally upon Locke, Madison, and Tocqueville—might contend that nothing like Rousseau's "civil religion" has ever disfigured the national landscape, one could argue that it is long past time to consult Rousseau for insight into our political enchantments. One could argue that, under the aegis of Protestantism, Americans proved more adept than Rousseau could have imagined at reworking Christianity into a civil religion. When G. K. Chesterton (a more discerning visitor than Tocqueville) observed in 1922 that the United States was "a nation with the soul of a church," he captured the religious character of American nationalism. Beginning with John Winthrop's Puritan (and Augustinian) image of a "city on a hill," American national identity had, until the early twentieth century, long been christened in the waters of Protestantism. As the historian Ernest Tuveson once put it, Protestant Americans fondly sacralized their homeland as a "Redeemer Nation," and even Catholics and Jews—whose allegiances were, until World War I, suspected in part on account of religion—slowly enlisted in the civil religion. From the Second Great Awakening to well after the Civil War, the nation's political culture formed part of an evangelical dispensation that ascribed salvific import to republican democracy and proprietary capitalism. When articulated by the northeastern middle classes who dominated the country's politics and culture, the evangelical dispensation became what Henry F. May has called "progressive patriotic Protestantism," a covenant theology for American nationalism. As a more cosmopolitan and secularizing "liberal" Protestantism split off from the evangelical dispensation, it preserved much of its ancestor's nationalist aura. Whether in the more religious form of the "Social Gospel" or in the more "secular" form of Progressivism, American nationalism retained a powerfully sacral character.[27]

Indeed, despite its "secular" veneer, the lineage of progressive-liberal nationalism is an unmistakeable pedigree of state fetishism and soteriology. Although Progressivism is often identified as a straightforwardly "secular" form of American political culture, its earliest partisans thought themselves acolytes of a new spiritual order. Usually fresh from the halfway covenant with modernity that characterized liberal Protestantism, the first generation of Progressives attributed a sacral character to American national community. When Jane Addams urged social workers in *Democracy and Social Ethics* (1902) to "love mercy," "do justly," and "walk humbly with God," she explained that the modern practice of the Christian verities lay not in organized religion but in a nation-state whose spiritual energies sought "simple and natural expression in the social organism." (Addams noted later that the "household service" held for a time by residents of Hull House, the Chicago settlement that made her famous, quickly became a "diluted form of worship.") Walter Lippmann asserted in *Drift and Mastery* (1914) that science and progressive politics could provide a sense of "modern communion," recover "the old sense of cosmic wonder," and kindle a "luminous passion" to make the nation more gentle and bountiful. In his work of the 1910s the Harvard philosopher Josiah

Royce espoused a "religion of loyalty," a species of benevolent nationalism in which the fulfillment of the individual self would come through a "wise provincialism," devotion to a "Beloved Community" constructed with the expertise of professional and managerial specialists.[28]

In an even more exalted vein, Herbert Croly—a founder of the *New Republic* and a lifelong dabbler in religious enthusiasms—filled *Progressive Democracy* (1914) with religious and even crypto-Augustinian imagery that parodied the ecclesial and salvific claims of traditional Christianity. Inspired by a "faith in the holiness of the city," modern progressive citizens, Croly believed, should possess a "common faith [which] sanctifies those who share it." This faith—rooted not in a desire for God but in "the will to live," that is, ultimately, in the love of self—put them on a "pilgrimage" toward a "holy city" or "consummate community" designed in accordance with the scientific principles of nature and social order. Croly did not shy away from the coercive but benevolent nature of this pilgrimage. "Pressure" from experts and leaders "economized the time of pilgrims, made their journey easier, improved their itineraries, and enriched their store of inventions and knowledge." This celestially-mandated pressure required the adoption of "scientific management" in industry, the need to impose "more exacting standards of behavior upon the citizens of an industrial democratic state," and an enormous increase in "the productive efficiency of human work." Croly concluded with an exalted peroration that democracy, "like the faith of St. Paul, finds its consummation in a love which . . . [is] a spiritual expression of the mystical unity of human nature."[29]

Croly's hope for a "common faith" was the point of departure for the pragmatist political thought of John Dewey and Richard Rorty. Decried by fundamentalists and celebrated by secularists as a purveyor of godless humanism, Dewey began his intellectual career as a liberal Protestant philosopher, and his subsequent work could be read as an attempt to reformulate that Protestant religiosity in the idioms of pragmatism and progressive social thought. In an early essay penned in 1887, Dewey had made the irreproachable and fateful observation that "whatever exiles theology makes ethics an expatriate." Dewey gradually exiled theology, but he strove ever after to repatriate ethics in the problem-solving, scientific culture of a democratic, progressive nation-state. Democracy, he surmised just a year later, was "a form of moral and spiritual association" which achieved "complete harmony with the universe of spiritual relations." Dewey's more mature writing of the 1920s and 1930s completed the trajectory begun in the 1880s. By demanding in his 1929 Gifford Lectures that religion "surrender once for all commitment to belief about matters of fact, whether physical, social, or metaphysical" and "leave such matters to inquirers in other fields"—inquirers, he made clear in *Individualism Old and New* (1930), such as "sociologists, psychologists, novelists, dramatists, and

poets"—he conferred episcopal status on these groups through his sacraliza-
tion of the national community. In *The Public and Its Problems* (1927), Dewey
envisioned a "Great Community" whose "life of free and enriching communion" bore a distinctly ecclesial quality.[30]

The high point of Dewey's progressive-nationalist fetishism came in *A
Common Faith* (1935) with its plea for a "religious faith that shall not be confined to sect, class, or race." Characterized by the historian Robert Westbrook
as an ideal of "consummatory experience," a kind of beatific vision for a secular, radical democracy, the pragmatist sacrality of *A Common Faith* ratified
the clerical status of democratic politicians and policy experts. In Dewey's
view, faith, or "the unification of the self through allegiance to inclusive ideal
ends," depended on the imaginative idealization of persons and events who
could "enlist devotion and inspire endeavor." But these symbols still required
a "final arbiter," a group endowed with cultural and sacral authority. Dewey
located these sacral powers in modern cultural and academic institutions
whose "revolution in the seat of intellectual authority" had been accepted by
most American citizens—"even," he emphasized, "those holding membership
in churches." Thus, though putatively democratic, Dewey's "Great Community" required the ministration of elites in industry, culture, and government.
Moreover, if we see "secularization" as the repression and concealment of the
enchanted or the sacred, then we can reinterpret Dewey's social and political
thought as the perverse enchantment of the modern state, an errant sacraliza-
tion which transferred to the nation-state and its battery of experts the ecclesial and redemptive powers once attributed to the church. As Bruce Kuklick
has observed, Dewey "transformed religious concerns into a new language," a
"lingua franca for those in the knowledge professions who sought power."[31]

With its direct appropriation of religious imagery and aura, Dewey's "common faith" might seem light-years distant from the self-conscious secularism
that marks contemporary American progressives. But the fetishism of the
state appears even in a writer as aggressively antireligious as Richard Rorty.
Though far less sympathetic than Dewey to traditional religion, Rorty has
called upon the American left to construct a "civic religion" that would revitalize social reform with the energies of democratic nationalism. Eager to repudiate the embarrassingly metaphysical (and Christian) idea of "holding reality and justice in a single vision," Rorty espouses a generous
"religion"—expounded, he believes, by Dewey, William James, and Walt Whitman—that appropriates Christian values while rejecting the ontological
claims on which they depend. Progressives must separate "the fraternity and
loving kindness urged by the Christian Scriptures from the idea of supernatural parentage, immortality, providence, and—most important—sin." These
theological antiques must be consigned to the flea market of "privatized reli-

gious belief, not the sort of religious belief that produces churches, especially churches which take political positions."[32]

What is revealing here is not Rorty's meager understanding of Christian theology, which dilutes charity into "loving kindness," mistakes church for "fraternity," and psychologizes sin into "self-loathing." (The maternal grandson of Walter Rauschenbusch really ought to know better.) Rather, what marks Rorty's overtly "secular" project as a desperate form of state fetishism and soteriology is his curious need to sacralize the democratic state. If the project of secularization is so urgent and straightforward, why does Rorty confuse the issue with the language of religion? Because, I suspect, he realizes that secularity will not mobilize the kind or degree of popular assent he considers necessary to "achieve our country." To his credit, Rorty forthrightly confesses that he "do[es] not think that there is a nonmythological, nonideological way of telling a country's story." Given this compromising of secularity, what Rorty appears to desire—given his open admiration for the attempt of early Progressive intellectuals to be, in his words, "ministers of [a] national church"—is clerical status for himself and his fellow reformers. Why else would Rorty be so keen on maligning, not "privatized religious belief"— twaddle whose adherents have the good manners to stay silent in public—but "the sort . . . that produces churches" and takes political stands? Still, because Rorty refuses to ground ethics in metaphysics, his "civic religion" remains an intellectually sophisticated form of positive thinking. This is why Rorty sounds, at times, like a liberal grotesque of Norman Vincent Peale. "You have to be loyal to a dream country rather than to the one to which you wake up every morning"—a counsel whose animating sentiment I would hope Rorty never directed to his wife.[33] Never has pragmatism been exposed as idealism in so saccharinely inept a manner.

One Progressive who discerned and eventually denounced the enchanted, ecclesial, and redemptive parodies of the modern state was Randolph Bourne. A student of Dewey's at Columbia, an admirer of Royce, and (before his dissent from the *New Republic*'s support for World War I) a writer for Lippmann and Croly, Bourne was an eager acolyte of Progressive religiosity. His pre-war essays vibrated with the hopes of progressive nationalism, whose expansive collective and personal ideals he envisioned as "the experimental life." Like many young intellectuals at the turn of the century, Bourne rejected a sclerotic Victorian culture whose claim on national identity was increasingly discredited by the realities of modern America. The immigration of Catholics and Jews from southern and eastern Europe, the interdependence fostered by corporate industrialism, the "new psychology" of psychoanalysis, the intellectual hegemony of evolution and relativity—all comprised an energetic coalition of dissent from an exhausted proprietary-evangelical dispensation of American nationalism. To revitalize the national spirit, Bourne looked to Deweyan pragmatism, whose amorphous blend of the scientific ethos and post-Protestant religiosity seemed a worthy successor to the pieties of evangelical nationalism. Indeed, Bourne invested pragmatic progressivism with lavish spiritual significance, proclaiming that Dewey's philosophy was "a great sermon" delivered by "a prophet dressed in the clothes of a professor of logic." Though leavened with the secular language of pragmatism—the plethora of "possibility," the method of "experiment," the conception of life as a "laboratory"—Bourne's youthful work typified the spiritual exuberance of Progressive civil religion.[34]

In Bourne's rendition of progressive nationalism—especially in "Trans-National America" (1915)—the United States assumed the roles of both the earthly and the heavenly cities. A magnificent and seminal document in the lineage of cultural pluralism, "Trans-National America" could also be read, in Augustinian terms, as a moving caricature of ecclesial aspiration, a creedal statement of state soteriology. Taking aim at the hallowed ideal of "the melting pot," Bourne attacked its implicit erasure of historical memory and its attendant erosion of critical vantage. Bourne proposed instead "dual citizenship," a "cosmopolitan ideal" in which immigrants would somehow preserve their distinctive backgrounds as they also embraced the possibilities offered by contact with other groups. In contrast to the "enmity and distrust" that marked the war-ridden Old World and the tension-ridden New—the sinful burdens of the earthly city—a new America would incarnate a "trans-nationality of all the nations," a dream that recalls the international composition of the pilgrim Church on earth. Bourne's conclusion accentuated the religious quality of his national ideal. Borrowing a phrase from Royce, Bourne asserted that trans-national America could enable "the good life . . . lived in the environment of the Beloved Community" and achieve "a spiritual moulding which should make us infinitely strong."[35] In Bourne's Progressive imagination, a cosmopolitan, multicultural democracy replaced the Protestant, proprietary republic as the beatific city of America.

But American entry into World War I, and the enthusiastic support it received from Progressive intellectuals, both undermined Bourne's buoyant faith and clarified the horrid sacrality of the nation-state. In two of his last essays—"Twilight of Idols" (1917) and an unfinished manuscript, "The State" (1918)—Bourne explored and tried to demystify the enchantment of modern nationalism. Over the spring and summer of 1917, Bourne watched in painful disbelief as his fellow progressives—especially his beloved Dewey—enlisted in the intellectual brigades and fouled themselves with "the sewage of the war spirit." Dewey's defense of the war in particular outraged Bourne. After a perfunctory acknowledgement of the bloodlust and misery war entailed, Dewey argued in the *New Republic* that the conflict offered Progressives an opportunity to experiment with the technical and managerial prowess they would need for peacetime social reconstruction. Bourne would have none of it. Studding "Twilight of Idols" with religious phraseology, Bourne issued a bull of apostasy from what he called "the pragmatic dispensation." To some of those like himself "who have taken Dewey's philosophy almost as our American religion," Dewey's militarism, as well as the facility with which "a younger intelligentsia" had undertaken the prosecution of the war, exposed the nihilistic sacrality at the core of the pragmatic dispensation. Although Dewey meant to "start with values," there was always, Bourne wrote mordantly, "that unhappy ambiguity" as to "just how values were created." As he wrote to the critic and fellow "malcontent" Van Wyck Brooks, the pragmatic disappointment indicated that America needed "a new gospel," a new civil religion—a new false worship, in Augustine's terms. Bourne argued that, in order to preserve what was best in (and what was left of) democracy, a principled but sympathetic opposition to the militarized popular moral imagination would be necessary. Rather than simply accept the popular will as an unassailable edict, the company of malcontents must educate popular desire and direct it toward genuine goods. "People must be appealed to to desire certain things mightily," Bourne wrote, and their educators had to be "those articulate souls who can express most convincingly those desired values."[36]

Read in an Augustinian light, Bourne's inability to envision "those desired values"—that is, to envision a different form of enchantment and redemption—is the major disappointment of "The State," a treatise left unfinished due to his death from influenza just before Christmas 1918. While this essay is often hailed as Bourne's approach to a Marxist theory of the state, it reads more like an expose of modern nationalism as a religion, a surrogate for the salvation once offered by the Church. Struck not only by the fervor but by the verbal and visual pageantry of war propaganda, Bourne could not avoid the conclusion that the State was primarily "a mystical conception." "The sanctity of the State" inhered in what Bourne perceived as the fetishism of modern political culture. The State was the "invisible grace" of which the government was "the visible sign, the word made flesh." Likening the State to an *ecclesia*, Bourne summarized what in theological terms would be its soteriology: "As the Church is the medium for the spiritual salvation of men," he wrote, "so the State is thought of as the medium for his political salvation." While this formulation retained the possibility of a tension between religious and national identity, Bourne soon suggested that the cultural and military strength of the modern nation-state enabled it to dissolve or destroy all rival devotions. "The State is a jealous God, and will brook no rivals," and its jealousy extended to the taking and sacrifice of life in war. By offering the individual a sense of existential completion—restoration of being—through sacrifice on the battlefield, war "achieved almost his apotheosis" and preserved its own facsimile of eternal life. Anticipating Taussig's insight into the death-dealing soteriology of modern nationalism, Bourne issued his imperishable maxim: "War is the health of the State." In what must have been one of the most painfully written passages of his life, Bourne concluded that despite its pretensions to enlightenment, pluralism, and progress, modern democracy was itself a perverse divinity, "no bright and rational creation of a new day." Indeed, its unprecedented capacity to mobilize the most primal impulses of herd-consciousness and violence revealed its continuity with the unenlightened irrationality of the past. As "the last decrepit scion of an ancient and hoary stock," democracy clung "tenaciously to [its] archaic and irrelevant spirit."[37] To put it in evangelical terms that even a Progressive like Bourne would have credited, even democracy hath no relish of salvation in it.

Extra agoram nulla salus: Enchantment, Redemption, and the Soteriology of Commodity Fetishism

Like modern politics, modern economics rests on repression of its redemptive hopes. Indeed, the repression required has been all the more forceful and pervasive. Dealing with money and commodities, economics—whether classical, marginalist, Marxist, or Keynesian—has always been considered the most manifestly materialist, "secular," and disenchanted of the social sciences. Thus, while economists and historians would agree that notions of providence and morality are clearly discernible in the work of James Steuart, Adam Smith, Thomas Malthus, and other pioneers of modern economics, they would also recoil from any suggestion that economic theory or economic culture retain powerful traces of belief in an enchanted world. Indeed, even Milbank, who has perhaps done more than any other theologian to uncover the theological (and especially theodical) roots of modern economics, concentrates wholly on the residue of providential design and the transvaluation of Christian virtue into sobriety, punctuality, and self-restraint.[38]

Yet historians of consumer culture are beginning to recognize the widespread persistence of enchantment in capitalism. Vestiges of the enchanted order survive, not only in such obvious venues as astrology, the occult, and the assortment of "New Age" spiritualities, but in the daily experience of commodity civilization. In megamalls, department stores, managerial workshops, and gambling casinos, one sees our shrines and devotions to the spirits of enchantment. While it is indisputable that a rationalized, "disenchanted" worldview is bound up with the history of capitalism, it is becoming equally apparent that disenchantment has assumed its purest form only in the precincts of modern intellectual culture. Among a variety of other figures—from admen,

gamblers, and marketing specialists, to management writers, business jour-
nalists, and corporate apologists—capitalism becomes a moral economy and
a sacral order, a vessel of desires for transfigured selfhood and common happiness. Much of the cultural power of capitalism derives from what Jackson
Lears has called its "fables of abundance"—what I would call the enchantments of Mammon—its beguiling perversion of our need for a sacramental
way of life.[39]

American literature abounds with tales of enchanted economics. In "The
Celestial Railroad" (1843), Nathaniel Hawthorne crafted a harrowing parable
of capitalist enchantment that explicitly recalled the Augustinian account of
the earthly and heavenly cities. The story's narrator recounts a dream in
which, accompanied by a "Mr. Smooth-it-Away," a railroad capitalist, he
boards a train for "the Celestial City." The most popular stop on the passage is
Vanity Fair, "the great capital of human business and pleasure." Many passen-
gers en route to the Celestial City disembark at Vanity Fair, but "such are the
charms" of the city that tourists mistake it for "the true and only heaven." Indeed, they become so "enchanted" that they exchange celestial "tracts of land
and golden mansions" for "small, dismal, inconvenient tenements." After
(barely) resisting Vanity Fair's blandishments, the dreamer passes through
"Beulah," a pastoral land whose luscious fruits and foliage bear a sacramental
character, having been "propagated by grafts from the celestial gardens." Perverse and second-hand, Beulah and Vanity Fair nonetheless bear the image
and likeness of the Celestial City. Arriving at the Celestial City's gates, the
dreamer's companion reveals his true identity as an "impudent fiend" with
smoke billowing from his nostrils and flames darting from his eyes. "Thank
Heaven it was a dream!" the narrator gasps.[40]

As Nathanael West saw a century later, dreams of redemption are the fuel of
consumer culture. In *Miss Lonelyhearts* (1946), a novel of extraordinary religious insight, West envisioned mass culture and its creators as both a substitute for religion and a new sacral order unto itself. Dreaming what he calls
"the Christ dream," the drunken advice columnist Miss Lonelyhearts hangs on
his bedroom wall a crucifix without its suffering figure—a Christ removed
from theological context, a "calmly decorative" therapeutic presence which
occasions only fitful reverence. In place of the "Christ dream," mass culture
becomes a new vehicle of enchantment, a new earthly city that perverts celestial desire. Columnists, Lonelyhearts' editor reflects, are among "the priests of
twentieth-century America," and Lonelyhearts himself observes that most of
the letters he receives are "humble pleas for moral and spiritual advice." But
even as he laments that "drams, once powerful . . . have been rendered puerile
by movies, radio, and newspapers," Lonelyhearts cannot despise these commodified and debased desires. Even the cheesiest ads, he says, compromise a

longing for perfection. "Guitars, bright shawls, exotic foods, outlandish cos-
tumes.... He had learned not to laugh at the advertisements offering to teach
writing, cartooning, engineering, to add inches to the biceps and to develop
the bust."[41] The newest earthly city, mass culture tendered its promises, not
only in money, but in a counterfeit currency of beatitude.

If these and other novelists are right, a scholarly rediscovery of capitalist enchantment is long overdue. But the major obstacles lie in the intellectual hegemony of Weber, Marx, and other invaluable students of capitalism, and in the
moralistic tradition of an assault on "materialism." Rather, we must maintain
that capitalism is the ritual enactment of the commodity fetish, and that our
best prophetic course lies not in fulminating about "materialism" but in embracing sacramental desire. Thus, we can translate the insights of fiction into
the idioms of history, theology, and prophecy by working through and not
around the nestors of disenchantment, extracting from their tales the repressed theology that lurks in the shadows.

In Weber's account, disenchantment commenced with prophetic Judaism,
stalled with Catholic sacramentalism, accelerated with Calvinist Protestantism,
and culminated in modern science, bureaucracy, and capitalism. As the central
figure in *The Protestant Ethic and the Spirit of Capitalism* (1904), the Calvinist
entrepreneur played the grim starring role in Weber's tale. Placing "no trust in
the effects of magical and sacramental forces on salvation," he practiced a "this-
worldly asceticism" in which the material world had no sacred or salvific character. If the world was providentially designed to serve human needs, it could
not bring one into contact with God—a conviction exemplified in the Calvinist doctrine of sacraments as signs of human faith, not bearers of divine grace.
Inheriting and transforming the providential and unsacramental world of
Calvinism, science, and technology destroyed the ontology of enchantment by
discrediting magic, sorcery, the occult, and animism. Yet Weber's autopsy of enchantment covered organized religion as well. If "one no longer need have recourse to magical means in order to master or implore the spirits," those "spirits" themselves—and, most importantly, the gods—had fallen victim, in his
view, to the juggernaut of scientific modernity.[42]

Still, it remains largely unnoticed that for Weber the prime suspect in the
death of enchantment was *capitalism*, not science. Since money—*not* science—was "the most abstract and impersonal element that exists in human
life," the pecuniary impersonality of capitalist relations demolished belief in
spirited goods and rendered the exchanges of material life "ever less accessible
... to any imaginable relationship with a religious ethic of brotherliness." The
enchanted assumptions of abundance, fluidity, and generosity receded before
the scarcity and competition postulated with disenchantment—that is, that of
capitalist economics. And as the spirits waned, their shamans, magicians, and

priests yielded to businessmen, bureaucrats, and technicians. As Weber wrote in his desolate conclusion to *The Protestant Ethic*, the modern culture of disenchantment produced "specialists without spirit, sensualists without heart" who presumed to have "attained a level of civilization never before achieved."[43] For Weber, the triumph of capitalism dispelled enchantment, mandated impersonality, and nullified the prospect of love.

Yet the sociologist who claimed that he was "religiously unmusical" heard faint chords of enchantment in capitalist culture, and a number of sociologists and theologians have attempted to recompose and play them. Weber himself mused that, despite the victories of disenchantment, the old deities had not simply hobbled off to die. "Many old gods ascend from their graves," he noted, to be transfigured into "the form of impersonal forces"—the laws of nature, the laws of the market. Noting the enthusiasm for size and quantity in American culture, Weber remarked on this "romanticism of numbers" without considering that he had discovered a vestige of enchantment, one that infused abstraction with spiritual import. And as some in the Weberian tradition have realized, even if moderns no longer located gods and spirits in the material world, the longing self could become the last refuge of enchantment in capitalist culture. In his cleverly titled *The Romantic Ethic and the Spirit of Modern Consumerism* (1989), the British sociologist Colin Campbell maintained that the perpetually unsatisfied desire for fulfillment that marks the consumerist consciousness is the subjective residue of enchantment, what I would call the contemplative mysticism of commodity culture. Milbank goes even further than Campbell by questioning the conceptual polarities on which Weber's account of disenchantment rests—the "charismatic" and the "bureaucratic," the "religious" and the "social," the "irrational" and the "rational." Just as religion cannot be reduced to "social forces" because it is a particular form of the social, so the "rationality" or "secularity" of capitalism cannot be easily set off against the irrationality or enchantment of premodern societies. If, Milbank writes, "these [conceptual] boundaries are not ahistorical absolutes,"[44] then the lines between the "enchanted" and the "disenchanted" are not as clear and impermeable as Weberian sociology makes them seem.

If this is true, then capitalist economic "rationality" is itself imbued with the traces of enchantment—a possibility explored by no less "secular" a thinker than Marx. Despite his early dictum that "the criticism of religion is the basis of all criticism," Marx supplies unlikely but auspicious resources for the rediscovery of enchantment. Marx considered capitalism the most arduous and liberating of modernity's disenchanting forces. "All that is solid melts into air, all that is holy is profaned," he declared in the *Communist Manifesto*. In its rage to accumulate, the bourgeoisie had "drowned the most heavenly ecstasies of religious fervor . . . in the icy water of egotistical calculation." But in the end

Marx could neither deny the religious nature of economics, affirm the secularity of capitalism, nor reject religion as a source of insight into its material and cultural mechanisms. If the capitalist is indeed "a sorcerer who is no longer able to control the powers of the nether world whom he has called up with his spells,"[45] then Marx can be a guide back to a sacramental, Augustinian critique of commodity civilization.

Marx's reliance on religious metaphors was more than sardonic flourish, for he not only framed his analysis of capitalism in religious language but ultimately resorted to religion to explain the commodity form. In the "1844 manuscripts," Marx reflected on the power of money in theological terms. "Thou *visible God!*" he exclaimed of money, citing Shakespeare's *Timon of Athens.* "The divine power of money" resided, Marx reflected, in its genius for metaphysical and moral transfiguration. Reducing all things, however incommensurate, to an abstract equivalence in its own image and likeness, money effected "the transformation of all human and natural properties into their contraries," procuring love for the unpleasant, education for the dull, travel for the indolent or parochial. Noting that money was first minted and stored in the temples of antiquity, Marx concluded in the *Grundrisse* (1857) that it was both "the god among commodities" and "the real community" of capitalist society.[46]

But as his exposition of "commodity fetishism" in *Capital* suggests, Marx's parallel between religion and economy subverted his attempt at a secular critique of capitalism. Marx's use of religious language in this celebrated passage highlighted what he considered the formal similarities between commodity exchange and religious practice. The commodity, he opened, is "a very queer thing, abounding in metaphysical subtleties and theological niceties." These subtleties and niceties arise from a particular form of "the mutual relations of the producers" which assumes the shape of a "social relation between the products." Because, under conditions of alienation, material products are invested with human qualities, they and their consumption can be endowed—enchanted—with promises of gratification and justice that can really be fulfilled, in Marx's view, only by a revolutionary transformation of society. But after stating the problem in this secular way, Marx almost immediately declared that to resolve it we must take "recourse to the mist-enveloped regions of the religious world." In the same way that "God" stands for the unrealized, projected, and distorted possibilities of humanity, so, too, do the products of alienated labor. The world of commodities, Marx concludes, is a world of "fetishism," the projection of the human into things. Just as an enlightened humanity will see a piece of bread instead of the Eucharistic host—a sacramental analogy Marx used earlier in *Capital*—so a classless world of unestranged producers will see use-values and social powers.[47]

But Marx's analogy between fetish and sacrament may have been all too clever, for it underlines his inability to banish "the religious" from his "scientific" account of commodities. In the end, Marx's futile effort to secularize and domesticate the language of enchantment suggests that we should follow some anthropologists and theologians in fudging the distinction between a scientifically disenchanted "reality" and an imaginatively enchanted realm of "values." In *The World of Goods* (1979), Mary Douglas, for instance, argues that goods compose "the visible part of culture." Material objects are always inextricably bound up with meanings and identities, and exchanges always create and foster human affairs. Commodities are, Douglas contends, "good for thinking." But if both "economics" and "religion" are practices in which material and symbolic actions are intertwined, then, as Milbank writes, "there is little reason for giving the one causal priority over the other."[48] So if we cannot define and patrol a boundary between a world of material goods and an "epiphenomenal"culture, then we cannot assert that a secular unmasking of an enchanted "fetishism" will reveal a transparent and disenchanted social "reality."

Thus, if religion works like an economy, then it forms an alternative community of ontology, goods, and desires. Also, if the erasure of distinctions between religion and economy suggests that desires to challenge or transcend capitalism must originate not, as in Marxist theory, from within the crucible of capitalism itself, but from what Milbank flatly dubs "a different desire," a distinctive longing and destination.[49] And if capitalism works like a religion, then we can study and critique it *as* a religion—that is, as a pattern of rituals, moral codes, iconography, and ideals. We might, that is, redescribe commodity fetishism as a religious practice unto itself—a caricature, an archetype, a *perverse imitatur*—irreducible to some distortion of a "secular" pattern of relationships.

Two students of money can help us here: Georg Simmel and Norman O. Brown. Simmel's sprawling *The Philosophy of Money* (1900) clearly hinted at a sacramental conception of money and economics. Money, Simmel wrote, possessed "a significant relationship to the notion of God." Just as God resolved "all diversities and contradictions" and thereby ensured "peace, security, and wealth of feeling" for His followers, so money, through its capacity for abstract equivalence, composed for its possessors all tensions among "the most opposed, the most estranged, and the most distant things." Yet it did so, Simmel thought, in a way that disenchanted and despiritualized the world. While this account of pecuniary disenchantment reaffirmed Weber and Marx, Simmel gestured, however abortively, to quite another perspective. If money was a substitute for God, it was also, Simmel realized, a surrogate for sacrament. If "every sacramental object embodies . . . the relationship between man and his God," then money was a secularized sacrament, a ritual object that embodied relations almong human beings. Simmel remarked on more than one occasion in *The Philosophy of Money* on "the similarity in psychological form" between money and sacrament, economic activity and religious ritual.[50] If we reject Simmel's reductionist assumptions about the "secular," we can use his psychology of money to justify an account, not of disenchantment, but of the perverse displacement and renaming of sacrament.

Simmel's mordant evasion of this possibility—the relationship between money and sacrament, he wrote, could be disclosed "only [by] psychology, which has the privilege of being unable to commit blasphemy"—points to the psychopathology of money, and here Norman O. Brown remains our most penetrating and theologically literate inquirer. Psychoanalysis has long understood economic pursuits as "anal" activities, a legacy epitomized in its association of money with excrement. But in *Life Against Death* (1959), Brown connected the psychoanalysis of money to an exploration of religious concerns. Noting how the standard psychoanalytical appraisal of money was "anchored in the domain of the secular," Brown concluded, after a survey of historical and anthropological literature, that money actually derived its power from "the magical, mystical, religious . . . the domain of the sacred." Besides, he continued, the "flat antinomy" of sacred and secular was misleading in any case. "Secularization," he asserted, "is only a metamorphosis of the sacred"—a point he made in the course of criticizing Simmel for accepting "the illusion that modern money is secular." The secular, Brown contended, is "the negation of the sacred"—negation, that is, in Freud's and Hegel's terms, in which negation affirms its opposite. In fact, Brown perceived that "the psychological realities of money" were "best grasped in terms of theology." In Brown's reading, neither capitalism nor secularism had disenchanted the world. Instead, Brown affirmed Luther's insight that, with capitalism, "power over this world has passed from God to God's negation, God's ape, the Devil." Like Luther, Brown saw in money "the essence of the secular, and therefore of the demonic." The "money complex"—the animating spirit, Marx might have said, of commodity fetishism—is "the heir to and substitute for the religious complex, an attempt to find God in things."[51]

But while Brown acknowledged that psychoanalysis "reaffirms ageless religious aspirations," he ultimately rejected theology, albeit no more convincingly than Marx. While he recognized that the Jewish and Christian traditions understood human destiny as "a departure from, and an effort to regain, paradise," he sided with Freud in locating this drama on a purely terrestrial, instinctual plane. The redemptive incompetence of religion lay in its cosmic pretensions, "delusions of grandeur" about the mere body that appeared most poignantly, for Brown, in the theology of Augustine. Citing Augustine's reflection on *cor irrequietum*—the "restless discontent" of the heart—as well as his account of the war between "true love on the one hand and the lust for power on the other"—the defining conflict, recall, in the *City of God*—Brown upheld Augustine's conviction that "the riddle of history is not in Reason but in Desire; not in labor, but in love." But Brown dismissed Augustine's faith that the end of this enigma depended on a supernatural power expressed through a community. Since religion, Brown concluded, saw the repressed "only in the form of projections,"[52] then the overcoming of capitalism and the money complex awaited the libidinal resolution of anality, not the repudiation of *libido dominandi*.

However sympathetic and ingenious in its appropriation of Augustine, Brown's call for the "resurrection of the body" remains a melancholy parody of the hope expressed in Christian eschatology. For if the secular refusal of that eschatology means acceptance of the finality of death, then does not life become *libido dominandi*, the quest for survival and power incarnate in the pursuit of money? Still, we can draw upon Brown's Pauline description of religion as "the wisdom of folly" to understand the "money complex" and the perverse desires that animate it.[53] For if, as Augustine would argue, desire *is* the riddle of history, and if not anatomy but redemption is destiny, then Augustine becomes an inescapable interpreter of longing, fetishism, and the enchantments of capitalism.

The closest to a secular Augustine that the twentieth century produced was the German Marxist Walter Benjamin, whose ambling through the streets of modern cities brought him to the threshold of theological enchantment. Benjamin's religiosity has long taxed the patience and ingenuity of those (from his Frankfurt School friends to contemporary scholars) eager to keep him on the manageable terrain of secularity. But Benjamin never completely embraced the secular materialism of Marxist metaphysics. "My thinking is related to theology as blotting pad is related to ink. It is saturated with it," he interjected in his "Arcades Project" sometime in the 1930s. "A theologian stranded in a secular age," as his friend Gershom Sholem thought, Benjamin was groping toward something quite different from that disenchanting "dialectic of enlightenment" out of which Adorno and Max Horkheimer could not, in the end, see a way.[54] Because Benjamin was attempting to disclose a divine presence that was latent and distorted in the world, he deserves to be called the Augustine of modern enchantment.

Evident in his earliest reflections on language, mimesis, and "the linguistic community of mute creation," Benjamin's enchanted sensibility recalls both the sacramental metaphysics of Augustine and his notion of perversion. Through the "mute magic of nature"—taste, fragrance, touch—"the word of God shines forth." Human beings translated this beatific conversation into the highest language of all through their powers of naming and mimesis. Though

reason uncovered "natural correspondences," the mimetic imagination pene-
trated more deeply to those complementary "magical correspondences and
analogies" divinely instituted as part of creation. Men corrupted their mimetic
and naming faculties, however, in their lust for power and judgment—that is, in
their thirst for *libido dominandi*.[55] Expelled from the Adamic state of commu-
nicative rapture, humanity embarked on history, the quest for the word whose
utterance would unlock the doors of enchantment, the gates of the heavenly city.

For all its "Marxism," Benjamin's subsequent work continued in this enchanted and eschatological vein. *One-Way Street* (1928), his miscellany of
aphorisms, dreams, and vignettes of urban life, abounded in perceptions of
enchantment hidden, displaced, and revealed. Ancient peoples, he wrote, realized that "they alone shall possess the earth who live from the forces of the
cosmos" and recognized that we "can be in ecstatic contact with the cosmos
only communally." As Augustine might put it, the meek on pilgrimage
through this sinful world shall together inherit the earth. Moderns, however,
obsessed with money, mastery, and autonomy, consigned this enchanted,
sacramental state to "the poetic rapture of starry nights." But their technical
and organizational genius represented a perverse order of enchantment, an
earthly city whose very "disenchanted" guise made it particularly reckless and
diabolical. Despite the conventional wisdom of disenchantment, the nation-
state's political and economic conduct betokened modernity's "unprecedented commingling with the cosmic powers." Though they embodied the allegedly disenchanted realm of money, bank notes, Benjamin observed,
illustrated the sacrality of capitalism. "Innocent cupids frolicking about numbers, goddesses holding tablets of law, stalwart heroes sheathing their swords
before monetary units"—all "ornamenting the façade of hell."[56]

During the 1930s, Benjamin relied increasingly on theology to fathom the
dream world of capitalism in the shops, exhibitions, and panormas—"sites of
pilgrimage to the commodity fetish," as he put it in the *Arcades*. Benjamin's incessant references to "dream," "sleep," and "awakening" signaled his pursuit of
the enchanted community lost in the Fall of powerlust. Indeed, if we read
through the maddeningly disheveled *Arcades* with an Augustinian lens, we can
understand Benjamin's epigrams, not only as notes toward a dialectic of enchantment, but as dispatches from a heavenward pilgrim trapped in an earthly
age. Benjamin realized that the cultural power of capitalism resided in its enlistment of the utopian, redemptive imagination. Utopia—for the younger
Benjamin, the state of transparent enchantment encountered and lost in paradise—"left its traces in a thousand configurations of life, from enduring ed-
ifices to passing fashions." Every atrium, dress shop, and voluptuous adver-
tisement bore the longing for what Augustine would call the celestial city.
Department stores, Benjamin wrote, were "temples consecrated" to "the reli-

gious intoxication of cities," the edenic and salvific fantasies of communion and abundance generated by urban commercial culture.[57] Thus, in Marxist terms, our awakening from ideological slumber *is* a disenchantment, a revelation of the commodified fetish in the sanctuary of capitalism. But, for Benjamin, the twilight of the fetish is also a *re*-enchantment, a discovery of the promise transparent in material life, a communal union with cosmic powers—what, in Augustinian terms, we might call the heavenly city on earth, a sacramental way of being in the world.

It was no accident that Benjamin hinted strongly near the end of his life that theology held the key to the master critique of commodity culture. Historical materialism could "be a match for anyone if it enlists the services of theology," he mused in "Theses on the Philosophy of History" (1940), adding wryly that secular intellectual culture insisted on theology's "keep[ing] out of sight." By raising the visibility of theology, Benjamin violated the fundamental protocol of disenchanted enlightenment, and in doing so allows us to align him with Augustine. Just as, in Benjamin's words, "our image of happiness is indissolubly bound up with the image of redemption," so too, in Augustine's words, the earthly city's vision of felicity perversely anticipates heavenly bliss. And in contending that our "cultural treasures" are stained by powerlust and its inexorable misery—"there is no document of civilization which is not at the same time a document of barbarism"—Benjamin restated Augustine's perception of the earthly city's perverted blessings.[58]

When the most doggedly "secular" modes of criticism cannot escape the specter of the sacred, we can stake a claim for Augustine as a contemporary. Having seen through the enchantments of Roman *imperium*, he can help us divine the fetishes of our allegedly secular age, fetishes whose enchantments lead only to death. We can see, in the service of the state, an ecclesial hope; in the hunger for riches, a sacramental longing; in both perverted loyalties, a celestial aspiration. Even in the fretful dreamlands of late capitalism, the world remains, as Gerard Manley Hopkins knew, charged with the grandeur of God, even as "all is seared with trade; bleared, smeared with toil." So if we follow Augustine, any renewal of political hope must rest in what Hopkins called "the dearest freshness deep down things." The first true thing we can say to our time is that it is wrongly but redeemably enchanted.

Notes

1. Max Weber, "Science as a Vocation" (1915), in Hans Gerth and C. Wright Mills, eds., *From Max Weber: Essays in Sociology* (New York, 1949), 129–56; *The Protestant Ethic and the Spirit of Capitalism* (New York, 1958 [1904]), 181. The historical narrative

of "disenchantment" that I've sketched is a staple of Western cultural history, examples of which can be found in Keith Thomas, *Religion and the Decline of Magic: Studies in Popular Belief in Sixteenth and Seventeenth Century England* (New York, 1997 [1971]), and Caroline Merchant, *The Death of Nature: Women, Ecology, and the Scientific Revolution* (New York, 1980). For a nice overview of tales of disenchantment, see Jane Bennett, *The Enchantment of Modern Life: Attachments, Crossings, and Ethics* (Princeton, 2001), 56–90. Bennett's valuable effort to recapture enchantment in daily life founders, in my view, on her reduction of enchantment to a "mood"—a move which, by locating the problem in subjectivity rather than in our accounts of the world, subtly reinforces the disenchantment narratives she tries to overcome.

2. The literature of "radical orthodoxy" includes John Milbank, *Theology and Social Theory: Beyond Secular Reason* (Oxford and New York, 1990), quote on 1; Milbank, Catherine Pickstock, and Graham Ward, eds., *Radical Orthodoxy: A New Theology* (New York and London, 1999); Ward, *Cities of God* (London and New York, 2000); D. Stephen Long, *Divine Economy: Theology and the Market* (London and New York, 2001); Michael Hanby, *Augustine and Modernity* (London and New York, 2003). The ur-text of "commodity fetishism" is, of course, Marx, *Capital*, Vol. 1 (New York, 1906), 81–961.

3. George M. Marsden, *The Outrageous Idea of Christian Scholarship* (New York, 1997), 51; Richard John Neuhaus, *The Naked Public Square: Religion and Democracy in America* (Grand Rapids, MI, 1984), esp. 3–93.

4. Andrew Shanks, *Civil Society, Civil Religion* (Oxford, 1995), 162; Augustine, *City of God*, trans. John O'Meara (London, 1985). The "melancholy conservative" line is exemplified in N. H. Baynes, *The Political Ideas of St. Augustine's 'De Civitate Dei'* (London, 1936); Herbert A. Deane, *The Political and Social Ideas of St. Augustine* (New York, 1963), quote on 151; and Peter Brown, "Augustine," in B. Smalley, ed., *Trends in Medieval Political Thought* (Oxford, 1965), 1–21. Hannah Arendt—who wrote her doctoral dissertation on Augustine—would have concurred with the Melancholy Conservative school. Because Christians possessed eternal life, Augustine, in Arendt's view, advised them to dismiss the cycle of historical change and "look with indifference upon the spectacles it offered": *On Revolution* (New York, 1963), 27.

5. Reinhold Niebuhr, "Augustine's Political Realism," in *Christian Realism and Political Problems* (New York, 1953), 119–46, quotes on 120–21, 127, 128–29. For a very similar view of Augustine, see John O'Meara, *The Charter of Christendom: The Significance of the 'City of God'* (New York, 1961), who writes that Augustine's position on the evils of earthly government is "so extreme as to be misleading" (101).

As the quotes indicate, Niebuhr did not conceal the liberal imperialism that informed (and arguably occasioned) his reading of Augustine. In this regard, Niebuhr's meditation on *The Irony of American History* (New York, 1952) should be read as a liberal reflection on the earthly city. Niebuhr had already praised Augustine's political vision as "very realistic" in his classic *Moral Man and Immoral Society* (New York, 1932), 70. For a range of historical discussions of Niebuhr and "Christian realism," see Donald Meyer, *The Protestant Search for Political Realism, 1919–1941* (Berkeley, 1960), 217–69; Richard Wightman Fox, *Reinhold Niebuhr: A Biography* (New York, 1985), esp. 136–223; and Eugene McCarraher, *Christian Critics: Religion and the Impasse in Modern American Social Thought* (Ithaca, NY, 2000), 48–50, 63–70, 93–111 passim. While I am greatly indebted to Fox's book in particular, I cannot agree that Niebuhr's essay on Augustine "breaks new ground" (255).

6. Niebuhr, "Augustine's Political Realism," 138; *Moral Man*, 263. For a forceful secular critique of Niebuhr, see Noam Chomsky, "Reinhold Niebuhr," *Grand Street* 6 (Spring 1982), 204–12. The best theological critiques of Niebuhrian realism are Milbank, "The Poverty of Niebuhrianism," in *The Word Made Strange: Theology, Language, Culture* (Oxford, 1997), 233–54, and Stanley Hauerwas,"The Irony of Reinhold Niebuhr: The Ideological Character of 'Christian Realism,'" in *Wilderness Wanderings: Probing Twentieth-Century Theology and Philosophy* (Boulder, CO, 1997), 48–61.

7. Jean Bethke Elshtain, *Augustine and the Limits of Politics* (Notre Dame, 1995), esp. 89–112, quotes on 91, 96, 98, 111. One could argue that Elshtain's recent enlistment in the "war on terrorism" signals her abandonment of even this anemic liberalism in favor of a decrepit "just war" Augustinianism. Elshtain makes much more suggestive use of Augustine elsewhere in her work. For example, in *Who Are We? Critical Reflections and Hopeful Possibilities* (Grand Rapids, MI, 2000), 42–43, she draws on Augustine to make the psychoanalytic-feminist point that we "deny our birth from the body of a woman" and "our dependence on her and others to nurture and tend to us."

8. R. A. Markus, *Saeculum: History and Society in the Theology of St. Augustine* (Cambridge and New York, 1970), esp. 164–86, quotes on 169, 171, 178, 185-86. For examples of "secular city" theology, see Harvey Cox, *The Secular City: Secularization and Urbanization in Theological Perspective* (New York, 1965), and Jurgen Moltmann, *A Theology of Hope* (Philadelphia, 1993 [1967]).

9. On the technocratic turn in liberal and social democratic politics after 1945, see Norman Birnbaum, *After Progress: American Social Reform and European Socialism in the Twentieth Century* (New York, 2001), 106–259 *passim*. For an example of the discourse of "maturity," see Daniel Bell, "The Mood of Three Generations," in *The End of Ideology: On the Exhaustion of Political Ideas in the Fifties* (New York, 1960), 299–314. Francis Fukuyama's contribution to the "end-of-ideology" lineage is in *The End of History and the Last Man* (New York, 1992).

10. Adrian Cunningham, Terry Eagleton, et al., *Catholics and the Left* (London, 1966), quotes from Eagleton, "The Roots of the Christian Crisis," 73–74, 81, and Cunningham, "The Failure of the Christian Revolution," 103; Eagleton, *The Body as Language: Outline of a 'New Left' Theology* (London, 1970), 12, 28.

11. On British Christian socialism, the most thorough study remains Peter D'Arcy Jones, *The Christian Socialist Revival in Britian, 1877–1914* (Princeton, 1968). Despite its many merits—lucidity, comprehensiveness, theological erudition, and critical sympathy—Jones's book awaits a worthy successor, especially one that examines the tradition after 1914 that included R. H. Tawney, William Temple, and Maurice Reckitt. Edward Norman, *The Victorian Christian Socialists* (New York, 1987), is competent but unoriginal.

12. Figgis, *The Political Aspects of St. Augustine's 'City of God'* (London, 1921), 29, 38, 42, 52, 56. See also Figgis's 1911 lectures at Harvard, published later as *Civilisation at the Cross Roads* (London, 1912), esp. *x*, where he refers to "that peculiar kind of social life we call the Christian Church." In those lectures, Figgis also observed of Nietzsche's philosophy (in contrast to later apologists such as Walter Kauffman) that in the

end "it comes to the Kaiser at last" (*Civilisation*, 114–15). Figgis's work merits renewed attention from scholars and fruitful appropriation by Christian intellectuals. The only book-length study of Figgis is M. G. Tucker, *John Neville Figgis: A Study* (London, 1950). For a discussion of the "sacramental socialism" espoused by Figgis and others in the Church Socialist League, see Jones, *Christian Socialist Revival*, 225–302, esp. 275–81 on Figgis.

13. Figgis, *Political Aspects*, 114–16.

14. *Ibid.*, 54, 113.

15. Milbank, *Theology and Social Theory*, 402, 407, 411, 418–20. This acknowledgement of Augustine's liberal moment takes some of the force out of Shanks's assertion that Milbank "wants all the sweetness of Augustine's rhetoric without any of the accompanying bitterness" (*Civil Society, Civil Religion*, 163). See also Ward, *Cities of God*, esp. 227–37, and Rowan Williams, "Politics and the Soul: A Reading of the *City of God*," *Milltown Studies* 19–20 (Winter 1987), 55-72.

16. Milbank, *Theology and Social Theory*, 389. Milbank's discussion of Marxism (177–205) is an incisive theological critique, much sharper, in my view, than anything in "liberation theology."

17. Milbank, "Can Morality Be Christian?" in *The Word Made Strange*, 225, 252 n. 10. See also Long, *Divine Economy*, 143–53.

18. Augustine, *City of God*, 852–57, 1086; Ward, *Cities of God*, 156–61, quote on 157; Milbank, "Can Morality Be Christian?" *op. cit.*, 230. Ward notes later (234) that Augustine was completing *De trinitate*—where he elaborates this doctrine of sacramental presence in creation—while he was composing *De civitate Dei*. I must also point out that Ward explicitly rejects any conception of sacrament as "a magical commodity, enchanting the material" (159). I hope it is clear that my difference from Ward is purely verbal, and that my account of "enchantment" can accommodate Ward's salutary caution.

19. Figgis, *Political Aspects*, 38; Milbank, *Theology and Social Theory*, 402–03. On the political character of the church, see Hauerwas, *In Good Company: The Church as Polis* (Notre Dame and London, 1995).

20. Augustine, *City of God*, 601, 878; Milbank, "On Complex Space," in *The Word Made Strange*, 268–92; Long, *Divine Economy*, 182–270, and *Goodness of God*, 233–60; Cavanaugh, "Beyond Secular Parodies," 194–98.

21. Augustine, *City of God*, 547–58, 1070–76; Oliver O'Donovan, "Augustine's *City of God* XIX and Western Political Thought," in Dorothy F. Donnelly, ed., *The City of God: A Collection of Critical Essays* (New York, 1995), 143.

22. Augustine, *City of God*, 71–72, 776–92. See also Bks. IV and VI in their entirety.

23. Milbank, *Theology and Social Theory*, 9–23; William Cavanaugh, "The City: Beyond Secular Parodies," in Milbank, Pickstock, and Ward, *Radical Orthodoxy*, 182.

24. Emile Durkheim, *The Elementary Forms of Religious Life*, trans. Karen E. Fields (New York, 1995 [1912]), 208, 215; Michael Taussig, *The Nervous System* (New York and London, 1993), 119–40, quote on 138. See also Milbank, *Theology and Social Theory*, 61–71 *passim*, on the religious character of Durkheimian sociology.

25. Taussig, 122.

26. Joshua Mitchell, *Not By Reason Alone: Religion, History, and Identity in Early Modern Political Thought* (Chicago, 1993), esp. 46–124 on Hobbes, Locke, and

Rousseau. Because Mitchell examines the political implications of biblical exegesis—an enterprise which is, as he rightly maintains, an underappreciated element of early modern political theory—his book is an invaluable text for historians and theologians. My own thoughts on Rousseau are indebted to his insight that much of modern political philosophy represents "the transposition of content *but not form*" of biblical (and especially eschatological) history (97). Cavanaugh, "Beyond Secular Parodies," 188. See also "'A Fire Strong Enough to Consume the House': The Wars of Religion and the Rise of the State," *Modern Theology* 11 (October 1995), 397–420, in which Cavanaugh challenges the entire conceptual framework through which the birth of modern political culture has been viewed. Rousseau, *The Social Contract* (Oxford and New York, 1999 [1762]), 78, esp. 158–68, quotes on 158, 162, 163, 166, 168. On Rousseau, see Mitchell, 116, who calls Rousseau's civil religion "a kind of Christology," and Cavanaugh, "Beyond Secular Parodies," 189.

27. G. K. Chesterton, *What I Saw in America* (New York, 1922), 11–12; Ernest Tuveson, *Redeemer Nation: The Idea of America's Millenial Role* (Chicago, 1990 [1962]). See also Robert T. Handy, *A Christian America: Protestant Hopes and Historical Realities* (New York, 1971), and Henry F. May, "The Religion of the Republic," in *Ideas, Faiths, and Feelings: Essay on American Intellectual and Religious History, 1952–1982* (New York, 1983), 171–80.

28. Jane Addams, *Democracy and Social Ethics* (Cambridge, 1964 [1902]), 69–70, 276–70; *Twenty Years at Hull-House* (New York, 1981 [1910]), 307–08; Walter Lippmann, *Drift and Mastery: An Attempt to Diagnose the Current Crisis* (New York, 1914), 152–57; Josiah Royce, *The Philosophy of Loyalty* (New York, 1908), esp. 241–48; *The Problem of Christianity*, Vol. II (New York, 1913), 430–31. On the meaning of "Beloved Community" to Progressive intellectuals, see Casey Nelson Blake, *Beloved Community: The Cultural Criticism of Randolph Bourne, Van Wyck Brooks, Waldo Frank, and Lewis Mumford* (Chapel Hill, 1990), 76–156. On the religious nature of Progressivism, see Richard Wightman Fox, "The Culture of Liberal Protestant Progressivism," *Journal of Interdisciplinary History* 23 (Winter 1993), 639–60, and McCarraher, *Christian Critics*, 9–16.

29. Herbert Croly, *Progressive Democracy* (New York, 1914), 191–93, 396–97, 399–404, 406, 414, 425, 427. On Croly's strange spiritual interests, see David W. Levy, *Herbert Croly of the New Republic: The Life and Thought of an American Progressive* (Princeton, 1985), esp. 32–37, 65-67, 290–95.

30. Dewey, "Ethics and Physical Science" (1887), cited in Robert Westbrook, *John Dewey and American Democracy* (Ithaca, NY, 1991), 32; "Ethics of Democracy" (1888), *ibid.*, 41; *The Quest for Certainty* (New York, 1929), 304; *Individualism Old and New* (New York, 1930), 131; *The Public and Its Problems* (Boulder, CO, 1956 [1927]), 143, 184.

31. Dewey, *A Common Faith* (New Haven, 1935), 31–33, 41, 62, 87; Westbrook, 418–28; Bruce Kuklick, "John Dewey, American Theology, and Scientific Politics," in Michael Lacey, ed., *Religion and Twentieth-Century American Intellectual Life* (New York and Cambridge, 1989), 90, 92.

32. Richard Rorty, *Achieving Our Country: Leftist Thought in Twentieth-Century America* (Cambridge, MA, 1998), 10–34, 142 n. 8; *Philosophy and Social Hope* (New

Chapter 12

York, 1999), 12. See also "Religion as Conversation-Stopper," *Common Knowledge* 3 (Spring 1994), 1–6, where Rorty dismisses Stephen Carter's contention that explicitly religious voices belong in public discussion.

33. Rorty, *Achieving Our Country*, 33, 50, 101.

34. Randolph Bourne, "The Experimental Life" (1914), in Olaf Hansen, ed., *Randolph Bourne: The Radical Will: Selected Writings 1911–1918* (Berkeley, 1992 [1977]), 149–58; "John Dewey's Philosophy" (1915), *ibid.*, 332.

35. Bourne, "Trans-National America" (1915),*ibid.*, 260, 262–63, 264.

36. Bourne, "Twilight of Idols" (1917), *ibid.*, 338–39, 342–43; letter to Van Wyck Brooks, March 27, 1918, in Eric J. Sandeen, ed., *The Letters of Randolph Bourne* (New York, 1981), 410–14, quotes on 414. For similar accounts of the Dewey-Bourne conflict, see Westbrook, 202–12, and Blake, 157–70.

37. Bourne, "The State" (1918), ibid., 355, 358–59, 361, 367, 382.

38. Milbank, *Theology and Social Theory*, 27–48.

39. Jackson Lears, *Fables of Abundance: A Cultural History of Advertising in America* (New York, 1994); see also his *Something for Nothing: Luck in America* (New York, 2003). Some examples of this work in cultural history include Rosalind Williams, *Dream Worlds: Mass Consumption in Late-Nineteenth Century France* (Berkeley, 1991); Roland Marchand, *Advertising the American Dream: Making Way for Modernity, 1920–1940* (Berkeley, 1985); Marchand, *Creating the Corporate Soul: The Rise of Public Relations and Corporate Imagery in American Big Business* (Berkeley, 1998); William Leach, *Land of Desire: Merchants, Power, and the Rise of a New American Culture* (New York, 1993). My own work-in-progress is entitled *The Enchantments of Mammon: Corporate Capitalism and the American Moral Imagination*.

40. Nathaniel Hawthorne, "The Celestial Railroad" (1843), in R. P. Blackmur, ed., *The Celestial Railroad and Other Stories* (New York, 1963), 185, 202.

41. Nathanael West, *Miss Lonelyhearts and The Day of the Locust* (New York, 1962 [1946]), 4, 8, 22, 32, 39.

42. Weber, *Protestant Ethic*, 95–154, quote on 104; "Science as a Vocation," *op. cit.*, 139.

43. Weber, "Religious Rejections of the World and Their Directions" (1915), *op. cit.*, 331; *Protestant Ethic*, 182.

44. Weber, "Science as a Vocation," *op. cit.*, 149; Colin Campbell, *The Romantic Ethic and the Spirit of Modern Consumerism* (Oxford, 1987); Milbank, *Theology and Social Theory*, 87–92, quote on 89.

45. Marx, "Contribution to the Critique of Hegel's Philosophy of Right" (1844), in Robert Tucker, ed., *The Marx-Engels Reader* (New York, 1978), 54; "The Communist Manifesto" (1848), *ibid.*, 475, 476, 478.

46. Marx, "Economic and Philosophical Manuscripts" (1844), in Tucker, *op. cit.*, 101–05; *Grundrisse*, Martin Nicolaus trans. (New York, 1973 [1857]), 221, 225.

47. Marx, *Capital*, 60, 81, 83, 90–91.

48. Mary Douglas, *The World of Goods: Towards an Anthropology of Consumption* (New York, 1996 [1979]), 33; Milbank, "'The Body by Love Possessed': Christianity and Late Capitalism in Britain," *Modern Theology* 3 (March 1986), 56–61, quote on 61.

49. Milbank, *Theology and Social Theory*, 193.

50. Georg Simmel, *The Philosophy of Money* (London, 1978 [1900]), 128–30, 228–38, quotes on 129, 237.

51. Ibid., 236; Norman O. Brown, *Life Against Death: The Psychoanalytical Meaning of History* (Middletown, CT, 1985 [1959]), 206–33, 240, 245, 252.

52. Ibid., 16, 98, 231.

53. Ibid., 227, 307–22.

54. Walter Benjamin, *The Arcades Project*, Howard Eiland and Kevin McLaughlin, trans. (Cambridge, MA and London, 1999), 459; Gershom Scholem, *Walter Benjamin: The Story of a Friendship*, Harry Zohn trans. (New York, 1981), 93; Theodor Adorno and Max Horkheimer, *The Dialectic of Enlightenment* (New York, 1972 [1944]).

55. Benjamin, "On Language as Such and on the Language of Man" (1916), in *Reflections: Essays, Aphorisms, Autobiographical Writings*, Peter Demetz ed. (New York, 1978), 314–32, quotes on 316–17, 326; "On the Mimetic Faculty" (1915), *ibid.*, 333–36, quotes on 333, 334.

56. Benjamin, *One-Way Street and Other Writings*, Edmund Jephcott and Kingsley Shorter, trans. (London, 1997 [1979]), 87, 93.

57. Benjamin, *Arcades*, 212–27, 893.

58. Benjamin, "Theses on the Philosophy of History" (1940), in *Illuminations: Essays and Reflections*, Harry Zohn trans. (New York, 1969), 253, 254, 256.

13

Machiavelli's *City of God:* Civic Humanism and Augustinian Terror

Paul R. Wright

An Exhortation to Penitence

But with what rock or what thorns shall we repress our itch for usury, or for shameful pleasures, or for the tricks we delight in playing on our neighbors? The only way is with gifts of charity, by doing honor to our neighbor, by doing good to him. But we are tricked ourselves by lust, tangled in error, caught in the snares of sin; and so we find ourselves in the grip of the devil. To escape, we must have recourse to penitence, we must cry with David, "Lord, have mercy on me!" and with Saint Peter we must weep bitterly, and repent of all the faults we have committed—
    "Repent and tune ourselves to this one theme
    That worldly pleasure is a short-lived dream."[1]

So ENDS AN *EXHORTATION TO PENITENCE* that began with an echo of Psalm 130: "*De profundis clamavi ad te, Domine; Domine, exaudi vocem meam*" ("From the depths, I cry out to you, O Lord; Lord, hear my voice") (*Ex. Pen.*, 119). The early modern voice that calls out from these recognizably Augustinian depths might well be mistaken for Thomas à Kempis, Martin Luther, or still another petitioner for the grace of God; the decisive hint might be the concluding quotation from Francesco Petrarca. That the author of the *Exhortation* is Niccolò Machiavelli should not only give us pause, but also demands further scrutiny than the usual efforts to explain the piece, or rather to explain it away. When the author of *The Prince* acknowledges and condemns our "itch" for those "tricks we delight in playing on our neighbors," our first instinct is no doubt skepticism. This cannot be the "real" Machiavelli, we assure ourselves, as if it were a matter of choosing between the *realpolitik* of *The Prince* and the Christianity of the *Exhortation*. But what if the choice, as it has been framed historically, were a false one?

So little is known about this rare piece of confessional prose by the author of *The Prince*, coming to us as it does via a solitary, undated manuscript in Machiavelli's hand. Machiavelli scholars have quibbled over the dating, authenticity, audience, and, not surprisingly, the sincerity of the *Exhortation* for years—to the extent that they acknowledge it at all.[2] Naturally, the various arguments run, the *Exhortation* is the product of a master ironist and cynic, and must be taken lightly; clearly it was produced as the script for a public rhetorical performance before one of the influential religious confraternities which greased the wheels of Florentine political, social, and economic life throughout the Quattrocento and Cinquecento.[3] As Robert Adams suggests, "Performances of this character did not necessarily imply an unusual measure of religious devotion in the speaker; they were part of the complex and long-continued initiation rituals by which a society in which money, family, and seniority counted overwhelmingly, prepared young men for formal positions of leadership and decision."[4] Adams rightly emphasizes the almost mundane quality of these rhetorical occasions in Renaissance Florence; and while he is hesitant to read the *Exhortation* as an exercise in mental reservation on the part of Machiavelli (whom he assumes wrote this long before *The Prince*), Adams nonetheless finds it to be of biographical rather than conceptual or ideological value.

Machiavelli joined the Company of Piety as early as 1495; the piece might well represent an accommodation not only to the social utility of the confraternities themselves, but particularly to the religious fervor that swept Florence during the Savonarolan phase of the republic founded in the wake of the 1494 expulsion of the Medici.[5] If written in the later stages of Machiavelli's life, it could similarly be accounted for as something written in the era of the Medici popes [Leo X (d. 1521) or Clement VII (d. 1534)], thereby performing the dual function of religious rhetoric and professional solicitation of the Medici papacy, that preferred instrument of Machiavelli's long-sought political rehabilitation. Lastly, if there is a camp that reads the *Exhortation* as socially obligatory (if not downright opportunistic), there have also been defectors content to date the piece near the end of Machiavelli's life precisely because it might represent penitence for his entire literary output from *The Prince* onwards. This impulse to read the *Exhortation* as a conversion or belated apology is genetically related to the enduring, unsubstantiated legend that on his deathbed Machiavelli recanted, much as was claimed for the heretical syncretist Pico della Mirandola before him.

What unites these otherwise disparate accounts is a single, problematic assumption—the *discontinuity* of the *Exhortation to Penitence* with respect to

Machiavelli's political writings, the pervasive sense that it must somehow be a product of irony, expedience, insincerity, deception, or the usual social-climbing. Even those whose wishful thinking leads them to a recanting Machiavelli presume that the *Exhortation* marks a break with something recognizably and decidedly Machiavellian in all that came before it. My aim in what follows is to answer (or at the very least to frame properly) a pressing and oft-overlooked question: What would it really mean to take the *Exhortation* seriously as evidence of both a genuinely Augustinian strain in Machiavelli's thought and of a related, fundamental continuity in his writings between a pessimistic anthropology of human desire and a political eschatology of Italian redemption? Put differently, is not Machiavelli's thought predicated on a certain imaginative reinvention, howsoever tortured, of Augustine's typology of the terrestrial and heavenly cities?

There have indeed been sporadic yet serious attempts to draw similar connections throughout the history of Machiavelli's reception.[6] And it is of course an historical absurdity to overlook the theological dimensions of the Reformation and Counter-Reformation reception of Machiavelli's thought: as unique as each of his interpreters was, Gentillet, Botero, Gentili, Bodin, and Boccalini all would have found it impossible to evaluate Machiavelli outside of the essential categories and disputes of the Christian tradition.[7] Nevertheless, it has often been the case that early moderns and moderns alike have reduced the Christian tradition to the background, context, or most often, the victim or foil of Machiavelli's presumed insurrection.[8] This leads us to what is at heart an historical problem of both methodology and content, that is, tracing the Augustinian lineage of Machiavelli's thought without sanitizing or over-simplifying the radical nature of his (or Augustine's) challenge to Western codes of morality and political order. Given that both Augustine and Machiavelli view themselves as revealers of things as they truly are, a second-order problem imposes itself—transcending the hackneyed opposition of Machiavelli and Augustine without effacing genuine points of contention that remain insoluble on the level of fundamental truth-claims.[9]

A Conversation Deferred

In tackling these difficulties I operate under the assumption that the theological scandal of Machiavelli, historically-inflected as it has been, is energized by a rich yet agonistic Augustinian understanding of political misery and religious salvation—which alchemically fuses with Machiavelli's peculiar incarnation of civic humanism to generate one of the most distinctive and influential examples of political theology in the West. To make sense of the rules of

combination by which this conceptual alchemy takes place, we must first eschew some of the more obvious approaches that have obscured as much as
they have explained the relationship between Augustine and Machiavelli. The
road most-traveled deploys Augustine's typology of the two cities as a way of
forestalling the connection: Machiavelli writes from, for, and to the earthly
city as an idolater of the ancients at best, as an atheist at worst—the historical
and political equivalent of the apples and oranges heuristic. The placement of
Machiavelli's writings on the Index of the Church in 1559 makes for a conve-
nient dividing line for readers so-inclined to use Augustine himself as a reason for Machiavelli not to be in dialogue with him. Much of the best modern
scholarship on Machiavelli still labors under the onus of this claim that
Machiavelli marks an epistemological break with the Christian order—and
thus puts out of bounds the very conversation I want to broker here.[10]

Another path of least resistance suggests that Machiavelli inherits his Augustine in the same spirit of resigned rebellion that furnished Hobbes and Nietzsche with so much grist for their mills; in this vein, Machiavelli becomes the
opening act for a set that concludes with the rousing encore of secularism in
the West. This amounts to rendering Christianity an incidental feature of
Machiavelli's march toward the promised land of modernity, while completely
overlooking the degree to which he is indebted to Augustine in his skepticism
about human nature and his convictions about the deep roots of human sin
and viciousness.[11] What of the missed opportunity to explore in more depth
why Augustine's genealogy of human failings meanders back to Adam and
Machiavelli's to the very moment the *polis* is born? Instead of taking seriously
the typological consistency (and the problems) inherent in this move, we are
usually content to chalk this up yet again to the dominant characterization of
Machiavelli as the border guard of the no-man's-land between premodern
Christianity and the modern secular state.

Here lies the interpretive danger of chaining the history of political thought
to the inescapable (and implicitly Hegelian) mechanisms of the *Annales*
School's *mentalitè*, Foucault's *episteme*, Gramsci's hegemony, or traditional
liberalism—whatever we seem to be reading at the moment becomes confirmation of both the reigning conceptual order and of the decisive break with
that order that our subject is made arbitrarily to represent.[12] This is a particular temptation in the case of Machiavelli, whose presumed wholesale rejection of Christianity is narrated via a discourse that effaces what Prezzolini
rightly called "the Christian roots of Machiavelli's moral pessimism."[13] This
temptation plays itself out recursively in a conversation between Augustine
and Machiavelli that is continually deferred on the assumption that they have
nothing to say to one another. Yet again, we see advanced a gross simplifica-
tion of the typology of the two cities to preclude analysis, forgetting Augus-

tine's conviction that "in truth, those two cities are interwoven and intermixed in this era, and await separation at the last judgment" (*De civitate Dei*, 1.35).[14] If Machiavelli's intuition tells him that the political order operates under rules, assumptions, and demands categorically different from those of the divine or the ideal, we would do well to consider that it is Augustine who helps to sharpen that instinct, among many others.[15] Hence while Machiavelli theorizes and Augustine deflates the earthly city, they are each keenly aware of the shared vocabulary that renders both cities meaningful.

Significantly, historians of early modern humanism have often been more generous in articulating these Augustinian dimensions of humanist classicism in the Renaissance, taking Petrarca's anxious conversation with Augustine in the *Secretum* as one benchmark for later humanists' guilty yet unrepentant pleasure in philology and *imitatio*.[16] In this light, one is hard pressed to read Augustine's elaborate exegesis of Varro, in which he criticizes Varro's account of "mythical" and "civic" theology in Roman religious practices (*De civ.*, bks. 6–7), without coming away convinced that Augustine was unwittingly presenting both a working method and a cautionary tale for Renaissance humanists. To the extent that our Machiavelli was a humanist (and a very odd one at that), the *City of God* must have been equally stimulating and exasperating as a work of historiography—one would like to know what he made of Book 18 of Augustine's treatise, with its polymathic incorporation of Old Testament and Mediterranean history that matches the encyclopedic scope of *The Prince* or the *Discourses on Livy*, not to mention what Machiavelli called his own "universal treatise," the first book of the *Florentine Histories*.[17] The shared preoccupation with Roman history—and the corresponding conviction that it could not only be narrated and explained but that it also *signified*—suggest that Machiavelli's most ambitious literary efforts are meant to rival not only Livy or Tacitus, but Augustine as well.[18]

Machiavelli's "Civic Humanism" Through the Lens of Augustine and Lucretia

And without doubt anyone who at present wishes to build a state will find it easier among mountaineers, where there is no culture, than among those who are used to living in cities, where culture is corrupt. (Machiavelli, *Discourses on Livy* 1.11)[19]

Ultimately, it is the oddity of Machiavelli's humanism that can at last give us purchase on the Augustinian terror implicit in and so vital to his thought. If my title makes clear from the outset that Machiavelli's humanism is "civic" in nature, it nonetheless glosses over the bugbear that civic humanism represents for historians of the Renaissance at large, let alone Machiavelli scholars who debate whether Machiavelli is properly called a humanist at all (with the absurd sub-text of the debate being that humanist credentials make him decidedly less modern, exceptional, original, or important). Hans Baron famously inaugu-rated the civic humanism controversy in *The Crisis of the Early Italian Renais-sance* when he read a narrative of liberty in (or onto) Florentine historiography of the early Quattrocento; he argued that the generation of humanists which included Coluccio Salutati and Leonardo Bruni gave the humanist paradigm a political content and a particular story about liberty in the face of the threat posed by the Visconti tyrants of Milan.[20] Baron upped the ante by claiming a direct lineage from Bruni's civic humanism to that of Machiavelli, an interpre-tation that has been pursued to this day.[21]

Paul Oskar Kristeller took issue with all such claims for Renaissance hu-manism that ascribed to it any content beyond its abiding interests in rhetori-cal training, philology, moral philosophy, and what he saw as a fascinating but fundamentally unsystematic account of metaphysics.[22] Kristeller's line has found enthusiastic adherents among those scholars who have insisted upon a skeptical reading of humanism's most lofty and most public claims that its ed-ucational agenda was the production of individual and civic virtues; this school has been equally adamant that the professional aspirations of the humanists and their search for preferment in the emerging modern state tell a far more coherent and plausible story about the transformation of early modern educa-tion.[23] As a way of framing anew the question of Machiavelli's humanism and Augustine, it is worth returning to Stephanie Jed's *Chaste Thinking: The Rape of Lucretia and the Birth of Humanism*,[24] still to my mind the most ambitious and provocative intervention in the civic humanism dispute (a dispute which not accidentally is yet another reincarnation of the recognizably Platonic anx-iety about the content, utility, and moral danger of all rhetoric).[25]

Jed recalls the tragic Roman matron Lucretia, whose rape by the son of the Tarquin king and subsequent suicide leads to the founding of the Roman Re-public by Junius Brutus. Jed examines representations of Lucretia's physical violation as a pretext not only for the civic humanist narrative, but also for "humanistic habits of handling and interpreting literary materials" which de-rive their traditions of textual purity from a kind of "chaste thinking" about the compensatory necessity of Lucretia's suffering to the political enfranchise-ment of Rome (and by extension to that of the Florentines who aspired to be Rome's inheritors). Jed aims to "break down the power of the *topos* of this rape into local and particular events of writing and, in doing so, to ask how our own practices of reading and writing, descended from those of the Flo-rentine humanists, discourage us from questioning the literary structures within which we work."[26] Jed delineates some key effects of humanism's response to the violation of Lucretia as a political narrative of liberation, suggesting how readers are made "complicitous in this displacement of the focus from the violated Lucretia to Brutus the liberator." As a result readers are conditioned, as is Brutus himself, to "a habit of feeling detached from the issues surrounding this rape."[27] The consequences include: the transference of these habits of feeling into the theorization of philology as a castigatory struggle against textual impurity; a resultant institutionalization of chaste thinking in "discriminations between 'literary' and other kinds of writing and between ideas and textual experience"; and the creation of an "autonomous 'literary' tradition" that decontextualizes and separates the private and the political.[28]

Despite its limitations, Jed's perspective remains a useful corrective to the civic humanism debate as it has been usually formulated. She contends that it has been framed too literally as a question of ideal and practice, rhetoric and reality. As she rightly points out, both Baron and Kristeller "have in common the search for idealized origins and filiation" on the trail of humanism's "genuine" roots and distinctive content. Further, we do well to remember that both Baron and Kristeller formed their interpretations as antifascist scholars who took refuge in the United States, such that their "idealization of their own origins in Florentine thought and activity was a means of dealing with their wartime suffering by means of writing."[29] As Jed sees it, despite their enormous intellectual gifts and pedagogical commitment, their experiences with Nazism blinded both scholars to the historical suffering implicit in the Renaissance: Baron to the suffering on which Florentine liberties rested and Kristeller to the violence inherent in the castigatory practices of "pure" classical philology. The corrective that I would add here (and one that brings Machiavelli and Augustine into a new arena with better acoustics) is the necessity of reading civic humanism not only as our troubled inheritance whose historical reality we might debate, but as an equally troubled inheritance of the humanists themselves from their classical, medieval, and more recent pasts. It is in fact *they* who are alternately fascinated by and doubtful of civic humanism's existence, and at times unsure of what it would actually be. My working assumption is that if civic humanism is a fictional reconstruction of the culture of Bruni after the fact, it is one that takes place at least as early as Machiavelli, who also lays the groundwork for a critique of the imaginative moves made possible by it.[30] To find the Augustinian vein of Machiavelli's civic humanism, we need only take our cue from the subject of Jed's intervention—Lucretia.[31]

To the extent that the founding of the Roman Republic contains the seeds of civic humanist rhetoric for Machiavelli, Jed's thesis is borne out in Machiavelli's reticence on the matter of Lucretia and his corresponding emphasis on the political challenges that face her avenger Brutus. In the *Discourses on Livy*,

Machiavelli famously praises the "pretended idiocy" of Brutus under the reign of the Tarquins, a feigned madness whose purpose was "to be noticed less, and to have more chance for overcoming the king and freeing his country whenever he might have an opportunity" (3.2). Retirement from the earthly city is not an option for Brutus, trapped as he is in a dilemma Tacitus would immediately recognize; simulation and dissimulation are the weapons of last resort here:

> It is not enough to say: "I do not care about anything, I do not desire either honors or profits, I wish to live in retirement and without trouble." Such excuses are heard but are not accepted. Men of rank cannot decide to sit quiet even when they decide truly and without any ambition, because they are not believed. Hence even when they do wish to be quiet, other people will not leave them quiet. You must, then, play the fool like Brutus, and often you play the madman, praising, speaking, seeing, and doing things contrary to your purpose, to please the prince. (3.2)

Not surprisingly, passages such as these are often picked clean by scholars invested in finding Machiavelli an enemy and "pretended idiot" to the Medici rulers to whom he addresses *The Prince*.[32] But what is more compelling for our purposes is the notion that, for "men of rank" at least, the earthly city offers no incentives and no quarter for the *vita contemplativa*, pagan or Christian. Retreat is never quite what it seems for Machiavelli, and it rarely goes unmolested.

In Machiavelli's transition here from a discussion of "the prudence of [Brutus] in regaining the liberty of Rome" to "his severity in maintaining it" (3.2–3), no mention is made of Lucretia's violation. At center stage are the measures Brutus must adopt to maintain the newly-founded republican order—the execution of his own sons who long for the perceived freedoms and licentiousness of the Tarquin era: "For he who seizes a tyranny and does not kill Brutus, and he who sets a state free and does not kill Brutus's sons, maintains himself but a little while" (3.3). This admixture of genealogical and political peril fuels so many of Machiavelli's meditations on corruption, the origins of political sin, and the price of stability. For Augustine of course, the spiritual price is usually too great, as he suggests in his own account of Brutus' sons (*De civ.* 3.16); yet importantly, there are also moments when Augustine invokes the willingness of Brutus to go so far in sin for the earthly city as a spur to Christians to go further in humility for the heavenly (5.18). And if Augustine entertains the symbolic utility of the Brutus narrative despite his condemnation of it, Machiavelli entertains his own moral doubts about Brutus despite being convinced that Brutus is doing what he must. Machiavelli's usual conviction that the price of order is worth paying is at times tempered by regret that the political calculus is precisely so inexorable: "It is true that I consider those princes unlucky who have to take unlawful methods for securing their positions for themselves, when the multitude are his enemies" (1.16). In itself, this statement might seem only to betoken Machiavellian resignation to *realpolitik*, but it also captures Machiavelli's nagging suspicion that Brutus' actions must somehow transgress legality in order to establish it.

In the *Discourses*, "killing the sons of Brutus" becomes a trans-historical metaphor for maintaining order that is extended to recent Florentine history—dangerous ground for Machiavelli in any event. Machiavelli compares Brutus to Piero Soderini, the *Gonfaloniere di giustizia* for life—chief executive of the Florentine Republic before the return of the Medici in 1512. Machiavelli chides his old friend and boss Piero, who deceived himself and "believed that with patience and goodness he could overcome the longing of Brutus' sons to get back under another government" (3.3). In underestimating the Medici resolve to reclaim Florence, Soderini so fatally miscalculates that thus runs Machiavelli's well-known epigram on his colleague's death:

> The night Piero Soderini died,
> He left for Hell via the common stair.
> But "Not for your sort!" was what Pluto cried;
> "We have a Hell for little boys. Go there!"[33]

Thus far we seem to be in familiar Machiavellian and anti-Christian territory, consonant with Machiavelli's letter of 1521 to Francesco Guicciardini, in which Machiavelli wishes for the Florentines not "a preacher who would show them the road to Paradise," but "one who would teach them the way to go to the house of the Devil."[34] The bluster of Machiavelli's demonic chic in such moments is meant to convey his exasperation with Florentines like Soderini and Savonarola, whom he saw as ambitious, full of good intentions, and completely unprepared to risk Hell for Heaven on Earth.[35]

All of this suggests that, instead of dismissing Machiavelli as an anti-Christian relativist and thereby evading the real thrust of his claims, it is far more accurate to describe what Machiavelli is doing throughout his writings as a reimagination (or less generously, usurpation) of Augustinian and Christian typology, an effort to reorient politics using the compass of the earthly city, but an orientation to a set of sincerely valued and deeply held *goods* nonetheless. This is substantiated by Machiavelli's paradoxical chastisement of Soderini in the *Discourses* for both failing to take extreme measures that would avert the return of the Medici and for seizing "extra-legal authority and [using] the laws to destroy equality among the citizens," all "in order vigorously to attack his opponents and crush his adversaries" (*Disc.* 3.3). In what strikes us at first glance as a profoundly mixed message, Machiavelli calls

Soderini to task in part because of his failure to attune himself to the times (cf. *Disc.* 3.9, 3.31; *Prince* ch. 25), but more importantly because of Soderini's misreading of political, if not moral, goods:

> [Soderini] should never have allowed an evil to continue for the sake of a good, *when that evil could easily crush that good.* And since his works and his intention would be judged by their outcome, he should have believed that if Fortune and life were with him he could convince everybody that what he did was for the preservation of his native city and not for his own ambition. He could also have regulated things in such a way that no successor of his could do for a wicked end what he had done for a good one [in becoming *Gonfaloniere* for life]. But he was deceived in his first opinion, since he did not know that malice is not mastered by time nor placated by any gift. Hence, not having the wisdom to be Brutus-like, he lost altogether with his native city his position and his reputation. (*Disc.* 3.3; emphasis mine)

This passage suggests something radically different from the perennial and reflexively uncritical reading of chapter 18 of *The Prince*, where Machiavelli is presumed to differentiate the infamous ends/means equation. We are reminded of what is obvious to all careful readers of Machiavelli, namely that ends for him are never formed in a vacuum, but rather embody a set of goods, however much in dispute those goods might be and however much they are indeed differentiated by their claims to individual or communal benefit. Soderini's failure, therefore, becomes a matter not of mere instrumentality, but the corruption of instrumentality by unjustifiable methods and poorly articulated or unpersuasive ends—the essence of political sin in Machiavellian terms. This goes to the heart of Machiavelli's distinction between success and renown in chapter 8 of *The Prince*, where Agathocles the Sicilian both wins the state and loses claim to *virtù*, for "it certainly cannot be called *virtù* to murder his fellow citizens, betray his friends, to be devoid of truth, pity, or religion; a man may get power by means like these, but not glory."[36]

It is finally "glory" that leads us to the real source of friction between Augustine and Machiavelli, a friction unaccounted for by the simplistic opposition of the good and pure instrumentality, truth-claims and technique, heavenly and terrestrial cities. Instead we must ask *both* Machiavelli and Augustine to unravel for us the nature of their goods, taking seriously Augustine's insight that the two cities are so intricate and interwoven that our best recourse is to ask what it is they each *love*:

> We see then that the two cities were created by two kinds of love: the earthly city was created by self-love reaching the point of contempt for God, the Heavenly City by the love of God carried as far as contempt of self. In fact, the earthly city glories in itself, the Heavenly City glories in the Lord. (*De civ.* 14.28; cf. 19.24)

Posing the question of Machiavelli and Augustine in this way, such that each is called to the stand, both the risk and the mandate of the civic humanist project emerge—Augustine's contention that Machiavelli's city serves "created things instead of the Creator" (*De civ.* 14.28); and Machiavelli's conviction that the prince who dares to be Italy's political redeemer has the friendship of Augustine's God, if only he will act knowing that "God will not do everything, lest he deprive us of our free will and a part of that glory which belongs to us" (*Prince* ch. 26).[37] Thus framed, the decisive issue becomes the nature of glory and how it is loved and pursued, with particular emphasis on the question of whether it rightly "belongs to us" at all.

The crux lies in these competing claims to "possession," which return us to the story of Lucretia, and to how the ingloriousness and irrational violence of her rape disturb both Augustine and Machiavelli, cementing each in his reading of the earthly city and at the same time fixing the lexicon they inevitably share. Where Machiavelli does acknowledge the role of Lucretia in the tragic founding of the republic, he is uncertain how much is owed her, as it were. In the *Discourses*, he suggests that Tarquin was not "driven out because Sextus his son raped Lucretia, but because he broke the laws of the kingdom and governed tyrannically" (3.5)—Machiavelli thus strips Lucretia of both agency and relevance. Elsewhere, however, Machiavelli as much as blames Lucretia for the crisis that Brutus resolves. This choice of language is significant in *Discourses* 3. 26, where Machiavelli speaks generally of how states fall on account of women, adducing Aristotle to show how "women have caused much destruction, have done great harm to those who govern cities, and have occasioned many divisions in them," especially where tyrants are "whoring them, or raping them, or . . . breaking off marriages." Here in Machiavelli's account of the republic we find the confluence of a tortured causality, the sexual politics of responsibility, and the dislocation of political glory from suicide to revolution; clearly Lucretia's "ownership" of Roman history is tenuous at best, and she remains the foil of Brutus' greatness and the symbol of political disorders for which he must be willing to kill even his own children, rather than being an emblem of resistance as she might.

In the *City of God*, Augustine is more overtly invested than Machiavelli in the story of Lucretia, tied as it is to his sustained discourse on suicide (*De civ.*, 1.16–28). Writing to Marcellinus in the wake of the sack of Rome by Alaric in 410, Augustine must not only defend Christianity against charges that it sapped Roman virtues and made Rome vulnerable to the attack, but moreover must pull off an adept bit of theodicy to account for and console the physical violation of women throughout the sack. Faced with the prevailing notion that suicide remained the best option left to dishonored women, Christian or pagan, Augustine develops an inquiry into suicide that is predicated on a reading of the Lucretia story made to serve multiple purposes. Like Machiavelli, Augustine senses that the lifeblood of the earthly city flows through the narrative of her violation; and like Machiavelli, Augustine tells a particular story about the ownership of her body, her virtue, and her history.[38]

Augustine holds that "Purity is a virtue of the mind ... [whose] courage decides to endure evil rather than consent to evil," such that "the violence of another's lust cannot take away the chastity which is preserved by unwavering self-control" (1.18). By this logic, Augustine takes Lucretia to task not for her violation, but for her self-slaughter as the slaughter of an innocent: "The highly extolled Lucretia also did away with the innocent, chaste, outraged Lucretia" (1.19). Unjustly subjecting herself to "heavier punishment" than the mere banishment endured by the Tarquins, Lucretia violates the fundamental Christian principle of the sanctity of life and exemplifies a corrupt Roman order that embraces death. Even if her desires were disordered and she consented secretly to the rape, Augustine insists "not even in this case ought she to have killed herself, if she could have offered a profitable penitence to false gods" (1.19). Ultimately, however, the suicide of Lucretia is deployed by Augustine to reveal the nature of the earthly city in one of the most complex arguments advanced in *City of God*:

> This suffices to refute those who, because any notion of chastity is alien to them, jeer at Christian women violated in captivity. They believe Lucretia to have been too good to be polluted by giving any consent to adultery. Her killing of herself because, although not adulterous, she had suffered an adulterer's embraces, was due to the weakness of shame, not to the high value she set on chastity. She was ashamed of another's foul deed committed *on* her, even though not *with* her, and as a Roman woman, excessively eager for honor, she was afraid that she should be thought, if she lived, to have willingly endured what, when she lived, she had violently suffered. Since she could not display her pure conscience to the world she thought she must exhibit her punishment before men's eyes as a proof of her state of mind. (1.19)

As with Machiavelli's account, we see Lucretia owed and in possession of nothing beyond her symbolic chastity. Yet where Machiavelli views her chastity as both the divisive pretext of conflict and the spoils of that conflict, Augustine maintains that she loses her chastity only when she compounds the sin of her rapist with the sin of her own suicide (1.25); her crime consists in trying to make visible to Rome what can only be visible to God, and in privileging civic honor and shame above life. Nevertheless, the relative generosity of Augustine's position shares with Machiavelli a troubling consistency—the relegation of Lucretia's very real trauma to the status of *exemplum*. Lucretia is again left empty-handed by being made to signify through negation another's patriarchal glory, be it God's or Brutus's; dispossessed of the semantic power of her own actions, she is summoned back to symbolic life by both Augustine and Machiavelli. In both cases Lucretia's suicide is never permitted to signify outside of the terms of their metaphysics or their politics, such that her claims to piety and loyalty are always disingenuous for Augustine and politically divisive for Machiavelli.

Still more baffling, it is Lucretia's confirmation of the sanctity of life and the moral vacuousness of Rome that leads to Augustine's unsettling juxtaposition of the discourse on suicide with his defense of state-sanctioned homicide. Chapters 20 and 21 of Book 1 of *City of God* arguably represent Augustine's own "Machiavellian moment." Where chapter 20 builds on the exegesis of the Lucretia incident to conclude that nowhere in Scripture can be found "any injunction or permission to commit suicide either to ensure immortality or to avoid or escape any evil," chapter 21 immediately qualifies the principle of life's inviolability with the caveat that not all homicide is murder:

> There are however certain exceptions to the law against killing, made by the authority of God himself. There are some whose killing God orders, either by a law, or by an express command to a particular person at a particular time. In fact one who owes a duty of obedience to the giver of the command does not himself "kill"—he is an instrument, a sword in its user's hand. For this reason the commandment forbidding killing was not broken by those who have waged wars on the authority of God, or those who have imposed the death penalty on criminals when representing the authority of the State in accordance with the laws of the State, *the justest and most reasonable source of power.* (1.21; emphasis mine)

If this passage were solely an effort to explain the willingness of Abraham to kill his son on God's command, any reader of Kierkegaard would recognize the road-map Augustine lays out here; if it were restricted to accounting for the brutality of Old Testament warfare in the Promised Land, the reader of Deuteronomy would also be on familiar ground. But Augustine's extension of his argument to homicide done at the behest of the State (either on the battlefield or the executioner's platform) is jarring indeed, especially when he warns us elsewhere, "It is a wicked prayer to ask to have someone to hate or to fear, so that he may be someone to conquer" (4.15).

Where Augustine's Lucretia was forced to bear responsibility for the murder of her own chastity (but never allowed to control its signification), his warrior or executioner is licensed to kill. These agents are safely distanced from the act of slaughter and exonerated as the instruments of a divine will that coincides with the will of the state, a rare find indeed in *City of God*. It would be tempting to explain away Augustine's position by adducing the political realities of his era and his great distance from our own sensitivities—his support of Theodosian measures which subjected to the death penalty those who performed pagan sacrifices is significant here—but this is as unsatisfying as efforts to explain away Machiavelli's "Exhortation to Penitence." What this passage does suggest, however, is that Augustine takes seriously the proposition that in the corrupt world of the earthly city, the state may have occasional claim to be "the justest and most reasonable source of power." Like Machiavelli, Augustine too has a taste for high-priced order but moral instincts enough to be troubled by it. This returns us to the problems explored of late by Giorgio Agamben, who has delved into the epistemology, theology, and politics by which the West has elevated the sacred inviolability of the human person at the expense of increasingly more individual lives.[39] In *City of God* 1.21, Augustine has not only opened the door to the killing of Isaac, but once again to killing the sons of Brutus; in the process, he has segued from a theological argument about the sanctity of life to a decidedly Augustinian, but by no means less civic, humanism. None of this is to deny those moments when Augustine develops his most focused critique of empire, sovereignty, and the murderousness and injustice demanded of earthly citizens (consider esp. 2.20; 4.15; 19.7–17). My purpose rather is to demonstrate how difficult it is for Augustine to *sustain* that critique in light of the infiltration of the earthly city's language into it; as we will see shortly, his problem is comparable to Machiavelli's, who cannot keep theology and eschatology out of his misanthropy.

The closest Lucretia herself may come to ownership of the conceptual turf Brutus, Augustine, and Machiavelli contest could well be Machiavelli's caustic *Mandragola*. The play's virtuous matron Lucrezia is no doubt an echo of the Roman matron, and like her historical counterpart, this Lucrezia is also the object of a sexual predator. The lustful Callimaco employs the Machiavellian Ligurio and a corrupt friar to assist him in bedding down Lucrezia, convincing her and her husband that their fertility woes will be resolved after the administration of the potent mandrake root—which will claim the life of her next lover, but guarantee pregnancy thereafter. The opportunistic Friar Timoteo first assuages Lucrezia's doubts by assuring her that she will become pregnant and "acquire a soul for the Lord" (*Mandr.* 3.11).[40] Finally, in what seems a direct echo of *City of God*, Timoteo twists the Augustinian logic of chastity and procreation to justify Lucrezia's adultery:

> As to the act, that it might be a sin, this is a fable, because the will is what sins, not the body; and what causes it to be a sin is displeasing your husband—but you please him; taking pleasure in it—but you have no pleasure from it. Besides this, the end has to be looked to in all things; your end is to fill a seat in paradise, to make your husband happy. The Bible says that the daughters of Lot, believing themselves alone in the world, lay with their father; and because their intention was good, they didn't sin. (*Mandr.* 3.11)

This is as fascinating and tortured a piece of logic as *City of God* 1.18–21, as Machiavelli's Friar reestablishes the incorruptibility of those who do not will but rather endure sin. If Lucrezia eschews pleasure for procreation, she will have fulfilled her duties to her patriarch and to her God. In a line of reasoning that ends with the incest of Lot and his daughters, we find the incestuous coupling of Augustinian arguments and a farcical version of the Machiavellian calculus of relational (but never quite relativistic) goods.[41]

Lucrezia ultimately accepts the Friar's interpretation, or at least rationalizes her acceptance. When Callimaco finally confesses the ruse and Lucrezia has looked to the "end . . . in all things," she actively chooses to embrace Callimaco and his offer to cuckold her husband indefinitely: "Since your astuteness, my husband's stupidity, my mother's simplicity, and my confessor's wickedness have led me to do what I never would have done by myself, I'm determined to judge that it comes from a heavenly disposition which has so willed; and I don't have it in me to reject what Heaven wills me to accept" (5.4). It is very much debatable whether this transformation of Lucrezia truly represents a singular instance of female empowerment in Machiavelli.[42] While it would be tempting to read this modern-day Lucrezia as the avenging spirit of both the Roman matron and the raped Fortuna of chapter 25 of *The Prince*, we cannot overlook how Lucrezia's newfound power depends on her resigned acceptance of a *fait accompli*—the "providential" seduction that has categorically (albeit not ethically) been cleared of the taint of rape by her very acquiescence to the Friar's arguments from Augustine. We do well to note also that it is *Callimaco* who reports Lucrezia's change of heart in the passage above—we are once again confronted with a Lucrezia who at the moment of crisis is given voice only in the retrospection of narrative, and only by a man.[43] Whether Lucrezia first agreed to the ruse out of deceived piety, self-interest, spousal devotion, or all of the above, she must now figure out how to find her own way in what has become the drama of Callimaco's sexual triumph. Denied interpretive control of events, Lucrezia's only option at play's end seems to be taking the starring role in that drama, which has now so uncomfortably become "comedic."

It seems that long-deferred conversation between Augustine and Machiavelli has finally been jump-started here, such that we find Augustine tempted by the order of the earthly city and Machiavelli usurping Augustinian typology and arguments in the service of his most unnerving insights. Through what glass is Machiavelli seeing Augustine so darkly (in every sense)? Is it the medieval "mirror of princes" genre?[44] The imperial nostalgia of that Augustinian comedian, Dante, who answers Augustine and Machiavelli alike by putting still-silent Lucretia in Limbo with the virtuous, noble, and wise pagans of *Inferno* 4? Is it the proto-nationalism of Petrarca, crying out to "Italia mia" in those *"Confessions"* to Laura, the *Canzoniere*? Is it Salutati or Bruni's civic humanism filtered through the *vita contemplativa* and the mercantilism of early Quattrocento Florence? The Medici-bankrolled Neo-Platonism of Ficino or Pico della Mirandola? Savonarola's millenarian fervor and raw ambition to reform the post-Medicean earthly city of Florence? Or Machiavelli's friend Guicciardini, with his skeptical, antihumanist, and anticlerical take on post-Republican Florence? Whatever Machiavelli's sources (and these are all plausible and not necessarily exclusive), the appeal of Augustine lies, I suspect, in Augustine's eloquent communication of the *terror* of the earthly city—built to last, destined to decay.

Restless Desire and Augustinian Terror

> For who is competent, however torrential the flow of his eloquence, to unfold all the miseries of this life? (Augustine, *City of God*, 19. 4; cf. 21.14)

The specter of barbarian invasions, theological civil war, and the reinvention of Roman sovereignty in the wake of both loomed over much of Augustine's lifetime, and there should be little surprise at his ambivalent terror in the face of the compensations and destructive excesses of earthly power. The costs of security and victory for both Church and Empire were never far from mind in the composition of *City of God*, nor was that potent mix of dread and anticipation that permeates the text, obscured as it often is for us by historical distance, linguistic alienation, and Augustine's relentless argumentation. Roughly 1100 years later, Machiavelli finds Italy at the mercy of transalpine and increasingly organized invaders, arriving under the banners not of tribes, but of emerging absolutist states. Having witnessed Florence in the throes of Savonarola's reformist zeal, republican mismanagement, and the reassertion of Medici dominance in Florence *and* Rome, Machiavelli will die the very year when the earthly citizens of Charles V's expanding empire transform into the homicidal marauders who sack Rome in 1527. The price of political freedoms and empire, the military integrity of the Italian peninsula, and the nature of political legitimacy where regime change is not an event, but a lifestyle—these are just some of the spurs to Machiavelli's own dread and anticipation, which as with Augustine, are so often obscured by distance and the veneer of technical rigor in Machiavelli's writing.

What, if not terror, unites Augustine and Machiavelli, who labor under terror, strive to mitigate it, and entertain its employment? If the typology of the two cities is meaningful at all, it is precisely because of their symbolic, almost genetic interpenetration—the earthly and heavenly cities do not so much place one another in sharp relief as much as they form the untidy canvas on which the West has represented its nightmares. If Machiavelli yokes the symbolic dualism of Augustine to the paradoxes of civic humanist realism, then this volatile blend of Christian typology and antiquarian pragmatism is key to tracing the roots of a particularly relentless anthropology of terror in the West.[45] As John Najemy has so persuasively demonstrated, Machiavelli throughout his career explored the poetic and political possibilities of historiography.[46] It might be helpful, however, to ask now a related question—What are the theological dimensions of Machiavelli's poetic historiography and his politics? The answer to this question might well be beyond the scope of this brief overview, but a good start can be made by creating a new context for understanding both the Augustinian terror and the political eschatology implicit in Machiavelli's thought. In order to flesh out the Augustinian dimensions of what is in essence a much larger problem than imagined, we must first sketch out Augustine and Machiavelli's overlapping (but by no means identical) anthropologies of desire.

We are reminded of Machiavelli's entrenched skepticism about the human capacity to choose the good, his certainty that it is necessary for any lawgiver to "presuppose that all men are evil and that they are always going to act according to the wickedness of their spirits whenever they have free scope" (*Disc.* 1.3); or as he puts it elsewhere, "It is a good general rule about men, that they are ungrateful, fickle, liars and deceivers, fearful of danger and greedy for gain" (*Prince* ch. 17). One cannot help but hear something of Augustine here, with his insistence that the earthly city must be studied precisely because it "aims at dominion, which holds nations in enslavement, but is itself dominated by that very lust of dominion" (*De civ.* 1.preface). For all of our gifts and our unique ontological status as beings shaped in the image of God, Augustine emphasizes our perpetual and restless desire: "The mind of man, the natural seat of his reason and understanding, is itself weakened by long-standing faults which darken it" such that "it is too weak to cleave to that changeless light and to enjoy it" (11.2). While Augustine does allow for the possibility of human renewal through Christ ["As God, he is the goal; as man, he is the way"] (11.2), he still finds us awash in time and corruption, praying but never at all certain that we are sons of Abel, "predestined by grace, and chosen by grace, by grace a pilgrim below, and by grace a citizen above" (15.1).

In the face of these uncertainties of predestination, Machiavelli fixes his attention squarely on the citizens below, the recognizable "natives" of the earthly city, whose disordered desires seem to cement human nature rather than speak to any imminent rectification of it. This takes on axiomatic weight for Machiavelli:

> Ancient writers say that men usually worry in bad conditions and get bored in good ones, and that either of these afflictions produces the same results. Whenever men cease fighting through necessity, they go to fighting through ambition,

which is so powerful in human breasts that, whatever high rank men climb to, never does ambition abandon them. The cause is that Nature has made men able to crave everything but unable to attain everything. (*Disc.* 1.37)

Framed in this Augustinian (and proto-Hobbesian) vein as the political and metaphysical itch that cannot be scratched, this restlessness of all desire necessitates "the chief foundations on which all states rest," that is, "good laws, good armies, and good examples" (*Prince* ch. 12; 24). Machiavelli takes as "given that men never do anything good except by necessity" and that "hunger and poverty make men industrious, and the laws make them good" (*Disc.* 1.3). And where the terrors of the earthly city demand the communal order of human laws backed by force, they also make individual guile possible and perhaps indispensable—that prudence, as Machiavelli most famously puts it, which makes "good use of both the beast and man," or the deceptions of the fox and the wrath of the lion. If "all men were good," he acknowledges, one would not need guile or violence and "this rule would be bad, but since they are a sad lot, and keep no faith with you, you in your turn are under no obligation to keep it with them" (*Prince* ch. 18).

Augustine not surprisingly would reject Machiavelli's regimen of prudence, or at the very least emphasize the limitations of prudence with respect to the determinative sinfulness of the earthly city on which he and Machiavelli do agree. Augustine sees prudence at best as a kind of intellectualized error correction, whose "vigilance in distinguishing good from evil" is employed "so that in our pursuit of the good . . . no mistakes may creep in"—nevertheless, "neither prudence nor self-control removes that evil from this life" (*De civ.* 19.4). Yet what truly distinguishes Machiavelli's all-purpose prudence from that of Augustine? Their conceptions of prudence are both in essence postlapsarian, whether the "original sin" is theological or political, born of Adam or Romulus, Eve or Lucretia.

Again, we are led to inquire into the loves and the glories Machiavelli and Augustine esteem. *City of God* 5.19 suggests that there is "a slippery slope from the excessive delight in the praise of men to the burning passion for domination," but that "the man who covets glory either 'strives by the right way' for it or 'struggles by trickery and deceit,' desiring to seem a good man without being so." Keying into the Machiavellian drama of simulation, Augustine tries to leave a space for glory as a check to the pure instinct to dominate, intimating that "the man who *despises* glory and is eager only for domination is worse than the beasts, in his cruelty or self-indulgence" [emphasis mine] (5.19). Hence the foxes and lions of Augustine's earthly city might find their way back to God, if only they will transfigure Roman values into their Christian counterparts—an act of hermeneutic as well as spiritual dexterity, and perhaps an answer to the civic humanism of Machiavelli. Yet note how this logic leads Augustine not only to account for God's toleration of the Roman Empire, but also to rationalize the empire's continued successes and expansion:

> I have now sufficiently explained, as far as I can, the reason why the one true and just God has assisted the Romans, who are good according to the standards of the earthly city, to the attainment of the glory of so great an empire. . . . However, it is the conviction of all those who are truly religious, that no one can have true virtue without true piety, that is without the true worship of the true God; and that the virtue which is employed in the service of human glory is not true virtue; still those who are not citizens of the Eternal City . . . are of more service to the earthly city when they possess even that sort of virtue than if they are without it. (5.19)

As with Lucretia and his discourses on suicide and homicide, Augustine once more teeters on the prudential borderline between transfiguring Roman glory and justifying it outright. The historical weight and the inspiring terror of Roman success seems to pull Augustine away from the full metaphysical and political implications of his typology of the two cities, such that while he insists on the fundamental divide between believers and the impious, he nevertheless makes what amounts to an argument from pure social utility in keeping citizens of the earthly city gainfully employed in the public service—no doubt as the warriors, executioners, and executors of the imperial will as in *City of God* 1.21. If the "sons of Brutus" are not to be killed here, their pursuit of glory is to be made *useful* to the state despite their inevitable damnation.

Augustine does openly hope that instead "those who are endowed with true piety and who lead a good life" might become "skilled in the art of government," for there would be "no happier situation for mankind than that they, by God's mercy, should wield power" (5.19). Yet while he makes clear that these ideal Christian princes should never ascribe to themselves the virtues supplied by God, their imagined and increasingly real domination of the Roman Empire represents Augustine's own "slippery slope" into the discourse of domination and the values of his putative opponents. In his own fear of disorder, Augustine does not hesitate to deploy the City of Man against the pagans who still, but not for much longer, are in its devoted service. I think ultimately this speaks to the earthly city's infiltration even of Augustine's eschatology, such that when Augustine asks himself whether the City of God will have "grades of honor and glory . . . appropriate to degrees of merit," he answers in the affirmative that "There will be such distinctions; of that there can be no doubt" (22.30).

Where Augustine negotiates this complicated and potentially compromised social contract with the earthly city, Machiavelli makes a similarly problematic move when he retreats from the absolutism of his own notions about the constancy of human nature to what seems an implicitly hopeful and profoundly idealistic account of humanism's capacity to save us from ourselves, even at very long odds. In what follows, Machiavelli maps out human character as an historical issue that finally transcends history. He suggests that his integrated analysis of classical Rome and modern Florence works precisely because of this paradox:

> He who considers present affairs and ancient ones readily understands that all cities and all peoples have the same desires and the same traits and that they always have had them. He who diligently examines past events easily foresees future ones in every country and can apply to them the remedies used by the ancients or, not finding any that have been used, can devise new ones because of the similarity of the events. But because these considerations are neglected or are not understood by those who read or, if they are understood, are not known to rulers, the same dissensions [*scandoli*] appear in every age. (*Disc.* 1.39)

How can new remedies be made both possible and impossible by the continuity of our natures? What is most compelling here is the perverse logic of social history implied, a "scandalous" logic completely in tune with Machiavelli's most misanthropic sentiments. The paradox of humanist *imitatio* lies in the degree to which misunderstanding the continuity of human nature confirms, reinforces, and perhaps even constitutes that nature—the paradox also lies in the extent to which imitation of the ancients is made possible only by the fact that, predictably, it has never been faithfully practiced.[47] In other words, human misprision and misreading become the very constants by which analysis of the past becomes actionable in the present, thereby leaving us with a negative definition of *imitatio* by which we only avoid or repeat the mistakes of others, usually the latter. Machiavelli's frustrated ambition is to reinvent imitation so that new remedies actually become plausible and human character might no longer be so mournfully constant.

It is in this sense that Machiavelli's understanding of *imitatio* is unique in early modern culture—as a mode of reading designed to escape from itself, that is, a planned obsolescence through which reliance on the past might somehow be tempered by innovation that is nevertheless consciously retrospective. This is an epistemological dance that would easily find a partner in the Augustine of *Confessions*, book 9. This temporal eccentricity of Machiavelli's hermeneutics is what drives his conception of political life at large, as Pocock has so ably demonstrated.[48] At his most despairing, Machiavelli denies the certainty of any remedy for political life, so that for him "it follows that an everlasting republic cannot be established; in a thousand unexpected ways her ruin is caused" (*Disc.* 3.17). At his most hopeful, Machiavelli still puts his faith in one who commands *and* who reads, in an idealized, redemptive lawgiver who "with his example would renovate [the republic's] laws, and would not merely stop it from running to ruin but would *pull it backward* [such that] it would be everlasting" [emphasis mine] (3.22). This is Machiavelli's only acknowledgment in the *Discourses* of the potential for an everlasting republic. What it demands of its earthly citizens is a reimagined countertemporality, a gesture by which going backwards interpretively is the only political means to go forward—this is truly the theology and epistemology of Machiavelli's civic humanism, inflected by Augustine's terror of disorder and his semantic agility in manipulating the typology of the two cities. Put in Augustine's terms, the mythical and civic theology of Varro have inseparably fused in Machiavelli's almost sacral channeling of the ancients.

In the preface to the second book of his *Discourses,* Machiavelli famously asks "whether I deserve to be numbered with those who deceive themselves if . . . I over-praise ancient Roman times and find fault with our own," perhaps giving voice to real doubts about his historical project and its attendant blindness to the text that is the present. Machiavelli is only able to escape this humanist equivalent of apostasy by rendering his implicit theology an explicit pedagogy: "For it is the duty of a good man to teach others anything of value that through the malice of the times and of Fortune you have been unable to put into effect, in order that since many will know of it, some of them more loved by Heaven may be prepared to put it into effect" (*Disc.* 2.preface; cf. *Prince,* dedication). Whoever might be ordained by Heaven to transform Machiavelli's earthly city is beseeched to make use of his insights, through which the mechanism of Christian grace transmutes into *virtù,* if only Fortuna can be cajoled, seduced, or beaten into submission (*Prince* ch. 25). As a result, Machiavelli's civic humanism is both the embodiment and the remedy of restless desire as it awaits a reader-redeemer "who is so great a lover of antiquity that he will rule Fortune in such a way that she will not have cause to show in every revolution of the sun how much she can do" (*Disc.* 2.30).

If Machiavelli's return to the ancients truly has this theological dimension, does it have a church to go with it? Here we are on the trail of Machiavelli's deepest reservations about all institutions, civil and ecclesiastical. What we will find, however, are vaguely Augustinian categories facilitating Machiavelli's skepticism. The *Discourses* are most notorious in their criticism of Christianity, making the religious opportunism of *The Prince* seem tame by comparison. Machiavelli hints at what is to come when he adduces the instrumentality and social utility of religion—as well as the cultural disaster courted by the ancients when their oracles and augurs "turned to speaking so as to please the powerful, and their falsehood was discovered by the people" (*Disc.* 1.12). But when the critique is most fully developed in the *Discourses* 2.2, Machiavelli seems torn between the truth, the utility, and the fragility of religious faith. "The difference between our religion and the ancient," he maintains, is that "ours, because it shows us the truth and the true way, makes us esteem less the honor of the world; whereas the pagans, greatly esteeming such honor and believing it the greatest good, were fiercer in their actions." Machiavelli is openly nostalgic for the "magnificence of their sacrifices, compared with the mildness of ours," so "full of blood and ferocity in the slaughter" that "this terrible sight made the men resemble it" (2.2).[49]

It is almost as if Machiavelli here usurps Augustine's critique of Varro and the Roman gods (*De civ.* 6–7), redeploying the discourse of sacrifice (which Augustine had reclaimed from the ancients to begin with) to bemoan a faith that "has glorified humble and contemplative men rather than active ones" (*Disc.* 2.2). By privileging an "abjectness and contempt for human things," Christianity's worst offense is that it enslaves us all the more to the corrupt earthly city, which has been weakened and "turned . . . over as prey to wicked men, who can in security control it, since the generality of men, in order to go to Heaven, think more about enduring their injuries than about avenging them" (2.2). This seems an echo in its own right of *City of God* 4.32, where Augustine takes issue with the Roman spiritual leaders who knowingly taught falsehoods under the guise of religion and "by this means . . . bound [men] tighter . . . to the citizen community, so that they might bring them under control and keep them there." Where Machiavelli and Augustine seem to meet (but never quite concur) is precisely this sense that misunderstanding the nature of sacrifice reduces faith to mere exploitation.

This "perversion" (literally a "turning through") of Augustinian typology resurfaces in the *Discourses* 3.1, as Machiavelli yokes civil and religious life to a unifying conception of reform that with true humanist élan equates change, renewal, and retrospection. A more mixed message is transmitted, however, as Machiavelli both celebrates and decries the Franciscan and Dominican renewals of Christianity, suggesting quite seriously that these movements represented simultaneously the preservation and the enervation of the faith:

> The power of their new orders is the reason why the improbity of the prelates and the heads of our religion does not ruin it; for still living in poverty and having great influence with the people because of hearing confessions and preaching, they give them to understand that it is evil to speak evil of what is evil, and that it is good to live under the prelates' control and, if prelates make errors, to leave them to God for punishment. So the prelates do the worst they can, because they do not fear that punishment which they do not see and do not believe in. This renewal, then, has maintained and still maintains our religion. (3.1)

Returning the institutions of the Church to their roots in poverty and the heavenly city, the reform movements ironically strengthen corrupt prelates' earthly hold on their charges. While we might be content to read this passage merely as sarcasm consistent with the spirit of the *Discourses* 2.2, the passage strikes me as genuinely ambivalent, even tortured. It is nearly impossible to pinpoint the logical transition by which Machiavelli segues in this passage from acknowledging the necessity and the truth-claims of these Christian renewals, to resigning himself to the reforms' confirmation of clerical tyranny; this is as incongruous and yet as deeply held as Augustine's discourse on suicide and homicide discussed above. If there is a turning point in the passage, it seems to be the familiar problem of rhetoric, for once it becomes "evil to speak evil of what is evil," it becomes good to be patiently enslaved by those who in essence do not believe in the evil that goes unnamed and unchallenged—the problem Machiavelli seems ultimately to have with the City of God is not that it cherishes universal goods, but that its goods are no longer vigorous or terrifying enough to be universally cherished.[50]

Machiavelli's Political Eschatology: "Leisure to Be Still"

Remove justice, and what are kingdoms but gangs of criminals on a large scale? What are criminal gangs but petty kingdoms? (Augustine, *City of God* 4.4)

From this came understanding of things honorable and good, as different from what is pernicious and evil, because if one injured his benefactor, there resulted hate and compassion among men, since they blamed the ungrateful and honored those who were grateful. . . . They undertook, in order to escape such evils, to make laws and to establish punishments for those who broke them. Thence came the understanding of justice. As a result, when afterward they had to choose a prince, they did not prefer the strongest, but him who was most prudent and most just. (Machiavelli, *Discourses* 1.2)

In light of this complex relationship between Augustine and Roman sovereignty, and Machiavelli and the Christian dispensation, perhaps we can approach the *Exhortation to Penitence* anew, taking Machiavelli far more seriously when he asserts, "Everything is created for the honor and benefit of man, and man is created only for the benefit and honor of God" (*Ex. Pen.* 120). This is the paradoxical and recalcitrant principle of Machiavelli's civic humanism—De Grazia is on to something in paraphrasing Machiavelli thus: "The Creator fashioned a man-centered world and a God-centered man."[51] The new accent is nevertheless matched by the conviction that "when he shows . . . ingratitude to God, man also changes himself from angel to devil, from master to slave, and human being to animal" (*Ex. Pen.* 120).[52] In this incarnation of Machiavelli's political cosmos, the foxes, lions, and predators of his other writings must continue to pursue order as a cherished good, yet continually live under the moral peril that "those who are ungrateful to God can hardly fail to be hateful to their neighbors" (121). Machiavelli fuses theological and political scandal here in the service of recalling both Christianity and the polis to their sacrificial, terrifying origins—Augustinian penitence rendered a Machiavellian ethic of fear.

It is indeed no accident that Machiavelli's guiding *exemplum* in the *Exhortation* is King David, the self-reliant, model warrior of chapter 13 of *The Prince*, of whom the *Exhortation* says, "There cannot possibly be united in any one person greater faults or greater penitence" (119). Suspended between the strictures of the two cities, David confirms an order of *realpolitik* and divine grace for Machiavelli—what scandalizes us most in our reception of Machiavelli is his ability to hold both orders in stasis, to tell sinful, opportunistic princes that "it is not sin, but perseverance in sin that will render [God] implacable" (*Ex. Pen.* 120). Read alongside *The Prince* chapters 15–19, does this not suggest that princes should sin *tactically* but in a spirit of civic penitence? Viewing the *Exhortation* thus as part of Machiavelli's political theology ultimately exposes his real intervention in the history of political thought, and moves us away from the dominant heuristic of Machiavelli scholarship, that is, reading everything through the prism of *The Prince*, or rather assumptions about it.

The last phase of our conversation between Augustine and Machiavelli builds on the premise that Machiavelli's political prose is *epistolary* at heart, implicitly (in the case of the *Discourses*) or explicitly (in the case of *The Prince*) addressing the Medici—no longer as natives of Florence, but as foreign conquerors whose political center of gravity has shifted from Florence to Rome as a result of the ascendancy of Giovanni de' Medici to the papacy as Leo X.[53] The transition from *The Prince* (ca. 1513), to the *Discourses on Livy* (ca. 1513–1517), and finally to the *Discourse on Remodeling the Government of Florence* (ca. 1520) is decisive here[54]—the *Exhortation to Penitence* may now be plausibly added to that constellation of texts and interests, whatever its actual date of composition or primary audience. In this strained, ongoing correspondence with the Medici and Florence at large, Machiavelli modulates between two possibilities—asking Leo (or his relatives as proxies) to assume the mantle of the mythical political redeemer and, more strikingly, asking them to become true lawgivers with extraordinary powers who would so reform the political life of Florence that it would no longer require their services or their domination. By asking the Medici to share his terror of disorder and his longing for stability, Machiavelli shares with them as well his vision for the earthly city of Florence transformed and perfected in their wake.

The first of these options, the redemptive prince, is of course most famously captured in the overt political eschatology of chapter 26 of *The Prince*.[55] Reminding Guiliano de' Medici (and by extension his brother the pope) that "it was necessary, to bring out the *virtù* of Moses, that the children of Israel should be slaves in Egypt," Machiavelli suggests to them that the redemption of Italy is not only possible but providential since Medici ambitions are as just and as favorable to God as any in the mythical past, however difficult the realization of those ambitions might prove to be. With *virtù* as the mechanism of political salvation through works alone, Machiavelli here deploys the Aristotelian dynamic of matter and form, with Florence and Italy providing the raw material for the seminal power of Medici order (cf. *Disc.* 3.8–9). In accounting for Machiavelli's transition from *The Prince* to the *Discourses*, John Najemy contends that Machiavelli ultimately abandons this myth of the redemptive prince for a more fundamentally communal (and republican) take on civic life.[56] I have some sympathy for this reading, and I suspect it is borne out by the *Discourses'* shift to talking about lawgivers and communal *virtù* as much as princes and individual glory, although Machiavelli conflates these categories often enough. My departure from Najemy on this score would be that if Machiavelli loses faith in redemptive princes, this does not render his political theology any less eschatological.

What seems to fuel the terrors of the *Discourses* is Machiavelli's dread of the Florentine factions born of partisan animosities and ambitions: "Hate went on to divisions; from divisions to parties; from parties to ruin" (1.8). This fear of faction informs Machiavelli's ambivalent understanding of mixed government, by which he does not mean the simple and historically unconscious amalgamation of political forms, or old and new laws. It is this kind of statecraft by accretion which leads him to conclude that Florence has gone its mad way "without ever having had a government [which] could truly be called a republic" (1.49). In his view, Florence has been a city misruled by a people who should be the prophetic "voice of God" (1.58), but are instead moved by and fed "as much on what seems to be as on what is" (1.25). The political salvation of any such republic, caught up as it is in the Platonic trap of mistaking evil for the good, is imagined by Machiavelli as the *conscious* engineering of the state in the face of inevitable ruin and revolution. This act of political will must be both interpretive and coercive, such that the republic partakes of princely, aristocratic, and popular government, but never tyranny per se (1.2). But what sort of leader evades the Polybian cycle of governmental decay without slipping into the half-measures and indecision so ridiculed by Machiavelli (2.15; 2.23)? Or as he wonders elsewhere, what truly good man would want the job (1.18)?

The agent of this social engineering is the lawgiver, be it a living, breathing sage or far less preferable and reliable, Fortuna herself. In either case the aim is to have "laws so planned that without any need for revision, [the republic] can live safely under them" (1.2). When Machiavelli entertains the possibility that the glorious lawgiver may devolve into the despised tyrant, his fixation on determinative origins and fatal choices betrays his most recognizably Augustinian instincts:

> Those men are infamous and detestable who have been destroyers of religions, squanderers of kingdoms and republics, enemies of virtue, of letters, and of every other art that brings gain and honor to the human race, such as the impious, the violent, the ignorant, the no-account, the lazy, the cowardly. . . . Yet in the end, almost all, *deceived by a false good and a false glory,* allow themselves to go, either willingly or ignorantly, into the positions of those who deserve more blame than praise. And though able, to their perpetual honor, to set up a republic or a kingdom, they turn to a tyranny. Nor do they realize how much fame, how much glory, how much honor, security, quiet, along with satisfaction of mind, they abandon by this decision, and into what great infamy, censure, blame, peril, and disquiet they run. (1.10; emphasis mine)

Nowhere in the Machiavellian corpus is this explosive alchemy of civic humanism and Augustinian dualism more pronounced. The reclamation of glory from its perversity, the reorientation to the true good, the relationship between *virtù* and letters, the fine line between laudable order and blameworthy despotism, the lawgiver's genuine repose and the tyrant's spiritual turmoil—all speak to a political theology whose contours Augustine would recognize, but whose consequences and goods he might soundly reject. Nevertheless, Machiavelli's "City of God," that "everlasting republic" which defies decay, relies on decidedly Augustinian signposts for its navigation, its coherence, and its eschatology.

Whatever lawgiver the *Discourses* imagine, be it the Medici pontiff or the republican sympathizers to whom the book is dedicated, salvation will be a matter of collaboration between the good works of a founding prince and the grace of a reformed populace—princes establish, while the people preserve and deepen legal and constitutional traditions (1.58). This insight puts Machiavelli in the decaying orbit of one of Augustine's key objections to Roman virtue, that is, its atomizing quality. When Augustine celebrates the patient, honorable suffering of Regulus at the hands of his Carthaginian captors as a counter-example to the pride of Lucretia, he nonetheless takes Romans to task for their privatized conception of the virtues, as they blithely ignore God's injunction to "aim at true virtue, which can bring happiness also to a community." With respect to Machiavelli's redemptive lawgiver, Augustine's question could fairly be posed to and by Machiavelli: "Now how are we to cope with men who are proud to have had such a fellow-citizen, but afraid to belong to such a community?" (*De civ.* 1.15).

The question suggests that in a world of transience, fragility, and terror, even those lawgivers who do not descend into tyranny may after death be relegated to a kind of symbolic isolation, leaving behind them a collection of mutually-suspicious, atomized citizens who fear to be a true community. Machiavelli's best effort at an answer is his *Discourse on Remodeling the Government of Florence*.[57] Written many years after *The Prince* and the *Discourses*, and to Pope Leo X directly rather than "middlemen" like Guiliano de' Medici or the Rucellai circle,[58] *Remodeling* insists that Florence has not only never been a republic (cf. *Disc.* 1.49), but has never been a true princedom either (*Rem.* 101). Machiavelli trots out many of his customary devices from earlier works: the eschatology of the everlasting republic, the divisiveness of factions, the political peril of half-measures, and the benefits and dangers of individual ambition. Yet the text represents a real sea-change and an intensification of Machiavelli's political theology. The transformation is inaugurated by his overt suggestion that the Medici are now profoundly alienated from the Florentine citizenry compared to the Quattrocento rule of Cosimo de' Medici or Leo's father, Lorenzo il Magnifico; the advantage of Leo's forefathers lay in being "educated and brought up among the citizens" whereas "now, they have grown so great that, since they have gone beyond all the habits of citizens, there cannot be such intimacy and consequently such favor" as before (105).

Essentially chastising the family for investing its political and cultural capital in Rome, for abandoning their Florentine identity for the papacy, Machiavelli is confident nonetheless that "Florence is a subject very suitable for taking [republican] form . . . and I know that Your Holiness is much inclined toward one" (107). The *Discourse on Remodeling* offers up an astounding compromise to Leo X—set up republican institutions as a hollow sham, rig them to favor all of your supporters and interests, yet allow that skeleton of republicanism to become a living reality after your death. Jacob Burckhardt read this plan with similar astonishment: "A more ingenious scheme of concessions to the Pope, to the Pope's various adherents, and to the different Florentine interests cannot be imagined; we might fancy ourselves looking into a clock."[59] It is quite telling how Burckhardt viewed Machiavelli's scheme in these mechanistic terms, thus fueling later understandings of his politics as the triumph of modern technique over classical morality. Yet Burckhardt's evocation of Machiavellian clockwork glosses over the strange theology of good faith at work in the *Discourse on Remodeling*. Offering Leo the equivalent of a monarchy while alive and well-deserved fame as a republican lawgiver after death, Machiavelli makes his most unique attempt to deal with the contingencies of time and the terrors of civil war. Giving Leo the tools to institutionalize an absolute princedom with an expiration date, Machiavelli develops the political equivalent of a *memento mori*, reminding the pontiff that "since you must cease to be," you should "leave behind a perfect republic made strong with all needed parts, which everybody will see and realize needs to be just as it is" (111). The dissimulation advised in earlier texts is missing here, for everyone in Florence will knowingly, quietly countenance a plan that will forever alter the rules of Florence's endemic zero-sum game. Leo and all Florentines alike will become conscious actors in the Polybian cycle of political corruption, knowing full well that a great deal of assembly will be required:

> And I am certain that in a short time, by means of the power of Your Holiness, who will steer everything, this present government will change in such a way into the other one, and the other into this, that *they will become one and the same, and all one body*, with peace for the city and everlasting fame for Your Holiness, because always your power can take care of such defects as arise. (113; emphasis mine)

Here Machiavelli makes his peace with Augustine and Plato alike,[60] and thus is consecrated the Eucharist of civic humanism, by which tyranny becomes the body and lifeblood of the republic to come. This is the Machiavellian dispensation of civil religion, Heaven's gift to the Medici prince and pontiff who holds the keys to Augustine's two cities—the gift of "power and material for making yourself immortal, and for surpassing . . . your father's and your grandfather's glory" (114). Peace and fame are the rewards of bridging the eschatological chasm that separates Machiavelli's two cities: Florence before and after radical, yet bloodless reform.

This *Discourse on Remodeling* is Machiavelli's exhortation to Medici penitence and the groundwork for their Davidic triumph over Florentine political sin. As with all Machiavellian opportunities, this one will not last indefinitely, as is suggested in Machiavelli's loose translation of Ausonius's "On Occasion":

> —Tell me then: who's this person by your side?
> —She's Penitence; and this you'd better note,
> Who misses me [Opportunity], gets her to be his bride.[61]

Penitence might be all that remains if the Medici family does not act immediately. One can hardly explain away the *Discourse on Remodeling* as Machiavelli playing the sycophant or the opportunist. The piece calculates to offend and unsettle too much, daringly marrying *realpolitik* to salvation, all in republican conviction that "The city institutions . . . will always stand firm when everybody has a hand in them, and when everybody knows what he needs to do and in whom he can trust, and no class of citizen, either through fear for itself or through ambition, will need to desire revolution" (115). Augustine and Machiavelli meet (and clash) where terrifying order becomes the price of participation in the new *ecclesia*, a term of assembly that has itself linguistically straddled the worlds of the Greek *polis* and the Christian Church. The risk that *both* Augustine and Machiavelli run is laid out in the *City of God*'s misgivings about Minerva's failure to save Troy: "The image did not preserve the men; the men were preserving the image" (*De civ.* 1.2). Hence we are left asking whether and when the typology of salvation (political or otherwise) descends into what is merely a delusional act of anthropomorphism.

If we are truly set on finding a kindred spirit for Machiavelli's inventiveness, we might well give Hobbes, Rousseau, and Nietzsche a respite, looking instead towards Blake's *Marriage of Heaven and Hell.* What at last are the terms of Machiavelli's marriage of Augustine and the ancients? For one, if Augustine helped to convince Dante that the virtuous ancients should remain in Limbo,[62] Dante induced Machiavelli to release them. Once released, however, what are the ancients to do and to mean? Machiavelli (unwittingly or not) follows Augustine in imposing upon the ancients a new order of signification and exemplarity, by which they are rendered proofs of Augustine's claim that "at least . . . the desire for human praise and glory makes [us], not indeed saints, but less depraved men" (*De civ.* 5.13). Machiavelli also accepts the ontological thrust of Augustine's anthropology, agreeing with him that "Everyone, since he takes his origin from a condemned stock, is inevitably evil and carnal." How much would Machiavelli really quibble with Augustine's corollary that "It is not the case that every bad man will become good, but no one will be good who was not bad originally" (15.2)?

Where Machiavelli extends the corruption of individual human agents to communal disorders, he is participating in a *lingua franca* that Augustine helped to develop. As a result, Machiavelli unhesitatingly follows Augustine's logic to the conclusion that imperial order is the inevitable consequence of our ingrained failings and the only terrestrial hope for checking them; this is not to say that Augustine and Machiavelli do not take issue with empire and its costs, but they each remain in thrall to it in important ways. In their terror of disorder, Augustine and Machiavelli entrust themselves to earthly sovereignty—one through faith in a divine sovereignty that trumps all others, another through faith in narratives of a past which ultimately both trumps and shapes the future. As competing eschatologists, Augustine and Machiavelli hope for the charges in their care a better city to come. Augustine's will be a city where free will is enfranchised and sin is made impossible—in human terms, a "when" as well as a "where." In that time, we will be "replenished and restored by [God's] blessing and sanctification"; in that place, "we shall have *leisure to be still*" [emphasis mine] (*De civ.* 22.30). While Machiavelli is profoundly uncertain whether Florence has the luxury of remaining still, his political theology in the *Discourse on Remodeling* nevertheless makes room for the conceit, if not the reality.[63]

Notes

1. Niccolò Machiavelli, "Exhortation to Penitence," trans. Robert M. Adams in *The Prince*, ed. Adams (New York: Norton, 1992), 119–22; subsequent references will be parenthetical with the abbreviation *Ex. Pen.* followed by the page number. The verse that completes this passage (and the entire piece) is from Petrarca's *Canzoniere*, l. 13–14. This Petrarchan connection echoes what Machiavelli does in concluding ch. 26 of *The Prince*, where he also quotes from Petrarca to exhort the Medici to free Italy from the barbarians; I will return to the political eschatology of ch. 26 in the conclusion of this essay.

2. For accounts that explicitly treat the *Exhortation*, see Paul E. Norton, "Machiavelli's Road to Paradise: *The Exhortation to Penitence*," *History of Political Thought* 4, no. 1 (1983): 31–42; and Douglas Kries, "A Question of Piety: Machiavelli's Treatment of Christianity in the *Exhortation to Penitence*," in *Piety and Humanity: Essays on Religion in Early Modern Political Philosophy*, ed. Kries and Mansfield (Lanham, MD: Rowman & Littlefield, 1998), ch. 1. Although Kries relies on some of the assumptions about the *Exhortation* that I am trying to get past here, he nonetheless does a fine job contextualizing the *Exhortation* and applying the same documentary attention to it as Machiavelli's other works have generated. See notes 6–8 for more on the broader question of Machiavelli's treatment of religion.

3. For more on the confraternities and their role in the ritual life of Florence, see Richard C. Trexler, *Public Life in Renaissance Florence* (Ithaca: Cornell UP, 1980), esp. 382–87, 403–18, 530.

4. "Exhortation," *The Prince*, trans. Adams, 119 (see note 1). One is tempted to reply that given Adams's criteria, there has never been an identifiably sincere piece of religious oratory. One avenue of inquiry in this essay will be the notion that the "sincerity" of Machiavelli's Augustinianism coincides, however jarringly, with the social utility of his rhetorical performance.

5. Adams seems most wedded to the thesis of an early composition. For more on Machiavelli's early years, see: Roberto Ridolfi, *La vita di Niccolò Machiavelli*, 6th ed., 2 vols. (Florence: Sansoni, 1969), 1: 3–23; Sebastia de Grazia, *Machiavelli in Hell* (Princeton: Princeton UP, 1989), esp. ch. 3; and Maurizio Viroli, *Niccolò's Smile*, trans. Antony Shugaar (New York: Hill & Wang, 2000), esp. chs. 2–3. Ridolfi opts for a later date of composition and reads the text as wholly sincere. Similarly, De Grazia guesses that the *Exhoration* is written late in life for a confraternity (59), as does Viroli (257–59). De Grazia is more generous toward the piece, while Viroli suggests instead that it is difficult to believe in an "image of Niccolò retreating to a cloister and exhorting his listeners to penitence" (258). Viroli's reading is symptomatic of the problem I describe in this essay—the assumption that the piece's conventionality makes it somehow less significant, "patched together" as it is "from homiletic commonplaces and paraphrases and quotations from the Psalms and Gospels." As a "commissioned text," the *Exhortation* is strangely discounted by Viroli despite the fact that the conclusion of his biography turns on a quote from the piece that Viroli uses to substantiate Machiavelli's purely secular "charity" (258–59). The expediency of this interpretive move begs a host of deeper questions that I will try to unravel here.

6. Of recent interest is Benedetto Fontana, "Love of Country and Love of God: The Political Uses of Religion in Machiavelli," *Journal of the History of Ideas* 60, no. 4 (1999), 639–58; this issue of the *Journal* is devoted to the question of Machiavelli and religion and includes a number of fine interventions. Fontana's analysis of the complexities of Machiavelli's views on religion is rich and compelling, but I take issue with his characterization of Machiavelli's Augustine, whose *caritas* and typology of the two cities are rendered an "exclusively political concept" by Machiavelli. Fontana rightly sees Machiavelli reinventing Augustine much as Augustine reinvented Cicero and the ancients, but I think he overstates the purely political nature of Machiavelli's move in returning to the ancients; as I argue here, Machiavelli has a civic *theology* that is not so easily categorized. More persuasive is John Najemy, "Papirius and the Chickens, or Machiavelli on the Necessity of Interpreting Religion," in the same volume as Fontana, 659–81. To my mind one of the most historically-sensitive Machiavelli scholars of the last twenty years, Najemy correctly sees that for Machiavelli, "Religion is never a given," but "always a matter of interpretation." Najemy does not mean this in the sense that this interpretation is optional (or so contingent as to be content-less) but rather that "the only unchanging truth about religion" for Machiavelli is the hermeneutic imperative to make sense of it; Najemy's close reading of the Machiavellian corpus draws the broad outlines of Machiavelli's theological context—what I attempt here is to sketch its Augustinian dimensions. See also Bjorn Qviller, "The Machiavellian Cosmos," *History of Political Thought* 17, no. 3 (1996): 326–53. Qviller borrows his title from Anthony J. Parel, *The Machiavellian Cosmos* (New Haven: Yale UP, 1992). Qviller is right to take Parel to task for overstating Machiavelli's atheistic cosmos, and he does a sound job of showing Machiavelli's indebtedness to Augustine for his anthropology. Qviller seems to err nonetheless in arguing that this genealogy becomes the pretext for Machiavelli's rejection of classical conceptions of justice—one comes away from Qviller and Parel alike feeling that Christianity remains the foil of Machiavelli rather than a true interlocutor. A more philosophically grounded account is given in Alfred Stern, "The Irreversibility of History," *Diogenes* 29 (1960): 1–15; this study connects Augustine and Machiavelli in terms of their understanding of temporality, and of the classical world's running debate on the eternity of the world; see also Gennaro Sasso's masterful "De aeternitate mundi," in *Machiavelli e gli antichi e altri saggi*, 3 vols. (Milan, 1987–8), 1: 167–399. Another provocative intervention is Giuseppe Prezzolini, "The Christian Roots of Machiavelli's Moral Pessimism," *Review of National Literatures* 1, no. 1 (1970): 26–27—Prezzolini's longer Italian study of Machiavelli, *Machiavelli anticristo*, uses Machiavelli's Christian lineage to demonstrate his ultimate divorce from that tradition [see *Machiavelli*, trans. Gioconda Savine (New York: Farrar, Straus, & Giroux, 1967)]. And although Augustine is by no means his explicit subject, one should not overlook the sensitivity to the Augustinian character of the temporal and political dilemmas facing Machiavelli in J. G. A. Pocock, *The Machiavellian Moment: Florentine Political Thought and the Atlantic Republican Tradition* (Princeton: Princeton UP, 1975), esp. pt. 1, ch. 1. Lastly, for passing insights on Augustine and Renaissance political theory, see Quentin Skinner, *The Foundations of Modern Political Thought*, 2 vols. (Cambridge: Cambridge UP, 1978), esp. vol. 1; and De Grazia, 203–5, 265–66 (see note 5).

7. For an account of the Continental reception of Machiavelli that is among the first to do real justice to the richness of early modern Machiavellianism (both pro and contra), see Victoria Kahn, *Machiavellian Rhetoric: From the Counter-Reformation to Milton* (Princeton: Princeton UP, 1994). For the English tradition specifically, see Felix Raab, *The English Face of Machiavelli: A Changing Interpretation, 1500–1700* (London: Routledge, 1964). More recently, see Graham Maddox, "The Secular Reformation and the Influence of Machiavelli," *The Journal of Religion* 82, no. 14 (2002): 539–63; and Cary J. Nederman, "Amazing Grace: Fortune, God, and Free Will in Machiavelli's Thought," same volume as Fontana (see note 6), 617–38.

8. This reductionism has had many sources, only some of which I can allude to here. Two obvious and related sources would be the nationalism of Italy's Risorgimento and nineteenth-century European historicism at large; Jacob Burckhardt facilitates this view of humanism and Machiavelli alike as anti-Christian in his *Civilization of the Renaissance in Italy*, 2 vols., trans. S. G. C. Middlemore (New York: Harper, 1958), esp. vol. 1, pt. 1. In the twentieth century, three otherwise excellent studies stand out, both for their insights in telling certain stories about modernity and their occasional misreadings of Machiavelli himself—Friedrich Meinecke, *Machiavellism: The Doctrine of Raison d'etat and its Place in Modern History*, trans. Douglas Scott (New Haven: Yale UP, 1957); Leo Strauss, *Thoughts on Machiavelli* (Chicago: Univ. of Chicago Press, 1958); and Ernst Cassirer, *The Myth of the State* (New Haven: Yale UP, 1973), esp. chs. 10–12. Different from one another as they are, all three see Machiavelli for better or worse as Cassirer does, standing "at the gateway of the modern world" (140) as the embodiment of modernity's privileging of pure technique over Platonic *techne*. The recurring narrative here is Machiavelli's wholesale rejection of Christianity and his overturning of even classical values. One corrective to this view is the cogent reevaluation of twentieth-century Machiavelli scholarship in Isaiah Berlin's "The Question of Machiavelli," in *Against the Current: Essays in the History of Ideas*, ed. Henry Hardy (Princeton: Princeton UP, 2001), 25–79; Berlin's thorough and comprehensive study is no mere summary—he brings much-needed nuance to Machiavelli studies, capturing the drama of his reception without drowning out Machiavelli himself. Lastly, there is a more recent and sorely understudied source for this misreading of Machiavelli's relationship to the Christian tradition—popular writings on business management, conflict resolution, social Darwinism, and contemporary politics. Just a few examples suffice. In the management genre, see Antony Jay, *Management and Machiavelli : Discovering a New Science of Management in the Timeless Principles of Statecraft* (San Diego, Pfeiffer, 1994); Stanley Bing, *What Would Machiavelli Do? The Ends Justify the Meanness* (New York: HarperBusiness, 2000); and *Machiavelli, Marketing, and Management*, ed. Harris, Lock, & Rees (London & New York: Routledge, 2000). For conflict resolution, see Fisher, Kopelman, & Schneider, *Beyond Machiavelli: Tools for Coping with Conflict* (New York: Penguin, 1996). For a wildly pseudo-scientific, social Darwinist take, see Bravata-Brozinsky & Gibson, *Eat or Be Eaten . . . The Truth about Our Species: The Marriage of Darwin and Machiavelli* (Patchogue, NY: Jake and Charlie Productions, 1999), the first in a promised series entitled *Unlearning Life*. And for a social Darwinist take from the mainstream (but one no less controversial), see Andrew Whiten and Richard Byrne's *Machiavellian Intelligence: Social Expertise*

and the Evolution of Intellect in Monkeys, Apes, and Humans (Oxford & New York: Oxford UP, 1988). Lastly, for two very problematic, yet arguably Machiavellian efforts to make the remote past speak to our political and economic present, see: Michael A. Ledeen, *Machiavelli on Modern Leadership: Why Machiavelli's Iron Rules Are as Timely and Important Today as Five Centuries Ago* (New York: St. Martin's Press, 2000); and Robert D. Kaplan, *Warrior Politics: Why Leadership Demands a Pagan Ethos* (New York: Random House, 2002). I am currently at work on a study of these popularizations of Machiavelli entitled "Satisfied and Stupid: Postmodern Princes and Machiavelli in Late Capitalism." My contention is that these popular writings are now as important a part of the tradition of Machiavellianism as any other; the interpretive failures of these texts have been little impediment to their "canonization."

9. I imagine this essay as an effort to account for the relationship without falling into what I perceive to be the pitfall of D.W. Robertson's otherwise masterful *Preface to Chaucer: Studies in Medieval Perspectives* (Princeton: Princeton UP, 1962). Robertson's erudition remains astonishing, but one comes away from his Augustinian reading of the Middle Ages with the sense that a template has overpowered what had been texts with lives of their own. With this caveat in mind, I will examine Augustine's impact on Machiavelli as one instance of Machiavelli's peculiar yet recognizably humanist appropriation of past models. In this vein, we will look at Augustine as but one of many influential sources on Machiavelli's political theology.

10. See note 8.

11. See Qviller, note 6.

12. On the *Annales* school, see Peter Burke, *The French Historical Revolution: The Annales School, 1929–89* (Stanford: Stanford UP, 1990); and Fernand Braudel's *On History*, trans. Sarah Matthews (London: Weidenfeld & Nicolson, 1980), esp. his key essay, "History and the Social Sciences: The Longue Durée." See also Michel Foucault, *The Order of Things: An Archaeology of the Human Sciences*, trans. A. M. Sheridan Smith (New York: Vintage Books, 1973); and Foucault, *The Archaeology of Knowledge and the Discourse on Lauguage*, trans. Smith (New York: Pantheon Books, 1972). For examples of how Marxism can both powerfully illuminate and threaten to constrain study of Machiavelli, see Antonio Gramsci, *The Modern Prince and Other Writings*, trans. Louis Marks (New York: International Publishers, 1957); Raymond Aron, "Machiavelli and Marx" in *Politics and History: Selected Essays*, ed. Miriam Conant (New York: Macmillan, 1978), 87–101; Benedetto Fontana, *Hegemony and Power: On the Relation between Gramsci and Machiavelli* (Minneapolis: Univ. of Minnesota Press, 1993); and Louis Althusser, *Machiavelli and Us*, trans. Gregory Elliott (London & New York: Verso, 1999). Lastly, for the problems and possibilities of reading Machiavelli through the lens of liberalism, see: Pierre Manent, *An Intellectual History of Liberalism*, trans. Rebecca Balinski, ed. Thomas Pavel & Mark Lilla, *New French Thought* (Princeton: Princeton UP, 1994), esp. chs. 1–3; Vickie Sullivan, *Machiavelli's Three Romes: Religion, Human Liberty, and Politics Reformed* (Dekalb, IL: Northern Illinois UP, 1996); Adam Danâel, *A Case for Freedom: Machiavellian Humanism* (Lanham, MD: UP of America, 1997); Robert Kocis, *Machiavelli Redeemed : Retrieving His Humanist Perspectives on Equality, Power, and Glory* (London: Associated University Presses, 1998).

13. See note 6.

14. St. Augustine, *Concerning the City of God against the Pagans*, trans. Henry Bettenson (New York: Penguin, 1984), 46. Hereafter, I abbreviate references to this text as *De civ.*, followed by book and chapter numbers as given in this edition.

15. We should of course include here Marsilius of Padua's *The Defender of Peace: The "Defensor pacis,"* trans. Alan Gewirth (New York: Harper, 1956). I would contend that Marsilius is caught up in many of the same theological problems and assumptions as Machiavelli; the decisive question is just how Machiavelli's humanism inflected the political discourse he inherited from medieval predecessors.

16. See, for example, Paul Oskar Kristeller, *Renaissance Thought and Its Sources*, ed. Michael Mooney (New York: Columbia UP, 1979), 75–78. This example alone reminds us that we should not underestimate the extent to which Machiavelli's Augustine is filtered through Dante and Petrarca.

17. Machiavelli identifies book 1 as his "trattato universale" in bk. 2, ch. 2 of the *Florentine Histories*, trans. Laura F. Banfield and Harry C. Mansfield, Jr. (Princeton: Princeton UP, 1988). Given that book 1 draws so heavily on late antique and medieval historiography, it is interesting to note how Machiavelli seemingly divides the remainder of the *Histories* from this apparently conventional introduction. It is difficult to tell whether he understands book 1 as a dispensable preamble or as the essential foundation for what is to come; if I am right about Machiavelli's relationship to Augustine, I think it is impossible not to assert the latter.

18. Although much is made of the library of Machiavelli's father Bernardo, especially its newly-bound volume of Livy to which the young Machiavelli no doubt had access (De Grazia, 5–6; see note 5), one is led to ask whether *City of God* or another Augustinian text was included in Bernardo's relatively modest but substantial collection. It would seem likely given the Greek and Roman authors mentioned in most allusions to the library.

19. Machiavelli, *Discourses on Livy*, in *Machiavelli: The Chief Works and Others*, trans. Allan Gilbert, 3 vols. (Durham: Duke UP, 1989). Subsequent references will be abbreviated *Disc.*, followed by the book and chapter number.

20. Hans Baron, *The Crisis of the Early Italian Renaissance: Civic Humanism and Republican Liberty in an Age of Classicism and Tyranny*, rev. ed. (Princeton: Princeton UP, 1966); see also Baron's *Humanistic and Political Literature in Florence and Venice at the Beginning of the Quattrocento: Studies in Criticism and Chronology* (Cambridge, MA: Harvard UP, 1955). Baron's final essays answered many of his detractors and clarified his position: see *In Search of Florentine Civic Humanism: Essays on the Transition from Medieval to Modern Thought*, 2 vols. (Princeton: Princeton UP, 1988). Among Italian scholars, see Eugenio Garin, *Italian Humanism: Philosophy and Civic Life in the Renaissance*, trans. Peter Munz (Oxford: Blackwell Publishers, 1965).

21. See Felix Gilbert, *Machiavelli and Guicciardini: Politics and History in Sixteenth-Century Florence* (New York: Norton, 1984); *Machiavelli and Republicanism*, ed. Gisela Bock, Quentin Skinner, & Maurizio Viroli (Cambridge: Cambridge UP, 1990); John Najemy, "Baron's Machiavelli and Renaissance Republicanism," *American Historical Review* 101, no. 1 (1996): 119–30; and Maurizio Viroli, *Machiavelli*, ed. Mark Philp, *Founders of Modern Political and Social Thought* (Oxford & New York: Oxford UP, 1998).

22. The major work in this vein was Paul Oskar Kristeller, *Renaissance Thought: The Classic, Scholastic, and Humanist Strains* (New York: Harper, 1955), a text which served an important purpose in delineating the competing modes of thought in the period as an antidote to the presumption of humanism's ubiquity or decisiveness. Later, in *Renaissance Thought and Its Sources* (see note 16), Kristeller insisted that humanism was fundamentally a literary program with a particular philological orientation to the past, having not much more than a passing, anecdotal interest in its political present. An indirect influence on Renaissance culture at large, less philosophy than rhetoric, humanism could be no more and no less than a professional vocation. In rejecting humanists as viable philosophers, he shares with Burckhardt doubts about the "moral" dimensions of humanist thought, citing humanists' adherence to the split between philosophy and rhetoric initiated by the Romans. A similarly skeptical tack was taken by Jerrold Seigel: see his "'Civic Humanism' or Ciceronian Rhetoric? The Culture of Petrarch and Bruni," *Past and Present*, no. 34 (1966): 3–48, and *Rhetoric and Philosophy in Renaissance Humanism: The Union of Eloquence and Wisdom, Petrarch to Valla* (Princeton: Princeton UP, 1968). Lastly, there is Mark Hulliung's *Citizen Machiavelli* (Princeton: Princeton UP, 1983), which explores the problematic imperialism underlying Florentine claims about humanism and liberty.

23. See Anthony Grafton and Lisa Jardine, *From Humanism to the Humanities: Education and the Liberal Arts in Fifteenth- and Sixteenth-Century Europe* (Cambridge, MA: Harvard UP, 1986); and Paul F. Grendler, *Schooling in Renaissance Italy: Literacy and Learning, 1300–1600* (Baltimore: Johns Hopkins UP, 1989). A recent and illuminating study of humanism's relationship to the professions is Douglas Biow, *Doctors, Ambassadors, Secretaries: Humanism and the Professions in Renaissance Italy* (Chicago & London: Univ. of Chicago Press, 2002); see esp. 160–74 on Machiavelli as Florentine secretary. Biow deftly avoids most of the simplifications that the civic humanism debate has fostered on both sides.

24. Stephanie Jed, *Chaste Thinking: The Rape of Lucretia and the Birth of Humanism* (Bloomington: Indiana UP, 1989).

25. See Siegel (note 22).

26. Jed, 4–5 (note 24). Jed is forthcoming about the aims of her methodology in looking at humanism "not from the perspective of what humanism may have meant to its cultural proponents in fifteenth-century Florence, but rather from the perspective of humanism's reception and continued transmission in intellectual and cultural settings in the United States today" (6). She claims an interest in "questions which the Florentine humanists themselves did not ask and could not have articulated, given the fact that this moment and place in the transmission of humanism are quite different from the historical context in which they worked" (6). An important question arises for all scholars who bridge past and present in this way: Does not this method ironically enough threaten a kind of violence upon the past commensurable with that done to Lucretia?

27. Jed, 10.

28. Jed, 8–13. For her understanding of Machiavelli's place in the history of mercantile writing as an implicit challenge to humanism's model of textual castigation, see 117–20.

29. Jed, 123.

30. Consider Machiavelli's relation of the fate of Stefano Porcari in the *Florentine Histories.* Member of a Roman patrician family, Porcari spent time in Florence as Capitano del Popolo from 1427–8, mediated between anti-papal forces and Eugenius IV in 1434, worked on and off for the Papacy, and was exiled to Bologna in 1448 on suspicion of conspiracy. Although it is unclear whether he was culpable in that case or not, Porcari decided to merit the charge by fomenting the revolt against Nicholas V that led to his execution as described in the *Histories* 6. 29 (see note 17) [Source for biography: J. R. Hale, ed., *The Thames and Hudson Encyclopaedia of the Italian Renaissance* (London: Thames & Hudson, 1981), 264]. Machiavelli essentially skewers Porcari for his naïve brand of civic humanism, and as much as implies that Dante and Petrarca led Porcari to his doom. I contend that this is symptomatic of Machiavelli's ultimate disillusionment with civic humanism—this question is beyond the scope of the current essay and its exploration of the uses made of Augustine in Machiavelli's earlier works. I deal with the *Histories* at length in an article submitted for publication, "The Alloy of Florentine Identity and Machiavelli's Entertainment of Xenophobia."

31. For more on Machiavelli and the Lucretia of both the *Discourses* and *Mandragola,* see Joseph M. Knippenberg, "Virtue, Honor, and Reputation: Machiavelli's Appropriation of Christianity in the 'Rape' of Lucrezia," in *Poets, Princes, and Private Citizens: Literary Alternatives to Postmodern Politics,* ed. Knippenberg & Lawler (Lanham, MD: Rowman & Littlefield, 1996); Mercedes Maroto Camino, "My Honor I'll Bequeath unto the Knife: Public Heroism, Private Sacrifice, and Early Modern Rapes of Lucrece," in *Imagining Culture: Essays in Early Modern History and Literature,* ed. Jonathan Hart (New York: Garland, 2001); Ronald Martinez, "The Pharmacy of Machiavelli: Roman Lucretia in *Mandragola,*" *Renaissance Drama* 14 (1983): 1–43; Patricia Vilches, "The Delegate Womb: Lucrezia's Body as Political Tool in Machiavelli's *La mandragola,*" *American Journal of Italian Studies* 22, no. 60 (1999), 99–124; and Melissa Matthes, *The Rape of Lucretia and the Founding of Republics: Readings in Livy, Machiavelli, and Rousseau* (University Park, PA: Pennsylvania State Press, 2000).

32. This sort of reading is consistent with the school of thought that makes *The Prince* a satire, a claim that can be traced back in spirit to the sixteenth-century jurist Alberico Gentili, the Italian-born Protestant who fled to England and became Regius Professor of Civil Law at Oxford. Reading *The Prince* against the grain, as it were, has found eloquent spokesmen in Gramsci (see note 12) and Garrett Mattingly [see "Machiavelli's *Prince*: Political Science or Political Satire?" *American Scholar* 27 (1958): 482–91]. I think there is *something* to Mattingly's argument in the sense that most of the examples in *The Prince* are either of ambitious failures (e.g., Cesare Borgia) or near-mythical success-stories (e.g., Moses)—in either case, it would seem the Medici prince reading the text would not necessarily be encouraged to action as much as paralyzed and overwhelmed by the prospect of failure. Still, at the end of the day I find myself coming back to the eschatology of ch. 26, and I am convinced that Machiavelli hopes and expects (at least here) that someone will rise to the occasion of Italy's redemption, no matter how difficult it might prove. The *Discourses* offer a whole other set of problems for the Mattingly thesis, particularly with Machiavelli's skepticism about conspiracies and crafty advisors; cf. *Disc.* 2. 31; 3. 16–17; 3. 35; and 3. 6. I think the best Machiavelli hopes for dissenters

under tyrants (as he may well view himself) is the feigned madness of a Brutus. Failing the dissenter's opportunity to act, his only compensation is being able to serve the state.

33. Machiavelli, "The Death of Piero Soderini," trans. Robert Adams in *The Prince*, 135 (see note 1).

34. Machiavelli, "Letter to Guicciardini of 17 May 1521," trans. Allan Gilbert in *The Letters of Machiavelli: A Selection*, trans. Allan Gilbert (Chicago: Univ. of Chicago Press, 1988).

35. For more on Machiavelli as critic of the Savonarola regime, see Marcia L Colish, "Republicanism, Religion, and Machiavelli's Savonarolan Moment," *Journal of the History of Ideas* 60, no. 4 (1999): 597–617.

36. Victoria Kahn is not convinced of the absolute nature of Machiavelli's moral distinction here, suggesting that the Agathocles scene enacts a complicated mechanism of value-opposition which Machiavelli deploys throughout his texts as a "revision" of the simplicity of "the humanists' prudential rhetoric" (*Machiavellian Rhetoric*, 37, see note 7). As a result, Machiavelli's rhetoric cannot be reduced to the elaboration of an ends/means equation as those contend who view him as the first modern "technician" of politics. Kahn argues: "In his demoralization of prudence, Machiavelli implies that the humanist view of politics is not rhetorical enough. For all the humanist emphasis on prudence as a faculty of deliberation about particulars, the insistence that prudence also be ethical amounts to a refusal to admit that to be ethical in every case is harmful and impractical" (38). *Disc.* 3. 40–41 might confirm or contradict Kahn's thesis; they certainly seem to contradict one another in their juxtaposition of two claims—that fraud cannot be glorious and that inglorious measures are demanded when survival of the state is at issue. Either Machiavelli is categorically separating glory from necessity knowing full well what each is and what each demands, or Kahn is right and Machiavellian prudence never truly settles on a stable (i.e., non-relational) definition of either. For more on prudence in Machiavelli, see Patricia J. Osmond, "Sallust and Machiavelli: From Civic Humanism to Political Prudence," *Journal of Medieval & Renaissance Studies*, 23 (1993): 407–38; and Eugene Garver, *Machiavelli and the History of Prudence* (Madison: Univ. of Wisconsin Press, 1987).

37. Machiavelli, *The Prince*, trans. Adams, 71 (see note 1). Subsequent references are parenthetical and by chapter number.

38. Of course, Augustine finds a similar exemplarity in those other violent myths of Roman origins—Romulus and Remus (*De civ.*, 15. 5), and the rape of the Sabine women (2. 17; 3. 13). What is most compelling about the Lucretia narrative, however, is the way in which Augustine and Machiavelli seem to converge over it as an evacuated *locus* of glory.

39. See Giorgio Agamben's wonderful *Homo Sacer: Sovereign Power and Bare Life*, trans. Daniel Heller-Roazen (Stanford: Stanford UP, 1998).

40. Machiavelli, *Mandragola*, trans. Mera J. Flaumenhaft (Prospect Heights, IL: Waveland Press, 1981), 36. Subsequent references are by act and scene.

41. See note 31, esp. Knippenberg and Martinez.

42. See note 31, esp. Vilches.

43. For a thorough account of Machiavelli's gendering of his politics at large, one of the best studies remains Hanna F. Pitkin, *Fortune Is a Woman: Gender and Politics in the*

Thought of Niccolò Machiavelli (Berkeley: Univ. of California Press, 1984); for Lucretia, see esp. 29–31, 112–19, 243–48.

44. For more on the "mirror of princes," see Allan Gilbert, *Machiavelli's Prince and Its Forerunners: The Prince as a Typical Book* De regimine principum (New York: Barnes & Noble, 1968); and Felix Gilbert, "The Humanist Concept of the Prince and 'The Prince' of Machiavelli," in *History: Choice and Commitment* (Cambridge: Harvard UP, 1977), 91–114.

45. Arno J. Mayer offers an analysis of the French and Russian Revolutions that takes as its mode a reconstruction of the history of terror. Mayer tells part of his story through the lens of early modernity and Machiavelli in particular, but one wishes he would flesh out the historical dimensions of Machiavelli's own arrival at an ethos of terror. See Mayer's *The Furies: Violence and Terror in the French and Russian Revolutions* (Princeton: Princeton UP, 2000), esp. ch. 4; and for more on the classical world and its conception of terror, N. Wood, "Sallust's Theorem: A Comment on 'Fear' in Western Political Thought," *History of Political Thought* 16, no. 2 (1995): 174–90. While the American academy has turned anew to terror since 2001, one is still left wondering whether we have adequately plumbed the historical, moral, or epistemological depths of terror in the many centuries prior to 9–11 (or in the many cultural contexts outside the limits of what has been crassly rendered an "American" tragedy).

46. John M. Najemy, *Between Friends: Discourses of Power and Desire in the Machiavelli-Vettori Letters of 1513–1515* (Princeton: Princeton UP, 1993), esp. 335–49.

47. For more on Machiavellian exemplarity in the context of the European tradition, consult Timothy Hampton, *Writing from History: The Rhetoric of Exemplarity in Renaissance Literature* (Ithaca: Cornell UP, 1990), esp. 31–80.

48. Pocock, *Machiavellian Moment* (see note 6).

49. This politics and language of spectacle at the scene of terror is worth comparing to *Prince* ch. 7, where Cesare Borgia's brutal mutilation of his ex-enforcer Remirro de Orco leaves citizens "satisfied and stupefied." Those sections of *The Prince* that deal with Cesare are in essence Machiavelli's most famous exploration of politics as a sacrificial ritual.

50. *Disc.* 1. 12 and 2. 5 emphasize Machiavelli's condemnation of the Church as an institution per se, not so much in terms of doctrine as misapplication of doctrine. It is also significant that side by side with Machiavelli's critique of the Church is an insistence that the Roman Empire bears equal responsibility for overwhelming the liberty of neighboring republics and reducing *virtù* in the world (*Disc.* 2. 2). What Machiavelli says about the sapping of communal *virtù* is comparable to claims made by Augustine in *City of God*, to the effect that the Roman state truly ceased to be once its already limited virtues had dissipated (*De civ.* 2. 21; 19. 21). Living on as a mere shadow of its former glory, Rome has mistaken "material" for "moral defenses," rendering itself "more hideous while it stood than when it fell" (*De civ.* 2. 2); Machiavelli might simply substitute the Church for Rome in Augustine's formulation.

51. De Grazia, *Machiavelli in Hell*, 59 (see note 5).

52. Machiavelli is clearly drawing not only on the Christian tradition here, but on earlier Florentine Neo-Platonism as well, particularly on the movement's speculations about the mobility of human beings in the ontological hierarchy that leads to pure contempla-

tion of God. The overall relationship between Machiavelli and figures such as Pico della Mirandola and Ficino has been underexamined for the most part, and in many cases dismissed outright in much the way the Augustine/Machiavelli connection has been, under the assumption that Machiavelli has little to say to these predecessors. Peter Godman has helped in telling a better story overall about Machiavelli's relationship to Florentine intellects of previous generations in his recent study, *From Poliziano to Machiavelli: Florentine Humanism in the High Renaissance* (Princeton: Princeton UP, 1998); a proper study of Neo-Platonism through the eyes of Machiavelli and Guicciardini awaits.

53. This understanding of the Medici as aliens is the subject of a recent essay of mine that has been submitted for publication entitled, "Topography and Colonization: The Medici as Foreigners in the Thought of Machiavelli." Also recommended is John Najemy, "Machiavelli and the Medici: The Lessons of Florentine History," *Renaissance Quarterly* 35, no. 4 (1982): 551–76.

54. I deliberately leave out the *Florentine Histories* here; see note 30. For more on the question of the unity of the Machiavellian corpus, see Marcus Fischer, *Well-Ordered License: On the Unity of Machiavelli's Thought* (Lanham, MD: Lexington Books, 2000). Despite the best efforts of this and other studies, the implicit separation of hermeneutic and rhetorical approaches to Machiavelli remains a real limit on our appraisals of him; Kenneth Burke tries intelligently to bridge the gap in *A Rhetoric of Motives* (Berkeley: Univ. of California Press, 1969).

55. For the important issues surrounding the dating and composition of ch. 26, see Hans Baron, "The 'Principe' and the Puzzle of the Date of Chapter 26," *Journal of Medieval and Renaissance Studies* 21, no. 1 (1991): 83–103.

56. Najemy, *Between Friends*, esp. chs. 4 & 7 (see note 46).

57. Machiavelli, *Discourse on Remodeling the Government of Florence*, trans. Allan Gilbert in *Machiavelli: The Chief Works and Others*, 3 vols. (Durham: Duke UP, 1989), 1: 101–15. Subsequent references are by page number as given in this edition.

58. For more on the circle of republican sympathizers to whom Machiavelli explicitly addresses the *Discourses*, see Felix Gilbert, "Bernardo Rucellai and the Orti Oricellari: A Study of the Origin of Modern Political Thought," in *History: Choice and Commitment* (Cambridge: Harvard UP, 1977), 215–46.

59. Burckhardt, *Civilization of the Renaissance in Italy*, 1: 105 (see note 8).

60. Machiavelli's understanding of Plato is slightly different in the *Remodeling* than in ch. 15 of *The Prince*; in ch. 15, Machiavelli famously divorced himself from Plato and the construction of ideal republics of any sort. Yet in the *Remodeling*, he insists that writing politics is the only compensation for not being able to put conceptions into practice, particularly when we fail not through "ignorance" but "impotence for putting [a free government] into practice" (114). The *Remodeling* as much as says that the Platos, Aristotles, and Machiavellis of the world ought to go on fantasizing that they will become lawgivers—in hopes that at least one of their readers truly will. This forbearing attitude toward Plato as idealist is also at work in the case of Augustine, who views Plato as the good Christian waiting to get out of every pagan (cf. *De civ.* 8. 5; 8. 11).

61. Machiavelli, "On Occasion," trans. Robert Adams, *The Prince*, (135) (see note 1).

62. One resource for Dante might be the discussion in *City of God* 18. 47, which addresses the issue of whether there were "any citizens of the Heavenly City outside the

race of Israel before the Christian era." Dante's exceptions to his own rules about the ancients notwithstanding, Augustine remains a key figure in the *Commedia*'s "urban planning" of the pagan Limbo.

63. I am particularly indebted to my teacher Albert Ascoli and to John Najemy for introducing me to the complexities not only of Machiavelli's *Discourse on Remodeling*, but of Machiavelli's counsel at large; the reading I develop of Machiavelli's political eschatology owes much to conversations with them and to colleagues met during the 1993 NEH Seminar, "Crisis and Evasion in Renaissance Italy, 1494–1527," led by Professors Ascoli and Najemy at Northwestern University. My debts to Najemy are obvious throughout these notes. Also highly recommended is Ascoli, "Machiavelli's Gift of Counsel," in *Machiavelli and the Discourse of Literature*, ed. Ascoli and Kahn (Ithaca: Cornell UP, 1993), 219–57. Writing of ch. 26 of *The Prince*, Ascoli argues that "in fact, Machiavelli's gift of prudential counsel is at its *most* pragmatic and realistic precisely in its prediction that it will be accepted and implemented only if it is indeed also a truly prophetic gift of the Holy Spirit—however unlikely that may appear to be in the terms of *The Prince*" (256). Let me suggest, therefore, that Augustinian eschatology fuels the "magical realism" of Machiavelli, which in the *Discourse on Remodeling* takes on its fullest, most perilous, and arguably most level-headed form.

BIBLIOGRAPHY

Texts and Translations of Augustine

Augustine. *Against the Academics*. Trans. and annotated by J. J. O'Meara. Ancient Christian Writers. Westminster, MD: The Newman Press, 1950.

———. *Arianism and Other Heresies*. Trans. R. Teske. Hyde Park, NY: New City Press, 1995.

———. *Concerning the City of God against the Pagans*. Trans. H. Bettenson. New York: Penguin, 1984.

———. *Confessiones*. Text and commentary by J. J. O'Donnell. 2 vols. Oxford: Clarendon Press, 1992.

———. *Confessions*. Trans. R. S. Pine-Coffin. New York: Penguin Books, 1961.

———. *Confessions*. Trans. J. K. Ryan. New York et al.: Image Books, 1960.

———. *de Civitate Dei*. Eds. B. Dombart and A. Kalb. *Corpus Christianorum, Series Latina*, vols. 47–48. Turnhout: Brepols, 1954.

———. *Exposition of the Psalms*. Trans. and notes by Maria Boulding. Hyde Park, NY: New City Press, 2001.

———. *The First Catechetical Instruction*. Trans. J. P. Christopher. Westminster, MD: The Newman Bookshop, 1946.

———. *Letters*. Trans J. G. Cunningham. *Nicene and Post-Nicene Fathers*, First Series, vol. I. T. & T. Clark, 1886.

———. *Letters*. Trans. Sr. Wilfrid Parsons. *The Fathers of the Church, A New Translation*. Washington, DC: The Catholic University of America Press, 1953.

———. *Of True Religion*. Trans. J. H. S. Burleigh. Chicago: Henry Regnery Company, 1964.

———. *On Christian Doctrine*. Trans D. W. Robertson, Jr. *Nicene and Post-Nicene Fathers*, First Series, vol. II. New York: Scribners, 1958.

———. *On Free Choice of the Will*. Trans. Thomas Williams. Indianapolis: Hackett Publishing Company, 1993.

———. *Sermons.* Trans. E. Hill. *The Works of Saint Augustine: A Translation for the 21st Century.* Hyde Park, NY: New City Press, 1995.

———. *Soliloquies* Trans. K. Paffenroth. Hyde Park, NY: New City Press, 2000.

———. *Tractates on the Gospel of John.* Trans. J. W. Rettig. *Fathers of the Church* 92. Washington, DC: Catholic University of America Press, 1995.

———. *The Trinity.* Trans. E. Hill. *The Works of Saint Augustine: A Translation for the 21st Century.* Hyde Park, NY: New City Press, 1994.

———. "The Work of Religious." Trans. S. Mary Sarah Muldowney. In *Saint Augustine: Treatises on Various Subjects.* New York: The Fathers of the Church, 1952.

Other Works

Addams, J. *Democracy and Social Ethics.* Cambridge: Belknap Press, 1964 [1902].

———. *Twenty Years at Hull-House.* New York: Macmillan, 1981 [1910].

Adorno, T. and M. Horkheimer. *The Dialectic of Enlightenment.* New York: Herder and Herder, 1972 [1944].

Agamben, G. *Homo Sacer: Sovereign Power and Bare Life.* Trans. D. Heller-Roazen. Stanford: Stanford University Press, 1998.

Althusser, L. *Machiavelli and Us.* Trans. G. Elliott. London: Verso, 1999.

Aquinas, Thomas. *Summa Theologica.* Trans. Fathers of the English Dominican Province. Reprinted by Christian Classics. New York: Benziger Brothers, 1981.

Arendt, H. *Between Past and Future: Eight Exercises in Political Thought.* New York: Viking, 1954.

———. *The Human Condition.* Chicago: University of Chicago Press, 1958.

———. *The Life of the Mind.* New York: Harcourt Brace Jovanovich, 1978.

———. *Love and St. Augustine,* ed. J. V. Scott and J. C. Stark. Chicago: University of Chicago Press, 1996.

Aristotle, *The Politics.* Trans. C. Lord. Chicago: University of Chicago Press, 1984.

Arquilliere, H.-X. *L'Augustinisme Politique.* Paris: J. Vrin, 1955.

Asad, T. *Genealogies of Religion: Discipline and Reasons of Power in Christianity and Islam.* Baltimore, MD: Johns Hopkins University Press, 1993.

Ascoli, A. "Machiavelli's Gift of Counsel." In *Machiavelli and the Discourse of Literature,* ed. A. Ascoli and V. Kahn. Ithaca: Cornell University Press, 1993. 219–57.

Atkins, E. M., and R. J. Dodaro, eds. *Augustine: Political Writings.* Cambridge, UK: Cambridge University Press, 2001.

Ayres, L. "Remember that You Are Catholic (Serm. 52.2): Augustine on the Unity of the Triune God." *Journal of Early Christian Studies* 8:1 (2000) 39–82.

Babcock, W. S. "Augustine's Interpretation of Romans (A. D. 394–396)." *Augustinian Studies* 10 (1979) 55–74.

Barnes, T. "Religion and Society in the Age of Theodosius." In H. Meynell, ed., *Grace, Politics, and Desire: Essays on Augustine.* Calgary: University of Calgary Press, 1990. 157–74.

Baron, H. *The Crisis of the Early Italian Renaissance: Civic Humanism and Republican Liberty in an Age of Classicism and Tyranny.* Rev. ed. Princeton: Princeton University Press, 1966.

———. *Humanistic and Political Literature in Florence and Venice at the Beginning of the Quattrocento: Studies in Criticism and Chronology.* Cambridge, MA: Harvard University Press, 1955.

———. "The 'Principe' and the Puzzle of the Date of Chapter 26." *Journal of Medieval and Renaissance Studies* 21:1 (1991) 83–103.

———. *In Search of Florentine Civic Humanism: Essays on the Transition from Medieval to Modern Thought.* 2 vols. Princeton: Princeton University Press, 1988.

Barr, R. "The Two Cities in Saint Augustine." *Laval theologique et philosophique* 18 (1982) 211–29.

Bashor, P. S. "Plato and Aristotle on Friendship." *The Journal of Value Inquiry* 2 (1958) 269–80.

Bastiaensen, A. A. R., ed. *Vita di Cipriano, Vita di Ambrogio, Vita di Agostino.* Rome: Fondazione Lorenzo Valla, 1975.

Bathory, P. D. *Political Theory as Public Confession: The Social and Political Thought of St. Augustine of Hippo.* New Brunswick: Transaction Books, 1981.

Baynes, N. H. *The Political Ideas of St. Augustine's 'De Civitate Dei.'* London: Historical Association, 1936.

Bell, D. "The Mood of Three Generations," in *The End of Ideology: On the Exhaustion of Political Ideas in the Fifties.* New York: Free Press, 1960. 299–314.

Benjamin, W. *The Arcades Project.* Trans. H. Eiland and K. McLaughlin. Cambridge and London: Belknap Press, 1999.

———. "On Language as Such and on the Language of Man." In *Reflections: Essays, Aphorisms, Autobiographical Writings*, ed. Peter Demetz. New York: Harcourt, Brace, Jovanovich, 1978.

———. *One-Way Street and Other Writings.* Trans. E. Jephcott and K. Shorter, London: Verso, 1997 [1979].

———. "Theses on the Philosophy of History." In *Illuminations: Essays and Reflections*, trans. H. Zohn. New York, 1969.

Bennet, J. *The Enchantment of Modern Life: Attachments, Crossings, and Ethics.* Princeton: Princeton University Press, 2001.

Berlin, I. "The Question of Machiavelli." In *Against the Current: Essays in the History of Ideas*, ed. Henry Hardy. Princeton: Princeton University Press, 2001. 25–79.

———. "Two Concepts of Liberty." In *Four Essays on Liberty.* Oxford: Oxford University Press, 1969. 118–172.

Berry, W. *Home Economics.* New York: Farrar, Strauss, and Giroux, 1987.

———. *Sex, Economy, Freedom, and Society.* New York: Pantheon Books, 1993.

———. *What Are People For?* New York: North Point Press, 1990.

Bing, Stanley. *What Would Machiavelli Do? The Ends Justify the Meanness.* New York: HarperBusiness, 2000.

Biow, D. *Doctors, Ambassadors, Secretaries: Humanism and the Professions in Renaissance Italy.* Chicago: University of Chicago Press, 2002.

Birnbaum, N. *After Progress: American Social Reform and European Socialism in the Twentieth Century.* New York: Oxford University Press, 2001.

Blake, N. *Beloved Community: The Cultural Criticism of Randolph Bourne, Van Wyck Brooks, Waldo Frank, and Lewis Mumford.* Chapel Hill: University of North Carolina Press, 1990.

Bock, G., Q. Skinner, and M. Viroli, eds. *Machiavelli and Republicanism*. Cambridge: Cambridge University Press, 1990.

Bori, P. C. *Chiesa Primitiva: L'immagine della comunità delle origini – Atti 2,42–47; 4,32–37 –nella storia della chiesa antica*. Brescia: Paideia Editrice, 1974.

Boswell, J. *Christianity, Social Tolerance, and Homosexuality: Gay People in Western Europe from the Beginning of the Christian Era to the Fourteenth Century*. Chicago: University of Chicago Press, 1980.

Bourke, V. *Augustine's View of Reality*. Villanova, PA: Villanova University Press, 1964.

———, ed. *The Essential Augustine*. 2nd ed. Indianapolis: Hackett, 1974.

Bourne, R. "The Experimental Life." In *Randolph Bourne: The Radical Will: Selected Writings 1911–1918*, ed. O. Hansen. Berkeley: University of California Press, 1992 [1977]. 149–58.

———. "John Dewey's Philosophy." In *Randolph Bourne: The Radical Will: Selected Writings 1911–1918*, ed. O. Hansen. Berkeley: University of California Press, 1992 [1977]. 332.

———. "Trans-National America." In *Randolph Bourne: The Radical Will: Selected Writings 1911–1918*, ed. O. Hansen. Berkeley: University of California Press, 1992 [1977]. 260–64.

———. "Twilight of Idols." In *Randolph Bourne: The Radical Will: Selected Writings 1911–1918*, ed. O. Hansen. Berkeley: University of California Press, 1992 [1977]. 338–39, 342–43.

———. "The State." In *Randolph Bourne: The Radical Will: Selected Writings 1911–1918*, ed. O. Hansen. Berkeley: University of California Press, 1992 [1977]. 355, 358–59, 361, 367, 382.

Bowlin, J. "Augustine on Justifying Coercion." *Annual Society of Christian Ethics* 17 (1997) 49–70.

Boyle, N. *Who Are We Now? Christian Humanism and the Global Market from Hegel to Heaney*. Notre Dame: University of Notre Dame Press, 1998.

Brown, N. O. *Life Against Death: The Psychoanalytical Meaning of History*. Middletown: Wesleyan University Press, 1985 [1959].

Brown, P. *Augustine of Hippo: A Biography*. Berkeley and Los Angeles: University of California Press, 1967. Rev. ed. 2000.

———. "St. Augustine's Attitude to Religious Coercion" in *Religion and Society in the Age of St. Augustine*, ed. P. Brown. New York: Harper and Row, 1972. 262–78.

———. "Political Society." In R. Markus, ed. *Augustine: A Collection of Critical Essays*. Garden City, NY: Doubleday Anchor Books, 1972. 311–35.

———. *Poverty and Leadership in Late Antiquity*. The Menahem Stern Jerusalem Lectures. Hanover, NH: University Press of New England, 2002.

———. *Power and Persuasion in Late Antiquity. Towards a Christian Empire*. Madison: University of Wisconsin Press, 1992.

Brunt, P. A. *Roman Imperial Themes*. Oxford: Clarendon Press, 1990.

Burckhardt, J. *Civilization of the Renaissance in Italy*. 2 vols. Trans. S. G. C. Middlemore. New York: Harper, 1958.

Burke, Peter. *The French Historical Revolution: The Annales School, 1929–1989*. Stanford: Stanford University Press, 1990.

Burnaby, J. *Amor Dei: A Study of the Religion of St. Augustine.* London: Hodder & Stoughton, 1947.

Burnell, P. J. "Is the Augustinian Heaven Inhuman? The Arguments of Martin Heidegger and Hannah Arendt." In *History, Apocalypse, and the Secular Imagination: New Essays on Augustine's* City of God, ed. M. Vessey, K. Pollman, and A. Fitzgerald. Bowling Green, OH: Philosophy Documentation Center, 1999. 283–92.

———. "The Problem of Service to Unjust Regimes in Augustine's *City of God*," *Journal of the History of Ideas* 54:2 (1993), 177–88.

———. "The Status of Politics in Augustine's *City of God.*" *History of Political Thought* 13 (1992) 13–29.

Burns, J. P. "Augustine's Role in the Imperial Action against Pelagius." *Journal of Theological Studies* (n.s.) 30 (1979) 67–83.

Burt, D. X. "Augustine on the Authentic Approach to Death." *Augustinianum* 28 (1988) 527–63.

———. *Friendship and Society: An Introduction to Augustine's Practical Philosophy.* Grand Rapids: Eerdmans, 1999.

Camino, M. M. "'My Honor I'll Bequeath unto the Knife': Public Heroism, Private Sacrifice, and Early Modern Rapes of Lucrece." In *Imagining Culture: Essays in Early Modern History and Literature*, ed. J. Hart. New York: Garland, 2001.

Campbell, C. *The Romantic Ethic and the Spirit of Modern Consumerism.* Oxford: Blackwell, 1987.

Cary, M., and H. H. Scullard, *A History of Rome: Down to the Reign of Constantine.* 3rd ed. London: Macmillan, 1975.

Cary, P. *Augustine's Invention of the Inner Self.* Oxford: Oxford University Press 2000.

———. "Believing the Word: A Proposal about Knowing Other Persons." *Faith and Philosophy* 13/1 (1996) 78–90.

———. "The Incomprehensibility of God and the Origin of the Thomistic Concept of the Supernatural." *Pro Ecclesia* 11:3 (Summer 2002) 340–55.

Cassirer, E. *The Myth of the State.* New Haven: Yale University Press, 1973.

Cavanaugh, W. "The City: Beyond Secular Parodies." In *Radical Orthodoxy: A New Theology*, ed. J. Milbank, C. Pickstock, and G. Ward. London: Routledge, 1999. 190–98.

———. "A Fire Strong Enough to Consume the House: The 'Wars of Religion' and the Rise of the State." *Modern Theology* 11:4 (October 1995) 397–419.

Chapman, E. *Saint Augustine's Philosophy of Beauty.* New York: Sheed & Ward, 1939.

Chappell, T. D. J. *Aristotle and Augustine on Freedom: Two Theories of Freedom, Voluntary Action and Akrasia.* New York: St. Martin's Press, 1995.

Chesterton, G. K. *What I Saw in America.* New York: Dodd, Mead and Co., 1922.

Cicero. *de Officiis.* Loeb Classical Library. Cambridge: Harvard University Press, 1975.

———. *The Letters of Marcus Tullius Cicero, with His Treatises on Friendship and Old Age.* Trans. E. S. Shuckburgh. New York: P. F. Collier, 1909.

Cipriani, N. "La precettistica antica e la regola monastica di s. Agostino." *Augustinianum* 39.2 (1999) 365–80.

Clark, M. T. *Augustine, Philosopher of Freedom.* New York: Desclee Company, 1958.

Constant, B. *Political Writings.* B. Fontana, ed. Cambridge: Cambridge University Press, 1988.

Cox, H. *The Secular City: Secularization and Urbanization in Theological Perspective.* New York: Macmillan, 1965.

Cranz, F.E. "*De Civitate Dei*, XV, 2, and Augustine's Idea of the Christian Society." In *Augustine: A Collection of Critical Essays*, ed. R. A. Markus. Garden City: Doubleday, 1972. 404–21.

Croly, H. *Progressive Democracy.* New York: Macmillan, 1914.

Cunningham, A. and Eagleton, T. *Catholics and the Left.* London: Sheed & Ward, 1966.

Deane, H. *The Political and Social Ideas of St. Augustine.* New York: Columbia University Press, 1963.

de Grazia, Sebastia. *Machiavelli in Hell.* Princeton: Princeton University Press, 1989.

DeLillo, D. *White Noise. Penguin Great Books of the 20th Century.* New York: Penguin Books, 1999.

Delmaire, R. "Cités et fiscalités au Bas-Empire. A propos du rôdes curiales dans la levée des impôts." In *La fin de la cité antique et le début de la cité médiévale de la fin du III siècle à l'avènement de Charlemagne*, ed. C. Lepelley. Bari: Edipuglia, 1996. 59–70.

de Lubac, H. *Augustinianism and Modern Theology.* New York: Crossroad, 1998.

———. *Catholicism: Christ and the Common Destiny of Man.* Trans. Lancelot Sheppard. San Francisco: Ignatius Press, 1988.

———. *Theological Fragments.* Trans. R. H. Balinski. San Francisco: Ignatius Press, 1989.

de Vogel, C. J. *Greek Philosophy.* 3 vols. Leiden: E.J. Brill, 1953–59.

Dewey, J. "Ethics and Physical Science" in R. Westbrook, *John Dewey and American Democracy.* Ithaca: Cornell University Press, 1991.

———. "Ethics of Democracy" in R. Westbrook, *John Dewey and American Democracy.* Ithaca: Cornell University Press, 1991.

———. *The Quest for Certainty.* New York: Minton, Balch, 1929.

———. *Individualism Old and New.* New York: Minton, Balch, 1930.

———. *The Public and Its Problems.* Boulder: A. Swallow, 1956 [1927].

———. *A Common Faith.* New Haven: Yale University Press, 1935.

Dihle, A. *The Theory of Will in Classical Antiquity.* Berkeley: University of California Press, 1982.

Dodaro, R. "Augustine of Hippo Between the Secular City and the City of God." In *Augustinus Afer. Saint Augustin: africanité et universalité. Actes du colloque international, Alger-Annaba, 1–7 avril 2001*, ed. P.-Y. Fux, J.-M. Roessli, and O. Wermlinger. Fribourg: Universitätsverlag, 2003.

———. "Augustine's Secular City." In *Augustine and His Critics*, ed. R. Dodaro and G. Lawless. London: Routledge, 2000. 231–59.

———. "Church and State." *Augustine through the Ages: An Encyclopedia*, ed. A. Fitzgerald. Grand Rapids: Eerdmans, 1999. 176–84.

———. "Eloquent Lies, Just Wars and the Politics of Persuasion: Reading Augustine's *City of God* in a 'Post-Modern' World." *Augustinian Studies* 25 (1994) 77–137.

———. "Language and Justice: Political Anthropology in Augustine's *De Ciuitate Dei*." Unpublished D. Phil thesis for Oxford University.

———. "Pirates or Superpowers: Reading Augustine in a Hall of Mirrors." *New Blackfriars* 72:845 (January 1991) 9–19.

Dodaro, R., and G. Lawless, eds. *Augustine and His Critics:Essays in Honor of Gerald Bonner.* London: Routledge, 2000.

Donnelly, D., ed. *The City of God: A Collection of Critical Essays.* New York: Peter Lang, 1995.

Dostoevsky, F. *The Brothers Karamazov.* Trans. C. Garnett. New York et al.: Penguin Books, 1958.

Douglas, M. *Purity and Danger: An Analysis of Concepts of Pollution and Taboo.* London 1966, 1978.

———. *The World of Goods: Towards an Anthropology of Consumption.* New York: Routledge, 1996 [1979].

Duchrow, U. "*Signum* und *superbia* beim jungen Augustin (386–390)." *Revue des Études Augustiniennes* 7/4 (1961) 369–72.

Durkheim, E. *The Elementary Forms of Religious Life.* Trans. K. E. Fields. New York: Free Press, 1995 [1912].

Dyson, R. W. *The Pilgrim City: Social and Political Ideas in the Writings of St. Augustine of Hippo.* Suffolk, UK: Boydell Press, 2001.

Eagleton, T. *The Body as Language: Outline of a 'New Left' Theology.* London: Sheed & Ward, 1970.

Ellul, J. *The Technological Society.* New York: Vintage, 1964.

Elshtain, J. B. *Augustine and the Limits of Politics.* Notre Dame: University of Notre Dame Press, 1998.

———, ed. *Just War Theory.* New York: New York University Press, 1992.

———. *Who Are We? Critical Reflections and Hopeful Possibilities.* Grand Rapids: Eerdmans, 2000.

Fabbrini, F. *La manumissio in ecclesia.* Milan: Dott. A. Giuffrè, 1965.

Feldmann, E., A. Schindler, and O. Wermelinger, "Alypius." *Augustinus-Lexikon,* vol. 1. Ed. C. Mayer. Basel: Schwabe & Co., 1986–1994. Col. 245–67.

Figgis, J. *The Political Aspects of St. Augustine's* City of God. London: Longman's, 1921.

———. *Civilisation at the Cross Roads.* London: Longmans, 1912.

Fiske, A. M. "St. Augustine and Friendship." *Monastic Studies* 2 (1964) 127–35.

Fitzgerald, A. D., ed. *Augustine through the Ages: An Encyclopedia.* Grand Rapids, MI: William B. Eerdmans Publishing Company, 1999.

Folliet, G. "L'affare Faventius. Examen du dossier (Augustin, Epist. 113–116)." *Revue des Études augustiniennes* 30 (1984) 240–50.

Fontana, Benedetto. *Hegemony and Power: On the Relation between Gramsci and Machiavelli.* Minneapolis: University of Minnesota Press, 1993.

———. "Love of Country and Love of God: The Political Uses of Religion in Machiavelli." *Journal of the History of Ideas* 60:4 (1999) 639–58.

Fortin, E. *Political Idealism and Christianity in the Thought of St. Augustine.* Villanova: Villanova University Press, 1972.

Foucault, M. *The Archaeology of Knowledge and the Discourse on Language.* Trans. R. Smith. New York: Pantheon Books, 1972.

———. *The Order of Things: An Archaeology of the Human Sciences.* Trans. R. Smith. New York: Vintage Books, 1973.

Fox, R.W. *Reinhold Niebuhr: A Biography.* New York: Pantheon Books, 1985.

———. "The Culture of Liberal Protestant Progressivism," *Journal of Interdisciplinary History.* 23 (Winter 1993), 639–60.

Fukuyama, F. *The End of History and the Last Man.* New York: Free Press, 1992.

Galindo, J. A. "La libertad como autodeterminación en san Agustín." *Augustinus* 35 (1990) 299–320.

Garin, E. *Italian Humanism: Philosophy and Civic Life in the Renaissance.* Trans. Peter Munz. Oxford: Blackwell Publishers, 1965.

Garver, E. *Machiavelli and the History of Prudence.* Madison: University of Wisconsin Press, 1987.

Gilbert, F. "Bernardo Rucellai and the Orti Oricellari: A Study of the Origin of Modern Political Thought." In *History: Choice and Commitment.* Cambridge, MA: Harvard University Press, 1977. 215–46.

———. *Machiavelli and Guicciardini: Politics and History in Sixteenth-Century Florence.* New York: Norton, 1984.

Gilson, É. *Introduction à l'étude de Saint Augustin.* Paris: Librairie Philosophique J. Vrin, 1949. English translation: *The Christian Philosophy of St. Augustine.* New York: Vintage, 1967.

Grafton, A. and L. Jardine. *From Humanism to the Humanities: Educatio and the Liberal Arts in Fifteenth- and Sixteenth-Century Europe.* Cambridge, MA: Harvard University Press, 1986.

Gramsci, A. *The Modern Prince and Other Writings.* Trans. L. Marks. New York: International Publishers, 1957.

Greer, R. *Broken Lights and Mended Lives: Theology and Common Life in the Early Church.* University Park: Pennsylvania State University Press, 1986.

Grendler, P. F. *Schooling in Renaissance Italy: Literacy and Learning, 1300–1600.* Baltimore: Johns Hopkins University Press, 1989.

Hadot, P. *Philosophy as a Way of Life.* Oxford: Blackwell, 1995.

Hagendahl, H. *Augustine and the Latin Classics.* Göteborg: Elanders, 1967.

Hale, J. R., ed. *The Thames and Hudson Encyclopaedia of the Italian Renaissance, World of Art.* London: Thames and Hudson, 1981.

Hampton, T. *Writing from History: The Rhetoric of Exemplarity in Renaissance Literature.* Ithaca: Cornell University Press, 1990.

Hanby, M. *Augustine and Modernity.* London: Routledge, 2003.

Handy, R. T. *A Christian America: Protestant Hopes and Historical Realities.* New York: Oxford University Press, 1971.

Hardt, M. and A. Negri. *Empire.* Cambridge, MA: Harvard University Press, 2000.

Harrison, C. "The Rhetoric of Scripture and Preaching: Classical Decadence or Christian Aesthetic?" In *Augustine and His Critics: Essays in Honor of Gerald Bonner*, ed. R. Dodaro and G. Lawless. London: Routledge, 2000.

Harvey, J. F. *Moral Theology of the* Confessions *of Saint Augustine.* Washington, DC: Catholic University of America Press, 1951.

Hauerwas, S. "The Irony of Reinhold Niebuhr: The Ideological Character of 'Christian Realism.'" In *Wilderness Wanderings: Probing Twentieth-Century Theology and Philosophy.* Boulder: Westview Press, 1997. 48–61.

———. *In Good Company: The Church as Polis.* Notre Dame and London: University of Notre Dame Press, 1995.

Havel, V. *Living in Truth*. Jan Vladislav, ed. London: Faber, 1987.

Hawthorne, N. "The Celestial Railroad," in R. P. Blackmur, ed., *The Celestial Railroad and Other Stories*. New York: New American Library, 1963. 185–202.

Hobbes, T. *Leviathan*. New York: Penguin Books, 1968.

Huisman, H. *Augustins' Briefwisseling met Nectarius. Inleideing, tekxt, vertaling, commentaar*. Amsterdam: J. Babeliowski, 1956.

Jacques, F. "Le défenseur de cité d'après la Lettre 22* de saint Augustin." *Revue des Études augustiniennes* 32 (1986) 56–73.

Jaspers, K. *Plato and Augustine*. New York: Harvest, 1962.

Jed, S. *Chaste Thinking: The Rape of Lucretia and the Birth of Humanism*. Bloomington: Indiana University Press, 1989.

John Paul II. *Pastoral Letter on St. Augustine*. Boston: St. Paul Editions, 1986.

Jolivet, R. *Le problème du mal d'après S. Augustine*. Paris: G. Beauchesne, 1936.

Jones, A. H. M. *The Later Roman Empire 284–602*. Oxford: Basil Blackwell, 1964.

Jones, P. D. *The Christian Socialist Revival in Britain, 1877–1914*. Princeton: Princeton University Press, 1968.

Kahn, C. "Discovering the Will: From Aristotle to Augustine," in *The Question of Eclecticism: Studies in Later Greek Philosophy*. J. M. Dillow and A. A. Long, eds. Berkeley: University of California Press, 1988. 234–59.

Kahn, V. *Machiavellian Rhetoric: From the Counter-Reformation to Milton*. Princeton: Princeton University Press, 1994.

Kaplan, R. *Warrior Politics: Why Leadership Demands a Pagan Ethos*. New York: Random House, 2002.

Knippenberg, J. M., and R. Lawler, eds. *Poets, Princes, and Private Citizens: Literary Alternatives to Postmodern Politics*. Lanham, MD: Rowman & Littlefield, 1996.

Kohler, G. "Selbstbezug, Selbsttranszendenz und die Nichtigkeit der Freiheit: Zur augustinischen Theorie des Bösen in *De civitate Dei* XII." *Studia Philosophica* 52 (1993) 67–79.

Kries, D. "A Question of Piety: Machiavelli's Treatment of Christianity in the *Exhortation to Penitence*." In *Piety and Humanity: Essays on Religion in Early Modern Political Philosophy*, ed. D. Kries and H. Mansfield. Lanham, MD: Rowman & Littlefield, 1998. 1–27.

Kries, D. and H. Mansfield. *Piety and Humanity: Essays on Religion in Early Modern Political Philosophy*. Lanham, MD: Rowman & Littlefield, 1998.

Kristeller, P. O. *Renaissance Thought: The Classic, Scholastic, and Humanist Strains*. New York: Harper, 1955.

———. *Renaissance Thought and Its Sources*. Ed. Michael Mooney. New York: Columbia University Press, 1979.

Kuklick, B. "John Dewey, American Theology, and Scientific Politics." In *Religion and Twentieth-Century American Intellectual Life*, ed. M. Lacey. New York and Cambridge: Cambridge University Press, 1989. 90–92.

Lafont, G. "Fraternal Correction in the Augustinian Community: A Confrontation Between the Praeceptum, IV, 6–9 and Matthew 18:15–17." *Word and Spirit* 10 (1988) 87–91.

Lamoreaux, J. C. "Episcopal Courts in Late Antiquity." *Journal of Early Christian Studies* 3:2 (1995) 143–67.

Lancel, S. *Saint Augustine*. Trans. Antonia Nevill. London: SCM Press, 2002.

Lawless, G. *Augustine of Hippo and His Monastic Rule.* Oxford: Clarendon Press, 1987.

Leach, W. *Land of Desire: Merchants, Power, and the Rise of a New American Culture.* New York: Pantheon, 1993.

Lears, J. *Fables of Abundance: A Cultural History of Advertising in America.* New York: Basic Books, 1994.

———. *Something for Nothing: Luck in America.* New York: Viking, 2003.

Ledeen, M. *Machiavelli on Modern Leadership: Why Machiavelli's Iron Rules are as Timely and Important Today as Five Centuries Ago.* New York: St. Martins Press, 2000.

Lenihan, D. A. "The Just War Theory in the Work of St. Augustine." *Augustinian Studies* 19 (1988): 37–70.

Lepelley, C., ed. *La fin de la cité antique et le début de la cité médiévale de la fin du III siècle à l'avènement de Charlemagne.* Bari: Edipuglia, 1996.

———. "Liberté, colonat et esclavage d'après la Lettre 24*: la jurisdiction épiscopale «de liberali causa»." In *Les lettres de saint Augustin découvertes par Johannes Divjak.* Paris: Études augustiniennes, 1983. 329–42.

Levick, B. *Tiberius the Politician.* New York: Routledge, 1976.

Levy, D. W. *Herbert Croly of the New Republic: The Life and Thought of an American Progressive.* Princeton: Princeton University Press, 1985.

Liebeschütz, W. "Cities, Taxes and Accomodation of the Barbarians: The Theories of Duliat and Goffart." In *Kingdoms of the Empire. The Integration of the Barbarians in Late Antiquity,* ed. W. Pohl. Leiden: Brill, 1997. 136–51.

Lienhard, J. T. "Friendship in Paulinus of Nola and Augustine." *Augustiniana* 40 (1990) 279–96.

Lippmann, W. *Drift and Mastery: An Attempt to Diagnose the Current Crisis.* New York: Prentice-Hall, 1914.

Lizzi, R. *Il potere episcopale nell'Oriente Romano. Rappresentazione ideologica e realtà politica, IV-V sec. d.C.* Rome: Edizioni dell'ateneo, 1987.

Locke, J. *An Essay concerning Human Understanding.* Amherst, NY: Prometheus Books, 1994.

———. *Two Treatises of Government.* New York: MacMillan, 1974.

Long, D. S. *Divine Economy: Theology and the Market.* London and New York: Routledge, 2001.

Lottman, H. R. *Albert Camus: A Biography.* Corte Madera, California: Gingko Press, 1997.

Lowith, K. *Meaning in History.* Chicago: University of Chicago Press, 1949.

Machiavelli, N. "The Death of Piero Soderini." Trans. R. M. Adams. In *The Prince,* ed. R. M. Adams. New York: Norton, 1992.

———. "Discourses on Livy." In *Machiavelli: The Chief Works and Others.* 3 vols. Ed. A. Gilbert. Durham, NC: Duke University Press, 1989.

———. "Exhortation to Penitence." Trans. R. M Adams. In *The Prince,* ed. R. M. Adams. New York: Norton, 1992.

———. "Letter to Guicciardini of 17 May 1521." Trans. A. Gilbert. In *The Prince,* ed. R. M. Adams. New York: Norton, 1992.

———. *Mandragola.* Trans. M. J. Flaumenhaft. Prospect Heights, IL: Waveland Press, 1981.

———. *The Prince*. Trans. L. P. S. de Alvarez. Prospect Heights, IL: Waveland Press, 1980.

MacIntyre, A. *Three Rival Versions of Moral Enquiry*. Notre Dame: University of Notre Dame Press, 1990.

———. *Whose Justice? Which Rationality?* Notre Dame: University of Notre Dame Press, 1988.

Maddox, G. "The Secular Reformation and the Influence of Machiavelli." *Journal of Religion* 82:14 (2002) 539–63.

Madec, G. "Le *De civitate Dei* comme *De vera religione*." In *Interiorità e intenzionalità nel "De civitate Dei" di Sant'Agostino*. Atti del III° Seminario Internazionale del Centro di Studi Agostiniani di Perugia. A cura di Remo Piccolomini. Rome: Institutum Patristicum "Augustinianum," 1991. 7–33.

Mandouze, A., ed. *Prosopographie chrétienne du Bas-Empire*. Paris: Éditions du CNRS, 1982.

Manent, P. *An Intellectual History of Liberalism*. Trans. Rebecca Balinski. New French Thought series. Princeton: Princeton University Press, 1994.

Marchand, R. *Advertising the American Dream: Making Way for Modernity, 1920–1940*. Berkeley: University of California Press, 1985.

———. *Creating the Corporate Soul: The Rise of Public Relations and Corporate Imagery in American Big Business*. Berkeley: University of California Press, 1998.

Maritain, J. *A Preface to Metaphysics: Seven Lectures in Being*. New York: Sheed & Ward, 1948.

Markus, R. A. "*De Civitate Dei*: Pride and the Common Good." *Augustiniana* 1990: 245–59.

———. *The End of Ancient Christianity*. Cambridge: Cambridge University Press, 1990.

———. *Saeculum: History and Society in the Theology of St. Augustine*. Cambridge, UK: Cambridge University Press, 1970.

Markus, R. A., ed. *Augustine: A Collection of Essays*. Garden City: Doubleday, 1972.

Marsden, G. *The Outrageous Idea of Christian Scholarship*. New York: Oxford University Press, 1997.

Martin, T. "'An Abundant Supply of Discourse': Augustine and the Rhetoric of Monasticism." *The Downside Review* 116 (January 1999) 7–25.

Martindale, J. R. *The Prosopography of the Late Roman Empire*. Cambridge, UK: Cambridge University Press, 1980.

Martinez, R. "The Pharmacy of Machiavelli: Roman Lucretia in *Mandragola*." *Renaissance Drama* 14 (1983) 1–43.

Marvin, C. and D. W. Ingle. *Blood Sacrifice and the Nation: Totem Rituals and the American Flag*. Cambridge, UK: Cambridge University Press, 1999.

Marx, K. *Capital*. Vol. I in *The Marx-Engels Reader*. Ed. Robert C. Tucker. 2nd ed. New York: W. W. Norton & Company, 1978.

———. "Contribution to the Critique of Hegel's Philosophy of Right," in R. Tucker, ed., *The Marx-Engels Reader*. New York: Norton, 1978. 54.

———. "The Communist Manifesto", in R. Tucker, ed., *The Marx-Engels Reader*. New York: Norton, 1978. 475–78.

———. "Economic and Philosophical Manuscripts", in R. Tucker, ed., *The Marx-Engels Reader*. New York: Norton, 1978. 101–5.

Bibliograpy

———. *Grundrisse*, Trans. M. Nicolaus. New York: Harper & Row, 1973 [1857].

Mattingly, G. "Machiavelli's *Prince*: Political Science or Political Satire?" *American Scholar* 27 (1958) 482–91.

May, H. F. "The Religion of the Republic," in *Ideas, Faiths, and Feelings: Essay on American Intellectual and Religious History, 1952–1982*. New York: Macmillan, 1983. 171–80.

Mayer, A. *The Furies: Violence and Terror in the French and Russian Revolutions*. Princeton: Princeton University Press, 2000.

Mayer, C., ed. *Augustinus-Lexikon*. Basel: Schwabe & Co., 1996.

McCarraher, E. *Christian Critics: Religion and the Impasse in Modern American Social Thought*. Ithaca, NY: Cornell University Press, 2000.

McGuire, B. P. *Friendship and Community: The Monastic Experience 350–1250*. Kalamazoo, MI: Cistercian Publications, 1988.

McLynn, N. B. *Ambrose of Milan*. Berkeley: University of California Press, 1994.

———. "Augustine's Roman Empire." In *History, Apocalypse and the Secular Imagination: New Essays on Augustine's City of God*, ed. M. Vessey, K. Pollman, and A. Fitzgerald. Bowling Green: Philosophy Documentation Center, 1999. 29–44.

McNamara, M. A. *Friends and Friendship for Saint Augustine*. Staten Island, NY: Alba House, 1958.

Meilaender, G. C. *Friendship: A Study in Theological Ethics*. Notre Dame and London: University of Notre Dame Press, 1981.

Meinecke, F. *Machiavellianism: The Doctrine of Raison d'Etat and Its Place in Modern History*. Trans. D. Scott. New Haven: Yale University Press, 1957.

Merchant, C. *The Death of Nature: Women, Ecology, and the Scientific Revolution*. New York: Harper, 1980.

Meyer, D. *The Protestant Search for Political Realism, 1919–1941*. Berkeley: University of California Press, 1960.

Meynell, H. *Grace, Politics, and Desire: Essays on Augustine*. Calgary: University of Calgary Press, 1990.

Milbank, J. "'The Body by Love Possessed': Christianity and Late Capitalism in Britain," *Modern Theology* 3 (March 1986), 56–61.

———. "The Poverty of Niebuhrianism." In *The Word Made Strange: Theology, Language, Culture*. Oxford: Blackwell Publishers, 1997. 233–54.

———. "Sovereignty, Empire, Capital, and Terror." Public lecture delivered at the Forum on Imperialism and Terror. University of Virginia, October 1, 2001.

———. *Theology and Social Theory*. Oxford: Blackwell, 1990.

———. *The Word Made Strange: Theology, Language, Culture*. Oxford: Blackwell, 1997.

Milbank, J., C. Pickstock, and G.Ward, eds. *Radical Orthodoxy: A New Theology*. New York and London: Routledge, 1999.

Miles, M. *Desire and Delight: A New Reading of Augustine's Confessions*. New York: Crossroad, 1992.

Mitchell, J. *The Fragility of Freedom: Tocqueville on Religion, Democracy, and the American Future*. Chicago: University of Chicago Press, 1995.

———. *Not By Reason Alone: Religion, History, and Identity in Early Modern Political Thought*. Chicago: University of Chicago Press, 1993.

Moltmann, J. *A Theology of Hope.* Philadelphia: Augsburg Fortress Publishers, 1993 [1967].

Momigliano, A. *On Pagans, Jews, and Christians.* Hanover, NH: Wesleyan University Press, 1987.

Mommsen, T., and P. M. Meyer, eds. *Theodosii libri XVI cum Constitutionibus Sirmondianis et Leges Novellae ad Theodosianum pertinentes.* Berlin: Weidmann, 1904–05. Reprinted Dublin and Zurich: Weidmann, 1970.

Monagle, J. F. "Friendship in St. Augustine's Biography." *Augustinian Studies* 2 (1971) 81–92.

Mondin, B. "L'Antropologia Cristiana di S. Agostino." *Sapienza* 54/1 (2001) 3–16.

Moreau, M. "Le dossier Marcellinus dans la Correspondance d'Augustin." *Recherches augustiniennes* 9 (1973) 5–181.

Morgenstern, F. *Die Briefpartner des Augustinus von Hippo. Prosopographische, sozial- und ideologie-geschichtliche Untersuchungen.* Bochum: Universitätsverlag Dr. N. Brockmeyer, 1993.

Munier, C. "Audientia episcopalis." *Augustinus-Lexikon,* vol. 1. Ed. C. Mayer. Basel: Schwabe & Co., 1986–1994. Col. 511–15.

Murdoch, I. *The Sovereignty of Good.* London: Routledge and Kegan Paul, 1970.

Najemy, J. "Baron's Machiavelli and Renaissance Republicanism." *American Historical Review* 101:1 (1996) 119–30.

———. *Between Friends: Discourses of Power and Desire in the Machiavelli-Vettori Letters of 1513–1515.* Princeton: Princeton University Press, 1993.

———. "Papirius and the Chickens, or Machiavelli on the Necessity of Interpreting Religion." *Journal of the History of Ideas* 60:4 (1999) 659–81.

Nederman, C. "Amazing Grace: Fortune, God, and Free Will in Machiavelli's Thought." *Journal of the History of Ideas* 60:4 (1999) 617–38.

Neuhaus, R. J. *The Naked Public Square.* 2nd ed. Grand Rapids: Eerdmans, 1996.

Niebuhr, R. "Augustine's Political Realism," in *Christian Realism and Political Problems.* New York: Scribner, 1953, 119–46.

———. *The Irony of American History.* New York: Scribner, 1952.

———. *Moral Man and Immoral Society.* New York: Scribner, 1932.

Nietzsche, F. *The Will to Power.* Trans. Walter Kaufmann and R. J. Hollingdale. New York: Vintage Books, 1967.

Nelson, J. O. "An Augustine for Our Age," *The University Bookman* 34:2 (1994) 77–138.

Noble, T. F. X., and T. Head, eds. *Soldiers of Christ. Saints and Saints Lives from Late Antiquity and the Early Middle Ages.* University Park: Pennsylvania State University Press, 1995.

Norman, E. *The Victorian Christian Socialists.* New York: Cambridge University Press, 1987.

Norton, P. E. "Machiavelli's Road to Paradise: *The Exhortation to Penitence.*" *History of Political Thought* 4:1 (1983) 31–42.

Nygren, A. *Agape and Eros.* 2 parts. Rev. ed. P. S. Watson, trans. London, 1953.

Oakeshott, M. "Introduction to *Leviathan.*" In *Rationalism in Politics and Other Essays.* Indianapolis: Liberty Press, 1991. 221–94.

———. "The Moral Life in the Writings of Thomas Hobbes." In *Rationalism in Politics and Other Essays.* Indianapolis: LibertyPress, 1991. 295–350.

———. *The Politics of Faith and the Politics of Scepticism*, ed. T. Fuller. New Haven: Yale University Press, 1996.

O'Connell, R. J. *The Origin of the Soul in St. Augustine's Later Works*. New York: Fordham University Press, 1987.

———. *St. Augustine's Early Theory of Man*. Cambridge: Harvard University Press, 1968.

———. *Soundings in St. Augustine's Imagination*. New York: Fordham University Press, 1994.

O'Connor, W. R. "The *Uti/Frui* Distinction in Augustine's Ethics." *Augustinian Studies* 14 (1983) 45–62.

O'Donnell, J. J. "Augustine: Christianity and Society, the Critique of Ideology (1)." Online: http://ccat.sas.upenn.edu/jod/twayne/aug3.html.

———. "The Demise of Paganism." *Traditio* 35 (1979) 45–88.

O'Donovan, O. "Augustine's *City of God* XIX and Western Political Thought." *Dionysius* 11 (December 1987) 89–110.

———. *Common Objects of Love: Moral Reflection and the Shaping of Community*. Grand Rapids: Eerdmans, 2002.

———. *The Problem of Self-Love in St. Augustine*. New Haven, CT: Yale University Press, 1980.

———. "*Usus* and *fruitio* in Augustine, De Doctrina Christiana I." *Journal of Theological Studies* (n.s.) 33/2 (October 1982) 361–97.

O'Donovan, O., and J. Lockwood, eds. *From Irenaeus to Grotius: A Sourcebook in Christian Political Thought, 100–1625*. Grand Rapids: Eerdmans, 1999.

O'Meara, J. J. *The Charter of Christendom: The Significance of the "City of God."* New York: Macmillan, 1961.

———. *The Young Augustine: The Growth of St. Augustine's Mind up to His Conversion*. London: Longmans, Green and Co., 1954.

Osmond, P. J. "Sallust and Machiavelli: From Civic Humanism to Political Prudence." *Journal of Medieval and Renaissance Studies* 23 (1993): 407–38.

Paffenroth, K. "Book Nine: The Emotional Heart of the *Confessions*." In *A Reader's Companion to Augustine's* Confessions, ed. K. Paffenroth and R. P. Kennedy. Louisville and London: Westminster John Knox Press, 2003.

———. "God in the Friend, or the Friend in God? The Meaning of Friendship for Augustine." *Augustinian Heritage* 38 (1992) 123–36.

———. *In Praise of Wisdom: Literary and Theological Reflections on Faith and Reason*. New York and London: Continuum International Publishing, 2004.

———. *Judas: Images of the Lost Disciple*. Louisville and London: Westminster John Knox Press, 2001.

———. "Tears of Grief and Joy. *Confessions* Book 9: Chronological Sequence and Structure." *Augustinian Studies* 28 (1997) 141–54.

Paffenroth, K., and K. Hughes, eds. *Augustine and Liberal Education*. Aldershot, UK: Ashgate Publishing, 2000.

Paffenroth, K., and R. P. Kennedy, *A Reader's Companion to Augustine's* Confessions. Louisville and London: Westminster John Knox Press, 2003.

Palamas, G. *The Triads*. Mahwah, NJ: Paulist Press, 1983.

Parel, A.J. *The Machiavellian Cosmos.* New Haven: Yale University Press, 1992.

Pegueroles, J. "Libertad como posibilidad, libertad como necesidad. Juliano y San Agustín." *Espíritu* 36 (1987) 109–24.

Peter, Damian. *Letters.* 4 vols., Owen J. Blum, trans. Washington, DC: Catholic University of America Press, 1989.

Pharr, C., trans. *The Theodosian Code and Novels and the Sirmondian Constitutions.* New York: Greenwood Press, 1952.

Philips, G. *La raison d'être du mal d'après S. Augustine.* Louvain: Editions du Museum Lessianum, 1927.

Pieper, J. *Leisure as the Basis of Culture.* Trans. Alexander Dru. New York: Random House, 1963.

Pinckaers, S. *The Sources of Christian Ethics.* Trans. Sr. Mary Thomas Noble. Washington, DC: The Catholic University of America Press, 1995.

Pitkin, H. F. *Fortune Is a Woman: Gender and Politics in the Thought of Niccolò Machiavelli.* Berkeley: University of California Press, 1984.

Pocock, J. G. A. *The Machiavellian Moment: Florentine Political Thought and the Atlantic Republican Tradition.* Princeton: Princeton University Press, 1975.

Pohl, W., ed. *Kingdoms of the Empire. The Integration of the Barbarians in Late Antiquity.* Leiden: Brill, 1997.

Prezzolini, G. "The Christian Roots of Machiavelli's Moral Pessimism." *Review of National Literatures* 1:1 (1970) 26–27.

———. *Machiavelli antichristo.* Trans. Gioconda Savine. New York: Farrar, Strauss, Giroux, 1967.

Qviller, B. "The Machiavellian Cosmos." *History of Political Thought* 17:3 (1996) 326–53.

Raab, F. *The English Face of Machiavelli: A Changing Interpretation, 1500–1700.* London: Routledge, 1964.

Rahe, P. A. "The Primacy of Politics in Ancient Greece." *American Historical Review* 89 (1984) 265–93.

Rahner, H. *Man At Play.* Trans. Brian Battershaw and Edward Quinn. New York: Herder and Herder, 1972.

Rahula, W. *What the Buddha Taught.* New York: Grove Press, 1974.

Raikas, K. "St Augustine on Juridical Duties: Some Aspects of the Episcopal Office in Late Antiquity." In *Collectanea Augustiniana,* vol. 1, *Augustine: Second Founder of the Faith,* ed. J. Schnaubelt and F. Van Fleteren. New York: Peter Lang, 1990. 467–83.

Ramsey, P. "Just War According to St. Augustine." In *Just War Theory,* ed. J. B. Elshtain. New York: New York University Press. 31–42.

Rawls, J. "Justice as Fairness: Political not Metaphysical." *Philosophy and Public Affairs* 14 (Summer 1985) 223–51.

Rebillard, E., and C. Sotinel, eds. *L'èvêque dans la cité du I^{ve} au Ve siècle. Image et autorité. Actes de la table ronde organisée par l'Istituto patristico Augustinianum et l'École française de Rome, 1er et 2 décembre 1995.* Rome: École française de Rome, 1998.

Ridolfi, R. *La vita di Niccoló Machiavelli.* 6th ed., 2 vols. Florence: Sansoni, 1969.

Rist, J. *Augustine: Ancient Thought Baptized.* Cambridge: Cambridge University Press, 1994.

Roberston, D. W. *Preface to Chaucer: Studies in Medieval Perspectives.* Princeton: Princeton University Press, 1962.

Romano, C. "La liberté sartrienne, ou le rêve d'Adam." *Archives de Philosophie* 63 (2000) 468–93.

Rommel, H. *Zum Begriff des Bösen bei Augustinus und Kant.* Frankfurt am Main: Pater Lang GmbH, 1997.

Rorty, R. *Achieving Our Country: Leftist Thought in Twentieth-Century America.* Cambridge: Harvard University Press, 1998.

———. *Philosophy and Social Hope.* New York: Penguin Books, 1999.

———. "Religion as Conversation-Stopper," *Common Knowledge* 3 (Spring 1994) 1–6.

Rose, G. *Mourning Becomes Law: Philosophy and Representation.* Cambridge: Cambridge University Press, 1996.

Rousseau, J.-J. *The Social Contract.* London: Penguin, 1968.

Royce, J. *The Philosophy of Loyalty.* New York: Macmillan, 1908.

———. *The Problem of Christianity*, Vol. II. New York: Macmillan, 1913.

Sandeen, E. J. ed. *The Letters of Randolph Bourne.* New York: Whitston Pub. Co., 1981.

Schall, J.V. "On the Place of Augustine in Political Philosophy." *The Political Science Reviewer* 23 (1994) 128–65.

Schnaubelt, J., and F. Van Fleteren, eds. *Collectanea Augustiniana*, vol. 1, *Augustine: Second Founder of the Faith.* New York: Peter Lang, 1990.

Scholem, G. *Walter Benjamin: The Story of a Friendship.* Trans. H. Zohn. New York: Schocken Books, 1981.

Scott, J.V. "Augustine's Razor: Public vs. Private Interests in *The City of God.*" In *The City of God: A Collection of Critical Essays*, ed. D. F. Donnelly. New York: Peter Lang, 1995.

———. "Political Thought, Contemporary Influence of Augustine." In *Augustine Through the Ages: An Encyclopedia*, ed. A. Fitzgerald. Grand Rapids: Eerdmans, 1999. 658–61.

Shanks, A. *Civil Society, Civil Religion.* Oxford: Blackwell Publishers, 1995.

Shaw, B. D. "The Family in Late Antiquity: The Experience of Augustine." *Past and Present* 115 (May 1987) 3–51.

Shklar, J. *Ordinary Vices.* Cambridge, MA: Harvard University Press, 1984.

Siegel, J. "'Civic Humanism' or Ciceronian Rhetoric? The Culture of Petrach and Bruni." *Past and Present* 34 (1966) 3–48.

———. *Rhetoric and Philosophy in Renaissance Humanism: The Union of Eloquence and Wisdom, Petrarch to Valla.* Princeton: Princeton University Press, 1968.

Simon, Y. R. *Freedom of Choice.* Ed. Peter Wolff. New York: Fordham University Press, 1969.

Skinner, Q. *The Foundations of Modern Political Thought.* 2 vols. Cambridge: Cambridge University Press, 1978.

Smith, T. W. *Revaluing Ethics: Aristotle's Dialectical Pedagogy.* Albany: State University of New York Press, 2000.

Stern, A. "The Irreversibility of History." *Diogenes* 29 (1960) 1–15.

Stout, J. *The Flight From Authority: Religion, Morality, and the Quest for Autonomy.* Notre Dame, IN: University of Notre Dame Press, 1981.

Strauss, L. *Natural Right and History.* Chicago: University of Chicago Press, 1953.

———. *Thoughts on Machiavelli.* Chicago: University of Chicago Press, 1958.

Taussig, M. *The Nervous System.* New York and London: Routeldge, 1993.

TeSelle, E. "Toward and Augustinian Politics" *Journal of Religious Ethics* 16 (1988) 87–108.

Teske, R. *Paradoxes of Time in Saint Augustine.* Milwaukee, WI: Marquette University Press, 1996.

———. "The World-Soul and Time in St. Augustine." *Augustinian Studies* 14 (1983) 75–92.

Testard, M. *Saint Augustin et Cicéron.* Paris: Études Augustiniennes, 1958.

Thomas, K. *Religion and the Decline of Magic: Studies in Popular Belief in Sixteenth and Seventeenth Century England.* New York: Oxford University Press, 1997.

Thompson, C. J. "Benedict, Thomas, or Augustine? The Character of MacIntyre's Narrative." *The Thomist,* 59:3 (July 1995) 379–407.

Torchia, N. J. "The *Commune/Proprium* Distinction in St. Augustine's Early Moral Theology." *Studia Patristica,* 22(1989). E. A. Livingstone, ed. 356–63.

Trexler, R. C. *Public Life in Renaissance Florence.* Ithaca: Cornell University Press, 1980.

Tucker, M. G. *John Neville Figgis: A Study.* London: SPCK, 1950.

Tuveson, E. *Redeemer Nation: The Idea of Americas Millenial Role.* Chicago: University of Chicago Press, 1990 [1962].

Ubl, K. "Verantwortlichkeit und autonomes Handeln: zur Entwicklung zweier Freiheitsbegriffe von Augustinus bis Thomas von Aquino." *Freiburger Zeitschrift für Philosophie und Theologie* 46.1–2 (1999) 79–114.

Vacca, R. "The Theology of Disorder in the *Iliad.*" *Religion and Literature* 23 (1991) 1–22.

Verheijen, L. *Nouvelle Approche de la Règle de saint Augustin.* Bégrolles en Mauges: Abbaye de Bellefontaine, 1980.

———. *Nouvelle Approche de la Règle de saint Augustin:* II. Chemin vers la vie heureuse Louvain: Institut Historique Augustinien, 1988.

———. *La Règle de saint Augustin.* Paris: Études Augustiniennes, 1967.

Vessey, M. "*Opus Imperfectum:* Augustine and His Readers, 426–435 A.D." *Vigilae Christianae* 52 (1998) 264–85.

Vessey, M., K. Pollman, and A. Fitzgerald, eds. *History, Apocalypse and the Secular Imagination: New Essays on Augustine's* City of God. Bowling Green: Philosophy Documentation Center, 1999.

Vilches, P. "The Delegate Womb: Lucrezia's Body as Political Tool in Machiavelli's *La mandragola.*" *American Journal of Italian Studies* 22:60 (1999) 99–124.

Viroli, M. *Machiavelli.* Oxford: Oxford University Press, 1998.

———. *Niccolò's Smile.* Trans. Antony Shugaar. New York: Hill and Wang, 2000.

Vismara, G. *La giurisdizione civile dei vescovi, secoli I-IX.* Milan: Dott. A. Giuffrè, 1995.

Voegelin, E. *The New Science of Politics.* Chicago: University of Chicago Press, 1952.

Von Heyking, J. *Augustine and Politics as Longing in the World.* Columbia: University of Missouri Press, 2001.

Ward, G. *Cities of God.* London and New York: Routledge, 2000.

Weber, Max. *The Protestant Ethic and the Spirit of Capitalism.* H. Gerth and C. Wright Mills, eds. New York: Scribner, 1958.

———. "Science as a Vocation." In *From Max Weber: Essays in Sociology*, ed. H. Gerth and C. Wright Mills. New York: Oxford University Press, 1949. 129–56.

Weismann, F. "La libertad como busqueda de la verdad en el joven Agustín." *Filosofía y Teología* (1990) 65–73.

Weithman, P. J. "Augustine and Aquinas on Original Sin and the Function of Political Authority," *Journal of the History of Philosophy* 30:3 (July 1992) 353–76.

———. "Toward an Augustinian Liberalism." *Faith and Philosophy* 8:4 (1991) 461–80.

West, N. *Miss Lonelyhearts and the Day of the Locust.* New York: New Directions, 1962 [1946].

Wetzel, J. *Augustine and the Limits of Virtue.* Cambridge: Cambridge University Press, 1992.

———. "Book Four: The Trappings of Woe." In K. Paffenroth and R. P. Kennedy, *A Reader's Companion to Augustine's* Confessions. Louisville and London: Westminster John Knox Press, 2003.

White, M. J. "Pluralism and Secularism in the Political Order: St. Augustine and Theoretical Liberalism." *University of Dayton Review* 22:3 (Summer 1994) 137–53.

Williams, R. *Lost Icons: Reflections on Cultural Bereavement.* Edinburgh: T&T Clark, 2000.

———. "Politics and the Soul: A Reading of the City of God." *Milltown Studies* 19.20 (1987) 55–72.

———. "*Sapientia* and the Trinity: Reflections on the *De Trinitate*." In *Collectanea Augustiniana*, ed. B. Bruning, et al. Leuven: Leuven University Press, 1990. 317–32.

Williams, R. *Dream Worlds: Mass Consumption in Late-Nineteenth Century France.* Berkeley: University of California Press, 1991.

Williams, S., and G. Friell, *Theodosius: The Empire at Bay.* New Haven, CT: Yale University Press, 1994.

Wolff, S. *Freedom within Reason.* Oxford: Oxford University Press, 1990.

Wood, N. "Sallust's Theorem: A Comment on 'Fear' in Western Political Thought." *History of Political Thought* 16:2 (1995) 174–90.

Worthington, G. "Michael Oakeshott and the *City of God*," *Political Theory* 28:3 (June 2000) 377–98.

Index of Citations

The asterisk (*) denotes the recently discovered Divjak letters. *Corpus Scriptorum Ecclesiasticorum Latinorum*, v. 88. Sancti Aureli Augustini opera; sect. II, pars VI . Ed. J. Divjak. Vindobonae: Hoelder-Pichler-Tempsky, 1981.

Index of Subjects

action: political, xii, 99–111, 202–5, 221, 265; and will, 68–69, 87
activism, political, xii, 99–111, 265
Adam, as origin of souls, 15–16
Adeodatus (son of Augustine), 38, 53, 182
aesthetics. *See* beauty
Africa: episcopal councils, 108–10; imperial administration, 100–108
Alexander II, Pope, 237, 251, 258n84
Alypius (bishop of Thagaste), 56, 104, 108
America. *See* United States
amicitia. See friendship
Anacletan schism, 252–53
Annales school, 300
Anselm da Baggio (Alexander II), 237, 252, 258n84
Anselm II of Lucca, 251–52
anthropology, political: of Augustine, xiv, 150, 220–30, 313, 325; of Machiavelli, xiv, 228, 313; modern, 272
Apringius (Proconsul of Africa), 102
Aquinas, Thomas: and the Church, 268–69; and consent, 94n64; and

happiness, 17; and lying, 39; and will, 86
Ariald of Cariate, 248–49
Aristotle: and ends and means, 73; and friendship, 226; and household, 146–48, 155, 160; and politics, 24, 220; and the will, 76
association, non-state, 222, 223–30
atonement, as sacrificial, 126–27
attachment, 220–21, 224–25, 227–29
Augustine of Hippo: as advocate, 102–8; as Christian Socialist, 266–69, 272; concubine, 7, 53, 174; and episcopal councils, 108–10; and father, 53; as Liberal Reformer, 264–65, 268–69; and marriage, 174–75; as Melancholy Conservative, 263–65, 268–69; and mother, 8–10, 59, 60, 174–75; and political activism, 99–111, 265. *See also The City of God*; *Confessions*; and Index of Citations
Aurelius (bishop of Carthage), 110
authority: civil, 100–101, 224, 309–10; in household, 22–23, 149–50, 153, 160, 201, 223; in monastic community,

and imperial power, 117–30, 132–33, 309–10; interpretive approaches, 188–91, 217–18; and love, 6–7, 306; and love and politics, xiii, 119, 134n6; and Machiavelli, 300–301; and modernity, 261–64; and ontology of peace, 17–20; and peace and war, 117–19, 123–25; and politics, xiii, 46–47, 99, 145–46, 188–205, 220–30, 261–65; and rape of Lucretia, 307–10, 322; and resident aliens, 197–202; and sin and death, 17; and soul and city, 121, 133; and terror, 312–19; and truthfulness, 46–49; and use of goods, 197–202; and will, 76, 85. *See also* just-war theory

civitas: and *domus*, 149, 151–52, 219; and harmony, 223–24, 227; and love, 221, 224; virtues, 170–81

class, and *concordia*, 174–75

classicism of Machiavelli, xiv, 301

clemency, appeals for, 100, 102, 103

Clement VII, Pope, 297

clergy, and sexuality, xiii–xiv, 237–38

coercion: in household, 149–50; and imperial power, 118–19, 268–69; and necessity, 77–78, 83

commodity-fetishism, xiv, 261, 271

common good (*bonum commune*), 169, 170–71, 172, 175, 178–81, 183, 222–24

communication: and community, 43, 44; and lying, 38

communitarianism, 222

community: in American Progressivism, 275–76; and friendship, 59, 173; and human nature, 166; and individual, 178–81, 203; and interpretation of Scripture, 43–44; and language, xii, 15, 37, 43–44, 49; and law, 4, 23, 224; and love, 4–8, 23, 44, 50, 57, 119, 121, 151, 196, 224; in Machiavelli, 322–23; monastery as, xiii, 163n38, 167, 169–84; and truthfulness, 36–37, 40, 43–46, 50; and unity, 4–8,

12–13, 221; universal, 152; and virtues, 170–81. *See also* household

compassion, and pity, 122–23

concordia, and community, 170–71, 173–78, 183

concubinage, clerical, 237, 241, 248–50

Confessions (Augustine), 5; and friendship, 7, 53, 58, 59–61, 62; and marriage, 174; and politics, 99; and soul and city, 121; and the stage, 122; and will, 68, 84–86

conflict, social, 13

consecration of churches, 251–53

consensus, and imperial power, 119, 129

consent, xii, 80–84, 85–87, 91

conservatism, 263–65, 268–69

consumption: and commodity fetishism, 283; and household, 156–60

conversion, moral, 103–4

councils, episcopal, 108–10

creation: goodness, 36, 269; sacramental view, 263, 269–70

criminals: and appeals for clemency, 100, 102–3; and right of sanctuary, 106. *See also* death penalty

Cyprian, 19–20

damnation, of earthly city, 3, 16, 26

Dante Alleghieri, 14, 56, 311, 325

Darius (military officer), 108

De libero arbitrio. See On Free Choice

death: of Christ, 126–27, 132; eternal, 9, 29n24; fear of, 193–96; in modernity, 272; as sacrifice, 124–27, 130–32, 195–96; and sin, 17, 19, 26

death penalty, 100, 102, 103, 177, 309–10

debt, financial, 106, 109

deception, and lying, 38, 39–40

defensores civitatum, 109–10, 111

delectatio (delight, enjoyment), 78, 79, 83, 90, 137n37

delight: and beauty, 90; and will, 78, 79, 83, 90, 137n37

democracy, 119, 129, 145, 222, 275–76, 280; Christian, 266

dependence, and freedom, 78–79, 89, 91

desire: common, 119, 196–97; and fetishism, 261, 271, 287; God as object of, 57, 117–18; in Machiavelli, 313–14, 317; and will, 76, 82, 87, 118; and worship, 197–99, 201, 204–5. *See also* restlessness

detachment, 220–21, 223–24, 225, 227–29

determinism, and freedom, 75, 76, 78, 80–83, 87–88

disobedience, civil, 101

dissent, 5, 7, 19, 100–101

distance, and separation, 10–11

domination. *See libido dominandi*

domus: and *civitas*, 149, 151–52, 219. *See also* household

Donatism: and Augustine's advocacy, 102, 108; and episcopal councils, 109; and grace, 7; and imperial sanctions, 99; and sacraments, 239; and sinful clergy, xiii–xiv, 237–53; and social unity, 4–5, 7–8, 19

Donatus (bishop of Carthage), 239

Donatus (Proconsul of Africa), 102

dualism, and Political Augustinianism, 187–88, 270, 322

duty, public, 222

earthly city: and Christian ruler, 24–25; and damnation, 3, 16, 26; and domination (*See libido dominandi*); and *domus*, 151–52; and household, 23–24, 223–24; and household of faith, 153–55, 158–60; and love of glory, 189–91, 192–97, 198–99, 201–2, 203–5, 306–7, 314–15; and love of self, 151, 220, 232n21, 264, 306; and Machiavelli, 300–301, 304, 313–18, 320–21; and peace, 21–25, 26, 151, 153, 221; and resident alienship, 199–202; and terror, 301, 312–19; and truthfulness, 46–49;

and use of goods, 197–99. *See also* politics

ecclesiology. *See* Church

economics, and commodity fetishism, xiv, 280–89

economy, and household, 147, 155–60

education, friendship as, 54–57

enchantment: and market, 280–89; and modernity, 261–63, 269; and state, 271–80

enjoyment: and use, 21, 73, 88–90, 197–202, 210n41; and will, 78

equality: in earthly city, 24; and friendship, 226; in household, 22, 24, 154; and ontology of peace, 20–21

error, and lying, 39, 40

eschatology, political, xiv, 313, 315, 319–25

ethics: and happiness 18; and love, 6

Eugippius of Lucullanum, 167

Eustochius (legal expert), 105, 108

evanescence, 197–98, 200

evil: and free will, 80, 85–87, 94–95n70, 137n37; hypostatization, 124, 125, 131, 188; in Machiavelli, 313–14, 319; providential purpose, 124

faction, in Machiavelli, 321, 323

faith: and will, 95n76. *See also fides*

fall: and grace, 122; language as result of, 15, 38; and loss of unity 15–16; politics as result of, 46–47, 150

Fascius (debtor), 106

Faventius (farmer), 106–8

fear, of death, 193–96

fetishism: of commodities, xiv, 261, 271; of state, xiv, 261, 271–80, 289

fides, and community, 170–73, 174, 183

Filmer, Robert, 32n87

flag, American, 130, 132

Flavius Marcellinus (military commander), 103, 108

Florence, and Machiavelli, 317, 320–25

Florentinus (officer), 106–8

Index of Modern Authors

Dewey, John, 275–76, 277–79
Dihle, Albrecht, 67–68, 70, 95n79
Divjak, Johannes, 113n20
Dodaro, Robert, O.S.A., 135n20,
    135–36n26, 139n59, 209–10n37,
    211n51
Douglas, Mary, 285
Durkheim, Emile, 272

Eagleton, Terry, 266–67
Ellul, Jacques, 233n29
Elshtain, Jean Bethke, 264, 265, 266

Figgis, John Neville, 267–268, 270
Fiske, A. A., 55, 63nn2,9
Fontana, Benedetto, 327n6
Foucault, Michel, 300
Fukuyama, Francis, 266

Galindo, J. A., 93n46
Gilson, Étienne, 76–77, 86, 90, 233n27
Godman, Peter, 334–35n52
Gramsci, Antonio, 300, 332n32
Greer, Rowan, 163n28

Hardt, Michael and Negri, Antonio, 119,
    127–28, 135n18, 139n60, 141n78
Haring, N. M., 258–59n94
Harvey, J. F., 64nn25,28
Havel, Vaclav, 235n61
Hawthorne, Nathaniel, 281
Hopkins, Gerard Manley, 289
Horkheimer, Max, 287

James, William, 276
Jameson, 139n60
Jaspers, Karl, 230n5
Jed, Stephanie, 302–3
John Paul II, 228–29
Jordan, Mark D., 44–45, 52n26,
    254–55n2, 256n29

Kahn, Charles, 94n64
Kahn, Victoria, 333n36
Kaplan, Robert, 142n81

Kaufmann, Walter, 291n12
Kirk, Russell, 217
Kohler, Georg, 70
Kristeller, Paul Oskar, 302, 303
Kuklick, Bruce, 276

Lears, Jackson, 281
Levick, Barbara, 174, 185n20
Lienhard, J. T., 54, 57, 60, 63nn4,14,
    64n28
Lippmann, Walter, 274, 277
Long, D. Stephen, 270

MacIntyre, Alasdair, 70
McLynn, N., 112–13n11
McNamara, M. A., 63n2
Madec, Goulven, 184n1
Maritain, J., 95–96n84
Markus, Robert A., 31n58, 32n82, 43–44,
    46–47, 59, 64n21, 160–61n3, 167,
    183, 186n43, 232n15, 265–66, 269
Marvin, Carolyn and Ingle, David W., 130
Marx, Karl, 75, 272, 282, 283–85, 286
Mattingly, Garrett, 332n32
May, Henry F., 274
Mayer, Arno J., 334n45
Meilaender, Gilbert C., 51n19, 53, 55, 60,
    64nn27,33
Milbank, John, 31n71, 129, 137n34,
    138n47, 140n66, 141n79, 232n15,
    262, 268–70, 272–73, 280, 283, 285
Miles, Margaret, 217, 230n4
Mitchell, Joshua, 273
Moltmann, Jurgen, 217, 265
Momigliano, Arnaldo, 171
Moore, R. I., 237, 238, 248, 251, 253,
    258n84
Murdoch, Iris, 71, 72, 74

Najemy, John M., 313, 321, 327n6,
    336n63
Neuhaus, Richard John, 160n3
Niebuhr, Reinhold, 188, 206n3, 264–65,
    266, 269
Nygren, A., 233n27

Oakeshott, Michael, 233nn29,31
O'Connell, Robert, 29–30n40, 30n52
O'Daly, Gerard, 94n58
O'Donnell, James J., 125, 208n23
O'Donovan, Oliver, 152, 162n18,
    163n28, 210n45, 211n47, 212n53,
    232n15, 232–33n25, 271
Orwell, George, 225

Parel, Anthony J., 327n6
Pegueroles, Juan, 78, 93n45, 96n86
Pieper, Josef, 89
Pinckaers, Servais O. P., 67, 71–72, 86
Pocock, J. G. A., 316
Prezzolini, G., 300

Rahner, Hugo, 89
Rauschenbusch, Walter, 277
Ridolfi, Roberto, 326n5
Rist, John, 94n58
Robertson, D. W., 329n9
Robinson, I. S., 255n11
Romano, Claude, 92n10
Rorty, Richard, 275, 276–77
Rose, Gillian, 125, 131, 139n60
Royce, Josiah, 274–75, 277, 278

Sartre, Jean-Paul, 69
Schlesinger, Arthur Jr., 264
Shanks, Andrew, 263, 292n15
Sholem, Gershom, 287
Simmel, Georg, 285–86

Simone, Yves, 88–89, 95–96n84
Smith, Thomas W., xiii, 160n1, 187–205
Strauss, Leo, 212n55

Taussig, Michael, 272–73, 280
Teske, Roland, 30n41
Tocqueville, A. de, 218, 273–274
Tuveson, Ernest, 274

Vacca, Robert, 194
Verheijen, L., 167
Vessey, Mark, 188–89, 231n13
Viroli, Maurizio, 326n5
Voegelin, E., 233n29
Von Heyking, John, 47

Ward, Graham, 269, 292n18
Warner, Margaret, 142n81
Weber, Max, 261, 282–83
Weismann, Francisco, 96n91
West, Nathanael, 281–82
Westbrook, Robert, 276
Wetzel, James, 76, 81, 87, 94n58,
    140–41n72
Whitman, Walt, 276
Williams, Rowan, 152, 160, 162n17,
    203, 203–4, 206n15, 208n26, 210n38,
    269
Williams, Stephen and Friell, Gerard,
    209n34, 211n49
Williams, Thomas, 70, 92n11
Wolff, Susan, 94n57

Index of Biblical Citations

About the Editors and Contributors

Todd Breyfogle received his B.A. from Colorado College in Classics-History-Politics (1988). At Oxford University he earned a second B.A. in Ancient and Modern History (1990) and an M.St. in Theology (1991). He graduated from the Committee on Social Thought at the University of Chicago, where his dissertation analyzed the intellect and will in St. Augustine's political thought. He is presently Director of the University Honors Program at the University of Denver and teaches in the program. He is the editor and a contributor to *Literary Imagination, Ancient and Modern: Essays in Honor of David Grene* (Chicago: University of Chicago Press, 1999), as well as a contributor to *Augustine through the Ages: An Encyclopedia* (Allan D. Fitzgerald, et al., eds.; Grand Rapids, MI: Eerdmans, 1999), and to the *Oxford Classical Dictionary* (3rd ed.; Oxford: Oxford University Press, 1996). He has also presented numerous papers on Augustine to learned societies.

Phillip Cary is Director of the Philosophy Program at Eastern University, where he is also Scholar in Residence at the Templeton Honors College and Associate Professor of Philosophy. He is the author of *Augustine's Invention of the Inner Self* (Oxford: Oxford University Press, 2000), as well as articles on Augustine in journals such as *Augustinian Studies*, and in *Augustine through the Ages: An Encyclopedia* (Allan D. Fitzgerald, et al., eds.; Grand Rapids, MI: Eerdmans, 1999). His audio- and videotaped lectures, *Augustine: Philosopher and Saint*, have been published by The Teaching Company. He is currently working on a book on Augustine's semiotics and its relation to the doctrine of grace.

Robert Dodaro, O.S.A., is Vice President and Professor of Patristics at the Patristic Institute, the Augustinianum, in Rome. He studied divinity at the Catholic Theological Union at Chicago and patristic theology in Rome at the Augustinianum. After a year of apprenticeship at the *Augustinus-Lexikon* in Wuerzburg, Germany, he began doctoral studies in Theology at Oxford University where, in 1992, he successfully defended a dissertation entitled, "Language and Justice: Political Anthropology in Augustine's *City of God*." Since that year he has been teaching at the Patristic Institute in Rome. He is an associate editor of the *Augustinus-Lexikon*. In addition to articles in scholarly journals, *Festschriften*, and books, he co-edited *Augustine and His Critics* (London: Routledge, 2000), and *Augustine. Political Writings*, (Cambridge: Cambridge University Press, 2001). He is currently completing a book on Augustine's political thought.

John A. Doody is Robert M. Birmingham Chair in Humanities at Villanova University where he serves as Associate Dean for Curriculum in the College of Arts and Sciences. He also directs the Core Humanities program. He has taught at Haverford College and the University of Notre Dame, where he received his degree in philosophy. His interests are in social and political philosophy and he has published work on Habermas and MacIntyre.

Louis I. Hamilton received his M.A. from the University of Virginia in 1994 where he wrote a thesis on Possidius *Vita Augustini*. He received his Ph.D. from Fordham University in 2000 and was a Fulbright Scholar in Italy, 1998-1999. He is revising his dissertation, "The Power of Liturgy and the Liturgy of Power in Eleventh- and Twelfth-Century Italy," for publication. His research considers how the medieval liturgy shaped spiritual experience, political power, and reflected contemporary social conditions.

Michael Hanby teaches in the Honors College at Baylor University and is Associate Director of the Baylor Institute for Faith and Learning. He is author of *Augustine and Modernity* (2003) and his work has appeared in several journals including *Modern Theology, Communio*, and *New Blackfriars*.

Kevin L. Hughes is Director of the Patristic, Medieval, and Renaissance Studies Converence and Assistant Professor in the Department of Theology and Religious Studies at Villanova University. He has published *Church History: Faith Handed On* (Loyola Press, 2001) and, with Kim Paffenroth, *Augustine and Liberal Education* (Ashgate, 2000). His articles have appeared in *The Heythrop Journal, Augustinian Studies, The American Benedictine Review*, and *Collectanea Franciscana*. He received his Ph.D. from the Divinity School of the

University of Chicago and is currently pursuing research in medieval Augustinianism, especially Bonaventure and the Franciscan School. He lives in Media, Pennsylvania with his wife and two daughters.

Robert P. Kennedy is currently an Assistant Professor in the Department of Religious Studies at St. Francis Xavier University in Antigonish, Nova Scotia, Canada. He received his doctorate in moral theology from the University of Notre Dame in 1997. The title of his dissertation was "The Ethics of Language: An Augustinian Critique of Modern Approaches to the Morality of Lying." He has contributed to *Augustinian Studies, Maritain Studies, Augustine through the Ages: An Encyclopedia* (Allan D. Fitzgerald, et al., eds.; Grand Rapids, MI: Eerdmans, 1999), and to the *New Catholic Encyclopedia* (forthcoming). He is also a co-editor and contributor to *A Reader's Companion to Augustine's Confessions* (Louisville, KY: Westminster John Knox Press, 2003). His current projects include translating a collection of Augustine's moral and ascetical works and research on Augustine's theory of the will.

Thomas F. Martin, O.S.A., is Director of the Augustinian Institute and Associate Professor of Theology/Religious Studies at Villanova University. His particular area of study involves the biblical and spiritual thought of Augustine. He has lectured on Augustine in the United States, Italy, England, The Philippines, Australia, and Latin America. He has published articles on Augustine in *Studia Patristica, The Downside Review, The Journal of Early Christian Studies,* and *Vigiliae Christianae,* and the monograph *Rhetoric and Exegesis in Augustine's Interpretation of Romans 7:24–25a* (Edwin Mellen Press, 2001).

Eugene McCarraher received his B.A. in history from Ursinus College, and his M.A. and Ph.D. from Rutgers University. He is the author of *Christian Critics: Religion and the Impasse in Modern American Social Thought* (Ithaca: Cornell University Press, 2000). Besides writing scholarly articles, he contributes essays and book reviews for *Commonweal* and *In These Times.* He is currently working on *The Enchantments of Mammon: Corporate Capitalism and the American Moral Imagination.* His article in this collection reflects his interest in Augustinian thought and its resources for cultural history.

Kim Paffenroth is Associate Professor of Religious Studies at Iona College. He is the author of *Judas: Images of the Lost Disciple* (Louisville, KY: Westminster John Knox Press, 2001), and a co-editor and contributor to *A Reader's Companion to Augustine's Confessions* (Louisville, KY: Westminster John Knox Press, 2003), and *Augustine and Liberal Education* (Aldershot, UK: Ashgate Publishing, 2000). He has also published articles on Augustine in *The Downside Review, Augustinian Studies,* and *Harvard Theological Review,* as well as translations of several of his works, including *Soliloquies* (Hyde Park, NY: New City Press, 2000). His most recent book is *In Praise of Wisdom: Literary and Theological Reflections on Faith and Reason* (New York: Continuum, 2004), in which he traces the development of the idea and practice of Wisdom through the bible, Augustine, and Pascal, as well as its expression in great works of literature.

David C. Schindler studied the Great Books as an undergraduate at the University of Notre Dame. He holds a master's degree in Theology from the John Paul II Institute, Washington DC Session, where he studied theological anthropology, and a master's degree and doctorate from the Catholic University of America in Philosophy. His dissertation was on the dramatic structure of truth in the philosophy of Hans Urs von Balthasar. Currently Assistant Professor of Humanities at Villanova University, he also works as a translator of French and German philosophy and theology.

Thomas W. Smith is Associate Professor in the Department of Political Science and Chair and Associate Professor in the Department of Humanities and Augustinian Traditions at Villanova University. He has published articles in ancient, medieval, and contemporary political philosophy in such journals as *Polity, The Review of Politics,* and the *American Political Science Review.* He is the author of *Revaluing Ethics: Aristotle's Dialectical Pedagogy* (SUNY Press, 2001). Currently he is working on a book entitled *Wisdom and Power: Three Rival Versions of Political Philosophy.*

Paul R. Wright took his Ph.D. in Comparative Literature from Princeton University, with an emphasis on English, Italian, and Latin literature of the Renaissance. He has lectured and written on Machiavelli, Milton, Vico, and the humanist tradition, with particular attention to the development of the public sphere in the wake of theoretical work by Habermas. He has taught at Princeton University, Osaka University, and is currently a Barbieri Fellow in the Core Humanities Program at Villanova University.